ROMANTICS
THEIR LIVES, WORKS AND INSPIRATION

ROMANTICS

THEIR LIVES, WORKS AND INSPIRATION

EDITOR

NATHANIEL HARRIS

WHSMITH

EXCLUSIVE
· BOOKS ·

House Editor Joey Chapter
Designer Kate Stuart-Cox
Picture Research Maureen Kane
Production Inger Faulkner

Produced exclusively for WH Smith Limited by
Marshall Cavendish Books Limited,
119 Wardour Street, London W1V 3TD

Concept, design and production by
Marshall Cavendish Books Limited

First printing 1991
1 2 3 4 5 6 7 8 9   99 98 97 96 95 94 93 92 91

Typeset by Litho Link Ltd, Welshpool, Powys, Wales
Printed and bound in Hong Kong

ISBN 1 85435 387 X

Some of this material was previously published in the
Marshall Cavendish partworks *Great Artists*, *Great Composers*
and *Great Writers*.

CONTENTS

INTRODUCTION

Colourful, passionate and intense, the lives and works of the great Romantics scandalized and thrilled the world. These writers, painters and composers were the standard-bearers of a movement whose influence went far beyond the arts, effecting a revolution in human consciousness.

Romanticism changed everything. As well as transforming the arts, it affected the way people thought and felt about childhood, nature, the past, the human personality and relations between the sexes. It influenced garden design as completely as landscape painting, fashions in dress as much as portraiture, politics as obviously as poetry. Over several generations it effected a revolution in consciousness that touched even those who ridiculed Keats's poetry or were outraged by Liszt's love-life.

Many of the Romantics were fascinating, daring, unconventional, even deviant personalities – artists in revolt such as Byron and Shelley, still known to millions of people who may never have read a line of their works. The appearance of such personalities was not a matter of chance, since a powerful impulse towards self-realization lay at the very heart of Romanticism. The Romantic exalted freedom – including free expression of the personality – and was in covert or open revolt against social and artistic constraints. Consequently even when we read the biographies of Romantic artists whose works were accepted and popular – figures such as Beethoven and Goya

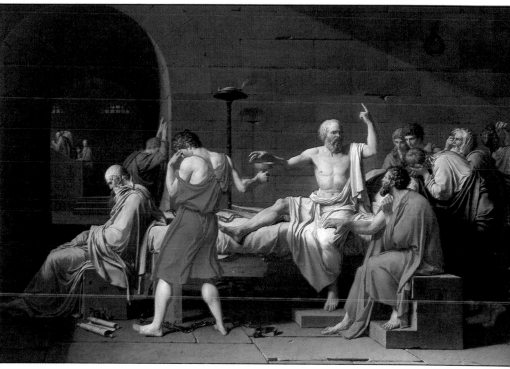

Classical
Jacques-Louis David's masterly Death of Socrates *(1787, above) epitomizes the Neo-Classical school of which*

reasoned about.

– we find abundant evidence that they too were fundamentally outsiders.

REVOLT AGAINST CLASSICISM

The Romantic revolt was directed against an early 18th century society that was in many respects admirable. Reacting against the religious wars and persecutions of the previous century, this society valued reason, order, sociability, urbanity and moderation. However, its emotional limitations are indicated by the fact that 'enthusiasm' was frowned upon, and the darker side of the spirit was largely ignored in favour of the sunlit world of consciousness.

The reigning artistic creed, Classicism, also emphasized reason and order, valuing the formal perfection of the sonata and, in verse, the neat finish of heroic couplets. In painting a certain idealization was permitted (for example in an historical scene), but the artist was exhorted to stick to the sane middle-ground of life, preferring the general and typical to the unusual, unhealthy or disturbing. The aim was harmony and balance, which could only be attained by emotional restraint, avoiding violence and extremes, and observing 'decorum' – the use of language

appropriate to the work in hand, so that, for example, grotesquerie was inadmissable in a 'noble' painting, and humour and dialect had no place in tragedy. As a rational enterprise, Classicism laid down the form, content and treatment of the arts in sets of rules that were believed to have a universal validity.

This was, in highly simplified terms, the state of affairs against which the Romantics rebelled. They embraced almost everything that Classicism had excluded – passionate self-expression, spontaneity and inspiration, unrestrained energy and imagination, violence and irregularity, the particular, the strange, the shocking, the elemental. Not surprisingly, Classicists were bitter in their denunciations of the new movement, which seemed wilfully to encapsulate everything that was artistically worthless and morally suspect. Pamphlet wars, venomous criticism and theatrical brawls enlivened the conflict. Confronted with the Classicists' weighty authorities – the revered achievements of ancient Greece and Rome – the Romantics rediscovered the hitherto despised 'Gothic' Middle Ages and, in literature, exalted Shakespeare as the supreme Romantic artist, blissfully indifferent to the supposedly inviolable rules of Classical drama. Taken up and translated by Continental Romantics, Shakespeare became for the first time a European figure, influencing Goethe and Mendelssohn in Germany and Berlioz and Hugo in France.

THE CULT OF NATURE

Perhaps the most extraordinary feature of Romanticism was its discovery of nature as a prime source of beauty, rapture and healing. Down to the 18th century, nature was perceived as hostile and unruly, except when tamed and organized into regular beds of flowers, smoothly barbered hedges and straight water-courses and lines of trees.

Beyond that, the countryside was good for farming, and really wild natural features such as mountains were simply viewed as barriers to travel and refuges for bandits.

The first identifiable signs of a change occurred

Resistance to the new

Elemental forces
Nature in all its forms enthralled the Romantics, and no one has equalled Britain's greatest painter, Turner, in his ability to evoke its elemental power. The picture above is titled Snow Storm: Hannibal and his Army Crossing the Alps *(1812); but whereas a painter working in the Classical tradition would have concentrated on the human drama, Turner's rendering of the mighty storm reduces the historical event to near-insignificance.*

quite new and, although written in the generalized language of the gentleman tourist, contains the seed of the full-blown Romantic attitude.

Nature is described with even greater rapture by the Swiss-born thinker Jean-Jacques Rousseau, whose writings reached a huge European audience in the middle decades of the 18th century. He was the first great Romantic outsider, articulating ideas about society, politics and education that were to have an extraordinary influence right down to the present day. Among these was an attitude to nature that earlier generations would have found incomprehensible: 'Never does a plain, however beautiful it may be, seem so in my eyes. I need torrents, rocks, firs, dark woods, mountains, steep roads to climb or descend, abysses beside me to make me afraid.' From here it is only a few steps to the particularized Suffolk scenery painted by Constable, Wordsworth's nature poetry, Turner's spectacular, light-bathed landscapes, and such musical equivalents as Beethoven's 'Pastoral' symphony and Mendelssohn's Hebrides-inspired *Fingal's Cave*.

The Romantic attitude to nature was essentially religious. Immersion in nature, union with nature, could be a mystical experience, doubly important in that it gave the worshipper some relief from the burden of his intensely self-conscious Romantic personality. To Wordsworth, nature was another self, the 'soul of all my moral being', and also the great teacher, for

> One impulse from a vernal wood
> May teach you more of man,
> Of moral evil and of good,
> Than all the sages can.

As this suggests, it became possible to elevate nature into the source of everything pure, in opposition to intellect, book knowledge, sophistication, town life, luxury and other aspects of civilization that had previously been regarded as certain signs of progress. And from this starting-point the Romantics developed a cluster of emotional convictions that have had a remarkably long run. One was that children and simple,

Sense of self
Many Romantic artists were intensely self-absorbed, expressing aspects of their own personalities. Here Delacroix portrays himself as Hamlet.

untutored people might be wiser than the learned. As a result, childhood not only entered literature as a subject, but was more sympathetically understood in life. Moreover, if simple people could be wise, their words and music were worth preserving; and despite the fact that interest in folk literature was confronted at an early stage with a resounding hoax – the ancient Celtic poems by 'Ossian', published (but also written) by James Macpherson in 1762 – modern collecting of ballads, songs and fairy tales owes everything to the Romantic movement.

Equally important was the Romantic cult of the simple life as an achievable ideal; despite the existence of an earlier pastoral tradition in literature which sentimentalized over the lives of shepherds and shepherdesses, Rousseau and Wordsworth were among the earliest actual cottage-dwellers to be admired for having high-mindedly chosen their way of life. The simple life offered its followers a range of new experiences including the most direct form of contact with nature. It comes as no surprise to learn that Rousseau, Wordsworth and Coleridge were pro-

Alpine grandeur
Mountains inspired Rousseau and later Romantics, who wrote with rapture of the Alps (left).

digious walkers; indeed, one of Coleridge's claims to fame is that he was the first true fell-walker, insouciantly ill equipped but regularly making long trips for pleasure in the Lake District.

Finally, the Romantic conception of nature gave rise to primitivism. If simple people were happier or wiser than the learned, surely primitive peoples, untainted by civilization, were even better off! Like so many ideas, this one derived from Rousseau, who gave it some intellectual substance by arguing at length that 'progress' had merely corrupted and enslaved people who were by nature good and free. The argument seemed to be confirmed by the discoveries of 18th century explorers, who were deeply impressed by the tropical abundance and sexual hospitality of the Tahitians . . . Rousseau's follower Bernardin de Saint Pierre wrote a best-seller, *Paul and Virginia* (1781), in which a boy and girl grow up in isolated innocence on an island modelled on Mauritius, while another French writer, Chateaubriand, made a similar impact with *Atala* (1800) and *René* (1802), stories with Amerindian settings. Admiration for primitive peoples and attempts to go 'back to nature' have enjoyed a long and fascinating history, stretching from Rousseau and Coleridge to Gauguin, D.H. Lawrence and *The Blue Lagoon*.

PASSION AND PERSONALITY

Cultivating intensity of emotion and expression, the Romantics were inevitably in love with love. Love – unhappy love – formed the chief subject of the first two Romantic novels to take Europe by storm, Rousseau's *Julie*, better known by its subtitle, *La Nouvelle Heloïse* (1762), and Goethe's *The Sufferings of Young Werther* (1774). Their popularity had nothing to do with the sexual content, which was unexceptional, but derived

Ossian
The poems of the Gaelic bard Ossian were admired

Solitary heroes
The Romantic hero stood apart from society, a prisoner of his own self-awareness. In Byronic guise be brooded on some secret guilt; but other Romantic loners included solitaries contemplating the void, as in Friedrich's Wanderer Looking over a Sea of Fog *(c.1815, left).*

climate and amiable, sexually uninhibited inhabitants, 'the South Seas' became the European's notion of paradise on earth.

...nal temperature, which ...and make overmastering ...omantic subjects.

...o tried to live out such ...ibility of sustaining them ...in sources of Romantic ...Byron, Berlioz, Liszt and others went through 'the Romantic agony' in such a fashion that their lives became more or less public property, and the line between life and art became far more blurred than it had been in the case of Classical artists, whose personalities were generally felt to be irrelevant to an appreciation of their works. Romantic art is shot through with autobiographical feeling and detail, and major works such as Rousseau's *Confessions*, Wordsworth's *Prelude* and Berlioz's *Symphonie Fantastique* are quite openly self-descriptive. *The Prelude*, describing 'the growth of a poet's mind', sounds another new Romantic note, bringing the creative process itself under scrutiny; and Wordsworth's friend and contemporary, Coleridge, even managed to make poetry out of his sense of fading powers. All in all, Romanticism placed the artist firmly in the centre of his own creation and fostered one of the most powerful and long-lived of modern myths – that the artist is a special kind of person, uniquely privileged and/or burdened.

William Blake and Samuel Palmer in England and Caspar David Friedrich in Germany.

In seeking to escape from the here and now, the Romantics ranged freely over time and space. Gothick novels often exploited the supposed 'darkness' of the Middle Ages to raise a shudder, but the true historical novel was the single-handed creation of Sir Walter Scott. His immediate followers included French writers like Alexandre Dumas and Victor Hugo, who also introduced a swashbuckling form of Romantic drama that ignited one of the rowdier conflicts between Classicists and Romantics. Like time, distance lent enchantment, and Northern artists flocked to the Mediterranean in search of light, colour and liberation; some, like Byron and Delacroix, went beyond the boundaries of 'civilized' Europe, looking for exotic scenes and experiences which they would later transmute into art.

Most of the great Romantics reached maturity between about 1750 and 1850, the dates adopted in this book. Romanticism in music was something of an exception, starting later and going on much longer than in the other arts. One reason was that the Classical era in music was singularly rich, and indeed Beethoven is its climactic figure. Yet he is also the first Romantic composer, responsible for introducing a new intensity of emotion into his music. Subsequently the Romantic impulse became still more apparent in phenomena such as the almost outlandish virtuosity of Chopin, Liszt and Paganini, in the expansion of the orchestra, and in the quest for new effects, intended to

NIGHTMARE AND CHIVALRY

Romanticism assumed many forms, but their common thread was avoidance of the middle ground – the everyday, the ordinary, the typical – in a quest for uniqueness and intensity. In Romantic literature, characters and situations tend to be exceptional and extreme. The Classical equation of deformity with evil, for example, is often reversed: Frankenstein's 'monster' is more sinned against than sinning, and if Victor Hugo's *Notre-Dame de Paris* has a hero, it is Quasimodo, the misshapen cathedral bellringer. The insight with which Goya and Géricault portrayed the insane is an example of the same phenomenon.

Dark places and unusual states of mind fascinated many Romantics from Goya to Edgar Allan Poe; some, like Coleridge and the English essayist Thomas De Quincey, experienced their day- and nightmares as a result of 'opium-eating'. The present-day horror novel has its roots in Romantic tradition, beginning with the 18th century 'Gothick' novels that Jane Austen satirized in *Northanger Abbey*, published in 1818. Coincidentally Mary Shelley's *Frankenstein* came out in the same year, raising the Gothick to new literary heights that were only subsequently reached by Poe's stories. In terms of pure supernaturalism, Coleridge's *Rime of the Ancient Mariner* has few peers in Romantic literature, but among painters an unexpected visionary art was created by

Nightmare
Turning from the rational, daylight world of Classicism, the Romantics tapped the unconscious, as in Fuseli's The Nightmare *(above).*

Style wars (2)
Romantic music could shock; this caricature (below, left) suggests that Richard Wagner's compositions were literally ear-splitting.

The tutu
In the Romantic era the tutu worn by Marie Taglioni (below) was a daring innovation, liberating dancers from long, stiff costumes.

The Revolution was eventually taken over by Napoleon Bonaparte, a military genius who proceeded to make himself emperor of France. An ambiguous personality – at once ruthlessly efficient tyrant and romantic dreamer – Napoleon fascinated even those Romantics who hated him on patriotic or libertarian grounds; for his tremendous energy and boundless ambition brought about a European upheaval that constituted an incomparably grand Romantic spectacle.

When Napoleon was defeated at Waterloo, Byron was 'damned sorry for it'. However, Romantic radicalism lived on, personified by the libertarian open-necked shirts of Shelley and Byron. And from 1821 there was a great new cause, the liberation of Greece from the Turks, in the pursuit of which Byron himself would die.

The Romantic liberation of the unconscious had its sinister side. An obsession with death, and love-in-death, pervades much Romantic art, sometimes rising to a frenzy of erotic violence, as in Delacroix's *Death of Sardanapalus*. Yearning for ecstasies that could never be sustained in the real world, Romantic artists were always liable to burn themselves out, and a surprisingly large number of them died young: of Byron, Shelley, Keats, Géricault, Mendelssohn, Schubert, Chopin and Poe, only Poe reached – barely reached – the age of 40. Romanticism too burned itself out. In literature and painting the movement was petering out by 1850, although diluted and respectable versions of Romantic art were produced throughout the Victorian period, and self-consciously 'decadent' works at the end of the 19th century drew on the most perverse and equivocal side of Romanticism. The movement itself has left an unbelievably rich artistic legacy, while Romantic emotions and attitudes live on, as powerful as ever, in all of us.

conjure up fairies or wit... episodes from the com... influenced music as never... great creations of Germa... (accompanied song), the... important as the music to... this was the age of 'programme music', in which the title or written notes enable the listener to follow the sequence of Romantic emotions or events that the score is intended to represent. Romanticism in music persisted beyond our period, becoming increasingly innovative in, for example, the works of Wagner and Mahler, and on into the 20th century.

Romantic politics tended to be utopian, and the French Revolution of 1789 attracted personalities as diverse as Blake, Wordsworth, Coleridge and Beethoven. Although it was much more than a Romantic occasion, the Revolution certainly had its Romantic side: Rousseau was its prophet, many of its great events smacked of political theatre, and a new spirit of naturalness and liberation led to interesting changes in everyday life such as the abandonment of wigs and the adoption of flowing hair and flowing garments. The development of revolutionary terror disillusioned many supporters such as Wordsworth, although years later he could still conjure up vivid memories of a time when 'Bliss was it in that dawn to be alive, but to be young was very Heaven!'

Sardanapalus *(1827, below).*

JEAN-JACQUES ROUSSEAU

1712-1778

Novelist, autobiographer, composer, philosopher and
educationalist, Jean-Jacques Rousseau was the great trail-blazer of
Romanticism and one of the most influential men who ever lived.
Himself an outsider in the sophisticated society of the 18th century,
he brought into literature and life an emotional intensity, a cult of
sincerity and a feeling for nature that swept his readers away and
transformed their ideas. At the same time, the political implications
of his writings undermined the established order and foreshadowed
the French Revolution.

The First Romantic

After an erratic vagabond youth, Rousseau became a Parisian celebrity when he was almost 40. Maintaining a prickly independence, he spent his last years in flight, exile and poverty.

Rousseau's birthplace
Rousseau's Geneva was a sovereign city, comfortable and industrious but still conscious of its stern, heroic past as the centre of Calvinism, the most rigorous of Protestant sects. Richard Parkes Bonington's painting shows Geneva as it was in the early 19th century, substantially unchanged since Rousseau's boyhood. The writer ran away from the city, but was marked by its spirit.

Jean-Jacques Rousseau was born on 28 June 1712 at Geneva, which was at that time an independent city-state. His mother, Suzanne Rousseau, died after giving birth to him, and her husband Isaac, a master watchmaker, brought up Jean-Jacques at home in haphazard fashion. For a time the little boy and his father constantly read novels to each other, an activity that gave Rousseau a premature sensitivity and 'the strangest and most romantic notions about life' which he claimed never to have shaken off.

After the death of his wife, who was of a higher social class, Isaac's fortunes declined rapidly, and to make matters worse he ran into trouble and was exiled from Geneva. However, the nine-year-old Jean-Jacques was taken in by his maternal uncle and had a happy enough childhood until 1725, when he was put in a notary's office as a trainee clerk. Unable to tolerate the stifling routine, he managed to get himself dismissed, upon which his uncle bound him as an apprentice to a brutal engraver, whose thrashings encouraged the boy to tell lies and steal.

To escape the miseries of reality, Rousseau read voraciously and acquired a lifelong addiction to the pleasures of fantasy and solitude. However, on many Sundays he happily joined other apprentices on jaunts into the countryside beyond the city walls; and his life was changed by the irregular hours at which the city gates were closed. Having twice been shut out for the night, he felt unable to face his master's rage when it happened for a third time, early in 1728, and ran away from Geneva to seek his fortune in the wider world.

YOUTHFUL ADVENTURES

A short walk took him across the border of Protestant Geneva and into the Duchy of Savoy. In Catholic territory and in urgent need of support, Rousseau allowed himself to be taken up as a potential convert and was sent on to the cathedral city of Annecy. There he presented himself to Françoise Louise, Baronne de Warens, and immediately fell under her spell. This 29-year-old aristocrat was herself something of an adventuress who had deserted her Swiss husband, converted to Catholicism, and now lived on the pensions with which her action had been rewarded. She was a charming, good-natured, pleasantly amoral and extravagant woman with a marked taste for hangers-on and dubious schemes that would eventually ruin her.

Although Mme de Warens played a formative role in Rousseau's life, on this occasion she merely received the 15-year-old boy sympathetically and arranged for him to be sent on over the Alps to a hospice at Turin. There he underwent a more or less sincere conversion, after which he was dismayed to be turned out into the street. He scraped along by doing simple engraving jobs,

Nature mystic
This engraving of Rousseau as a young man (left) is an ideal rather than a true-to-life portrait. But it does convey something of the almost mystical rapture that he always experienced in the presence of nature.

Protégé and lover
Rousseau's relationship with Mme de Warens (right) dominated his life for over ten years. She educated him, polished him, and took him as her lover. His feelings, however, were more those of a devoted son.

worked for a time as a valet, and finally walked back over the Alps to Annecy.

Luckily Mme de Warens was as kind-hearted as he hoped, and allowed him to stay. Soon he was in a position of comfortable, adoring dependence, and they were calling each other 'Mama' and 'little one'. Mme de Warens had no idea of her protégé's gifts since, although not unattractive, he was tongue-tied and easily made to look foolish on social occasions. He was sent back from a seminary as too stupid to make a village priest, and even failed as a trainee musician, although he had a passion for the subject and real but hidden gifts.

On each occasion Rousseau was happy to return to Mama's; but she may have been less enthusiastic about having an extra mouth to feed. At any rate she persuaded Rousseau to accompany the local choirmaster on a journey to Lyons, from which he returned to find her gone. In fact she had left for Paris to try to obtain

'That lovely lake'
'I wanted to feast my eyes on that lovely lake' (above), wrote Rousseau of his visit to Lausanne. The lake, and the island Château de Chillon, also inspired Byron's Prisoner of Chillon.

Music master
For some years Rousseau earned his living by giving music lessons. The master-pupil relationship (left) was often potentially amorous – a danger from which Rousseau's 'Mama' decided to 'save' him.

backing for a hare-brained political scheme which came to nothing. Left to his own devices, Rousseau ended up spending some time at Lausanne because 'I wanted to feast my eyes upon that lovely lake'. There, with the brazen effrontery that sometimes unaccountably replaced his shyness, he passed himself off as a Parisian music teacher until his ignorance was exposed. Moving to Neuchâtel, Rousseau was more successful: 'Insensibly I learned music by teaching it.'

But his adventures were far from over. Lured by his love of travel, Rousseau became secretary and interpreter to a Greek priest who was touring Europe to collect funds for the restoration of the Holy Sepulchre. Shortly afterwards a French diplomat exposed this 'Archimandrite' as a charlatan, but took Rousseau under his wing, finding him a job in Paris. When that fell through, Rousseau walked from Paris to Lyons and in the autumn of 1731 managed to contact Mme de Warens, who arranged for him to join her at her new house at Chambéry in Savoy.

MOTHER AND MISTRESS

Rousseau lived for most of the next ten years with Mme de Warens, helping to run her estate or teaching music to the young ladies of Chambéry. He was still sexually naive enough to be surprised by the discovery that Mama's steward, Claude Anet, was her lover – and even more surprised when she decided that to save her 'little one' from being corrupted by one of his predatory clients, she had better initiate him herself.

Rousseau and Anet shared Mme de Warens' favours until Anet's death in 1734. In the following year Rousseau persuaded his mistress to lease an estate at Les Charmettes, in the countryside outside Chambéry. Returning every year, he formed a taste for country life that his writings would later transmit to generations of readers. It was here, too, that he had his first severe illness, and a consequent change of heart that turned him towards study, writing and composing.

In later years Rousseau took an idyllic view of the brief period in which he had Mme de Warens to himself at Les Charmettes. By 1737 there was another young man on the scene, and when Rousseau returned from a trip to Montpellier – on which he himself had had a gratifying amorous experience – he found his rival fully installed. Mme de Warens was perfectly happy to continue on the old footing with Rousseau, but he preferred to terminate a sexual relationship which he had always felt to be uncomfortably incestuous. His feeling for Mama – 'the best of mothers' – was essentially filial, doubtless because he had been deprived of his natural mother; and he preferred to believe that Mme de Warens' easy-going attitude to sex was the result of indifference – a 'chaste heart and icy disposition' – rather than enthusiasm.

Nevertheless Rousseau's position became increasingly awkward, and reluctantly he went out into the world once more. He remained devoted to Mme de Warens, and in later life did what he could to help her as her fortunes declined. But in leaving for Paris in the summer of 1742, the 30-year-old Rousseau entered a new phase of his unusual life story.

Rousseau's hopes of winning immediate fame and fortune were dashed when his scheme for a new musical notation was received by the Academy with lukewarm politeness. Then in 1742-43 he served as secretary to the

Country idyll
Rousseau remembered his years with Mme de Warens at Les Charmettes (left) as the happiest period of his life. There he could botanize, study and write in peace – until another young man came upon the scene. After working for a year as a tutor at Lyon, Rousseau left to start a new life in Paris.

neurotically unstable French ambassador in Venice, returning to Paris disgusted with subservience and worse off than before.

During the next few years Rousseau maintained a penurious independence while he composed an unsuccessful opera and lived in a boarding house. There he began a relationship with the establishment's laundry maid, Thérèse Levasseur, who became his life's companion. Compassion and convenience, rather than passion, attached Rousseau to this near-illiterate girl, who was incapable even of telling the time; yet he did value her companionship and the simple pleasures that they shared.

Over the years Thérèse had five children by Rousseau, who, by his own account, got rid of each new baby by sending it to the foundlings' home in Paris. In his *Confessions* Rousseau put forward several half-hearted arguments to justify his conduct, but he ended by admitting that it had always troubled his conscience. Thousands of indigent Parisians actually behaved in this fashion, but were not as candid – or naive – as Rousseau in making the fact public.

There was now another, more sophisticated side to Rousseau's life. He was making his way in intellectual society and becoming accepted in Parisian salons where, despite his continuing sense of being a clumsy outsider, he made a fair showing. He also learned much, socially and intellectually, by working as a researcher for wealthy friends with literary ambitions who paid badly but entertained him stylishly in their town houses and châteaux. All this brought him into fruitful contact with

Parisian pleasures
Eighteenth-century Paris (above, top) was a hard school of experience for most newcomers. Rousseau found comfort in his relationship with Thérèse Levasseur (above), an almost illiterate but shrewd laundry maid who became his lifelong companion. Later he mixed simple home pleasures with forays into the salons and châteaux of his wealthy and clever friends.

the *philosophes* – 'philosophers', or liberal intellectuals, such as Denis Diderot and Jean d'Alembert, whose witty, intelligent writings aimed to undermine France's caste-ridden, intolerant social and political order.

The *philosophes'* most potent weapon proved to be the *Encyclopédie*, a seemingly harmless, multi-volume encyclopedia into which they smuggled a range of subversive facts and opinions. The appearance of the first volume in 1751 caused a sensation, making celebrities of the editors, Diderot and d'Alembert, and of contributors such as Rousseau, who had written most of the music articles. Almost simultaneously Rousseau published his first substantial work, the *Discourse on the Arts and Sciences*. This had already won first prize in an essay competition set by the Academy of Dijon, and now stirred up a tremendous controversy by praising primitive simplicity and condemning culture and society as instruments of corruption.

FASHIONABLE PHILOSOPHER

Having come to these conclusions, Rousseau determined to live accordingly. He began to dress plainly, sometimes appeared unshaven, signed himself plain 'citizen of Geneva', and presented himself as a simple, straightforward 'bear' who scorned the artifice and insincerity of polite society. Paradoxically, the result seems to have boosted his self-confidence, and to have given him a good deal of social success as a fascinating eccentric.

Rousseau even presented himself in this fashion at court when the King ordered a performance of his opera *The Village Soothsayer* in 1752. This too was a triumph for

Daring Diderot
Denis Diderot (below) was a close friend of Rousseau, although Rousseau's mounting persecution complex eventually convinced him that Diderot was part of a plot against him. During his lifetime Diderot was mainly known as the editor of the subversive Encyclopédie, *published – often clandestinely – between 1751 and 1772. Posthumous publication of literary works such as* Rameau's Nephew *gave Diderot a new reputation as a highly original imaginative writer.*

Subversive knowledge
Rousseau contributed to the great Encyclopédie *(above), an epoch-making compendium of liberal thought that undermined France's 'Old Regime'.*

D'Alembert
The mathematician Jean de la Rond d'Alembert (right) co-edited the Encyclopédie, *but withdrew in the face of official hostility.*

17

Royal audience
Under Louis XV (above), the French monarchy lost much of its prestige, although crowned heads all over Europe copied the great royal palace at Versailles (above, top). Restless and easily bored, the King moved from one residence to another, and the command performance of Rousseau's opera took place at Fontainebleau.

'Rousseauist' simplicity, its pastoral story and tuneful songs captivating the sophisticated audience at Fontainebleu. Afterwards Rousseau avoided meeting the King, who would almost certainly have rewarded him with a useful pension. In this way he preserved his independence – and also avoided a formal interview at which he might make a fool of himself and would certainly feel acute physical discomfort. For Rousseau suffered from an embarrassing and at times agonizing malady: a partly-blocked bladder that compelled him to make frequent use of a chamber pot. His discomforts encouraged him in one of his more notable eccentricities, the wearing of Armenian costume, consisting of a fur hat and conveniently loose caftan.

Over the next few years Rousseau wrote a second *Discourse* and took a vigorous part in musical controversy while continuing to earn his living at the humble but reliable trade of music copyist. Weary of Paris, he visited his native city, renewed his citizenship rights by returning to Protestantism, and considered settling there; but eventually he moved into the Hermitage, a rustic cottage a few miles outside Paris, which had been offered to him by his friend Mme d'Epinay. Although most of his other friends wagered that he would be back within three months, on 9 April 1756 Rousseau 'left Paris never to live in a town again'. Life in the country suited him and stimulated his creativity, although visitors from Paris, Thérèse's parasitic relations and Mme d'Epinay in her nearby château all made demands on his time.

Fur-capped philosopher
This portrait of 1766 shows Rousseau in his celebrated 'Armenian' outfit. Comfortable and convenient, it also suited his chosen image as a Romantic outsider.

LOVE AND FLIGHT

Feeling that he was growing old, and afraid of 'dying without ever having lived', Rousseau was ready to fall passionately in love for the first time. When he did so, it was with Mme d'Houdetot, the exquisitely charming although by no means beautiful sister-in-law of Mme d'Epinay. Unfortunately Mme d'Houdetot already had a complaisant husband and a devoted lover who was Rousseau's friend. While the lover, St Lambert, was absent with the French army, Rousseau and his beloved developed a painfully intense, platonic relationship that inevitably came to nothing, although it seems to have inspired the story of Rousseau's famous novel *La Nouvelle Héloïse*.

Perhaps because of this episode, Rousseau quarrelled with Mme d'Epinay and felt obliged to leave the Hermitage at the end of 1757. His relations with other old friends also showed signs of deteriorating, and he began to believe that dark plots were being hatched against him – a paranoid conviction which was partly responsible for his subsequent misfortunes, but which remained curiously compartmentalized, leaving his literary genius unimpaired.

Nevertheless Rousseau still received generous offers of hospitality, and was able to live in the country while he entered upon a period of intense creativity. But, having published the sensationally popular *Nouvelle Héloïse* (1761) and other major works, he fell foul of the powerful French law courts, which in 1762 condemned his writings and issued a warrant for his arrest. He fled to Switzerland, avoiding Geneva – where his writings were also disliked – but found only temporary havens before being forced to move on from one territory to the next.

Driven from Switzerland, in 1766 Rousseau accepted an invitation to settle in England, secured for him by the Scottish philosopher David Hume. Having been given a pension by George III, he settled for the winter at Wootton in Staffordshire, where he began his last major work, the *Confessions*. Appalled by the English climate and convinced that Hume was part of the grand conspiracy against him, he returned surreptitiously to France, where he moved restlessly from place to place, living incognito. Finally, in 1770, he was allowed to return to Paris.

The rest of Rousseau's life was relatively peaceful, and his paranoia seems to have abated. In Paris he and Thérèse lived in poverty, supported by his music copying. He had married Thérèse in 1768, despite the fact that his ailment had terminated their sexual relations years before and that she had been notoriously unfaithful to him. He wrote little now except for some final, mutedly eloquent *Reveries*. Near to the end of his life he moved back to the country, and he died of a stroke at Ermenonville on 2 July 1778. His influence lived on in the Romantic spirit he had fostered throughout Europe, and in the Revolution which, only 11 years later, proclaimed him as its greatest inspiration.

Beloved

In his forties, Rousseau fell in love with Mme d'Houdetot (above), the wife of a nobleman. Marital obligations were taken lightly in 18th-century French society, but she was faithful – to her lover.

Mme d'Epinay

(above, right) offered Rousseau a rustic cottage where he could live the philosophic life. To his friends' surprise, he did – until his relationship with his patron deteriorated.

David Hume

Rousseau settled in England on the invitation of the Scottish philosopher David Hume (right). But persecution mania and English weather soon drove him away again.

Final refuge

After years of wandering and an impoverished old age spent in Paris, Rousseau found a final, appropriately picturesque refuge in a cabin at Ermenonville (left).

Inspired Outsider

Doggedly independent, and content not to write unless inspired, Jean-Jacques Rousseau published only a handful of books – but almost every one was an extraordinary, eloquent, original, world-changing achievement.

Whatever his faults as a man, Rousseau was fearlessly independent as a writer. He avoided literary coteries and, rather than become a professional author, preferred to earn his living as a music copyist. Since he was not dependent on literature for his bread, he was never obliged to write against the clock, publish regularly, or set out to please his readers. 'I feel that writing for a livelihood would soon have stifled my genius and killed my talent, which lay less in my pen than in my heart . . . It is too difficult to think nobly when one only thinks for a living.' The paradoxical outcome was that freedom from commercial pressures enabled Rousseau to produce the kind of fresh, original work that made him one of the most widely read authors of his time, although his attitude ensured that the financial benefits would be relatively small.

He also fitted the popular image of the Romantic artist in being completely at the mercy of inspiration – or of the lack of it. Ideas 'arrive when they please, not when it suits me. Either they do not come at all, or they come in a swarm, overwhelming me with their strength and their numbers'. However, like many other writers he discovered that inspiration could be encouraged by providing the most favourable conditions for its arrival, which in Rousseau's case meant taking a walk, preferably in the country; in fact he claimed that his thoughts advanced only while his legs continued to do the same. Above all, walking in a forest stimulated him, and it was not an accident that his most prolific years, the late 1750s and early '60s, coincided with his quiet life in the country close to the forest of Montmorency, just before he was driven from France. A true Romantic, Rousseau felt a sense of liberation in the presence of nature, declaring that he 'never liked to pray in a room' because 'walls and all the little works of man come between myself and God'.

Although ideas came readily enough in the right surroundings, the words in which they were to be expressed were less easy to find. Surprisingly, Rousseau – one of the great French stylists – was not a fluent writer. He composed everything slowly and with great labour, endlessly striking out, altering and correcting, so that all his works had to be written out again four or five times; however, his final manuscript, intended for the printer,

was a masterpiece of elegant calligraphy. He also did a good deal of mental 'writing' in bed during periods of insomnia, but found that his poor memory caused him to forget his painstakingly constructed paragraphs even before he could get to pen and paper. He devised an effective, if characteristically eccentric, solution to the problem, arranging for the mother of his mistress Thérèse to be present at his bedside every morning, ready to receive dictation before he got up!

THE NOBLE SAVAGE

Rousseau began his career as a literary man in his thirties, after settling in Paris; but for years he seemed unlikely to produce anything more significant than skilfully written encyclopaedia articles for his friend Diderot. Then in 1750 the Academy of Lyons announced that it would award a gold medal for the best essay written in answer to the question 'Has the progress of the arts and sciences had a purifying effect upon morals?' Walking out to Vincennes to

Noble savage

Rousseau gave wide currency to the idea that civilization corrupts, and that only simple folk or primitive peoples are happy, noble and free. Rousseau's readers admired Tahitians and Corsicans; later writers such as Chateaubriand found similar qualities in the North American Indian (left).

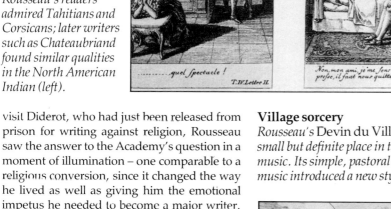

.... *quel spectacle !*

T.IV.Lettre II.

Non, mon ami, je me sens bien la mort me presse, il faut nous quitter.

T.IV.Lettre XXII.

O grand Être! Être éternel, Je le sais je m'en réjouis, je vais paroître devant ton trône.

T.IV.Lettre XXII.

Julie

Rousseau's novel Julie *(left), better known by its subtitle,* La Nouvelle Héloïse, *was a landmark in the evolution of sensibility. Its now dated raptures and deathbed dramatics (left) brought a new intensity into life and literature.*

visit Diderot, who had just been released from prison for writing against religion, Rousseau saw the answer to the Academy's question in a moment of illumination – one comparable to a religious conversion, since it changed the way he lived as well as giving him the emotional impetus he needed to become a major writer. His *Discourse on the Arts and Sciences* – a substantial pamphlet rather than an essay in the modern sense – roundly declared that the arts and sciences had corrupted, not improved, humanity. And in a subsequent, more cogently argued discourse, Rousseau pinpointed the source of corruption more precisely, indicting organized society, and in particular the inequalities produced by a system of private property, as the cause of human vices and follies.

Although Rousseau did not invent the myth of an ancient golden age, his version of it achieved an unparalleled emotional impact. The idea of 'the noble savage' – of a desirably unspoiled primitive existence that it might be possible to recapture – has haunted Western man ever since.

Rousseau always insisted that the discourses were simply analyses, and not programmes of action, since it was simply not possible to turn back the clock and revert to a state of nature. But they were also rather more than theoretical exercises since they did imply a set of values that were relevant to Rousseau's own time, and that he himself tried to live by. Rules, conventions, codes of manners and other artificial restraints were evidently bad: simplicity, spontaneity and sincerity were good. And while society corrupted, contact with nature elevated. This essentially Romantic creed found its clearest expression in Rousseau's novel *La Nouvelle Héloïse* (1761). Although too lengthily high-minded for most present-day tastes, this was the most sensationally successful of all Rousseau's books, describing a ménage à trois set against a splendidly painted Alpine background, in which the characters spoke and behaved with a passionate intensity new in fiction.

A few years earlier Rousseau had played a

Village sorcery

Rousseau's Devin du Village *(below) has a small but definite place in the history of music. Its simple, pastoral story and tuneful music introduced a new style.*

similar pioneering role as a composer. His opera *The Village Soothsayer* (1752) had moved the court (the ladies sighing 'Every note speaks straight to the heart') precisely because of its pastoral setting and simple melodies, so unlike the portentous sonorities of the French classical tradition. Rousseau had initially been influenced by the sprightly tunefulness of the operas he had heard in Venice; and later, when an Italian company came to Paris, he wrote in

Rameau

In Rousseau's day, the outstanding French composer was Jean Philippe Rameau (right), whose operas and opera-ballets dominated the stage. Rameau was a musical conservative by comparison with Rousseau, and performances in Paris by the Italian opera led to a bitter controversy between the two men.

A disciple

This delightful painting by Joseph Wright of Derby shows Sir Brooke Boothby (left), a fervent follower of Rousseau, in an appropriately arcadian setting; he holds a copy of Rousseau's Emile *in his elegantly gloved hand. Boothby defended Rousseau's character against a 'wanton butcherly attack' mounted by Edmund Burke.*

its defence during the controversy that arose over the merits of the two national schools. Joining battle with France's most distinguished composer, Rameau, Rousseau insisted upon the priority of melody – the principle of freedom and spontaneity – in opposition to the older composer's championship of harmony, the Classical principle of order and control. The controversy bore fruit, since the great operatic composer Gluck was influenced by Rousseau's arguments; while the minor but charming *Village Soothsayer* inspired the young Mozart's *Bastien and Bastienne*.

One of Rousseau's longest-meditated works – he claimed he had been thinking about it for 20 years – was *Emile* (1762). This was a treatise on education thinly disguised as a novel, and another of Rousseau's works that profoundly influenced people's lives. Believing in natural goodness and freedom, he rejected traditional methods of teaching and discipline, showing Emile learning by doing, making discoveries for himself, and acquiring knowledge as and when he genuinely needed it. Widely studied and imitated in its own time, *Emile* remains a classic text of the 'progressive' approach to education.

Rousseau returned to the political issues implicit in the discourses in *The Social Contract* (1762), one of the most influential works of political philosophy ever written. It opens with the rousing sentence 'Man is born free; yet everywhere he is in chains', and goes on to ask whether there is any way of organizing a state so that its citizens could be considered truly free. Rousseau's answer is that the laws and government of such a state would represent 'the General Will' rather than the will of an individual or class. In spite of philosophical

objections and qualifications, these ideas became widely known and their effect was deeply subversive, since all could see that the monarchies of Europe were hopelessly unrepresentative of the General Will. Rousseau's writings can hardly have caused the French Revolution, but they permeated its atmosphere, giving the participants readily understood ideals and slogans, couched in what became the characteristic rhetorical style of the era.

THE CONFESSIONS

In 1766, in the gloom and bitter cold of an English winter at Wootton in Staffordshire, Rousseau began the most quintessentially Romantic of all his projects: an autobiography, intended for posthumous publication, in which he tried to relate his life with complete truthfulness. He rightly called this 'an enterprise which has no precedent', since earlier autobiographers mainly concerned themselves with events, dwelling very little on their psychological development; while those who went so far as to mention their sins and shortcomings were usually motivated by a religious zeal to convert rather than to inform the reader.

By contrast, Rousseau wanted to make a complete record of his life and personality because they were his own, and therefore unique, although he did not necessarily suppose that they were admirable: 'I am made unlike anyone I have ever met; I will even venture to say that I am like no one in the entire world. I may be no better, but at least I am different.'

The difference appears throughout this extended self-portrait, with its immense

psychological acuteness and uncomfortable candour, although inevitably its most celebrated passages are those describing Jean-Jacques' sexual peculiarities and some of his more shameful actions. The *Confessions* was published in 1782, four years after Rousseau's death. If he was correct in believing that it had no precedent, he was far from the mark in supposing that it would 'have no imitator'. Not the least of Rousseau's achievements was to have blazed a trail that has since been followed by legions of autobiographical novelists and confessional writers who have brought to light hitherto hidden areas of the human personality. In this, as in so many other respects, Rousseau was a true original.

FRANCISCO DE GOYA

1746-1828

Francisco de Goya was the greatest painter of 18th century Spain. Born in an isolated village, he went to Madrid at 18 to work in the studio of Francisco Bayeu, whose sister he later married. Madrid was the centre of Spanish culture and society, but Goya was slow to make his name, becoming a royal painter only when he was 43. From then on his future was assured, and he quickly rose to even higher eminence.

Goya first earned his reputation painting cartoons for tapestries, and further success came from portraits. But his most remarkable works were produced after a serious illness left him permanently deaf. Paintings and etchings of his bizarre, fantastic 'imaginings' were followed by satires on high society and ghastly visions of the horrors of war. His late 'black paintings' were more dramatic still, with immense, if sombre impact.

The 'Deaf Man' of Madrid

At the age of 47 – four years after his appointment as painter to the Spanish king – Goya was struck by deafness. He lived to witness the downfall of the monarchy and to chronicle the disasters of war.

Francisco Jośe de Goya y Lucientes, the son of a gilder, was born on 30 March 1746 in the desolate village of Fuendetodos in western Spain. When he was 14, the family moved to Saragossa, the capital of his native region of Aragon, and Francisco was apprenticed to the painter José Luzán, at that time the leading artist of Saragossa. (One of his specialities was adding drapery to nude figures in religious pictures, for which he was given the official title of 'Reviser of Indecent Paintings'.) In Saragossa, Goya also met the painter Francisco Bayeu, who was 12 years older than him and enjoying the rapidly growing success that in 1763 led him to the court of Madrid. Goya moved to Madrid soon after Bayeu and worked in his studio.

MADRID, CENTRE OF THE ARTS

To be established at Madrid was, at this time, virtually the only way in which a provincial Spanish artist could gain more than merely local recognition. The great wealth of the Spanish monarchy and its lavish patronage of the arts also attracted major painters from elsewhere in Europe. In the 1760s and 1770s the two most important artists at the court were the Venetian Giambattista Tiepolo and the German Anton Raffael Mengs, both of whom had a major influence on Goya's evolution as an artist.

In 1763 and 1766 Goya made unsuccessful attempts to enter the recently founded Madrid Academy of Art and then, probably in 1770, he did what was customary for ambitious young artists: he went to Italy. Here he enjoyed his first minor success, getting an honourable mention in a

The Spanish capital
When Goya moved to Madrid in 1764 to work with his future brother-in-law, Francisco Bayeu, he entered one of Europe's most modern cities, already equipped with both street lights and sanitation. This view across the River Manzanares shows a panorama stretching from the Royal Palace on the left to the magnificent Church of S. Francisco el Grande on the right.

Josefa Bayeu
In 1773 Goya married Josefa Bayeu, the sister of his teacher. She bore him several children, but only his son Javier reached maturity. Josefa, painted here by Goya, died in 1812 at Madrid.

The family home
Goya grew up in the rocky, arid region of Aragon. His birthplace, a two-storey stone house in the village of Fuendetodos, has been preserved as a memorial to him.

In the 1790s, with the tapestry designs completed, Goya devoted himself principally to the types of work by which he is best known today: portraits and imaginative compositions. Towards the end of 1792 a traumatic change occurred in his life when he developed a mysterious illness, variously and unconvincingly interpreted as syphilis, lead poisoning from using white paint, and even a severe nervous breakdown. At any rate, it caused him temporary paralysis and partial blindness, and left him permanently deaf.

The illness also had a significant effect on the development of Goya's art. While convalescing in 1793 he painted a series of small oil paintings of bizarre subjects of 'fantasy and invention', as Goya himself described them, telling the Academy later that he had produced them 'in order to occupy an imagination mortified by the contemplation of my sufferings'.

Goya's increasingly introverted and morbidly imaginative tendencies as an artist were not greatly appreciated by his contemporaries. But they did not in any way hinder his worldly success. In 1795, on the death of Bayeu, he was promoted to Director of Painting at the Academy,

A tapestry for the King

Goya's first important commission in Madrid was to design tapestries for King Charles III. The Swing was woven by the Royal Tapestry manufactory from a painting by Goya in 1779.

painting competition organized by the Art Academy of Parma. In 1771 he returned to Spain, and two years later married Bayeu's sister, Josefa. The following year he was summoned to work, first under Mengs and then under Bayeu, on cartoons for tapestries to be woven at the Royal Factory of Santa Barbara in Madrid. This task was to occupy him sporadically until 1792.

Goya's beginnings as an artist were slow and unremarkable. It was not until the 1780s, when he was already in his mid-30s, that important official recognition came his way. In 1780 he was elected a member of the Madrid Academy, and five years later he was made Deputy Director of Painting there. After Charles IV was crowned in 1789, Goya was at last appointed as one of the royal painters, a promotion which he celebrated by adding the aristocratic 'de' to his name.

The Royal Family
(left) Goya painted The Family of Charles IV *in 1800. His avoidance of flattery led one critic to comment that the King and Queen looked like 'the corner baker and his wife after they have won the lottery'. Prince Ferdinand is in blue on the left; his bride-to-be has her face averted, as their engagement had not been officially announced. Goya himself is in the background at his easel.*

The Escorial Palace
(right) As court painter, Goya often visited this royal residence in the Guadarrama mountains outside Madrid. This palace-monastery, built in 1563 as a retreat, is where the Spanish monarchs are buried.

and in 1798 he received the prestigious commission to decorate the church of S. Antonio de la Florida in Madrid. The following year he was appointed First Painter to the King. By now he could count among his friends and patrons many leading intellectuals and aristocrats in Madrid.

THE NAKED MAJA

Goya was on particularly close terms with the widowed Duchess of Alba, a beautiful, intelligent and powerful woman. Their relationship was the source of much gossip, especially after Goya spent the summer of 1796 on her estate in Andalusia, where the Duchess had moved after the death of her husband. One of the most popular legends in art history – almost certainly wrong – holds that she was the model for Goya's famous pair of paintings, *The Naked Maja* and *The Clothed Maja*.

Such speculations have often been used to flesh out our rather meagre information about the less public aspects of Goya's personality. He has been depicted variously as a relentless womanizer, a manic-depressive, a revolutionary, and a sort of Hamlet-like figure, viewing society with growing scepticism and pessimism and ultimately achieving an almost other-wordly detachment from it. However, the evidence for all this is scanty. The known facts of Goya's life reveal little more than a great concern with his social standing, financial shrewdness, a love of pigeon-shooting, and an unwillingness to allow political or other forms of idealism to get in the way of the practical business of living.

The first half of Goya's life was a time of political stability in Spain. But the reign of Charles IV (1789-1808) saw mounting unrest, made even worse by the international repercussions of the French Revolution. Charles was a weak and lazy ruler, greatly influenced by his strong-minded wife, Maria Luisa, who in turn was led by the upstart favourite, Manuel de Godoy. The rule of this 'trinity on earth', as the queen described it, was highly unpopular with both the nobility and the public.

Eventually, in 1808, mass disturbances caused the downfall of Godoy and forced Charles IV to resign in favour of his son Ferdinand VII.

However, during this period of intrigue and confusion the French had secured a foothold in the peninsula, and Ferdinand was almost immediately forced to hand over his throne to Napoleon's brother, Joseph. The French occupation provoked serious rioting in Madrid and led to a bloody civil war. Goya's own allegiances are not clear, but he was appalled by the brutality of the fighting, and in his horrific series of etchings, the *Disasters of War*, he portrayed atrocities committed by both sides.

HONOURED BY THE ENEMY

Whatever Goya's political views, he also had to make a living, and it was therefore prudent, if not perhaps principled, for him to swear allegiance to the French king and in 1811 to accept from him the Royal Order of Spain. This caused trouble for him after Ferdinand VII was restored to the throne in 1814, following the intervention of British troops under the Duke of Wellington – whom Goya was also quite happy to portray. But the painter

The Second of May, 1808 (1814) *(below) Goya commemorated the uprising of the people of Madrid against Napoleon's cavalry in one of the most terrifying and convincing battle scenes in the history of art. There is no sense of good triumphing over evil; instead Goya shows ghastly and bloody confusion. His theme is not patriotism, but horror at man's inhumanity.*

The Beautiful Duchess

In 1796, Goya's relationship with the widowed Duchess of Alba caused scandal in Madrid. At 34, this high-born lady was nearly 16 years younger than Goya, and famous for her capricious nature. She and her husband had been Goya's patrons, and when the Duke died that summer, she retired with the artist to her country estate at Sanlucar. Here it has been supposed they became lovers. Certainly his notebook conveys an idyllic atmosphere, and some of his sketches depict erotic poses for which the Duchess may have modelled.

The Duchess in love
Goya's portrait of the Duchess, dated 1797, suggests a close relationship between them. The names inscribed on her two rings are 'Alba' and 'Goya' and she points to the words 'Solo (only) Goya', written in the sand.

The Naked Maja (c.1800)
Legend has it that the Duchess of Alba posed for this erotic painting, which later led Goya into the hands of the Inquisition.

escaped the punishment meted out to some of his liberal friends by claiming that he had never worn the medal awarded to him by the French. In addition he offered to paint for the king his two famous scenes of the Madrid rioting that had led to the war: *The Second of May, 1808* and *The Third of May, 1808*.

The gloom of Goya's later paintings may well reflect the morbidly represssive atmosphere in Spain following the restoration of Ferdinand VII. Universities and theatres were closed down, press censorship was introduced, and the dreaded religious tribunal, the Inquisition, was re-established. No sooner had Goya been exonerated from the charge of having 'accepted employment from the usurper' than he found himself summonded in front of the Inquisition to explain why and for whom he had painted the allegedly obscene *Naked Maja* and its companion piece. The artist had other problems to contend with. His wife had died in 1812, and he was now embarked on an affair with a married woman, Leocadia Weiss, which made him the subject of malicious gossip.

WITHDRAWAL FROM PUBLIC LIFE

Ferdinand VII took hardly any interest in Goya, but kept him on as his First Painter; and when Goya eventually retired from the post, the King awarded him a generous pension which enabled him to live comfortably until his death. He virtually withdrew from public life after 1815, and worked almost exclusively for himself and for a circle of close friends.

In 1819 serious illness struck Goya again, and

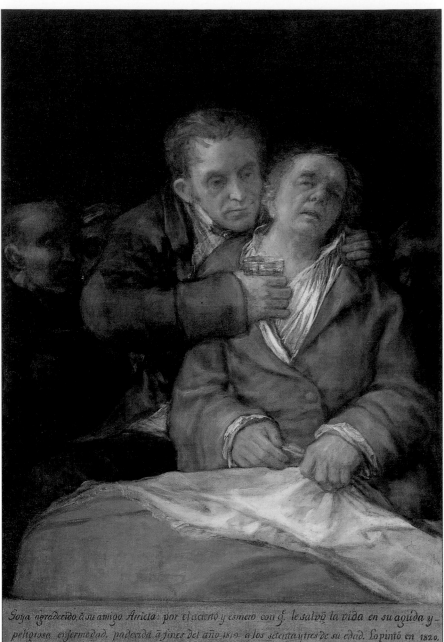

Goya agradecido, á su amigo Arrieta: por el acierto y esmero con q. le salvó la vida en su aguda y peligrosa enfermedad, padecida á fines del año 1819, á los setenta y tres de su edad. Lo pintó en 1820.

The Court of the Inquisition (1815)

Goya's chilling painting (detail, left) captures the ritual nature of the Inquisition's proceedings and the misery of its victims, condemned to wear tall conical hats and robes painted with flames. Under royal patronage the Inquisition was particularly active in Spain, where unnumbered thousands of heretics – actual or imaginary – were tortured and burned alive. Goya himself had to answer to the Inquisition in 1815 for painting The Naked Maja, *but emerged unscathed.*

he recovered only thanks to the intervention of a fashionable Madrid doctor, Eugenio García Arrieta. In gratitude, Goya painted an extraordinary double portrait, showing himself half-dying in bed being supported by Arrieta, who is offering him a draught of medicine; in the background is a group of dark and sinister figures. Similar reflections on death and old age are to be found in the 'black paintings' that he executed between 1820 and 1823 on the walls of his newly acquired house (the 'Quinta del Sordo' or 'House of the Deaf Man') in the country outside Madrid.

The three years during which the artist was engaged on these works, perhaps the most terrifying and technically astonishing in his career, saw a brief moment of liberalization in Ferdinand's regime. However, by the end of 1823 reaction had set in again, and many of Goya's liberal friends sought refuge in France. A number of them went to Bordeaux, including Leocadia Weiss, who took with her the child she had supposedly had by Goya. He joined her there soon afterwards, having

The Sleep of Reason Produces Monsters
Designed originally as the frontispiece to his Caprichos *series, this etching, dated 1797-98, sums up Goya's view of humanity. When reason is allowed to sleep, monsters of the irrational take over.*

Self-portrait with Dr Arrieta (1820)
(left) As the inscription beneath the picture explains, Goya painted this moving portrait of himself and his doctor after recovering from 'an acute and dangerous illness suffered at the end of 1819, at the age of 73'.

The Bullfight (c.1827)
(below) In many of his works Goya applied his paint very freely, leaving out details and avoiding precise outlines. Here, this method expresses the chaos and excitement in the arena as the crowd of cape-waving would-be matadors floods into it.

La Manola (1820)
(above) This portrait is thought to be of Leocadia Weiss, who lived with Goya until his death. Although one of the 'black paintings' decorating the walls of the Quinta del Sordo, it has none of the nightmarish quality of the others.

been granted temporary leave of absence by the King on the pretext that he needed to take the waters at Plombières for his health.

Goya was found by his friends now to be 'deaf, old, slow and feeble'. But his enthusiasm for life was apparently as strong as ever, and his artistic powers were undimmed. He still had enough strength to make an extended sight-seeing trip to Paris, and even began experimenting with the new medium of lithography in his series the *Bulls of Bordeaux*. To the surprise of his fellow exiles, he made two brief return trips to Spain, on the first of which (in 1826) he officially handed in his resignation as court painter.

In the spring of 1828, he was visited in Bordeaux by his daughter-in-law and grandchildren. The excitement caused by their visit made him, in his own words, a 'little indisposed'. He died on 16 April following a paralytic stroke, aged 82. His mortal remains were returned to Spain in 1900 and interred in the cemetery of San Isidro in Madrid.

The Dark Side of Humanity

Goya began his career designing colourful tapestries for royal palaces. But his own traumatic illness and the dreadful events of the war against France led him to depict scenes of horrific violence.

Goya is almost universally regarded as the greatest European painter of his period. The originality, emotional range and technical freedom of his work set him apart from other artists. Indeed, among his contemporaries we have to look to Beethoven to find his equal in grandeur of imagination and power of expression.

Although Goya produced a huge amount of work as a painter and a graphic artist, he was slow to develop, and it was not until he was well over 30 that he produced work that was especially remarkable or original. His early career was taken up mainly with the repetitive task of designing tapestries to be executed at the Royal Factory of Santa Barbara in Madrid.

A TRAUMATIC ILLNESS

Goya was employed on the tapestry designs until 1792, but by that time the direction of his art had changed radically. In the 1780s he had some success as a religious painter, and in 1789 he was appointed one of the painters to the king, which meant that painting portraits would be one of his major tasks. But the most significant change in his approach to art came with the severe but mysterious illness which he suffered in 1792-93.

The traumatic effect this had on him deepened his awareness of the pain and suffering in human life, and he turned increasingly to sombre or sinister subjects.

In the two fields for which he is best known – portraiture and imaginative subjects – Goya showed both his links with the great masters of the past and his startling originality. He is reputed to have said that his only masters were 'Velázquez, Rembrandt and Nature'. These two painters (the leading artists of Spain and Holland in the 17th century) were among the greatest portraitists who ever lived, and Goya followed them in their penetrating depiction of character. Goya also shared with them a virtuosity in the handling of paint that distinguishes him from most contemporary artists, who favoured a smooth, detailed

An unorthodox painter
(left) This is a detail from a self-portrait Goya painted in about 1790. His lack of orthodoxy is seen not only in his odd appearance, but also in the vigorous sketching technique and the way in which Goya has boldly silhouetted himself against the golden light.

The Third of May, 1808 (1814)
By the eerie light of a large, square lantern, Spanish rebels are executed by a French firing squad. A row of faceless soldiers, all in the same brutal, impersonal attitude, takes aim. The condemned men react with a mixture of terror, defiance and despair. Goya focuses our attention on a larger-than-life figure in a white shirt, his arms thrown out in a Christlike gesture.

The Straw Manikin (1792)
(left) Between 1775 and 1792
Goya made 63 full-size cartoons
for the royal tapestry works. The
designs had to be bold and
colourful to make suitable wall-
hangings. Some of them are
huge, the largest being more than
20 feet wide; this one is 8ft 9in by
5ft 3in.

The master engraver
(below) Goya made almost 300
engravings in his career, but was
over 50 when he published the
first of his great series, the
Caprichos, in 1799. Three other
major series followed: the
Disasters of War (begun 1810),
Tauromaquia (begun 1815)
and the Proverbios (begun 1816).

31

The Madhouse (c.1800)
(above) Goya was not the first artist to depict madhouse scenes but no one before him had evoked such pain and pity. There was a tradition of including lunatics who crown themselves as monarchs or popes, as shown on the right of the picture. Goya's madmen, however, are not stock characters but disquieting portrayals of individuals in genuine mental torment.

finish. 'Where does one see lines in nature?' he asked. 'I see no lines or details, I don't count each hair on the head of a passer-by, or the buttons on his coat. There is no reason why my brush should see more than I do.'

In his imaginative scenes Goya also drew on a rich tradition, for Spain was a country of religious fervour, and the agonies and ecstasies of the saints had been celebrated in art for centuries, often with a grisly concentration on the suffering of martyrs. Two centuries before Goya, the Spanish king Philip II had avidly collected the bizarre works of the Flemish painter Hieronymus Bosch, and Goya would have seen the work of his great spiritual predecessor in the royal collection.

THE BLACK PAINTINGS

Goya's probing of the darker side of human nature began to emerge in his series of etchings, the *Caprichos*, in which he combined caricatures of contemporary life with gruesome fantasy. The ultimate development of this kind of theme came in the so-called 'black paintings' which he executed on the walls of his own house soon after recovering from his near-fatal illness of 1819. In these virtually colourless works depicting morbid and terrifying scenes, Goya handled paint with a freedom that could almost be called ferocious. Here Goya was painting purely for himself – a startling notion at this time, when the Romantic conception of artistic self-expression was still

unknown in Spain.

Goya's technical virtuosity and resourcefulness are as apparent in his graphic work as in his painting. He drew in pencil, in ink and in brush wash, among other media, and as a printmaker he excelled in aquatint, etching and lithography. Aquatint and etching both use acid to 'bite' into a metal printing plate a design that the artist has brushed or drawn on to it; lithography involves drawing on stone with a wax crayon and then printing from it, using an oil-based ink that adheres only to the parts that have been touched by the wax. Lithography was invented in 1798 and Goya was the first great master of the technique.

SERIES OF ETCHINGS

As well as the *Caprichos*, Goya produced three other great series of etchings: the *Disasters of War*, which records the appalling events following the French invasion of 1808; the *Tauromaquia*, a series on bullfighting; and the *Proverbios*, an enigmatic series showing various aspects of human folly. Of these, the *Disasters of War* are perhaps the most devastating. There are no heroes in Goya's war, and no glory – only death and mutilation, pain and degradation. His prints still have a shocking impact today, even though we have become accustomed to seeing such brutalities recorded in photographs and films. They stand as timeless portrayals of the conflicting forces of life and death, light and darkness.

JOHANN WOLFGANG von GOETHE
1749-1832

The greatest of all German poets, Goethe was probably the last
'universal man', able to take on the roles of author, artist and
scientist, man of the theatre, courtier, state minister and lover. His
writings gave an immense impetus to the Romantic movement, and
two of the figures he created would assume an almost mythical
significance: Werther, who dies for love, and Faust, who risks
damnation for knowledge and power. Goethe himself became
a majestic literary Olympian, living into a long and fruitful old age.

The Universal Genius

Goethe's life has been described as his greatest work of art – a carefully shaped odyssey of self-realization, crammed with experiences and emotions, stern duties and sudden flights.

Johann Wolfgang von Goethe was born on 28 August 1749 at Frankfurt-am-Main, an important Free City within the Holy Roman Empire – the empire being a patchwork of kingdoms and petty states occupying roughly the territory of modern Germany. Although his grandfather had been a shrewd and successful wine dealer, Goethe was born into a solidly comfortable upper-middle-class background. By his own account his childhood was a happy one, unspoiled even by the French occupation of Frankfurt during the Seven Years War (1756-63). In fact, performances by the troupes of actors who arrived in the wake of the French army fired a passion for the theatre that lasted throughout Goethe's life. His own talents became apparent when his grandmother presented him with a puppet theatre and he conceived and performed shows for his family and friends.

However, Johann Kaspar Goethe was determined that his son should follow in his footsteps by studying the law. For his part, the young Goethe never dared openly to defy his stern, authoritarian father, and duly went up to the University of Leipzig in October 1765; but, now and later, he used his generous allowance to lead an interesting life, devoting the minimum necessary attention to the law. At Leipzig, a much more sophisticated city than Frankfurt, he acquired some social graces, had a love affair, studied art and began to write poetry in the rather artificial style of the period.

In 1768 Goethe's stay at Leipzig was cut short by a serious illness, and he went on with his studies only after a long convalescence. At Strasbourg University he met an older writer, Johann Gottfried von Herder, who introduced him to folksong and other 'primitive' literary forms. As a result, Goethe produced verse of a new

A poet's parents
(below) Goethe's father, Johann Kaspar, was a cultivated but stern and cold man who bent his much younger wife, Elizabeth Textor, to his will. The young poet, too, found it advisable to make a show of doing as his father wished.

freshness and spontaneity, and began to emerge as a lyric poet of unsurpassed gifts.

POETRY AND LOVE

The best of these Strasbourg poems were inspired by Goethe's passion for Friederike Brion, the daughter of a pastor at nearby Sesenheim. This was his first serious romance, and breaking it off was painful to him and, he believed, almost cost Friederike her life. Class and culture placed almost insuperable barriers between them, but in any case Goethe was not looking for a wife. He was intensely susceptible, and valued emotional experience as a source of literary inspiration, but was fundamentally disinclined to commit himself to any one woman. He took a curiously detached view of his own feelings, as if they existed in a sealed-off compartment of his being, so that he could write that 'It is a very pleasant sensation when a new passion begins to stir within us, before the old one has quite passed away.' Some of his finest lyrics represented a 'self-tormenting penance' after which he gave himself 'inward absolution' for letting the loved one down! After Friederike he most often managed to fall in love with women who were engaged or married, combining the maximum emotional satisfaction with the minimum danger of permanent entanglement.

Goethe failed to get a degree at Strasbourg, but did manage to secure a licence to practice. But on his return to Frankfurt he threw himself into literature and journalism, becoming the leading figure of the 'Storm and Stress' movement. In reaction against the smooth-

Frankfurt
*Goethe's birthplace (left)
was an Imperial Free City,
basically self-governing
within the Holy Roman
Empire. Like most of
Germany it was sleepy,
conservative, and as yet
untouched by new ideas.*

University days
*Goethe studied at the
universities of Leipzig
(below) and Strasbourg.
At Leipzig he began to
shed his provincial
manners, but Strasbourg
introduced him to passion
and made a poet of him.*

ness and order of 18th-century writing, Goethe, F.M.
von Klinger, J.M.R. Lenz and other Storm and Stress
writers went to the opposite extreme, filling their poems
and plays with exaggeratedly violent emotions and
events. The period is often called the *Geniezeit* – age of
geniuses – but in reality Goethe was the only creative
genius among the Storm and Stress writers. Under the
influence of Shakespeare, whose works he had begun to
study avidly during his convalescence, Goethe wrote a
sprawling historical play, *Götz von Berlichingen*, whose
publication in 1773 made him famous.

Meanwhile his legal practice had been so sparse that
his father sent him for further training to the Imperial
Supreme Court at Wetzlar. His few summer months
there in 1772 were momentous because he met and fell
in love with a girl named Charlotte Buff. She was
betrothed to a lawyer, Johann Christian Kestner, who
was confident – or weak – enough to tolerate Goethe's
attentions to Charlotte, although he grew rather tired of
visiting her after a hard day's work and finding the poet
already in possession. Even when Charlotte told him
plainly that they could never be more than friends,
Goethe lingered – until the morning when, having
dined with Charlotte and Kestner the night before, he
left Wetzlar without a word of warning.

The significance of this episode became clear in the
autumn of 1774, when Goethe published a novel, *The
Sufferings of Young Werther*. This was patently based on
his relations with Charlotte and Kestner – with the
difference that, unlike Goethe, the hero cannot conquer
his pain and shoots himself. *Young Werther* was probably
the most sensationally successful book published during
the 18th century. It was amost immediately translated
into a dozen languages and, working on emotions
sensitized by the writings of Rousseau, changed the
lives of its readers. Young men affected gloom and wore
the same costume as Werther (round grey hat, yellow
waistcoat and hose, blue coat, topboots); and more than
one ended by killing himself, leaving a copy of the novel
in his pocket by way of explanation.

Just before *Young Werther* made Goethe famous

Young genius
*Famous even as a young
man, Goethe impressed
others as a privileged
being. In addition to his
literary gifts, he was a
polished man of the world
with many social
accomplishments –
including, as this
watercolour (above)
indicates, a graceful
skating style.*

Charlotte Buff
*While studying at
Wetzlar, Goethe met and
fell in love with Charlotte
Buff (right). Later, when
Goethe's novel* Young
Werther *appeared,
Charlotte and her fiancé
were embarrassed to find
that it told their story – but
with Goethe cast as
Charlotte's truly beloved.*

Young Werther
The melancholy hero of Goethe's novel (left) killed himself for love. Following the book's vogue, many young men dressed like Werther and even embraced the same fate.

throughout Europe, he met a banker's daughter, Lili Schönemann, at a party in Frankfurt. True to form, he immediately fell in love with her and, since she was not spoken for, the couple became engaged. Goethe nevertheless bolted once more, leaving without warning or farewell for a two-month visit to Switzerland. Even this might not have disentangled him; but in December 1774 he received a visitor who changed his life.

GOETHE AT WEIMAR

Duke Karl August of Saxe-Weimar was not quite 18, but his rank and his effusive admiration for Goethe flattered and charmed the 26-year-old poet. After a relatively brief acquaintance, Goethe accepted the Duke's offer of hospitality and on 7 November 1775 arrived at Weimar, intending to stay for a month or so. In the event, it became his principal home for the rest of his life.

At first Goethe was simply a boon companion for Karl August, who was so eager for the poet to settle at Weimar that he appointed him a salaried privy councillor and provided a house for him to live in. Soon, however, Goethe began to take over an expanding range of ministerial duties, organizing the finances, transport system and mines of the tiny duchy and making extended tours of inspection and supervision. He became effectively chief minister, and in 1782, on the Duke's request, the Holy Roman Emperor ennobled him. Henceforth he was no longer plain J.W. Goethe but the Geheimrat Johann Wolfgang *von* Goethe.

This was a remarkable career for a commoner in 18th century Germany, where the nobility were regarded as a caste apart, infinitely superior to the wealthiest and most cultivated of ordinary mortals. Goethe owed his success in part to his literary fame and practical ability, but at least as important were his personal charm, handsome presence and fascinating brown eyes. He acquired a final aristocratic polish from his relationship with an older woman, Charlotte von Stein, with whom he had a ten-year intimacy that seems to have been strictly platonic. The wife of the Duke's Grand Equerry, Charlotte was Goethe's intellectual equal, a quiet, serious woman whose companionship stimulated him to go on with his writing and his studies of chemistry, botany, anatomy and mineralogy. Despite his duties, he was a serious (if sometimes wrongheaded) scientific

Weimar
Goethe's meeting with Duke Karl August was a watershed in his life. The two men developed an extraordinary rapport (right) and Goethe left Frankfurt – and Lili Schönemann – to live at the Duke's court in Weimar (below).

Enter the actress
A beautiful professional actress, Corona Schröter, came to Weimar to play opposite Goethe in his Iphigenia in Tauris; *the scene below shows them together. Corona's stay lasted for several months, during which she caused several cross-currents of passion and jealousy at the little court.*

Muse and mentor
At Weimar, Charlotte von Stein (below) was Goethe's muse.

investigator, and in 1784 made a significant contribution to anatomy by demonstrating the existence of the intermaxillary bone in human beings. And although he published nothing during these years, Goethe wrote a good deal – exquisite lyrics inspired by his devotion to Charlotte; *Iphigenia in Tauris*, a play reflecting his abandonment of Romanticism; and an uncompleted novel, *Wilhelm Meister's Theatrical Mission*. However, the difficulties he experienced in finishing his more ambitious projects did suggest that he was dispersing his energies unwisely.

At Weimar the years passed laboriously but with no greater upheavals than the coming and going of a glamorous actress, Corona Schröter, who played opposite Goethe in performances of *Iphigenia* and stirred up a flurry of rivalries and jealousies: when the play was premièred, the coolly platonic Charlotte von Stein was conspicuous by her absence. His years of practical work and responsibility may well have saved Goethe from burning himself out prematurely as so many Romantic writers did; but by 1786 he had begun to feel jaded and oppressed by his administrative routines and the narrow circle in which he moved.

TRAVELS IN ITALY

Characteristically he took refuge in sudden flight. Goethe managed matters so that only the Duke had any inkling of his departure, and even he merely received a letter informing him that his friend and minister intended to lose himself 'in places where I am totally unknown'. Goethe slipped away from Weimar at three o'clock in the morning of 3 September 1786, boarding a stagecoach with a rucksack and valise and travelling to Italy under the name of Möller.

For Goethe, as for so many northerners, the warmth and colour of the South were a revelation. He also found a personal – and perhaps a sexual – liberation in leading a more leisurely life, incognito, in Rome, where he lodged with the painter Tischbein and moved in more mixed society than had been possible at Weimar. His studies of Greek and Roman art confirmed his development away from Romanticism and towards a form of Classicism, and in his new surroundings he was able to complete a number of long-neglected works.

Goethe's Italian wanderings took him as far south as Naples and Sicily, and then back again to Rome. In June 1788 he left Italy and settled again at Weimar, but only

Italian interlude

After 11 years as a minister in the little duchy of Saxe-Weimar, Goethe spent almost two years in Italy, where he was able to live incognito for long periods. For him it was a time of self-renewal, new experiences, writing and study. Goethe in the Campagna *(above) is so famous that the artist is remembered simply as 'Goethe' Tischbein. 'Tischbein's sketch is ready', wrote Goethe; 'it shows me life size, wrapped in a white cloak, seated on a fallen obelisk while I look at the ruins in the Roman countryside.'*

after the Duke agreed to put their relations on a new footing. Goethe was no longer to be burdened with administrative duties, but was to retain his privy councillor's office and the salary that went with it. From now on he would be a writer and scientist before all else – and, as the years passed, a revered figure who attracted pilgrims of all ages to Weimar.

Although life seemed to go on as usual at Weimar, Goethe's position was rather different after his return from Italy. His unannounced flight had alienated such old friends as Charlotte von Stein, and the extent to which he had changed became clear when he made a new choice of female companion. She was Christiane Vulpius, a 23-year-old brunette who was employed in a workshop making artificial flowers. She met the great man in the ducal park, handing him a petition on behalf of her indigent brother, and was soon installed in his house. On Christmas Day 1789, at 40, Goethe became a father; Christiane bore him a son, named August after the Duke, who became the baby's godfather. Despite this sign that Goethe continued to be high in Karl August's favour, Christiane's unwedded state meant that much of Weimar society was closed to her – a situation that may well have suited Goethe. He remained active not only as a writer and scientist but also as the Duke's friend and adviser, the director of Weimar's first public theatre, founded in 1791, and an impressive but still intensely susceptible sage.

REVOLUTION AND WAR

By 1792 the French Revolution was in its third year and the Bourbon monarchy was about to fall. Alarmed by the threat to the traditional order, Austria and Prussia determined to march on Paris, and Duke Karl August supported the Prussians with his miniature army (less than 300 strong, thanks to cost-cutting by Goethe some years before). Goethe was invited to accompany the

Friendly rival
Friedrich von Schiller (left) was the only contemporary German writer whose stature was comparable with that of Goethe. Initially wary of each other, the two men became close friends and collaborators in the 1790s.

Historic meeting
(below) In 1808 Goethe was introduced to the all-conquering Emperor Napoleon. Each of the two great men impressed the other, Napoleon claiming to have read Young Werther *seven times.*

Christiane
Soon after returning from Italy, Goethe met Christiane Vulpius (left) and made her his mistress. She bore him a son and lived with him for almost 20 years before he decided to regularize their union, apparently in recognition of her courage when the poet's life was endangered during the French occupation.

claimed to have read *Werther* no less than seven times, pressed Goethe to come to Paris, and at the end of their encounter, in his typically incisive fashion, indicated the poet and remarked 'There is a man!'

Goethe never went to Paris, and the fall of Napoleon made no great difference to his · life of writing, experimenting, collecting, and entertaining admirers. Nor did marriage prevent him from forming a series of sentimental attachments to young women such as Minna Herzlieb, who partly inspired the novel *Elective Affinities*, and Marianne von Willemer. But in other respects he was rapidly becoming a national institution. He began publishing his autobiography, *Poetry and Truth*, and in 1823 acquired his own Boswell, Johann Peter Eckermann, whose *Conversations with Goethe* became a German classic.

Yet even when he was over 70 Goethe still had a single youthful folly left in his heart. At Marienbad, one of the spas he patronized every year, he met Ulrike von Levetzow, a girl still in her teens, fell in love with her, and failed to manage his emotions with his accustomed skill. Since Christiane had died in 1816, Goethe was unencumbered, and he actually persuaded Duke Karl August to propose on his behalf. Ulrike's mother sensibly vetoed the match, and Goethe consoled himself on the journey back to Weimar by composing a late masterpiece, the *Elegy to Marienbad*.

Famous and honoured, Goethe worked to the end of his long life, completing the second half of *Faust* in 1831 and sealing up the manuscript for posthumous publication. He took the passing of the Duke (1828) and of his only son August (1830) with apparent stoicism. His own death came on 22 March 1832. His last words were a simple request that the shutters of his room should be opened. But the human faculty for myth-making has transformed the incident into a passionate cry from the heart: 'More light! More light!'

Duke and was present at the battle of Valmy on 20 September 1792, when the French 'nation in arms' defeated Prussia's drilled and disciplined professional soldiers. Goethe grasped the symbolic importance of what had happened, and told his companions that 'Here and today begins a new epoch; and you will be able to say that you were present.'

Goethe witnessed more fighting the following year, and – indefatigable writer that he was – published two books about his war experiences. Once back at Weimar, however, he became absorbed in the literary life. Thanks to the close friendship he formed with Friedrich von Schiller, the only comparably gifted German writer, he became immensely productive, reworking his earlier unfinished novel as *Wilhelm Meister's Apprenticeship* and completing Part One of *Faust*, the longest meditated and most famous of all his works. When Schiller died in 1805, Goethe felt as though he had lost 'half of his being'.

War finally reached Saxe-Weimar in 1806, when the French army – now led by the Emperor Napoleon – won a crushing victory over the Prussians on the soil of the duchy, at Jena. The first French troops to enter Weimar were unruly and threatening, and after they broke into his house Goethe believed that he owed his life to Christiane's courage and presence of mind. Presumably for this reason – and perhaps also to signify his loyalty to the established order – he married her a few days later, on 19 October 1806.

Two years later, when French victories had converted Saxe-Weimar and other German states into satellites, Karl August entertained Napoleon, and during the festivities a meeting took place between the Emperor and the almost equally celebrated poet. Goethe was politically conservative, but the Romantic side of his personality responded to Napoleon's demonic energy and unbounded ambition. For his part, the Emperor

A turning-point
In 1789 a revolution began in France that was soon perceived as a threat to the entire European order. Austria and Prussia – and little Saxe-Weimar – dispatched troops to disperse the revolutionary 'rabble'. But Valmy (above) was a victory for the French; and, as Goethe predicted, it marked the dawn of a new era.

Serene old age
Few men have enjoyed an old age of such fame, honour and protracted creativity as Goethe. His later years were also fundamentally serene, although he continued to allow his heart to be agitated (to good literary effect) by a series of young women. His crowning achievement, Faust, was completed less than a year before his death in 1832.

Romantic Classicist

Although famous throughout Europe as a Romantic writer, the mature Goethe turned his back on the movement. However, underlying his entire life's work was an essentially Romantic belief in action and dynamic change.

Goethe was – if such a thing exists – a born writer. As an adolescent he seems to have composed a mass of works which later went up in smoke on a bonfire; and as a young man he published able but conventional verses before he was caught up in the first wave of German Romanticism. Curiously enough, the early Romantics of the Storm and Stress movement were more extreme – more drawn to violence, bombast and irrationalism – than their successors. Goethe's first major contribution was *Götz von Berlichingen* (1773), a sprawling drama based on the life of a 16th century robber-knight; among other things Götz was famous for the iron hand with which he replaced the hand lost during one of his adventures. Like other Romantic dramas, Goethe's play, with its swiftly changing scenes and loose structure, is strongly influenced by Shakespeare, whose works broke most of the 'rules' devised by later theorists. Much more than Shakespeare, Goethe shared the Romantic vice of radically changing inconvenient historical facts, making Götz, who actually lived to a ripe old age, die young for freedom in the best Romantic style.

'THE AUTHOR OF WERTHER'

Young Werther (1774) was an epistolary novel – a novel in which the narrative is revealed through letters supposedly written by one or more of the characters. Initially this device gave the story a convincing 'documentary' feeling, but as letter followed letter it tended to become increasingly clumsy and artificial; although there were famous examples, including Rousseau's *Nouvelle Heloïse* and Laclos' *Liaisons Dangereuses*, the genre hardly survived the 18th century. Goethe wisely kept *Werther*

His manuscript
This fair-copied poem in Goethe's handwriting (left) hardly suggests the effort that it must have cost.

short enough to read in a sitting; and the outcome was a European sensation.

Werther was Romantic in its subject – the young man who kills himself for love – and its essentially autobiographical nature. As well as calling his heroine Lotte (the original of the character being Charlotte Buff), Goethe actually used letters, diaries and newspapers verbatim, and in German literary society the identity of the principals was an open secret.

Young Werther was imitated by a host of young men anxious to perish for love, and was even exploited as a promotional gimmick

The work of a lifetime

Goethe is shown at his desk (left), his mind filled with thoughts of the characters in his great epic, Faust, *a work that occupied him for most of his adult life. Ranging from passion and melodrama to allegory, and written in an astonishing variety of poetic styles, it is one of the supreme works of European literature.*

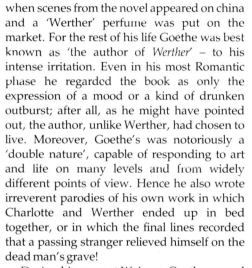

Faust

Goethe's famous work has attracted composers and artists such as Monticelli, whose painting (above) evokes the doomed love of Faust and Gretchen and the malevolent scarlet presence of Mephistopheles.

when scenes from the novel appeared on china and a 'Werther' perfume was put on the market. For the rest of his life Goethe was best known as 'the author of *Werther*' – to his intense irritation. Even in his most Romantic phase he regarded the book as only the expression of a mood or a kind of drunken outburst; after all, as he might have pointed out, the author, unlike Werther, had chosen to live. Moreover, Goethe's was notoriously a 'double nature', capable of responding to art and life on many levels and from widely different points of view. Hence he also wrote irreverent parodies of his own work in which Charlotte and Werther ended up in bed together, or in which the final lines recorded that a passing stranger relieved himself on the dead man's grave!

During his years at Weimar, Goethe moved away from Romanticism, placing less value on unrestrained passion and increasingly appreciating the Classical qualities of clarity, harmony and balance. On occasion he dismissed Romanticism out of hand: 'I call Classical that which is healthy, Romantic that which is sick.' This 'Weimar Classicism' – by no means appreciated by all the *Werther*-admirers at Weimar – was at its strongest during and after Goethe's trip to Italy, where he made a first-hand acquaintance with the ancient Greek and Roman art on which Classicists modelled their works. However, Goethe's 'double nature' and constantly evolving attitudes ensured that few of his writings could be considered purely 'Classical'; and he is so hard to pigeonhole that some critics have been driven back on formulas such as 'Romantic Classicism' to describe his final position.

At a fundamental level Goethe remained a Romantic artist – in his awareness of clashing opposites as creative forces, giving birth to the new, and in his profound belief in individual self-development and a general human evolution to ever-higher levels through active striving. His own development can be traced in the two parts of his great verse drama *Faust*, composed over a period of 60 years. The basic situation derived from the legend of a learned man, Heinrich Faust, who sold himself to the Devil in return for a lifetime of power, pleasure and knowledge. But in Goethe's version Faust becomes an alienated, disillusioned individual of a now-familiar modern type; and the bargain he makes is that his life and soul shall be forfeited if Mephistopheles can give him a single moment so fulfilling that he would wish to stay its passing. Neither wine nor love have the desired effect, although Faust seduces, abandons and finally attempts to rescue from prison the innocent Gretchen, whose imminent death and assured salvation form the climax of Part One.

THE FAUSTIAN MYTH

Completed in 1808, Part One was received as a thoroughly Romantic work, and in time overtook *Werther* in reputation, so that Goethe became 'the author of *Faust*'. But Part Two (1832) was a very different production, diffuse and filled with difficult symbolic and allegorical episodes; understandably, it has never

Drawings of Italy

A talented artist, Goethe brought back a large portfolio of his own drawings from Italy. He was delighted with Rome, the heart of the classical civilization he revered; among the views of the city by him is one showing the dome of St Peter's in the distance (above, top). He also sketched one of Rome's more curious monuments, the pyramid of Cestius (above), raised by an ancient Roman with a taste for the monuments of the exotic eastern Mediterranean.

41

Wilhelm Meister's Apprenticeship
(left) In this novel, Goethe's wandering hero gets to know every level of German society.

Goethe's busy social and official life, a fact that may partly explain his extraordinary creative habits. He constantly took up projects and then set them aside in favour of some other task, which might in its turn be set aside and taken up again at a later date. In some instances – for example *Faust* – he might add scenes or chapters intermittently over a period of decades rather than years. On occasion this could lead to a result lacking real unity, but it did reflect the various phases of its author's outlook and his philosophy of unceasing self-development. Characteristically Goethe never referred to one of his works as finished, but only, more provisionally, as 'coming into existence'.

The fact remains that no other author has worked in such a fashion, apparently never totally absorbed by his subject. The *Wilhelm Meister* novels in particular have an incredibly tangled history. Goethe worked on *Wilhelm Meister's Theatrical Mission* from time to time, writing about one part a year, in the 1780s; effectively abandoned it on going to Italy; then took it up again in 1794, completely recasting it as *Wilhelm Meister's Apprenticeship* (1795-96). An unsatisfactory sequel, *Wilhelm Meister's Travels* (1829), was even more completely a product of cutting and pasting.

Nevertheless *Wilhelm Meister's Apprenticeship* was Goethe's most influential novel, in the long run more important than *Young Werther*. It was originally intended to be a picture of theatrical life and a means to make the public understand the social and cultural value of the drama. But in reworking the story Goethe altered its focus, so that it became an account of a young man's apprenticeship to – and education by – life. This 'novel of education' (*Bildungsroman*) became a distinctive modern genre, and one of Goethe's many achievements was to have explored territory since occupied by *The Way of All Flesh*, *Portrait of the Artist as a Young Man* and *Sons and Lovers*.

achieved anything like the same popularity. In this, Faust travels back in time to ancient Greece (in pursuit of Helen of Troy and perhaps, like Goethe, of the Classical ideal), but ultimately devotes himself to an ambitious scheme of land reclamation. Goethe commented that Part One was subjective, being concerned with one man's personal experiences, whereas Part Two offered an objective, broader view of the world, with a Faust who has become a universal figure representing modern man. Significantly, he achieves fulfilment, and utters the fateful words, when working for the benefit of others. But he is saved, not damned, in spite of all his sins and errors, because he has never adopted Mephistopheles' negative attitude to existence, but has striven constantly to understand himself and the world – a religiously unorthodox but eminently Romantic conclusion.

As reworked by Goethe, *Faust* became one of the prime Romantic myths, inspiring Berlioz, Liszt and Gounod, whose opera has become the best-known, though hardly the most profound, treatment of the subject. In *Faust* and many other works, Goethe displayed an extraordinary mastery of every mode of verse, from galloping doggerel to sublime lyrics. His poetry had an all-pervasive influence on German Romanticism, and was set so frequently by composers such as Schubert, Schumann, Brahms and Wolf that the development of the outstanding 19th-century German song (Lied) tradition is unthinkable without it.

PIECEMEAL COMPOSITION

Goethe's enormous output included poems and plays, novels, travel books, war diaries, volumes of research in optics, botany and geology, essays and criticism, a huge correspondence and a famous autobiography, *Poetry and Truth*. These were created in the course of

Literary dictator
Goethe remained prolific in his old age, dictating to a secretary with such fluency that it seemed he was reading aloud.

WILLIAM BLAKE

1757-1827

One of the most distinctive of all English artists, William Blake was a brilliant poet as well as a great painter. A fiercely independent man, he started his career as a commercial engraver, but in his thirties began illustrating his own poems. He soon created a completely personal style and an original technique that perfectly expressed the full intensity of his visionary experiences.

Blake is now recognized as one of the giants of the Romantic period, but in his lifetime his genius was appreciated by only a small circle of admirers. He had few patrons and much of his life was spent in poverty. But lack of worldly success was of little consequence to Blake – he was completely dedicated to his work and lived in the world of the imagination and the spirit, rather than in the material world.

The Visionary Engraver

Blake spent most of his life working as an engraver in London. He was always poor, but derived strength from a happy marriage, deep political convictions and an exceptionally rich spiritual existence.

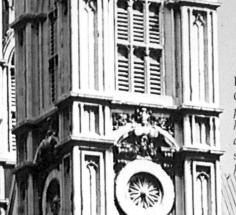

Blake by his wife
Catherine Blake made this pencil drawing of her husband shortly before his death. It shows Blake as she remembered him 'in his fiery youth'.

William Blake was born on 28 November 1757 at 28 Broad Street, off Golden Square in London. He was the second child of a fairly prosperous hosier, and the family occupied a spacious old house in a district made up of private houses and respectable shops. Blake's father positively encouraged his son's artistic leanings. He bought him a few plaster casts, gave him pocket money to buy his own prints, and sent him, at the age of ten, to Henry Pars' drawing school in the Strand, then the best and most fashionable preparatory school for young artists. Here Blake learned to draw by copying plaster casts of classical statues.

When the time came for him to be apprenticed, Blake's father was unable to afford the cost of his entrance to a painter's studio, and anyway he wanted his son to have the security of a craft. And so, for a premium of 50 guineas, he arranged for Blake to join the workshop of James Basire, master-engraver to the Society of Antiquaries, in Lincoln's Inn Fields.

THE MASTER ENGRAVER

Blake worked under Basire for seven years, becoming himself a master of all the techniques of engraving, etching, stippling and copying. He helped Basire with his engravings for books, among them Jacob Bryant's then-famous *New System of Mythology*, which introduced him to the world of ancient religions and legends. Another profound influence was the study he made, at Basire's suggestion, of Gothic architecture and sculpture in Westminster Abbey and other old churches in London. Blake's lifelong love of Gothic art dates from these visits to the Abbey.

After this seven-year apprenticeship, Blake set out to earn his living as an engraver. He continued to live in his father's house, working on commissions for such publications as the *Ladies' Magazine*. He enrolled as a student at the newly-founded Royal Academy, but could not tolerate the life drawing he was required to do there. According to him, 'copying nature' deadened the vigour of his imagination.

In 1782, at the age of 25, Blake married. His wife, Catherine Boucher, was the illiterate daughter of a Battersea market gardener, a choice of partner that did not please his father. The couple moved to a house in nearby Green Street, but two years later Blake's father died, and William and Catherine returned to Broad Street, living at No. 27, next door to his old home. They were joined by Blake's younger brother, Robert, who became his pupil as well as a member of the household.

For two and a half happy, though not financially successful, years this much-loved brother was Blake's professional and intellectual companion. Then, tragically, Robert fell ill and died, leaving Blake broken-hearted; he had nursed Robert so selflessly that he is said to have gone without sleep for a fortnight. At the moment of death Blake claimed he had seen 'the released spirit ascend heavenward, clapping its hands for joy'. He continued to communicate with his brother's spirit throughout the rest of his life, deriving much comfort from their conversations. Living constantly on the borderland between the material and the invisible world, Blake also communicated freely with angels and characters from the Bible.

A Londoner, born and bred

Blake was born in this spacious corner house in Soho, where he lived until he was 25. Two years later he set up a small print-selling shop next door to his old home.

Westminster Abbey

(left) During his seven-year apprenticeship to the engraver James Basire, Blake often made drawings in Westminster Abbey. According to his earliest biographer, this 'kindled a fervent love of the Gothic which lasted throughout his life'.

The Abbey monuments

(right) This coloured drawing is one of a series Blake made in 1775; they were used as the basis for engravings illustrating the Abbey's monuments, published in 1780.

Nebuchadnezzar (1795)
This powerful image symbolizes the bestial aspects of humanity. In the Bible, Nebuchadnezzar 'was driven from men, and did eat grass as oxen'.

After Robert's death, Blake moved to a house in Poland Street, Soho, where he struggled to fulfil the few commissions that came his way. He was too unworldly in his commercial dealings and too proud in his relations with clients to make himself rich. In his politics he was an extreme radical, and took to wearing a red bonnet when the French Revolution broke out. As both a man and an artist, he was a visionary whose imaginative world was far more splendid and inspiring than anything he encountered in the real world. Above all, he was a deeply religious man, for whom everything possessed its own spiritual essence.

In 1788 Blake made his first experiments with 'illuminated printing'; that is, combining words and images together on a single copper plate. For some time he was unable to hit on a technique that was both cheap and suitable, and it worried him deeply. Then one day his dead brother appeared to him in a vision and gave him explicit directions,

Blake's Soho

Blake lived most of his life in the district of Soho, in the West End of London. Built in the 18th century, this has consistently been a home for craftsmen, artists and writers – among them Canaletto and Shelley as well as Karl Marx and the critic William Hazlitt.

Today Soho is best known as a red-light district and the centre of London's Chinatown, but in Blake's time it was a typical urban mixture of grand houses – in the squares – and terraces for artisans' families. There was also a work-house in the district.

Soho Square
(right) In Blake's day, Soho Square was an elegant residential area not far from open fields. Blake lived nearby, first in the family home in Broad Street (now Broadwick Street), then with his wife in Green Street and later in Poland Street.

which he promptly put into action. They proved to be exactly what he needed. Using this method, he printed copies of *Songs of Innocence* the following year and taught Mrs Blake how to bind them.

In 1794 he wrote and illustrated his *Songs of Experience*, which betrays a much bleaker and more pessimistic outlook. It is believed that he never issued it separately, but always combined it with *Songs of Innocence* in order to show 'the two Contrary States of the Human Soul', as he put it on the title-page. Helped by his wife, he continued until the time of his death to make and colour sets of the prints as they were commissioned by his customers.

'PARADISE' IN LAMBETH

Shortly before the death of his mother in 1792, the Blakes had left Poland Street and moved to 13 Hercules Buildings in Lambeth. This was evidently a pretty terraced house, with a strip of garden behind in which Blake allowed a wandering vine to grow unpruned and form a little arbour. Here, according to legend, a friend once discovered Mr and Mrs Blake as naked as Adam and Eve, reading aloud from *Paradise Lost*. The seven years they spent in Lambeth were certainly happy and productive. It was in this house, in 1795, that Blake designed the magnificent series of colour prints, including *God Judging Adam*, which are generally thought to mark the high water of his genius as a print-maker.

By and large Blake was not lucky in his patrons, but there was one man who never failed him: Thomas Butts, a civil servant and art collector. Blake referred to him as 'my employer', but in fact Butts seems to have left Blake free to follow his creative impulses. He simply placed a standing order, asking for 50 small pictures at a guinea each.

Visionary powers
(above) Blake claimed that he was frequently visited by spirits and angels. The Ghost of a Flea *(c.1819) is a blood-curdling record of one of his most bizarre visionary experiences. According to his friend John Varley, this extraordinary monster visited Blake twice.*

Engraver at work
Blake used various methods of engraving, but they all involved cutting a design into a plate of metal or block of wood, rolling ink over it and taking an impression. Before the development of photography this was the main way to reproduce an image many times.

Blake was able to confide in Butts, and was a frequent visitor to his house, which by the end of the artist's life overflowed with his pictures.

William Hayley, a country gentleman and minor poet, was another of Blake's patrons. He commissioned Blake to engrave plates for his proposed life of the poet William Cowper, and invited the Blakes to move to Felpham in Sussex to be near his own house. In 1800 Blake left London for the first time to begin what he later called his 'three years' slumber on the banks of the ocean'. At first Blake thought his new cottage a little paradise, and both he and Catherine loved to go for walks, exploring the countryside.

DAUGHTERS OF INSPIRATION

Blake was overwhelmed by the beauty of nature, but he did not take up landscape painting, nor did he ever see nature in anything other than visionary terms. 'Everything is human! Mighty! Sublime!' he wrote. During this period he not only communed with his 'daughters of inspiration', who descended from the tops of trees to talk with him, but he also discovered that the vegetable world was inhabited by fairies. 'Did you ever see a fairy's funeral, madam?' he asked an astounded lady at a party, and proceeded to describe one he had witnessed the previous night.

Meanwhile, his relationship with Hayley was not proving easy. He worked loyally at the jobs he was given, but found them imaginatively unrewarding. By 1802 he was getting restive and would probably have fallen out with Hayley if events had not intervened. In the summer of 1803 Blake had a fight with a soldier who had been sent to cut the grass in his garden. Blake, who was opposed to the war against France, was reported as saying, 'Damn the King, and damn all his soldiers, they are all slaves.' He was tried for assault and

The Patron's Reward

In 1809 Blake held an exhibition at his brother's shop in Soho, showing his new painting, the *Canterbury Pilgrims*, together with 15 other pictures. Subscribers were invited to order engravings, but not one order was taken. His ever-faithful patron Thomas Butts bought the *Canterbury Pilgrims* – one of Blake's masterpieces – for just £10.

The loyal patron
(left) The minor civil servant Thomas Butts filled his house with Blake's pictures.

Canterbury Pilgrims
(right) Blake's painting shows a scene from Chaucer's Canterbury Tales. *The procession presents a picture of 'universal human life'.*

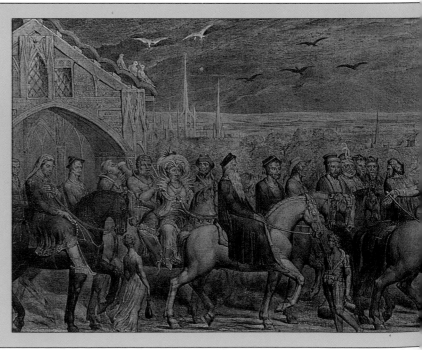

about etching plates for this book, and also began work on his etchings for *Jerusalem*, a book which he continued to expand until as late as 1820. In the end, he illuminated only one copy.

For the next ten years Blake's life is difficult to trace. He lived in obscurity, continuing to write and paint, but selling very little except his water-colours to Butts. However, in the summer of 1818 his life was radically changed by meeting John Linnell, a young portrait and landscape painter, who began to pay him regular sums of money in exchange for a large part of his output. Linnell also introduced him to a group of young admirers, including Samuel Palmer, the painter who came closest to inheriting Blake's visionary inspiration, and John Varley, a landscapist who was fascinated by Blake's accounts of his visionary experiences.

POOR BUT HAPPY

In 1821 the Blakes moved to No. 3 Fountain Court, a house off the Strand that was owned by William's brother-in-law. Although they still lived in very poor circumstances, he seems to have been much happier at Fountain Court. He continued to be an object of veneration to his younger friends, Samuel Palmer going so far as to kiss the bell-handle whenever he called. And when Blake was 65, Linnell commissioned him to execute the 22 magnificent engravings illustrating *The Book of Job*,

The Ancient of Days (1794)
Blake used this design as an illustration to his poem Europe, *and it proved to be one of his most popular prints; he hand-coloured this particular impression for a customer 30 years later. The image was inspired 'by a vision which he declared hovered over his head at the top of the staircase'.*

Beatrice Addressing Dante (1824-27)
Heavy with symbolism (above), this is one of Blake's illustrations for Dante's great poem The Divine Comedy.

sedition. Hayley managed to get him acquitted, but Blake had to leave Felpham.

He was now 45. On his return to London he chose to live in South Molton Street, but could only afford to rent one floor of a house. Here he lived for the next 17 years, mostly in poverty. He brought back from Felpham his long poem, *Milton*, which he claimed had been dictated to him by angels, with some assistance from Milton himself. He set

Blake's last design
Blake completed his final engraving in 1827, the year of his death. It took the form of a visiting card for his friend George Cumberland, and although tiny (only three inches long), it is full of vitality.

paying him £5 per plate. Linnell was also responsible for the second masterpiece of Blake's last years, his illustrations for Dante's *Divine Comedy*. He worked on these until his death, completing over 100 large watercolour designs but engraving only seven plates.

A friend who visited Blake during his last days recorded that, after finishing a piece of work, 'his glance fell on his loving Kate, no longer young or beautiful, but who had lived with him in these and like humble rooms, in hourly companionship, ever ready helpfulness, and reverent sympathy, for 45 years. "Stay!" he cried. "Keep as you are! you have ever been an angel to me: I will draw you!" ' This was his last work and, sadly, it has been lost. Blake died at Fountain Court on 12 August 1827. To the last he sang his own songs of praise and joy.

The Power of the Imagination

An engraver by trade, Blake developed original techniques to illustrate his own poems – and those of Shakespeare, Milton and Dante – with images of strange and unusual power.

The art of illumination
These 'illuminated' pages come from Blake's Songs of Innocence *(far left), published in 1789, and its sequel,* Songs of Experience *(left), which appeared in 1794. They combine words and images in a way that recalls medieval manuscripts, but Blake's intensity of vision is completely personal. He finished each copy of the book by hand, so no two copies are identical.*

William Blake was as great a poet as he was a painter, and it is no exaggeration to say that for a time he painted his poems and wrote his pictures, combining the two media in an almost unique fashion. From the beginning he was intent on developing his own personal symbolism, both in words and pictures, but by the end of his life his poetic world had become highly complicated and difficult to interpret. For this reason, his later poetry is not much read today. His art, however, retained a brilliant visual clarity, even if the ideas behind it are sometimes obscure.

Blake's apprenticeship to James Basire gave him the chance to study engravings by the Old Masters, of whom he most admired Michelangelo and Raphael. Their influence, spiced with a fashionable interest in the horrific, is to be seen in his earliest engravings. But it was his taste for medieval art, stimulated by his visits to Westmins-ter Abbey, which showed most strongly in *Songs of Innocence* (1789), his first truly original work, not only as a painter and poet, but also as a printer.

The printing method Blake used – which he believed had been revealed to him by his dead brother – had the advantage of being cheap, although it called for an exceptional degree of skill and patience. First, he laboriously transferred the text of his poem, in reverse of course, on to a prepared copper plate. Then he added his design and marginal decorations. When these images had been etched into the plate by the use of acid, he made a print, using one or sometimes two tinted inks. Finally, he added his watercolour 'illumination' to the page, with pen or paintbrush.

This extraordinary method turned each copy of *Songs of Innocence* into a separate work of art, for Blake was able to vary his colours from volume to volume. Early copies have the translucent delicacy

Satan, Sin and Death (1808)

(right) The power and imaginative grandeur of Milton's Paradise Lost *made a strong appeal to Blake. This watercolour illustration shows the crowned Satan about to fight with Death when Sin intervenes, telling him Death is their son.*

Jerusalem

The title-page to Blake's most famous poem (left) is dated 1804, but he worked on the illustrations until about 1820.

Horror and anguish

This painting, The Body of Abel found by Adam and Eve *(1826, below), is the culmination of Blake's long obsession with the subject. An accursed Cain flies from his murdered brother's body; his father looks on in anguish (right).*

of a rainbow, while some later volumes are more jewel-like, and glow with gold paint. In 1794, using the same technique, he created *Songs of Experience*, always thereafter printing the two sets of *Songs* as a single book. The designs for *Experience* are noticeably darker and more severe, in accordance with the grimmer mood of these poems, which probably arose from political disillusion and long-endured domestic difficulties. However, Blake's final verdict, as the joint title indicates, is that innocence and experience are 'the Two Contrary States of the Human Soul'.

A SECRET TECHNIQUE

Meanwhile, Blake had been experimenting with a new method of print-making, using thick pigments of his own invention based on carpenter's glue. He claimed that this secret had been revealed to him by Joseph, the carpenter father of Jesus. And in 1795 he composed a series of 12 large colour prints which were not associated with any text. Their bold images, clear-cut forms and rich texture put them among his finest works.

These prints of 1795 draw their subject matter from a bewilderingly wide range of sources, including the Old and the New Testaments, Shakespeare and Milton. Nevertheless, Blake evidently conceived the series as a whole. Their precise meaning has still to be discovered, although it is generally thought that each print represents a stage in the Fall of Man as Blake conceived of it. Thus *Newton* shows man as slave to

pure reason, unenlightened by the imagination, a state of mind that Blake detested. By contrast, the crawling, bestial figure in *Nebuchadnezzar* shows man as a slave to the senses.

FREEING THE SPIRIT

All his life Blake fought against oppression, whether it took a political, intellectual or religious form. What he valued above all was imagination and its power to liberate the human spirit from its earthly confines. Throughout his work, humanity under many different guises struggles to escape from the tyranny of Urizen, who is always depicted as a ferocious, bearded old man, symbol of both the authoritarian father and God, the unfeeling creator of systems and laws. Opposed to him is 'Jesus, the Imagination', otherwise called 'the God within', who reigns in every human soul.

Blake set himself the impossible task of creating a symbolism with which to express his spiritual visions, which owed nothing to ordinary existence. It is perhaps for this reason that some of the

finest work he did towards the end of his life was inspired by visions other than his own – especially those of the Biblical writers and Dante. Blake's engravings for the *The Book of Job* amount to a new interpretation of Job's character; he created some unforgettable images for this series, especially the fearsome *Satan Smiting Job with Sore Boils*. The critic John Ruskin declared that Blake had surpassed even Rembrandt in rendering the effects of strong flickering light.

Blake's last years were occupied by his illustrations to Dante's *Divine Comedy*. This series was to have been engraved too, but at his death Blake had finished only seven plates. However, he did draw over 100 large designs, some of them painted in glowing watercolours. These beautifully delicate paintings display a new sensuousness and variety of mood; they provide a fitting climax to a career of ceaseless and fiercely independent creativity.

To sum up Blake's work, one cannot do better than quote his own words: 'The imagination is not a State: it is the Human existence itself.'

Satan Smiting Job with Sore Boils (c.1826)
(above) Blake simplifies the forms of the human body and creates bold contrasts between different shapes and textures. The mounds of thick, twisted hair set against Job's sinewy flesh are highly characteristic. Blake often returned to the same subject, and this is the final and most powerful version of a story he had treated twice before.

**WILLIAM
WORDSWORTH**
(1770-1850)

**SAMUEL TAYLOR
COLERIDGE**
(1772-1834)

LORD BYRON
(1788-1824)

**PERCY BYSSHE
SHELLEY**
(1792-1822)

JOHN KEATS
(1795-1821)

THE ROMANTIC POETS

Reacting against the formal, rational elements of 18th-century
verse, five writers emerged who, within decades, changed the face
of English poetry. Wordsworth, with his belief in the inspiration of
Nature, and Coleridge, who was fascinated by the supernatural,
were 'first-generation' Romantics. Byron, Shelley and Keats, who
followed, were tragically short-lived – but not so their art. They
created some of the most angry and most lyrical of English poems,
and revolutionized ideas on beauty, truth and imagination.

William Wordsworth

In the course of his long life Wordsworth changed from a young rebel to a pillar of the Establishment. His literary eminence made the Lake District – where he spent most of his life – a place of pilgrimage.

The aged poet
(right) Ironically, as Wordsworth's imaginative powers declined, his popularity soared. Passionate youth gave way to sober middle age in his poetry and personality alike, but the public lionized him. However, his younger contemporaries Byron and Shelley mocked the simplicity of his poetry, and abused him as a reactionary.

Wordsworth was of the first generation of Romantic poets. His life was a model of artistic dedication and persistence – most of it spent quietly, frugally and laboriously in the Lake District, while metropolitan critics savagely abused his work. But he lived to achieve universal recognition, and in his old age became Poet Laureate.

William Wordsworth was born on 7 April 1770 at Cockermouth, a little Cumbrian market town on the edge of the Lake District. He lost his mother when he was seven, but his schooldays at Hawkshead were happy. However, when his father died in 1783, the five young Wordsworths found themselves impoverished and dependent on the charity of relatives. William was sent to St John's College, Cambridge, but, rapidly disillusioned by university life, deliberately neglected his studies. Despite his slender resources, he refused to take up a conventional career, dedicating himself to poetry and adopting radical opinions.

On a visit to France and Switzerland in 1790, he was overawed by the Alps and fired by the French Revolution. Returning to France in 1791, Wordsworth had a love affair at Orléans with a girl named Annette Vallon, who bore him a daughter. Late in 1792 he left for England to raise money, possibly intending to go back and marry Annette; but war broke out between Britain and France, ending the relationship by cutting off all communication for years. This 'scandalous' episode in the poet's life remained a closely-guarded secret until the 1920s.

A CHANGE OF FORTUNES

Wordsworth's early publications had aroused little interest, but a turning-point in his fortunes occurred in 1795, when a young admirer died and left him £900 – enough for the 'plain living and high thinking' that appealed so strongly to Wordsworth. It was also enough to support his sister Dorothy, who now shared his home and became his closest companion. Dorothy Wordsworth proved to be a remarkable observer, and her journals – works of literature in their own right – often served as source-books, recording shared memories, on which William drew for poems such as the famous 'I wandered lonely as a cloud'.

At about this time the poet Samuel Taylor Coleridge entered Wordsworth's life. When William and Dorothy became the Coleridges' neighbours at Nether Stowey in Somerset, the two poets stimulated each other to an intense pitch of creativity. Local antagonism to their bohemian lifestyle and radical friends eventually persuaded them to move on.

To finance a trip to Germany, Wordsworth and Coleridge published *Lyrical Ballads* (1798), a selection of their work now recognized as a landmark in English

A devoted sister
(left) One year younger than William, Dorothy Wordsworth lived with her brother from 1795 until his death 55 years later. Coleridge described himself, Dorothy and William as 'three people with one soul'.

poetry. Nineteen out of the 23 poems were by Wordsworth, although the volume appeared anonymously. ('Wordsworth's name is nothing', Coleridge explained, 'and mine stinks.') Wordsworth's intention was 'to choose incidents and situations from common life, and to relate or describe them, throughout, as far as possible in a selection of language really used by men'. But although the collection contained masterpieces such as *Tintern Abbey*, its novel poetic language and subject matter won only a small public at first.

The German trip was a failure, and William and Dorothy returned to England in February 1799. They settled in the Lake District, and rented – for £8 a year –

Love and loyalty
(above) Wordsworth first met his wife Mary when they were at infants' school together. They were married for almost 50 years, and had five children – two of whom died tragically in the same year, 1812.

Tintern Abbey
Wordsworth wrote his famous lines on Tintern Abbey in 1798, after revisiting these enchanting Welsh ruins (below) for the first time in five years. The poem charts his changing attitude to nature.

Rydal Mount
(below) Wordsworth's move to his last home, Rydal Mount, coincided with his assumption of the government post of Distributor of Stamps for Westmorland. He lived in this 'modest mansion of sober hue' until his death.

the most famous of all their homes, Dove Cottage in Grasmere. The years at Dove Cottage (1799-1808) saw Wordsworth at his creative peak. Many great poems from this period, such as *Intimations of Immortality*, chronicle moments of almost mystical rapture.

Time made Wordsworth a more staid, less inspiring figure. In 1802 he married Mary Hutchinson, whom he had known since childhood, and fathered five children. He became a political conservative, now attacked as a turncoat by younger radicals such as Byron and Shelley. In 1813 he accepted a post – from the government he had once detested – as Distributor of Stamps for Westmorland, and moved into his last and grandest home, Rydal Mount. The government post brought him the highly respectable sum of £400 a year, and in his later life he was a wealthy man; in 1827 his friend Sir George Beaumont left him a legacy, and in 1842 he was awarded a pension of £300 a year.

FAME AND HONOURS
By this time Wordsworth had become one of the most famous and honoured of English writers, for by the 1820s the critics had begun to veer about and hail him as a great poet. Thomas de Quincey, author of *Recollections of the Lake Poets* (1834-39), summed up the poet's change of fortunes when he wrote: 'Up to 1820 the name of Wordsworth was trampled underfoot; from 1820 to 1830 it was militant; from 1830 to 1835 it has been triumphant.' An increasingly venerated figure, Wordsworth composed a *Guide to the Lakes* (1822) and in old age became one of the district's chief tourist attractions. He outlived all his great contemporaries to become Poet Laureate in 1843, seven years before his death on 23 April 1850.

A few months later, Mary Wordsworth published the most ambitious of all her husband's works – *The Prelude* – completed years before but reserved for posterity. This record of 'the Growth of a Poet's Mind' made a fitting climax to the English Romantic movement.

Samuel Taylor Coleridge

Eloquent, idealistic and with wide-ranging talents, Coleridge nevertheless failed to find the love and fulfilment he craved – except, perhaps, in his inspiring friendship with the Wordsworths.

Coleridge's brilliant mind and eloquent tongue fascinated almost everyone who met him. Wordsworth, though often impatient with his friend's weaknesses, described him as 'the most wonderful man I have ever known'. Although Coleridge's splendid genius began to flag early in life, undermined by opium and unhappiness, he left a handful of magical, incantatory poems that place him among the greatest spirits of English literature.

Samuel Taylor Coleridge was born on 21 October 1772 at Ottery St Mary in Devon. On the death of his father, the village vicar and schoolmaster, he was sent to Christ's Hospital, a London school where he rapidly attracted attention as a prodigious scholar, omnivorous reader and spellbinding conversationalist. At Jesus College, Cambridge, he seemed certain of a great future, until events revealed the flaws in his curiously helpless, childlike character. In debt and rejected by Mary Evans, the girl he loved, Coleridge ran away and joined a regiment of dragoons under the fanciful name Silas Tomkyn Comerbache. Although bought out by his elder brother, he failed to settle down again at Cambridge and left without taking a degree.

Another curious episode occurred shortly afterwards, at Bristol, when Coleridge fell in with a fellow-poet, Robert Southey. These two idealistic young men planned to set up a utopian community in the wilds of America. Since there would have to be women in the community, they rather hastily became engaged to two sisters, Sara and Edith Fricker. Coleridge evidently had qualms about the arrangement, drifted off to London and even proposed again – without success – to Mary Evans. But when Southey tracked him down, Coleridge tamely allowed himself to be taken back and wedded to Sara Fricker. The utopian community never materialized, and Coleridge soon discovered that he and his wife were hopelessly mismatched.

The couple settled close to the Quantock Hills, at Nether Stowey in Somerset. By now, Coleridge had produced a political journal, *The Watchman*, and toyed with the idea of becoming a Unitarian minister. His

Spiritual pilgrimage
Coleridge (left) was the son of the vicar of Ottery St Mary in Devon (below) and seemed destined to follow in his father's clerical footsteps. But with his new friend Robert Southey, the 21-year-old Coleridge was captivated by the idea of a utopian community, in which there would be complete political and religious freedom. Later in life, however, Coleridge became increasingly conservative, and spent his last years studying the Bible.

led relationship with her gave him little happiness, and it was to her that he addressed *Dejection: An Ode*, which has been called the saddest poem in the language. It was also to be his last major poem.

Racked by illness and hopelessly addicted to opium, Coleridge seemed to be deteriorating fast. In 1804 he went to Malta for three years as secretary to the governor, but returned in no better health and spirits. He separated from his wife, and for two years lived with the Wordsworths at Dove Cottage – a relatively stable episode during which he brought out a periodical, *The Friend*, dictated to Sara Hutchinson.

When Sara left the Lake District, Coleridge moved to London. He was to be deeply wounded by Wordsworth's reported remarks about his trying domestic habits, and the ensuing breach between the two poets was never fully healed. Despite his apparent decline, Coleridge was to live for many years, mainly thanks to Dr James Gillman, who in 1816 took him into his own family and looked after him until the poet's death on 25 July 1834.

In his later years, Coleridge had made a new reputation as a lecturer and produced much distinguished philosophical and critical writing, including a famous literary autobiography, *Biographia Literaria* (1817). His poetic output was tiny compared with that of his fellow-Romantic Wordsworth, yet it includes at least two of the most famous and most frequently anthologized poems in the English language.

Fruitful friendship

In 1797 the Wordsworths rented Alfoxden House (left) near Nether Stowey in Somerset in order to be near Coleridge. The two poets talked, walked and wrote, roaming the Quantock Hills for inspiration.

Wife and daughter

Against his better judgement, Coleridge married Sara Fricker (below, left) in 1795. He separated from her some years later, having fathered three sons and the clever and beautiful Sara (below).

association with William and Dorothy Wordsworth, however, reaffirmed and revitalized his poetic vocation. Coleridge contributed only four poems to *Lyrical Ballads*, of which 'it was agreed, that my endeavours should be directed to persons and characters supernatural, or at least romantic'. But one of these poems was an awesome, parable-like story of unsurpassed potency, *The Rime of the Ancient Mariner*.

In 1797 Coleridge stayed for a time at a farm near Porlock in Somerset. There, according to a note he wrote in 1816, suffering from 'a slight indisposition' for which he had taken laudanum (opium in liquid form), he fell into a reverie or drugged dream in which he 'read' a long poem about the Khan Kubla. On waking, he began to write it down but, according to his own account, he was interrupted by 'a person from Porlock' and lost the thread. Wildly beautiful, exotic and enigmatic, *Kubla Khan* remained a fragment – but, nevertheless, an imperishable masterpiece.

In 1800 Coleridge and his family moved to Keswick in order to be closer to the Wordsworths. Another strong attraction of Grasmere was Sara Hutchinson, Wordsworth's sister-in-law. But Coleridge's unfulfil-

Lord Byron

Byron was both famous and infamous for his audacious poetry, his scandalous love life and his liberal ideals. Ostracized by English society, he died during the fight for Greek independence.

The family seat
(above) Newstead Abbey in Nottinghamshire came into Byron's possession when, at the age of ten, he inherited the title and estate of his great-uncle, the 5th Lord Byron. The building, which had originally been presented to the Byrons by Henry VIII in the 16th century, was in a semi-ruined state, but the young Byron fell in love with its romantic atmosphere. In 1818, however, he sold Newstead for almost £100,000 to pay off his debts.

Byron made a unique impression on 19th-century Europe, not only as a poet but as a legendary personality: a great lover and solitary outsider, brooding against a landscape of wild romantic scenery. The real Byron was more complex, alternating his romantic role with that of a fashionable society man, and writing sustained masterpieces of comic and satirical verse.

George Gordon Byron was born on 22 January 1788 in a furnished room in London. His mother, a Scottish heiress, had seen most of her money spent by her wild, fortune-hunting husband, Captain John Byron. The family fled from its creditors to Aberdeen, and the Captain soon decamped to France, where he died.

Until he was ten, Byron was sent to school in Aberdeen. Meanwhile a succession of doctors tried in vain to correct his deformed right foot, of which he always remained acutely conscious. Byron's lameness may account for his need to prove himself in love and action, and it became an important element in his romantic image.

An unexpected death promoted Byron to the ranks of the aristocracy as Baron Byron of Rochdale, with Newstead Abbey as his family seat. He was sent to Harrow, and went on to Trinity College, Cambridge, graduating in 1808. He appeared to be a typical Regency buck, deep in debt and prone to reckless dissipation; but he was also publishing a good deal of verse. When the *Edinburgh Review* dismissed it with scorn, he lashed out at the critics in a long, immensely funny poem, *English Bards and Scotch Reviewers* (1809).

In July 1809 Byron left England on a Mediterranean tour which lasted for two years. He was delighted with the exotic, untamed Balkans, and above all with Greece. 'If I am a poet,' he said, 'the air of Greece has made me one.' Back in England, he spoke out in the House of Lords against government repression of working-class discontent. Then in March 1812 he published the first two cantos of *Childe Harold's Pilgrimage*, which narrates the travels and adventures of the first distinctively 'Byronic' hero, whom contemporaries rightly assumed to be a disguised self-portrait. *Childe Harold* made Byron famous virtually overnight, and gave added allure to his extraordinary good looks and mercurial character. One of the many women who pursued him was the unstable Lady Caroline Lamb. Despite her famous description of him

Indiscreet passions
(right and below) Byron insisted that he was the victim, rather than the seducer, of women, but his stormy love life shocked his contemporaries. His most famous affair was with Lady Caroline Lamb (below), and he was rumoured to have had an incestuous relationship with his adored step-sister Augusta (right), who was said to have had his child.

under the sun. This, rather than his gloomy romantic narratives, is now regarded as Byron's master-work. Claire, meanwhile, had given birth to Byron's daughter, Allegra. Mother and child travelled to Italy with the Shelleys in 1818, and Byron took on responsibility for Allegra's care. He put the little girl in a convent, but she died of typhus at the age of five.

In 1819 Byron met Teresa, the 19-year-old wife of the elderly Count Guiccioli. They became lovers, and Teresa eventually left her husband. For a few years Byron led a relatively settled life with Teresa. But in 1823 he answered appeals to help the Greek revolt against Turkish rule. He was financing and training troops at Missolonghi when he fell ill with a fever. After ten days' illness, on 19 April 1824, a clap of thunder rang out and the Greeks in the streets of the town looked at one another and said, 'The great man is gone.' Byron had died, but a legend was born.

An exotic image
(left) Byron was fascinated by the colour and romance of the East and the more remote areas of Europe, and he delighted in having himself painted in exotic costume. He was proud of his remarkable good looks, but he was also highly self-conscious about his club foot, which is here artfully concealed by the draperies among which he reclines.

Greece's sufferings
(below) Byron was not alone in supporting the Greeks in their fight for freedom against the Turks; artists and intellectuals all over Europe sympathized with their plight. The great French Romantic Delacroix painted this picture of the victims of a Turkish massacre at Chios in 1824, the year in which Byron died.

as 'mad, bad, and dangerous to know', she created a series of public scandals in her frantic attempts to hold on to him.

Over the next few years, *The Giaour*, *The Corsair* and similar narrative poems, with eastern settings and mysterious, tormented heroes, reinforced the Byronic image. Yet Byron himself was trying to settle down, and in January 1815 he married Annabella Milbanke. She bore him a daughter but the marriage broke down within 15 months. Annabella, a rather solemn intellectual, was quite unable to handle Byron's moods and erratic behaviour.

Stung by the campaign of innuendo and insult that followed his separation from Annabella, Byron left England – as it proved, for ever – on 24 April 1816. He had already succumbed to the determined attentions of Claire Clairmont, who renewed their relationship in Switzerland and introduced Byron to her step-sister Mary, and Mary's husband, Percy Bysshe Shelley. The poets struck up a friendship, living as neighbours at Lake Geneva.

After Shelley returned to England, Byron settled in Italy. The sale of Newstead Abbey cleared his debts, and his prolific literary output brought in huge sums. Everyone was reading Byron, though his reputation was such that a lady novelist fainted with fright in a salon when his name was announced. In the summer of 1818 he began *Don Juan*, a long, rollicking, novel-like poem in which he perfected a discursive conversational style that enabled him to treat every subject

Percy Bysshe Shelley

A radical and apostle of free love, Shelley spent his life in virtual exile for his beliefs. Before his early death, he had expressed his Romantic and political idealism in pamphlets, essays and poems.

Shelley was above all an idealist, and in his restless, complicated private life, ideals and realities constantly clashed. His poetry is a reflection of this conflict, exalting personal and political freedom but also mirroring Shelley's own struggles with failure and disillusion.

Percy Bysshe Shelley was born on 4 August 1792 at Field Place in Sussex. His family were wealthy members of the gentry, and Shelley was sent to Eton and Oxford, where he became a fine classical scholar. But he was a rebel and misfit even at school, where he was bullied mercilessly. As one schoolmate reported, 'I have seen him surrounded, hooted, baited like a maddened bull, and at this distance of time I seem to hear ringing in my ears the cry which Shelley was wont to utter in his paroxysm of revengeful anger.'

At Oxford, Shelley published a pamphlet entitled *The Necessity of Atheism*, for which he was sent down. At 18, the future poet was already a political radical, a vegetarian, an apostle of free love, and an atheist. He was also a tousled eccentric, subject to hallucinations and fits of sleep-walking, but his transparent sincerity and enthusiasm won over most of the people he met.

In London, Shelley encountered Harriet Westbrook, who attended the same boarding school as his sister. They eloped and were married in Edinburgh on 28 August 1811. Shelley was 19, and Harriet 16. From this time, Shelley led a wandering life, rarely staying in the same place for more than a few months. Having quarrelled with his father, he was often short of money and deep in debt.

During a stay in Dublin, Shelley wrote pamphlets denouncing English rule in Ireland and discrimination against Catholics. He and Harriet lived variously in Wales, England and Scotland, while Shelley composed *Queen Mab*, his first sustained poetic statement.

Meanwhile, the incompatibility between Shelley and Harriet had become increasingly obvious – to Shelley, at least. Though Harriet was pregnant with their second child, he left her for Mary Godwin, the daughter of two people Shelley admired intensely: the radical philosopher William Godwin and his long-dead wife, the feminist Mary Wollstonecraft. In July 1814, Shelley and Mary eloped to the Continent, accompanied by Claire Clairmont, the daughter of Godwin's second wife. Shelley had already displayed a taste for group living, and Claire was to stay with him and Mary, on and off, for years.

Lack of money brought Shelley and his companions back to England within six weeks, but in 1816 they set out again for Switzerland. Claire Clairmont steered them to Lake Geneva, where she hoped to resume her affair with Lord Byron (she was already pregnant by him). The two poets met and formed an important,

Florentine vistas
Enamoured of Italy, Shelley composed 'Ode to the West Wind' near the banks of the river Arno (above). When his only surviving son was born there in November 1819, he and Mary named him Percy Florence to commemorate his birthplace – to Shelley, 'the most beautiful city I ever saw'.

Rebel poet
The most radical of all the English Romantic poets, Percy Bysshe Shelley was the scion of Sussex gentry but became a democrat, an atheist, a vegetarian and an advocate of free love. After Shelley's death, his family promoted a more acceptable view of him as an 'ineffectual angel' who wrote exquisite verse. The ironic result was that he became one of the Victorians' favourite poets.

Eton schooldays
Shelley's time at Eton (above) was not happy – his fellow students tormented him because of his eccentricities, while his teachers were alarmed by his dangerous chemical and occult experiments, including attempts at raising the Devil.

Jane Williams
(below) *Shelley was one of Jane Williams's many admirers, writing poems to her such as 'When the lamp is shattered'. Later, when both he and her husband had lost their lives, Mary Shelley seems also to have fallen under Jane's extraordinary spell.*

stimulating friendship. A tour of the lake with Byron inspired Shelley to compose his first unmistakably great poem, *Hymn to Intellectual Beauty*.

In September 1816 Shelley returned to England. Three months later the unlucky Harriet, pregnant by an army officer, drowned herself. Shelley and Mary were married a few days later, but this gesture towards respectability failed to procure Shelley the custody of his children by Harriet.

After a year in England, Shelley was in poor health, stifled and discouraged by the atmosphere of political repression. In March 1818 the Shelleys, their children and Claire Clairmont left for Italy, where renewed contact with Byron inspired Shelley's *Julian and Maddalo*, a vivid verse portrait of the two men. Shelley was now at the height of his powers, and *Prometheus Unbound, The Cenci, Ode to the West Wind* and *The Mask of Anarchy* were all composed in 1818-19. Much of his late verse was political, but in May 1821 the news of Keats's death prompted the elegiac *Adonais*.

THE FINAL JOURNEY

By this time, Shelley's relations with Mary were often strained. All but one of their children died, and Shelley continued to find inspiration in other women, the last being Jane Williams to whom he wrote many poems, including 'When the lamp is shattered'.

Edward and Jane Williams were new friends who moved in with the Shelleys in April 1822 and shared their home at Lerici, on the Bay of Spezia. Although unable to swim, Shelley had a lifelong passion for the water, and he intended spending the summer sailing with Edward Williams and Byron. But on 8 July, on a trip from Livorno to Lerici, Shelley's boat disappeared. Ten days later, the bodies of Shelley, Williams and their boat boy were washed ashore. Shelley was identified by the copy of Keats's poems in his pocket. Byron was one of the small party that was present when the remains of his friend were cremated on the beach. At his death, Shelley was not quite 30.

The fateful voyage
Edward Williams shared with Shelley a love of the sea, and the two eagerly awaited delivery of their boat – Williams even painted her (below) in full, resplendent sail. Their first trip, however, was to be their last. Sailing from Leghorn on 8 July 1822, they were caught in a storm and drowned.

John Keats

Although his life was tragically short, Keats was blessed with an exquisite poetic gift which triumphed over both his personal suffering and savage criticism.

K eats was the youngest of the great Romantics, and the first to die. Yet because of his precociously mature genius, he left a substantial body of work, including poems whose sensuous loveliness demonstrates his cherished belief that Beauty and Truth are one and the same.

John Keats was born in London on 31 October 1795. His father ran a prosperous livery stables in the parish of Moorfields, and at the age of seven Keats was sent to a good private school at Enfield. But both his parents died by the time he was 14, and in 1810 his guardian apprenticed him to a surgeon and apothecary at Edmonton, Middlesex. Although he qualified in 1816 and spent a few months studying surgery at Guy's Hospital, the lure of poetry proved too strong for Keats. For the rest of his brief existence he lived precariously as a professional writer, sometimes desperately short of money and working with great intensity while his health lasted.

A PRECOCIOUS GENIUS

As a teenager Keats steeped himself in English poetry, and his first efforts at verse – probably made at about 18 – were predictably lush and imitative. But by 1816 he was maturing fast. In April, Leigh Hunt's magazine *The Examiner* published Keats's sonnet *To Solitude*. By the end of the year he had shown further skill and subtlety with *On First Looking into Chapman's Homer* (a poem about a poem – George Chapman's early 17th-

Joseph Severn
A true friend to Keats, Joseph Severn (right) was a frequent visitor at his house, and the only one of their circle who was prepared to leave England for Italy when Keats's health failed. In Rome, Severn tended him night and day, cooking, reading to him, and trying to make his final days as comfortable as possible. He even reputedly stopped Keats from committing suicide on one particularly bleak occasion. Severn painted Keats (far right) during happier days.

century translation of the *Iliad* and the *Odyssey*), and Hunt was confidently prophesying greatness for him.

Leigh Hunt, himself a distinguished essayist and journalist, gave Keats invaluable encouragement, introducing the inexperienced young poet to his literary circle, which included Shelley and the critic William Hazlitt. However, most of these men were regarded as dangerous radicals by powerful establishment periodicals such as *Blackwood's*, and Keats was later to suffer for his association with what they sneeringly labelled 'the Cockney school of poetry'.

When his first collection of poems appeared in March 1817, it was ignored rather than abused. Un-

discouraged, Keats moved out of London to Hampstead – then a country village – and worked for months on an epic poem, *Endymion*. The result was flawed in parts, but the disciplined effort involved seems to have brought Keats to the verge of his astonishingly early artistic maturity. In the spring of 1818, he completed another long narrative poem, *Isabella; or, the Pot of Basil*.

That summer, Keats and a friend embarked on a 42-day walking tour of the Lake District, Ulster and Scotland which overtaxed the poet's strength. When he reached Inverness, a local physician insisted that he return home at once. This ominous incident was

Hampstead Heath
During the winter of 1816-17, Keats left London and joined his brothers in the village of Hampstead (left) to be near his friend and fellow-writer Leigh Hunt. The Heath was his back garden, and he delighted in strolling across it, watching the wind ruffling great fields of barley like the motion of 'the inland sea'.

Roman requiem
With books and a piano to distract him, Keats spent his final weeks in a corner room by the Spanish Steps in Rome's Piazza di Spagna (below).

followed by the death of Keats's brother Tom, whom he nursed devotedly through the last stages of consumption – the disease that in just three years would take the poet's own life.

Meanwhile, the Tory reviewers had begun to single out Keats for attack. *Blackwood's* snobbishly derided the poetic efforts of footmen, farm-servants and apothecaries, sardonically lamenting 'the calm, settled, imperturbable drivelling idiocy of *Endymion*'. It advised, 'It is a better and wiser thing to be a starved apothecary than a starved poet; so back to the shop Mr John, back to the "plasters, pills and ointment boxes".'

Shelley's *Adonais* implies, and legend has it, that such savagery broke Keats's heart and killed him. In reality, the reviews appeared just when he was entering his 'Great Year', 1818-19, when he produced one masterpiece after another, including *Hyperion*, *The Eve of St Agnes*, all his great Odes (including *Ode to a Nightingale* and *Ode to a Grecian Urn*), and *La Belle Dame Sans Merci*.

After this supreme creative output, Keats was unwell in the winter of 1819-20, and in February 1820

Keats's love
Fanny Brawne (left), who met Keats in November 1818, was five years younger than the poet. Keats was immediately and completely enthralled by her, expressing his passion in many poems and letters. She was the 'sweet home of all my fears,/ And hopes, and joys, and panting miseries . . .' They became secretly engaged in 1819, but his illness marred any happiness they might have had. She wore mourning for several years after his death, but finally married in 1833.

began to cough blood. He immediately recognized this as his 'death warrant'. The blow was all the more cruel because he had met and become engaged to a young neighbour named Fanny Brawne. Their relationship was stormy, since Keats, realizing he was to die, suffered agonies of jealousy. But it was among the Brawne family that he spent his last weeks in England.

A PAINFUL DEATH

By September 1820 Keats's condition was desperately serious, and his friends believed that only the southern sun might cure him. A close friend, the painter Joseph Severn, travelled with him to Rome, and the two men took rooms on the Piazza di Spagna, at the bottom of the Spanish Steps. Here, after terrible suffering, Keats died in Severn's arms on 23 February 1821. He was buried in Rome's Protestant cemetery, where his tombstone was inscribed, as he had instructed, with the gloomy words 'Here lies one whose name was writ in water'. But his name was not disappeared. Instead, posterity has endorsed his defiant response to the reviewers: 'I think I shall be among the English poets after my death.'

LUDWIG VAN BEETHOVEN

1770-1827

Beethoven's story is one of triumph over personal tragedy, and of supreme musical achievement. He is at once the last great master of the Classical tradition and pioneer of musical Romanticism.

Beethoven's birthplace
Beethoven was born in this house, No. 515 Bonngasse, Bonn, on 16 December 1770. Not surprisingly, his place of birth has been a focus of interest: this pencil drawing was made in 1889 by R. Beissel, two generations after the death of the composer.

A modern view
A modern photograph of the same house, now a shrine as well as a Beethoven museum. The only major structural changes made since the composer was born have involved enlarging it on the garden side and altering the roof.

Ludwig van Beethoven is widely regarded as the greatest of all composers, even by people who are not temperamentally in sympathy with his work. The reasons are not hard to discover. No other composer's output has contained so large a proportion of indisputable masterpieces. Moreover Beethoven took music out of the 18th century and gave it a radical new direction; and in doing so he broke many rules which were considered sacrosanct. Finally, despite all that has happened since his death, his music continues to influence composers today.

EARLY YEARS

For a man who was destined to be lionized by the aristocracy, Beethoven's start in life was singularly inauspicious. He was born in Bonn, probably on 16 December 1770, the son of an obscure tenor singer in the employ of the Elector of Cologne. Few facts are known about his childhood, and traditional accounts may or may not be reliable. His father is said to have been a violent and intemperate man who returned home late at night, much the worse for drink, and dragged young Ludwig from his bed in order to beat music lessons into the boy's sleepy head. There are also stories of Beethoven's father forcing him to play the violin for the amusement of his drinking cronies. Despite these and other afflictions – which might well have made a lesser man loathe the subject – the young Beethoven developed a passion for music.

When Ludwig began to show signs of promise, other teachers were called in, and by the age of seven he was advanced enough to appear in public. A year or so later the composer Christian Gottlob Neefe took over his musical training, and progress thereafter was rapid. Beethoven's Nine Variations for piano in C minor was published, and it was listed later in a well-known Leipzig catalogue as the work of 'Louis van Betthoven [sic], aged ten years'.

In 1787 Beethoven met Mozart. Beethoven was visiting Vienna, a great European capital and notable musical centre, and must have felt a little out of place, for he was clumsy and stocky; his manners were unrefined, his black hair was unruly and he habitually wore a surly expression on his swarthy face. By contrast, the great Mozart was dapper and sophisticated. He received the boy sceptically, but once Beethoven started playing the piano his talent was evident. 'Watch this lad', Mozart remarked. 'Some day he will make the world talk about him.'

PREPARING FOR GREATNESS

With the death of his wife the last steadying influence on Beethoven's father was removed. The old singer unhesitatingly put the bottle before any thoughts of duty to Ludwig, his two younger brothers and his one-year-old sister. The situation became so bad that by 1789 Beethoven was forced to show his mettle. He went resolutely to his father's employer and demanded – and got – half his father's salary, so that the family could be provided for; his father could drink away the rest. In 1792 the old man died. The event occasioned no great grief: as his employer put it, 'That will deplete the revenue from liquor excise.'

For four years Ludwig supported his family. He also made some good friends, among them Stephan von Breuning, who became a friend for life, and Doctor Franz Wegeler, who wrote one of the earliest biographies of Beethoven. Count Ferdinand von Waldstein also entered Beethoven's circle; he received the dedication of a famous piano sonata in 1804.

In July 1792 the great Austrian composer Haydn passed through Bonn on his way to Vienna. He met Beethoven and was impressed, and perhaps disturbed, by his work. Clearly, he felt, this young man's talent needed to be disciplined before it could be developed. Consequently Beethoven left Bonn for good early in November 1792 to study composition with Haydn in Vienna. However, if Haydn had hoped to discipline Beethoven's talent he was fighting a losing battle. Beethoven's music strode towards the next century, heavily influenced by the strenuous political and social tensions that ravaged Europe in the wake of the French Revolution.

His first weeks in Vienna were hard for Beethoven. Opportunities were not forthcoming; expectations were unfulfilled. In addition it must have irked him, fired as he was by the current egalitarian spirit, to have to live in a tiny garret in his patron Prince Lichnowsky's mansion. Soon, however, the Prince gave him more spacious accommodation on the ground floor, and, mindful of the young man's impetuous nature, instructed his servants that Beethoven's bell was to be answered

An idealized portrait
Beethoven (above), painted by Joseph Carl Steiler in 1819, when the composer was 49 years old. He is shown at work on the score of the Missa Solemnis. *By this time he was already totally deaf.*
Beethoven was deeply attached to his mother, Maria Magdalena (left), referring to her as his 'best friend'. She died of tuberculosis in 1787, when Beethoven was 17. A pious and conventional woman, she tried to shield Beethoven and her other children from their drunken father's violence.

65

were secure enough for him to set up his own apartments. He was the first composer to become a freelance by choice, rather than being dependent on the bounty of patrons. However, it was his virtuosity as a pianist rather than his genius as a composer that brought him recognition during his twenties.

THE ONSET OF DEAFNESS
Beethoven's career as a virtuoso pianist was soon to be terminated. In a letter written to his friend Karl Amenda on 1 July 1801, he admitted he was experiencing signs of deafness:

How often I wish you were here, for your Beethoven is having a miserable life, at odds with nature and its Creator, abusing the latter for leaving his creatures vulnerable to the slightest accident . . . My greatest faculty, my hearing, is greatly deteriorated.

Apparently Beethoven had been aware of the problem for about three years, avoiding company lest his weakness be discovered, and retreating into himself. Friends ascribed his reserve to preoccupation and absentmindedness. In a letter to Wegeler he wrote:

How can I, a musician, say to people 'I am deaf!' I shall, if I can, defy this fate, even though there will be times when I shall be the unhappiest of God's creatures . . . I live only in music . . . frequently working on three or four pieces simultaneously.

Many men would have been driven to suicide by such an affliction, and Beethoven may indeed have

Master and pupil
Joseph Haydn (above), the great classical composer, attempted to guide the young Beethoven's talent; however, Beethoven later claimed to have learned little from the older composer. The miniature (above right) shows Beethoven in 1803, at about the time when he was composing the 'Eroica'.

even before the Prince's own!

Impetuosity was also a feature of his piano playing at this time. In those days pianists were pitted against each other in front of audiences to decide who could play the more brilliantly and improvise the more imaginatively. Beethoven's rivals always retired, defeated, from such combats. While he made enemies of many pianists in Vienna, the nobility flocked to hear him. Personally and professionally his future looked bright. Compositions poured from him, and he gave concerts in Vienna as well as Berlin, Prague and other important centres. His finances

A noble friend
Therese, Countess of Brunswick (right), was Beethoven's pupil and developed an 'intimate and warm-hearted' friendship with him. She gave him this portrait, and this gesture has been interpreted as evidence that she was his 'Immortal Beloved': the great and secret love of his life.

contemplated it. But his rock-like nature gave him strength, and he came to terms with his deafness in a dynamic, constructive way. Another letter to Wegeler, written five months after the despairing missive just quoted, makes it clear that Beethoven, always stubborn, unyielding and struggling against destiny, had come to see his deafness as a challenge to be faced and overcome:

Free me of only half this affliction and I shall be a complete, mature man. You must think of me as being as happy as it is possible to be on this earth – not unhappy. No! I cannot endure it. I will seize Fate by the throat. It will not wholly conquer me! Oh, how beautiful it is to live – and live a thousand times over!

With the end of his career as a virtuoso pianist inevitable, he plunged into composing. It offered a much more precarious living than that of a performer, especially since his compositions were already in advance of popular taste. In 1802 his doctor sent him to Heiligenstadt, a village outside Vienna, in the hope that its rural peace would help his hearing. The new surroundings reawakened in Beethoven a love of nature and the countryside, and hope and optimism returned. Chief among the sunny works of this period was the charming, exuberant Symphony No. 2. However, when it became obvious that there was no improvement in his hearing, despair returned. By autumn Beethoven felt so low, physically and mentally, that he feared he would not survive the winter. Consequently he wrote his will, leaving instructions that it was to be opened only after his death. This 'Heiligenstadt Testament' is a moving document that reveals his state of mind more directly

Beethoven's 'testament'
The last page of the 'Heiligenstadt Testament' (above), which Beethoven intended to be both a will and a statement of his personal philosophy. By now his deafness was growing worse, and he believed that he would soon be dead.

Music publishing
(left) The first really professional composer, Beethoven developed a close business relationship with his publishers, Artaria & Co., who occupied premises in Vienna's Kohlmarkt (foreground right of picture).

than the music he was writing at the time:

O ye men who accuse me of being malevolent, stubborn and misanthropic, how ye wrong me! Ye know not the secret cause. From childhood my heart and mind were disposed towards feelings of gentleness and good will, and I was eager to accomplish great deeds; but consider this: for six years I have been hopelessly ill, aggravated and cheated by quacks in the hope of improvement but finally compelled to face a lasting malady . . . I was forced to isolate myself. I was misunderstood and rudely repulsed because I was as yet unable to say to people, 'Speak louder, shout, for I am deaf' . . .
With joy I hasten to meet death. Despite my hard fate . . . I shall wish that it had come later; but I am content, for he shall free me of constant suffering. Come then, Death, and I shall face thee with courage. Heiglnstadt [sic], 6 October, 1802.

Just how bad was Beethoven's malady? At first the disturbance in his hearing was intermittent, or so faint that it worried him only occasionally. But by 1801 he reported that he was constantly troubled by

whistling and buzzing sounds. Low speech tones became an unintelligible hum, shouting an intolerable din. Delicate sounds were drowned out and stronger ones distorted. There may have been short periods of remission, but for the last ten years of his life Beethoven was totally deaf.

BEETHOVEN IN MATURITY

The mature Beethoven was a short, well-built man. His dark hair went grey, then white, but was always thick and unruly. Reports differ as to the colour of his eyes. His skin was pock-marked, and his mouth, which had been a little petulant in youth, later became fixed in a grim, down-curving line, as if in a permanent expression of truculent determination. He seldom took care of his appearance, and, as he strode through the streets of Vienna with hair escaping from beneath his top hat, his hands clasped behind his back and his coat cross-buttoned, he was the picture of eccentricity. His moods changed constantly, keeping his acquaintances guessing, and they could never be sure that a chance remark might not be misconstrued by him.

By nature Beethoven was impatient, impulsive, unreasonable and intolerant; deafness added suspicion and paranoia to these attributes. He would often misunderstand the meaning of a facial expression and accuse faithful friends of disloyalty or conspiracy. He flew into a rage at the slightest provocation, and

A second home
This delightful silhouette shows Frau von Breuning, widow of a court councillor, and her family. Their house was a second home for Beethoven while he lived in Bonn. There he gave lessons to two of her four children and made important artistic and intellectual contacts.

Family man
Beethoven's emotional involvement with his family was, like all his involvements, intense to the point of unreason. One of his brothers, Carl, ran the composer's business affairs, but was thrust aside when he married a woman of whom Beethoven disapproved. A very similar situation led to a rift between Beethoven and his brother Johann (left), a Linz apothecary. However, Beethoven felt even more strongly about his nephew Karl (above left), who seems to have been something of a scamp; in one surviving letter (above) he apologizes for misbehaving at school.

Years of fame
A portrait of Beethoven painted by Ferdinand Schimon in 1818-19, when the composer was at the height of his fame.

The music room
(below) in Johann Beethoven's house at Gneixendorf. Beethoven and his nephew Karl spent eight weeks here after Karl, oppressed by his uncle's emotional demands, attempted suicide. Their subsequent parting proved to be final: Karl went into the army, and Beethoven died soon afterwards.

would turn on intimates, dismissing them as unworthy of his friendship. But, as likely as not, he would write a letter the next day calling them noble and good, and admitting that he had misjudged them.

A TEMPESTUOUS LIFE

After his return from Heiligenstadt, Beethoven's music deepened. He began creating a new musical world. In the summer of 1803 he began work on his Third Symphony, the 'Eroica'. It was to be a paean to Napoleon Bonaparte, whom Beethoven admired as the military and political leader of republican France. Like its subject, the Eroica was revolutionary. It was half as long again as any previous symphony and its musical language was so uncompromising that it provoked a good deal of resistance among its earliest audiences. It broke the symphonic mould, yet it established new, logical and cogent forms. This was a miracle Beethoven was to work many times.

In December 1804, news arrived that Napoleon, the republican hero, had proclaimed himself Emperor. In a fury, Beethoven strode over to his copy of the symphony, which bore a dedication to Napoleon, and crossed out the 'Bonaparte' with such violence that the pen tore a hole in the paper. 'Is he, too, no more than human?' he raged. 'Now he will crush the rights of man. He will become a tyrant!' When the Eroica was published it bore the inscription 'To the memory of a great man'!

For the next few years in Vienna, from 1804 to 1808, Beethoven lived in what might be described as a state of creatively valuable uproar. His relationships suffered elemental rifts, his music grew ever more profound and he was always in love with one woman or another. The women were usually high-born, sometimes unattainable, always unattained. He never married.

Beethoven's Fifth and Sixth Symphonies were completed by the summer of 1808. The Fifth indeed 'takes fate by the throat'; the Sixth ('Pastoral') is a portrait of the countryside around Heiligenstadt. These and other works spread his name and fame.

In July 1812 Beethoven wrote a letter to an unidentified woman whom he addressed as 'The Immortal Beloved'. It is as eloquent of love as his 'Heiligenstadt Testament' had been of despair:

My angel, my all, my very self – a few words only today, and in pencil (thine). Why such pro-found sorrow when necessity speaks? Can our love endure but through sacrifice – but through not demanding all – canst thou alter it that thou art not wholly mine, I not wholly thine?

So moving an outpouring might perhaps have resulted in some permanent arrangement – if the lady in question had been free, and if the letter had been sent. It was discovered after Beethoven's death in a secret drawer in his desk.

His brother Caspar Carl died in November 1815. The sequel brought about something that neither deafness nor the fire from Napoleon's guns outside Vienna could achieve: it almost stopped Beethoven composing. He was appointed guardian of his brother's nine-year-old son, Karl – a guardianship he shared with the boy's mother Johanna. Beethoven took the appointment very seriously, and was certain that Johanna did not. He believed her to be immoral, and immediately began legal proceedings to obtain sole guardianship of his nephew. The lawsuit was

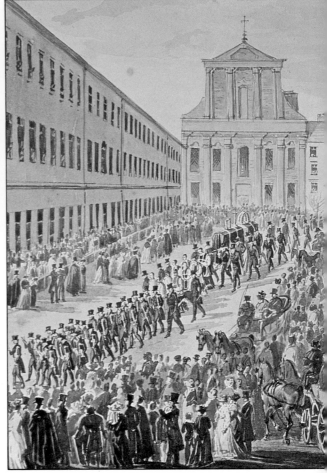

Always in love
There were many women in Beethoven's life, for he was almost always in love with someone. Both Countess Giulietta Guicciardi (top) and Josephine von Brunswick (above) were pupils with whom he became infatuated. Antonie Brentano (above, right) is most likely to have been the mysterious 'Immortal Beloved' to whom he wrote, making the painful confession that, in the conflict between art and love, he would have to choose his art.

Eccentric genius
As he strode through the streets of Vienna, deep in thought and unkempt in appearance, Beethoven was the picture of eccentricity and a delight to caricaturists. Some sketches, such as one (right) by Lyser, succeeded in capturing the determination so characteristic of the composer.

painful, protracted and frequently abusive, with Johanna asking 'How can a deaf, mad bachelor look after the boy's welfare?' Beethoven repeatedly fell ill because of the strain. He did not finally manage to secure custody of Karl until 1820, by which time the boy was 20.

The Ninth ('Choral') Symphony was completed in 1823, by which time Beethoven was completely deaf. There was a poignant scene at the first performance. Despite his disability Beethoven insisted on conducting; but unknown to him another conductor sat out of his sight, giving the time. As the last movement ended, Beethoven, unaware even that the music had ceased, was also unaware of the tremendous burst of applause that greeted it. One of the singers took him by the arm and turned him round so that he might see the ovation.

THE FINAL DAYS
In the autumn of 1826 Beethoven took Karl to Gneixendorf ('The name', said Beethoven, 'sounds like the breaking of an axe') for a holiday. A servant there left a graphic picture of Beethoven, the demonic genius, working on his last string quartet:

At 5.30 a.m. he was at his table, beating time with hands and feet, humming and writing. After breakfast he hurried outside to wander in the fields, calling, waving his arms about, moving slowly, then very fast, then abruptly stopping to scribble something in his notebook.

In early December Beethoven returned to Vienna with Karl. The journey brought the composer down

Vienna's last respects
At 3 pm on 29 March 1827, Beethoven's funeral took place in Vienna. The Viennese turned out en masse: at least 20,000 people crowded into the square in front of the Schwarzpanierhaus, Beethoven's last residence. There were eight pallbearers, dozens of torchbearers and a choir which sang to the accompaniment of sombre trombones.

with pneumonia; he recovered, only to be laid low again with cirrhosis of the liver, which in turn gave way to dropsy. His condition had deteriorated dramatically by the beginning of March and, sensing the worst, his friends rallied round: faithful Stephan brought his family, and Schubert paid his respects.

If a report by Schubert's friend Hüttenbrenner is to be believed, Beethoven's final moments were dramatic in the extreme. At about 5.45 in the afternoon of 26 March 1827, as a storm raged, Beethoven's room was filled with light and shaken with thunder:

Beethoven's eyes opened, and he lifted his right fist for several seconds, a serious, threatening expression on his face. When his hand fell back, he half-closed his eyes . . . Not another word, not another heartbeat.

Schubert and Hummel were among the 20,000 people who mourned the composer at his funeral three days later. He was buried in Währing Cemetery, but in 1888 his remains were removed to Zentral-friedhof in Vienna, a great resting-place for musicians where he lies side by side with Schubert.

Beethoven revolutionized music, breaking many rules which had been considered inviolate for centuries. His work represents the culmination of the Classical tradition of Haydn and Mozart, and also the beginning of the new, dynamic Romantic movement. At the height of his powers he declared: 'Strength is the morality of the man who stands out from the rest, and it is mine.' His work is perhaps the most powerful and splendid body of music ever to be put together by one composer; and it is eternal.

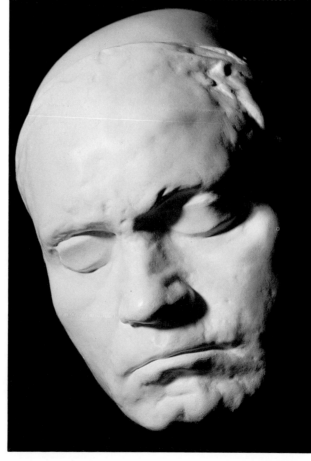

The death mask
Two days after Beethoven's death the young painter Danhauser took this death mask of the composer. Parts of the temple bones had been removed at the post mortem the previous day, giving the head a curious formlessness.

Symphony no.5 in C minor, op.67

This dynamic symphony is one of Beethoven's greatest achievements. Driven on by an irresistible energy, the music sweeps the listener along from the menacing opening to a triumphant conclusion.

The arresting opening bars of Beethoven's Fifth Symphony must be among the most memorable in all music. Beethoven was supposedly alluding to these four violent hammer blows in his famous remark 'Thus fate knocks at the door', although it was made many years after the symphony was composed. On an earlier occasion, according to his friend and pupil Czerny, he simply attributed his inspiration for the opening notes to a yellowhammer's song which he had heard when strolling through the Prater park in Vienna.

Not surprisingly, audiences have preferred the 'Fate' myth to Czerny's story, as it accords perfectly with the dynamic nature of the symphony. The unremitting drive of the first movement conveys a dramatic conflict which is only resolved in the heroic finale, and which has caught the public imagination ever since it was first performed.

THE FIRST PERFORMANCE

The first performance took place on 22 December 1808, at the Theater an der Wien, during a concert which by present-day standards seems gargantuan. First came the Sixth Symphony ('Pastoral'), which was also receiving its first performance; the aria, 'Ah Perfido', part of the Mass in C, and the Third Piano Concerto – it was to have been the new Fourth Concerto, but the pianist was unable to learn it in time. Then in the second half the Symphony in C minor – listed as No. Six but known ever since as the Fifth – was followed by another movement from the C major Mass, and finally by the Fantasia for piano, chorus and orchestra; its piano introduction was apparently improvised by Beethoven on the spot. This marathon concert began at half past six and continued for four hours in a freezing cold hall: 'There we sat from 6.30 until 10.30 in the bitter cold,' wrote Reichardt, the composer and journalist, 'and found from experience that one could have too much even of a good thing . . .'

It is hardly surprising that the standard of the performances left much to be desired – all the more so since Beethoven's fiery temper had antagonized the orchestra and they had only agreed to rehearse if he absented himself from the hall. He was therefore banished to an ante-room, where, in what must have been desperate frustration made even worse by his deafness, he had great difficulty following what was going on; he was only kept in touch by visits from the orchestra leader, Seyfried. However, Beethoven does seem to have conducted the actual concert himself.

Contemporary reports of the evening focus not on the Fifth but on a mishap which occurred during the Choral Fantasia, when the orchestra ground to a halt over a misunderstanding in the wind section. An exasperated Beethoven abandoned his piano to try to sort the problem out, while the long-suffering audience waited for the concert to start again. Reichardt does, however, refer to 'a great symphony, very elaborate and too long'. Perhaps by this time the audience had simply begun to run out of patience.

CRITICAL REACTION

Nevertheless, when the work was played at Leipzig in 1810, E.T.A. Hoffmann, writing in the *Allgemeine Musikalische Zeitung*, the leading musical journal of the day, described the new symphony as 'one of the most important works of the master, whose foremost position among instrumental composers probably no one would now dispute'; and he finishes by describing the work as a 'concept of genius executed with profound deliberation, which in a very high degree brings the Romantic content of the music to expression'.

On the other hand the composer Spohr, discussing a performance of the symphony at Munich in 1815, felt that 'with all its individual beauties it does not form a classical whole', and found the famous opening phrase 'wanting in the dignity which to my mind is indispensable for the opening of a symphony'.

The new work reached London in a concert by the Philharmonic Society on 15 April 1816. During the rehearsal the simplicity of the opening bars seems to have provoked gales of laughter among the members of the orchestra; but the Society was to perform it every year for the next 55 years.

THE PROCESS OF COMPOSITION

As always with Beethoven, the gestation

The master symphonist
Beethoven at about the age of 34, when he had just begun work on the Fifth. Ideas for it appear in sketches dated April 1804.

period was a long one. The first ideas appear in his sketchbooks as early as 1804, alongside similar sketches which found their way into the Fourth Piano Concerto.

Further ideas appear at the end of the sketchbooks for the Third Symphony ('Eroica'), which was finished and first performed in 1805. This symphony, twice as long as any of the great symphonies by Haydn or Mozart and tremendous in the impact of its musical content, revealed to the public the extraordinary dynamic and revolutionary nature of Beethoven's music.

The Fifth Symphony was probably intended to succeed the rugged 'Eroica', but Beethoven's mood may have been influenced for a time by his relationship with the Countess Therese of Brunswick. During 1806 he worked on the lighter Fourth Symphony, which evidently reflects his happier frame of mind. But he took up work on the Fifth Symphony

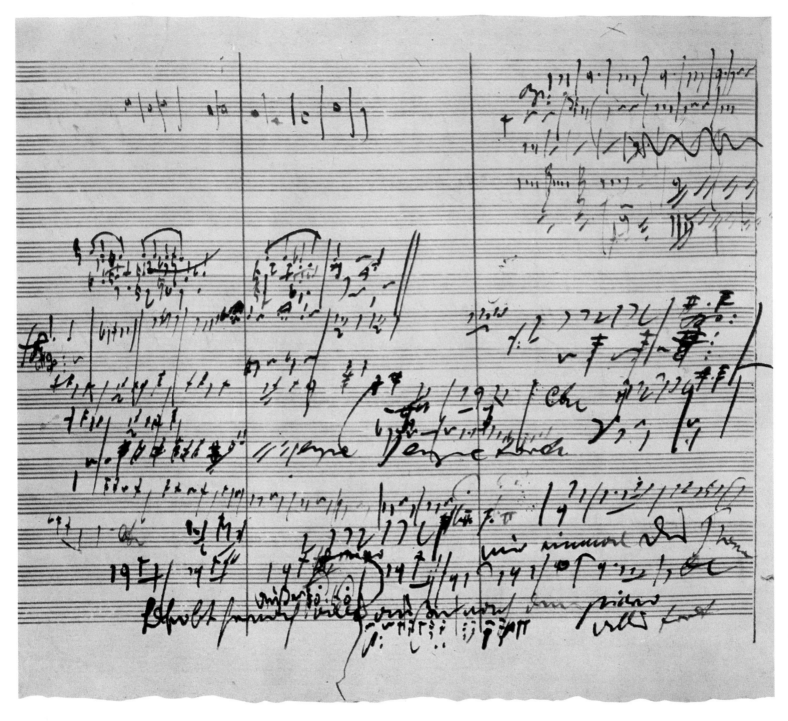

again in 1807 and completed it either later that year or early in 1808. Strangely, during this period he was working simultaneously on the charming and lyrical 'Pastoral' Symphony.

To us, hearing the Fifth in its final form, the symphony seems to surge onwards in a completely spontaneous manner from one idea to the next. Yet it caused Beethoven a great deal of trouble. Even the famous hammer-blow opening went through several transformations before he arrived at the utterly simple and emphatic statement with which the symphony now begins.

MUSICAL INFLUENCES

Beethoven's genius was so distinctive that we tend to underestimate the influence on him of his great predecessors. Haydn's series of 104 symphonies, begun in 1755 and completed in 1795, had developed the form of the symphony from a simple serenade – a harmonious composition divided into different stylized dance forms – into something more complex and personal. As his former pupil, Beethoven must have been very familiar with Haydn's works. Also influential were the compositions of Bach's most famous son, Carl Philip Emmanuel Bach, whose music has a dramatic cut and thrust which is quite individual, and whose keyboard works helped to shape the style of Beethoven's piano sonatas. Mozart's great symphonies were also, inevitably, a

'The Fifth'

Beethoven's numerous sketches for the Fifth Symphony (above) show how much effort went into its composition. Even the opening bars – stunning in their apparent simplicity – underwent several transformations.

source of inspiration.

Moreover, in the Fifth Symphony Beethoven is not really breaking old moulds and creating a new form. In fact the form of the first movement is not only conventional but, like the great classical compositions of Haydn and Mozart, is perfectly balanced in being divided into four equal parts. The exposition – the opening section in which the musical themes are set out – lasts for 124 bars, the

Generous patrons
*Count Razumovsky (above) shared the
dedication of the Fifth Symphony with Prince
Lobkowitz (above right). Both men were great
music lovers and enthusiastic patrons of
Beethoven's art. Razumovsky, long-serving
ambassador to the Austrian court, was a fine
violinist, quite capable of taking his part in a
quartet; Beethoven dedicated the 'Razumovsky
Quartets' of 1805-06 to him. Lobkowitz was
one of three aristocratic patrons who
guaranteed Beethoven an income when he
thought of quitting Vienna.*

*Beethoven told his pupil Czerny that the
opening bars of the Fifth were inspired by the
rhythmic pattern of the yellowhammer's song.*

development – in which these themes are
expanded and explored – 123 bars, the
recapitulation – basically a variation on the
opening section – 126 bars, and the coda –
the concluding section (coda is the Italian
word for 'tail') – 129 bars. It was rather the
originality of the ideas contained within
this strict formal plan, the brightness of
the inspiration and the energy of the
music that were new.

Programme notes

The Fifth Symphony is often described
with warlike terms such as heroism,
conflict and triumph. Yet the conflict is
usually seen as an essentially personal
one: between the physical world, which in
Beethoven's case included his increasing
deafness and inner tensions, and the
divine as Beethoven conceived of it.

The symphony is divided into four
movements: an *Allegro con brio* (meaning
lively and with verve) which moves at a
very brisk pace; an *Andante con moto*
('walking' pace, with animation), a
steady, flowing movement; another
Allegro, traditionally known as the
Scherzo (vigorous and playful in character), which leads into the final movement,
also an Allegro, by way of a long
transitional passage of stunning power.

FIRST MOVEMENT –
ALLEGRO CON BRIO

Example 1

Beethoven begins the symphony by
throwing down the tremendous challenge: 'Thus fate knocks at the door'. But
neither this famous four-note motive nor
its repetition a tone lower down tells us
the key of the symphony. It is not until

after the phrase has been repeated several
times by the strings that the full orchestra
establishes the key of C minor. The full
orchestra here means two flutes, oboes,
clarinets, bassoons, horns and trumpets,
plus timpani and strings. Constant repetition of the initial phrase builds up
magnificently towards a powerful climax.

The mood changes with the introduction on the violins and woodwind of a
new and gentler theme, more flowing and
lyrical than the opening, but still with the
hammer-blow phrase sounding in the
bass. Through constant repetition this
again builds up to a great climax, bringing
the first section to a close. The very
terseness of the opening makes it seem
completely natural that it should be
repeated before the exposition section
gives way to the exploration of these
musical ideas in the development section.

The horns and clarinets once again give
out the main theme with great force, and
the music charges on with irresistible
energy, still repeating the little phrase
over and over, while the moving harmo-
nies create a distinct feeling of unrest, as if
anticipating a storm. Strings and wind
instruments alternate in sequences in a
passage of extraordinary tension; then for
a short period the energy seems to be
spent, only to return with added impact
when Beethoven forcefully drums home
his 'Fate' theme, this time using the sound
of the full orchestra, as we pass into the
recapitulation.

But now comes one of Beethoven's
masterstrokes. The music suddenly
relaxes its unremitting energy, and a solo
oboe gives out a strange lyrical cry. Is this
the 'still small voice' at the centre of all
creation? Beethoven's own creed, taken
from an Egyptian temple inscription, was
on his desk when he worked: 'I am that
which is, I am everything that is, that was,
and that will be. No mortal man has raised
my veil. He is himself alone, and it is to
this aloneness that all things owe their
being.' This brief, poignant oboe solo,
suddenly making itself heard amid the
tumult, is surely a musical expression of
that 'aloneness'.

But immediately the pounding energy
starts up again, mounting to another
grand climax. Just before the second,
lyrical theme reappears, the 'Fate' theme
is played loudly by the horn section.

The concluding section, the coda,
which occupies the last part of this
movement, contains still further development of the opening phrase, driven to the
final climax with incessant, almost
demonic energy. This first movement has
long been regarded as one of the miracles
of music. The great French Romantic
composer Berlioz said it revealed Beethoven's 'most private griefs, his fiercest
wrath, his most lonely and desolate
meditations, his midnight visions, his
bursts of enthusiasm'. Yet all this is
expressed with that tiny 'Fate theme'

repeated hundreds of times, and with a passion and fire that overwhelm everything in their path.

SECOND MOVEMENT – ANDANTE CON MOTO

The second movement is in complete contrast to the fiery energy of the first. It is a series of variations on a long, stately melody which starts on the violas and cellos and gradually unfolds in several directions. Violas and cellos are soon joined by the woodwind and the upper strings, and then the addition of the brass brings it to a triumphant climax. But within this theme is embedded the rhythm of the 'Fate' theme from the first movement, now greatly slowed down but present in the second section of this long melody, heard first on clarinets and bassoons, and then with full force on the horns and trumpets.

Example 2

In the first variation, violas and cellos weave a chain of notes about the theme,

Symphonic venue

The magnificent Theater an der Wien (below), where the Fifth Symphony was first performed on 22 December 1808. The programme consisted of four hours of music, the concert hall was bitterly cold, the orchestra ill rehearsed and out of tune. All in all, the Fifth Symphony had less impact than it now invariably carries.

which rises once again to a powerful statement on the brass. A strange and mysterious change of mood follows, beneath which cellos reiterate an ominous rhythm which acts as a bridge to the second variation. The running notes now double their speed, while the accompanying chords only hint at the framework of the theme, and, as the whole orchestra joins in, all but obliterate the running notes in cellos and basses.

There is now a pause in the flow of the music while in the third variation Beethoven indulges in some whimsical variants for woodwind on the opening notes of his theme, before the whole orchestra returns fortissimo (very loudly) with the second half of the theme. Another pause occurs while Beethoven again plays with these four notes. But this capriciousness is swept aside for a last grand, full statement of the main theme. There follows a most beautiful and touching moment on the strings, achieved by the slightest alteration to the melody. It soon ends, and Beethoven brings the movement to a calm, triumphant close.

THIRD MOVEMENT – ALLEGRO (SCHERZO)

The last two movements are run together without a break, according to the practice of the time. The third movement returns to the main key of the symphony and is traditionally referred to as the Scherzo. The word literally means 'joke' in Italian. But the quiet, mysterious opening, whose theme seems like a ghostly memory of the finale of Mozart's 40th Symphony, does not seem particularly humorous. (The

Mozart theme does appear in Beethoven's sketchbook adjacent to this scherzo theme, so the resemblance is not coincidental.) The air is cleared by the horns boldly giving out a theme, fortissimo, whose relationship to the first movement's 'Fate' motive is obvious:

Example 3

These two contrasting themes are developed at some length.

The middle section of this movement is more scherzo-like in character. Cellos and basses set off a busy, bumbling motive which frequently cuts across the main theme in a vigorous, lively rhythm. For a few brief seconds at the end of this passage, the woodwind affectionately transform this theme into a charming lyrical idea, before the mysterious opening returns. But now Beethoven, against all formal procedures, maintains this atmosphere, not repeating the opening of the movement. The violins play the second theme pizzicato – with strings plucked rather than bowed – and an atmosphere of almost comic expectancy pervades the music. There is a long-held note, above which the violins wander, which seems to hint that something significant is about to happen.

The music gradually grows louder and louder in an enormous crescendo and

A perceptive critic
The Romantic writer and musician E.T.A. Hoffmann (left) had a real understanding of the Fifth Symphony. Writing about it in 1810, he drew attention to the way in which the entire first movement is built up from one small but inspired idea: 'There is no simpler idea than that on which the composer based the entire Allegro, and we see with admiration how he succeeded in using rhythm to link all the subsidiary ideas to that theme, so that they serve only to unfold more and more the character of the whole, which the theme could only hint at.'

His inner world
A romantic image of Beethoven (below), slumped over the piano, utterly exhausted by his mental exertions. He is surrounded by the many spirits that people his inner world – spirits of torment as well as of inspiration.

Beethoven requires the whole of this section to be repeated, although later in the 19th century it became traditional to omit the repeat and go straight into the development.

A great deal is made of the dance theme in the first part of the development. It is thrown around from one instrument to another, and built into a climax of tremendous force – and then, suddenly, everything comes to a halt. Now comes another of Beethoven's great master-strokes: he reintroduces a ghostly echo of the theme from the third movement (Example 3). 'Fate' is still present, and, as at the end of the Scherzo, it exists in the insistent repetition of one chord, although this time without the colourful wanderings of the violins in the string section.

Now all the themes of triumph return and are developed at length to produce an effect of boundless energy and joy. The final section starts with a variant of the leaping horn theme, and at a gradually increasing pace we rush headlong into the final pages, with the hymn-like theme (Example 4) played at tremendous speed.

What other resolution could there be to all this joyous energy than the final 29 bars based entirely on the triumphant C major chord? If the performance has fully realized the passion and excitement of Beethoven's score, then this thundering reiteration is the only possible ending.

LATER INTERPRETATIONS
More than any other work by Beethoven, the Fifth Symphony is seen as a personal statement, describing his titanic inner struggle to master his fate. His friend and biographer Anton Felix Shindler identified the quality that set the composer apart: 'Beethoven is a force of nature; and this battle of elemental power against the rest of nature is a spectacle of truly Homeric grandeur.'

This symphony has always been a favourite with both audiences and conductors. In France, François-Antoine Habeneck was one of its earliest interpreters, although Berlioz castigated him for omitting the repeat in the last movement. It was possibly at one of his performances that the famous singer Malibran first heard the work, and was so overwhelmed by it that she had a fit of convulsions and had to be carried from the concert hall.

Wagner adapted the bassoon part for the horns in the first movement, and indulged in great exaggerations of Beethoven's markings, if his recommendations are anything to go by. 'The life blood of the note must be squeezed out of it to the last drop, with force enough to arrest the waves of the sea and lay bare the bed of the ocean' – all this and more about the fourth note of the score!

More recent interpretations have been content to follow Beethoven's original scoring, finding it rich in drama and immensely powerful as it stands.

then, in triumphant style, the heroic finale arrives. What is more, the orchestra has suddenly grown in size: a piccolo, double bassoon and, most impressively, three trombones add to the clamour. This was the first time that trombones had been used in the concert hall; Mozart had introduced them into the opera house for the damnation scene of *Don Giovanni* in 1787, but it was Beethoven who added them to the symphony orchestra.

FOURTH MOVEMENT – ALLEGRO
The finale is a great march of triumph; but is this triumph a military one, despite the martial terms in which Beethoven expresses it? The 'Fate' motive is still present, but now transformed into a dancing melody – only the rhythm remains. Perhaps the triumph that Beethoven is depicting here is the ultimate triumph of the fully realized human

being, reconciled with his fate and at one with God.

New ideas pour out during this final movement in generous profusion. The triumphant hymn on the now-enlarged orchestra is soon followed by a leaping theme on the horns, then by the dance-like theme and yet another hymn-like theme, which itself has the 'Fate' motive embedded in it, somewhat quieter at first but soon matching the preceding themes in its power and grandeur.

Example 4

SIR WALTER SCOTT

1771-1832

A Romantic as well as a chronicler of real events, Sir Walter Scott had a lifelong passion for Scotland's colourful history, which permeates his poetry and prose. His seemingly effortless ability to relive the past made him a pioneer of the historical novel, a key figure in the development of Romanticism, and an influence on novelists as diverse as Victor Hugo and Tolstoy. Scott's literary fame was coupled with immense personal popularity, and at his death he was designated by the historian Thomas Carlyle as the 'pride of all Scotchmen'.

'Wizard of the North'

The most famous and admired Scot of his time, Scott became renowned for extraordinary literary achievements that won recognition far beyond the borders of his native land.

In Princes Street, the main thoroughfare of Edinburgh, stands a 200-foot-high monument to Sir Walter Scott. Few British writers have been so conspicuously honoured in their native city. But the tribute is not excessive – it is a testimony to the enormous influence exerted by Scott, both as a writer and as a celebrator of his country's history, traditions and landscape.

Walter Scott was born in Edinburgh on 15 August 1771. On both sides of the family he was descended from ancient Border yeoman families. His father, also named Walter Scott, was the first member of his family to live in a town and adopt a profession – he was a respected solicitor. Scott's mother, Anne Rutherford, was the daughter of a professor of medicine at Edinburgh University. From his father, a stern but just man, Walter acquired his disciplined attitude to work, while the example of his cultivated mother helped to develop his imaginative gifts.

LAMED IN CHILDHOOD

Walter was the fourth of six surviving children. When he was a baby the family moved from Edinburgh's picturesque but dirty Old Town to the much healthier New Town – an area of splendid contemporary Georgian buildings. Despite the move, while still a toddler Walter was struck by an illness (probably poliomyelitis) that left his right leg permanently lame. He was therefore sent to live at his paternal grandfather's farmhouse at Sandy-Knowe in the country air of the Border moorlands. Various remedies were tried to cure his lameness, and one of his earliest memories was of lying on his grandfather's parlour floor, wrapped in the skin of a newly-killed sheep.

His disability remained, but young Walter grew up strong and vigorous in all other ways. One of his greatest pleasures was listening to the tales of Border history and legend that the old folks told. His memory for these tales was phenomenal, and this early period at his grandfather's house was important in nurturing his historical imagination.

In 1778 Walter entered the High School in Edinburgh, where he acquired a proficiency in Latin and modern languages that was directly inspired by his desire to read stories and poems in these languages. Naturally high-spirited and outgoing, he quickly made himself popular with the other boys with his inexhaustible gift for storytelling. This popularity was to last throughout his life; indeed, he came to be loved and admired by virtually everyone he met, from kings to peasants.

Walter spent six months at Kelso Grammar School before proceeding to Edinburgh University at the age of 12, which was not at that time unusual. Like many students, he did not read for a degree, but simply attended classes in which he was interested. However, his studies were interrupted by a serious illness, described by his later son-in-law and biographer, John Gibson Lockhart, as 'the bursting of a blood vessel in the lower bowels'.

After his convalescence (during which he was forbidden to speak), young Scott embarked on a five-year legal apprenticeship to his father. He later said he would have become a soldier if he had not been lame; instead he submitted to 'the dry and barren wilderness of forms and conveyances'. Unlike his father, he decided to become an advocate (barrister) and in 1792 was admitted to the Bar.

Although Scott's heart was not in the law, he made a living at it, and found that life as a young advocate had many pleasant aspects. He travelled a great deal around his native countryside, and so added to his knowledge of Scottish history, folklore and traditions. When he was 24 he became curator of the Advocates' Library, where

A varied childhood
(above and right) Scott was born in this street of rather ramshackle houses, but by the time he was six (when the portrait above was painted) he had moved several times – first to the New Town, then to his grandfather's Border farmhouse, and then to Bath, where he spent a year with an aunt in the hope – which unfortunately was not realized – of curing his lameness. When Scott was six, the writer Alicia Cockburn called him 'the most extraordinary genius of a boy I ever saw'.

Old Town, New Town
(above) Edinburgh in the late 18th and early 19th centuries was one of the most cultivated cities in Europe, and many splendid buildings were constructed in Scott's lifetime. This view of 1825 shows Princes Street, at the far end of which Scott's monument now stands. On the right is the Old Town with its tightly-packed buildings; on the left the regular façades of Princes Street mark the edge of the spaciously laid out Georgian New Town.

he spent many happy hours studying old documents. His busy social life included membership of literary and debating societies, and in 1792 he joined a German class in order to read German Romantic literature. His enthusiasm bore fruit in his first book, a translation of some German poems which was published anonymously in 1796.

A HAPPY MARRIAGE

At this time, Scott was also experiencing the pleasures and pains of love. In the early 1790s he was smitten by Williamina Belsches, who was from a higher social class than he, but seemed to return his feelings. In 1796, however, she married a rich young banker, and Scott

said that although he could put together the pieces of his broken heart, 'the crack will remain to my dying day'. He did, indeed, remember his first love all his life, but in the following year he not only paid court to another woman, but married her. She was Charlotte Carpenter or Charpentier, who had been born in France but brought to England as a girl. Their relationship was companionable rather than passionate – 'it was something short of love in all its fervour', he wrote – but it apparently made for a very happy marriage.

In 1799 Scott's father died, leaving a sizeable legacy to each of his children, and in the same year Scott was appointed Sheriff-Depute of Selkirkshire, a post which paid £300 a year in return for fairly light duties. The

Parental influence
Scott's solicitor father was a formal and temperate man, but he was also kind-hearted and extraordinarily scrupulous in his business dealings. Scott, who inherited his father's integrity and concern for others, said 'He had a zeal for his clients which was almost ludicrous.' Scott's mother was privately educated to be 'well-bred in society', and her son also grew up to be at ease in any company.

Laird of Abbotsford

(above and right) Scott loved his life as a country gentleman at his beautiful Abbotsford estate (above). A most generous host to his many guests, he was also extremely popular with the local people. In this painting (right) by the leading Scottish artist Sir David Wilkie, Scott has had himself and his family depicted as a group of peasants. Scott was devoted to his dogs, who often appear in portraits with him.

improvement in his financial circumstances allowed him to devote more time to writing, and in 1802-03 he published to great acclaim his first major work, the three-volume *Minstrelsy of the Scottish Border*.

Meanwhile, the war with Napoleon's France had sparked off fears of an invasion, and in 1797 Scott joined the Royal Edinburgh Volunteer Light Dragoons. He became 'Paymaster, Quartermaster and Secretary' and took part in drilling and exercises; for although he was lame, his strength was such that he could walk 30 miles a day, and he was an excellent horseman.

However, Scott's military exploits were not appreciated by the Lord Lieutenant of Selkirkshire, who thought that he was devoting too much of his time to soldiering and invoked an old rule that the Sherrif-Depute of the county must live within the area of his jurisdiction for at least four months of the year. So in 1804 Scott rented a house called Ashestiel, a few miles from Selkirk and pleasantly situated on the Tweed. By this time he had two daughters and a son; a second son, born in the following year, completed the family.

Scott's work in editing medieval romances encouraged him to try a similar type of composition himself. In 1805 he published a long narrative poem, *The Lay of the Last Minstrel*, set in the 16th century and based on a Border legend about a goblin. This, his first original literary work of any importance, was an immediate success, running to five editions in a year. Over the next few years Scott published several other best-selling poems in the same vein, notably *Marmion* and *The Lady of the Lake*. The vogue of the latter set off an extraordinary tourist stampede to Loch Katrine, the setting of the poem.

Scott was prospering in other ways. In 1804 an uncle left him some property which he sold for £5000, and in

Scotland's tourist image

(right) Virtually single-handed, Scott created the glamorous public image of Scotland's history and landscape, and in so doing he gave birth to Scotland's tourist industry. The Edinburgh publisher Robert Cadell described the 'extraordinary sensation' caused by Scott's poem The Lady of the Lake *(1810), which is set at Loch Katrine (right). 'The whole country rang with the praises of the poet – crowds set off to the scenery of Loch Katrine, till then comparatively unknown; and as the book came out just before the season for excursions, every home in that neighbourhood was crammed with a constant succession of visitors.'*

1806 he was appointed a Clerk of Session, an important official in Scotland's supreme civil court. The duties carried a salary of £1300 a year but were not too arduous, and Scott often used his time in court to catch up with correspondence (he was even accused of writing his books in court, but he denied this).

In 1811 Scott bought a farmhouse on the Tweed. The site was originally called Clarty Hole, but he renamed it, more romantically, Abbotsford. This was to be his home for the rest of his life, although he had to spend a good part of the year in Edinburgh because of his court duties. He bought neighbouring land to create an estate and built up a palatial country house, complete with a large library. Scott realized that, even with his sherrifship and clerkship, he needed to keep up a prolific literary output to finance Abbotsford, and he continued to pour out narrative verse. In 1813 he was offered, but declined, the poet laureateship.

A CHANGE OF DIRECTION

That same year, quite by chance, the direction of his career changed completely. According to Scott's own account, he was searching for some fishing tackle in a drawer when he came across the manuscript of a novel he had begun eight years earlier. He had laid it aside then, because of adverse comments by a friend whose judgement he valued. Now he decided to complete it,

Companion and wife
Charlotte Carpenter or Charpentier married Scott in 1797. He said that their love increased with the years, but he never forgot his first, lost love, and his marriage 'was something short of love in all its fervour which I suspect people only feel once in their lives'.

Pensive chronicler
This portrait by Raeburn shows Scott in pensive mood, holding notebook and pencil while one of his beloved hounds looks at his master with mystified devotion.

and, warming to his task, wrote the last two-thirds during the evenings of three weeks. The book was *Waverley*, which on its publication in 1814 proved even more successful than *The Lady of the Lake*, and marked the beginning of one of the most remarkable series of novels in English literature.

The book was published anonymously, and its successors always carried on the title page the words 'by the author of Waverley'. Various explanations have been suggested as to why Scott wanted to keep his authorship secret – one being that the novelist's 'lowly' status conflicted with his dignity as an important legal official. Another possible reason is that speculation about the identity of 'the Great Unknown' kept interest in the books alive and boosted sales. In literary circles Scott's secret was an open one. In the year that *Waverley* was published, Jane Austen wrote: 'Walter Scott has no business to write novels, especially good ones. It is not fair. He has Fame and Profit enough as a Poet . . .' Yet to outsiders it seemed scarcely credible that someone who already had an extraordinarily full business and social life could find time to write substantial novels at a rate of almost two a year.

Scott accomplished this by rising early in the morning and doing several hours' work at his desk while the rest of the household slept. His many guests at Abbotsford, to whom he was the perfect host, never suspected the labours he performed before they came down to breakfast. Many of the 'Waverley Novels' dealt with Scottish history, so Scott already had much of the material in his head and wrote with astonishing fluency. But with hard study he also mastered English and French sources for novels such as *Ivanhoe* and *Quentin Durward*. Although he did not publicly acknowledge his authorship of the Waverley novels until 1827, he was by

Son-in-law biographer
The writer John Gibson Lockhart who, like Scott, was a lawyer by training, married Scott's daughter Sophia in 1820. This portrait of them was painted much later, in fact after Sophia was dead. Lockhart knew his father-in-law intimately and his extremely long, minutely detailed Life of Sir Walter Scott *is one of the classics of literary biography. Many critics rank it next to Boswell's* Life of Johnson.

now the most famous living Scot. In 1820 he was made a baronet and in 1822 he supervised George IV's visit to Scotland.

Scott enjoyed his busy and energetic life to the full, and his happiness reached a peak in 1825 when his beloved elder son, also called Walter, married a pretty young heiress, Jane Jobson. 'There is gold in her garters', wrote Scott, and although his attitude was not really as mercenary as it sounds (he had a deep affection for her), the subject of money was always at the forefront of his mind. As 1825 drew close it was an increasing source of worry. His fortune was, in fact, built on very shaky foundations, and in the following year it toppled like a house of cards.

FINANCIAL RUIN

This extraordinary reversal can be explained by the complex nature of Scott's literary dealings at a time when publishing was becoming big business and fortunes could be made or lost overnight. Since 1805 he had been involved as more than just an author, for he had gone into partnership with the printer James Ballantyne, an old school friend. Four years later he founded the firm of John Ballantyne and Co., booksellers and publishers, with James and his brother John. Both the printing and the publishing sides of the business ran into financial trouble. Scott was able to steer business their way, but he also lost money for them by prompting them to produce unsaleable antiquarian texts.

When the first financial crisis occurred, Scott and the Ballantynes were rescued by another Edinburgh publisher, Archibald Constable, who from 1814 onwards issued Scott's novels. After this the financial arrangements linking the Ballantynes, Constable and Scott became extremely involved, and Scott often spent money that he did not really have. He borrowed large sums and was in the habit of getting advances from Constable in the form of post-dated bills of exchange, which he would immediately sell at a discount for cash. In December 1825 Constable's London agents, Hurst Robinson & Co., went bankrupt, and in a chain reaction Constable and Ballantyne (and thus Scott himself) were brought down.

Scott had kept his involvement in publishing a secret, and when it suddenly became known that he was ruined – with personal debts of over £100,000 – his

Robert Burns

Scott's greatest contemporary among Scottish writers was Robert Burns, who also loved their country's heritage. They met only once, when Scott was 15. This painting records an earlier incident, with young Scott gazing at Burns in an Edinburgh bookshop.

Royal pageantry

(left) Scott was one of the guests at the coronation of George IV in London on 19 July 1821. He wrote that it was 'impossible to conceive a ceremony more august and imposing in all its parts, and more calculated to make the deepest impression both on the eye and the feelings'. In the following year Scott was given the honour of organizing the ceremonials for the King's visit to Scotland.

A nation mourns

(below) Scott was so popular that his death caused widespread sorrow. His son-in-law Lockhart recorded that at his funeral at Dryburgh Abbey 'when the coffin was taken from the hearse, and again laid on the shoulders of the afflicted serving-men, one deep sob burst from a thousand lips.'

friends were shocked and dismayed. A group of them offered to lend him money, but with a magnificent resolve that would have done credit to any of his fictional heroes, Scott refused, saying 'No, this right hand shall work it all off!' Such was his reputation that trust arrangements were made to give him the necessary time, and he was even allowed to keep Abbotsford, and he settled down to a regime of work that was gruelling even by his standards. The death of his wife in 1826 was another bitter blow, but he worked on indomitably, and in the space of two years his writing paid off nearly £40,000 of his debts. His astonishing output included not only novels, but also a nine-volume biography of Napoleon and a two-volume history of Scotland.

As a result of the strain of such a workload, the quality of Scott's writing declined and his health began to give way. He had a stroke in 1831 and, in the hope of recovery, made an eight-month voyage to the Mediterranean. It is a mark of the esteem in which he was held that his ship was provided by the Government.

Scott had further strokes on the voyage and, realizing he was dying, could think of nothing but getting back to his beloved Scotland. His son-in-law Lockhart has movingly described the long journey home – how Scott, bemused and feeble though he was, rose in spirits as he recognized places he knew and murmured their names. He arrived back at Abbotsford on 11 July and died on 21 September 1832, with all his children at his bedside. 'It was so quiet a day', wrote Lockhart, 'that the sound he best loved, the gentle ripple of the Tweed over its pebbles, was distinctly audible as we knelt round the bed and his eldest son kissed and closed his eyes.'

Sir Walter Scott was buried at Dryburgh Abbey, a few miles from his home, and Lockhart records that the newspapers 'had the signs of mourning usual on the demise of a king'. His copyrights and remaining liabilities were taken over by the publisher Robert Cadell, who made a fortune from them. But his beloved home, Abbotsford, passed to Scott's eldest son and still belongs to his direct descendants.

Celebrating The Past

Sir Walter Scott virtually invented the modern historical novel. In a rapidly produced succession of best-sellers, he brought to life the colourful, turbulent history of Scotland, England and France.

Sir Walter Scott was the first British novelist to make a fortune by writing. The 'Waverley Novels' were tremendous best-sellers, composed at great speed and in rapid succession. In all, he wrote 27 novels in 18 years, and his enormous literary output also included tens of thousands of lines of poetry, a voluminous collection of ballads, massive editions of Dryden and Swift, a nine-volume biography of Napoleon, a three-volume child's history of Scotland, a long and fascinating *Journal*, and quantities of letters, reviews and stories.

Scott wrote fast, fluently and with a certain large carelessness that sometimes irritated critics. In the *Edinburgh Review*, the severe Francis Jeffrey praised *Waverley* almost in spite of himself: 'Here is a thing obviously very hastily, and, in many places, very unskilfully written . . . and yet, by the mere force, and truth, and vivacity of its colouring, already casting the whole tribe of ordinary novels in the shade.'

Scott worked best under pressure, with the printer almost waiting at his elbow. A passage from the *Journal*, itself hasty and under-punctuated, tells us that 'I love to have the press thumping, clattering and banging in my rear – it creates the necessity [which] almost always makes me work best – needs must when the Devil drives.'

Driven on by his fertile imagination, Scott drew on his amazing memory and extraordinary command of language to create a succession of sprawling masterpieces, compelling stories as various and unshaped as life itself.

Recreating the past *(left) Scott's home, Abbotsford, reflected the love of history which inspired his writing. He indulged his passion for the past almost to the point of mania, filling his rooms with a vast collection of armour, relics and curios. Surrounded by such stimulating images, he set about creating a monumental series of historical novels, most of them written in early-morning, pre-breakfast sessions in his study (inset).*

He cheerfully admitted that, although he initially planned and plotted his books, they ran away with him:

'I think there is a demon who seats himself on the feather of my pen when I begin to write, and leads it astray from my purpose. Characters expand under my hand; incidents are multiplied . . . when I light on such a character as Bailie Jarvie [in *Rob Roy*], or Dalgetty [in *The Legend of Montrose*], my imagination brightens, and my conception becomes clearer at every step which I take in his company . . . If I resist the temptation . . . my thoughts become prosy, flat and dull . . . I am no more the same author . . . than the dog in a wheel, condemned to go round and round for hours, is like the dog merrily chasing his tail.'

'A WINNING GAME'

Money was an important incentive for Scott. He denied that it was his main motive for writing, although he declared himself 'not displeased to find the game a winning one'. His huge earnings financed the building mania that kept him always short of ready cash and eventually led to his bankruptcy. After this, rapid and continuous literary production was

Historic landscapes
Scott's fascination with history was paralleled by his love of Scotland's landscape. Indeed, the two were associated in his mind: though the old days had passed, the landscape in which historic events had taken place remained unchanged.

Rational historian
(above) The philosopher David Hume (1711-76), a leading figure in Scotland's Enlightenment, wrote a massive History of Great Britain. *Scott was affected by the rational climate of the Enlightenment, but also delighted in Scotland's wild past.*

Unknown Scot(t)
Supposedly 'unknown' as a writer, Scott was cheered through Dublin's streets in 1825.

more of a necessity than ever.

In spite of his success and his prodigious capacity for hard work, Scott's literary career was completely unplanned. He was well into his thirties before he published his first original literary work of any significance, *The Lay of the Last Minstrel*. But before then he had shown that even as an antiquarian scholar he had a golden touch, for his collection of old ballads, *The Minstrelsy of the Scottish Border* (1802-03), was a best-seller.

Chance played a part in the composition of *The Lay of the Last Minstrel*. The subject of the poem was suggested by the Countess of Dalkeith, who had heard a legend about a goblin named Gilpin Horner, and thought it was ideal material for Scott. He jumped at the suggestion and set off on a series of poems that made him the forerunner of those 20th-century authors whose blockbusters are fought over by publishers. *The Lay of the Last Minstrel* was such a runaway success that the publisher, Constable, offered Scott 1000 guineas for his next poem, *Marmion*, before he had seen a single line of it.

Scott realized he was not a great poet (he told his children not to waste their time reading

his verse), but the fast movement, colour and romance of his work caught the public imagination. The stirring ballad *Lochinvar* that Scott included in *Marmion* is a good example. The poem tells with tremendous verve how the bold Lochinvar rescues his beloved Ellen as she is about to be married to a rival – 'a laggard in love and a dastard in war'. Lochinvar triumphantly carries her off on his horse:

So faithful in love and so dauntless in war,
There never was knight like the young Lochinvar.

Scott continued publishing long narrative poems until 1817, but by then it was Lord Byron's poetry that was on everyone's lips. In comparison with Byron's melancholy, introspective heroes rebelling against conventional morality, Scott's characters seemed wooden and juvenile. His switch to novel-writing – though evidently accidental – came at an opportune moment and gave him a new outlet for his enormous, casual erudition in Scottish history and legend. It is clear that from boyhood he was a compulsive storyteller of 'old unhappy times'.

One of Scott's proclaimed motives for writing 'romances' was to make Scotland

The Jacobite Rebellion

The Battle of Culloden (1746), the final defeat of Bonnie Prince Charlie and his Jacobite army by English troops under the 'Butcher' Duke of Cumberland (above), was a moment in Scottish history which fascinated Scott. It focused his interest in the Jacobites – the supporters of the exiled Stuart kings, who feature in some of his finest novels. He was first introduced to Jacobite tales and songs as a boy, and developed 'a very strong prejudice in favour of the Stuart family'. This prejudice increased when he heard about 'the cruelties exercised . . . in the Highlands, after the Battle of Culloden. One or two of our own distant relations had fallen on that occasion, and I remember detesting the name of Cumberland with more than infant hatred. Mr Curle . . . husband of one of my aunts, had been present at their execution; and it was probably from him that I first heard these tragic tales which made so great an impression on me'. In Waverley *Scott was intent upon recreating the romance as well as the tragedy of the Highlanders' struggle in the 1745 Jacobite Rebellion.* Rob Roy *goes further back to the Jacobite Rebellion of 1715; and in* Redgauntlet *Scott mixed history with fantasy to write about the imagined secret return from exile of Bonnie Prince Charlie.*

better known to the English, and to 'introduce her natives to those of the sister kingdom, in a more favourable light than they had been placed hitherto'. His first nine novels were set in his homeland, and include several of his finest books. *The Heart of Midlothian, Old Mortality* and other tales of Scotland's turbulent history are his most profound and subtly characterized works. They present moving conflicts based on fact, and the author's shifting sympathies reflect his special place at a crossroads in his country's evolution.

SCOTLAND'S HISTORY

In Scott's day, the country had become settled and 'civilized'. Edinburgh in particular – 'the Athens of the North' – boasted a society as urbane as any in Europe, and had produced such internationally renowned thinkers as the philosopher David Hume and the economist Adam Smith. Yet in 1745, only a generation before Scott's birth, wild Highlanders had risen for Bonnie Prince Charlie, occupied the Lowlands, and invaded England. Scott himself interviewed many of the survivors, and drew heavily on their memories. And, hardly further away in time, royalist and robber, stern Covenanter and swaggering Jacobite had fashioned Scottish history into a pageant of wild passions and forlorn loyalties.

As a man of the Enlightenment, Scott detested fanatics and upheld civilized order; but his imagination responded powerfully to the appeal of the old wild ways, and his novels pull our sympathies first one way and then another. It is this tension between glamorous, ruinous romanticism and a saving but prosaic

realism that gives Scott's fiction much of its strength. The conflict exists between individuals, and even within individuals – in characters such as Edward Waverley, who begins as a soldier in the English army but later transfers his allegiance to Bonnie Prince Charlie.

Scott had a sure grasp of his strengths and weaknesses as a novelist, and in a revealing passage in his *Journal* he compared himself, to his disadvantage, with Jane Austen: 'That young lady had a talent for describing the involvements and feelings and characters of ordinary life, which is to me the most wonderful I ever met with. The Big Bow-wow strain I can do myself like any now going; but the exquisite touch, which renders ordinary commonplace things and characters interesting, from the truth of the description and the sentiment, is denied to me.'

A BROAD VIEW

Scott's talents lay in quite another direction. He brought to history a new breadth of understanding whose importance went far beyond the writing of fiction; and his influence on the European imagination would be very difficult to overrate. In purely literary terms he is a major figure as the creator of the modern historical novel, which aims to 'get inside' a past age and describe it as it seemed to those who lived through it. In his own time he made the novel respectable and novel-writing a potentially well-paid if uncertain profession – achievements which make him the father-figure of Dickens, George Eliot and other literary giants of the 19th century.

CASPAR DAVID FRIEDRICH

1774-1840

The greatest of the German Romantic artists, Caspar David Friedrich devoted his life to landscape painting, creating mysterious and compelling images of remarkable spiritual intensity. A serious, melancholy figure whose forbidding appearance was softened by a childlike simplicity, he was only truly content when contemplating the rugged landscapes of his Pomeranian homeland or the lovely German countryside.

Friedrich spent most of his life in Dresden, where he enjoyed moderate success as an artist, attracting the patronage of the Prussian and Russian royal families. But after a severe stroke in 1835 he was forced virtually to abandon oil painting. He died in 1840, his reputation temporarily – but only temporarily – in eclipse.

Landscapes of the Spirit

Friedrich transformed the landscape of his native Pomerania into a mystical place, alive with religious feeling. From precise studies of natural objects he created strange, otherworldly images.

Caspar David Friedrich was the outstanding German artist of the Romantic era. He lived at a time when landscape painting took on a new significance, to become a means of celebrating the natural world and the divine power that created it. 'The divine is everywhere,' wrote Friedrich, 'even in a grain of sand.' For him, the mystical experience of nature was such a central concern that he even painted a landscape for an altarpiece.

ART FROM THE INNER DARKNESS

Before beginning a picture, Friedrich advised an artist to 'close his bodily eye' and then bring to light what he saw in the inner darkness. Accounts of the artist in his studio suggest that he did in many respects put this into practice. As the painting by Georg Kersting shows (below), he had nothing but the barest essentials around him so that he would not be distracted. His friend Carus records that Friedrich would stand silently before his canvas until the image of a picture stood 'lifelike before his soul'. Then he would sketch it on to the blank canvas in outline and proceed directly to the painting.

However, Friedrich did not work entirely from his imagination, for in his pictures he consistently

A grounding in sepia
(left) Before he began to paint in oils Friedrich worked mainly in sepia ink. As well as ambitious landscape views, he produced small-scale works such as The Wanderer at a Milestone *(1802).*

Spiritual imagery
(right) Friedrich often used natural elements as religious symbols. In Oak Tree in the Snow *(1829), the leafless tree is a symbol of death, but also of the hope of resurrection. The dead branch on the ground resembles the crucified Christ.*

Friedrich's studio
(left) Georg Kersting's picture of Friedrich in his Studio *(1812) shows the artist standing quietly before a canvas in his bare room. Friedrich felt that ornaments would distract him from his vision.*

Morning in the Riesengebirge (1810-11)
Friedrich painted this religious landscape on his return from a walking tour of the Riesengebirge mountains. He built up the composition from sketches he had made on the trip, as well as drawings he had done up to ten years earlier.

used sketches he had made for individual features such as rocks and trees. But he does seem to have used the contemplative method to arrive at his compositions, for although his drawings have survived in great numbers there are virtually no compositional sketches among them.

This reliance on the mental image highlights the visionary nature of Friedrich's work. However, he was not unique in this respect: such methods were common among painters of 'ideal' landscapes. What was unusual about Friedrich was that he employed the process to create images with a powerful, almost hypnotic, impact – images that would remain forever fixed in the mind.

Early in his career he began to use contrast as an important element in his designs, silhouetting a central image, such as a tree, against an indefinite background. And he made a point of choosing evocative subjects: 'moonlight, sunset glow, the ocean, the beach, snowy landscapes, church-yards, bleak moors, forest torrents, rocky valleys and the like'. Contemporaries were struck by the haunting, enigmatic quality of his work, and searched his paintings for hidden meanings.

RELIGIOUS SYMBOLS

Friedrich often used his landscapes to convey religious ideas. In his description of the *Cross in the Mountains* altarpiece, for example, he wrote that the rock was a symbol of unshakeable faith, while the evergreen fir trees represented the eternal hope of mankind. But he also recognized that his paintings could be interpreted on another, naturalistic level. Describing one of his landscapes, he wrote: 'On a bare stony seashore there stands, raised on high, a cross – to those who see it as such, a consolation, to those who do not, simply a cross.'

For the detailed forms in his pictures, Friedrich drew freely on the sketches that he made on his many journeys through northern and central

Time of Day (1820/21)
(right) These evocations of Morning *and* Evening *are part of a four-picture series showing 'Times of Day', which – like the four seasons – were traditionally seen as allegories of the stages of life. In* Morning, *a fisherman pushes his boat out through the mists into the deep waters of life. In* Evening, *the setting sun foreshadows darkness and eternity.*

Man and Woman Gazing at the Moon (1830/35)

(left) In this intimate work, the dark moonlit landscape becomes the natural setting for spiritual contemplation. The couple stand together, by the rock of faith, looking at the waxing moon – a symbol of Christ. The ridge of evergreens beyond the dead tree symbolizes mankind's undying hope of salvation.

Germany. By and large it seems that these studies were made because the objects interested him, rather than because he had a particular composition in mind. For the most part they were of single objects or small groups; overall views are much rarer. Nor was Friedrich concerned with fidelity to the original location of the forms he combined in his paintings. Without any apparent qualms he would incorporate rocks and fir trees from northern Bohemia with dolmens and oak trees from Pomerania. It seems that his overriding purpose was to achieve the most striking effect.

A RANGE OF TECHNIQUES

Friedrich was never very happy painting the people in his landscapes, and in his early works his friend Kersting sometimes drew them for him. Later, Friedrich almost invariably chose to show his figures in back view.

Friedrich only began to paint in oils after ten years of working in watercolours and sepia. From the first he had thought of these media as the means of colouring or tinting drawings, and this outlook affected his way of using oils. He painted very thinly, using small brushes. When working with sepia he had been in the habit of 'stippling' areas – covering them with minute dots, to give a sense of texture and vibrancy. In his early oils he used a similar method to convey the brilliance of sunlight or the shimmer of moonlight.

Over the years Friedrich gradually extended his range of colours and the breadth of his brush strokes. In the 1820s he came under the influence of his friend J.C. Dahl, whose working method was to use oils to make direct studies from nature, and Friedrich followed suit on a number of occasions. His enchanting picture of his wife looking out of the window of his studio was

painted in this fashion.

Friedrich appears to have abandoned this practice after 1824, but he did not forget the lessons he had learnt. His last oil paintings are executed in a richer, thicker manner, and show an enhanced sense of colour. This is particularly true of works like *The Large Enclosure* and *The Stages of Life*. In these the purples, yellows and deep blues of the evening sky are conveyed by means of broad, smooth areas of paint.

Friedrich also continued to paint in watercolour and sepia throughout his life, but he tended to use these media more for topographical than for imaginative work. Only after his stroke in 1835 did he return to mainly using sepia, painting images which are often meditations on death.

Woman in the Setting Sun (c.1818)

(above) In some of his more visionary works Friedrich used a balanced, symmetrical composition. Here, a woman stands transfixed before the sinking sun, an image of God the Father. Like most of Friedrich's figures, she is shown with her back towards us.

J.M.W. TURNER

1775-1851

J.M.W. Turner was one of the greatest of all British artists. He worked extremely quickly, but the brilliance and originality of his painting is unsurpassed. By the age of 30 he was a successful artist and a prominent member of the Royal Academy, yet he remained a gruff, reclusive and intensely secretive character, renowned for his unkempt dress and meanness with money.

Brought up in London, he was fascinated by the Thames: water and ships were always his strongest inspiration. The riverside area of the city remained his home base all his life, but he travelled extensively – throughout Britain and Europe – in search of new dramatic landscapes to paint. When he died at the age of 76, he left a vast legacy of over 20,000 works.

Genius at the Academy

Despite his abrupt, unconventional manner and daringly original style of painting, Turner was proud of his prominence in the Royal Academy, the home of Britain's artistic establishment.

Turner's 'Daddy'
The artist and his father were devoted to each other. 'Daddy' encouraged his son's gift from the beginning, and exhibited Turner's youthful drawings in his barber shop. He also encouraged the carefulness with money for which the artist became notorious. When Daddy died in 1829, Turner said he felt as if he had lost an only child.

Joseph Mallord William Turner was born on 23 April 1775. His father was a barber and his mother the daughter of a butcher. They lived above his father's shop in Maiden Lane, Covent Garden, an area then, as now, closely associated with the arts.

Little is known of his mother except that she was liable to break out in furious rages. When Turner was 15 she was put into the Bethlem Hospital for the insane, and she died four years later in a private asylum. As an adult Turner never spoke of her.

With his father, on the other hand, Turner had a very close relationship. 'Dad never praised me for anything but saving a halfpenny', he once remarked. Nor was this praise ineffective, since Turner grew up to be both parsimonious and extremely astute in all his financial dealings. In reality his father did encourage him in other ways, not least by exhibiting his drawings in his shop.

As a boy Turner came to love the river, which

Final voyage
The Fighting Téméraire *(1838) has always been one of Turner's most popular works. It records the last voyage of a famous warship which is being towed up the Thames to a breaker's yard. The picture also reveals Turner's delight in the effects of light on water, and his enduring love for the river, near which he spent most of his life.*

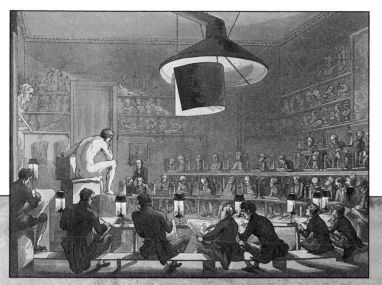

A life class at the RA
Turner entered the RA school at the age of 14 and became a professor there at 32. He remained fiercely loyal to the Academy throughout his life, referring to it as his 'mother'. His own mother had died in an asylum when he was 19.

The artist at 21
While at the RA school, Turner earned money in the evenings by copying other artists' works at the 'academy' run by Dr Monro, who sketched this portrait of his talented employee in 1796. In the same year Turner exhibited his first oil painting at the RA.

was within a few minutes' walk of his home. The restless water of the Thames, the ever-shifting play of light on its surface, the fog and mist rising to veil the ships' sails and rigging and, too, the busy bustle and business of the dockside, were scenes which haunted him all his life. He saw something of the countryside too when he was sent for the sake of his health to stay with his butcher uncle at Brentford, where he attended the Free School.

Turner received no specific education designed to make him an artist. Such training as he did pick up, however, combined with his great natural talent, was enough to qualify him at the age of 14 for free tuition at the Royal Academy school. The following year (1790) he successfully submitted a drawing for the Academy's annual exhibition. During the next ten years he not only worked hard but learned fast, and he soon attracted both critical approval and patronage.

While at the Royal Academy he also studied with Thomas Malton, who painted detailed watercolours of architectural subjects. And for three years, from 1794, Turner worked at the 'Monro School', copying other artists' works for 2/6 (12½p) an evening. Among the artists whose work he copied was J.R. Cozens. Turner's contemporary (and rival) Thomas Girtin copied the outlines; Turner added watercolour washes. Cozens's wild, romantic landscapes of Switzerland and Italy fired the young artist. By 1798 Turner had more commissions than he could carry out.

A MOROSE, SECRETIVE CHARACTER

In stature Turner was short, and he later grew stocky and heavy, though he never lost his formidable energy. His face was dominated by a prominent nose and a pair of vigilant eyes. Most portraits show him somewhat dishevelled, probably as a result of his lifelong habit of saving money by buying cheap clothes. In manner he was abrupt and taciturn, even morose, and he only revealed the warmer side of his character with people he knew very well. He allowed an air of mystery to surround his working methods and he was notoriously secretive about his private life.

In the year he joined the Academy school Turner made the first of the innumerable journeys that were to form the pattern of his professional life. He displayed a tremendous stamina when travelling, to which he added an indefatigable capacity for making rapid, incisive sketches in his notebooks. These became the basis of many 'topographical' watercolours: the detailed studies of Gothic buildings he painted until 1796, when he first exhibited an oil painting. This picture, *Fishermen at Sea*, is a moonlit scene in which fishermen struggle for survival in a gale just off the Needles of the Isle of Wight.

After only his second application, Turner was elected an Associate of the Royal Academy on the last day of the 18th century. Unlike his near-contemporary Constable, Turner was by this time financially independent. As a result he was able to leave home in 1800 and take lodgings in Harley Street. Around this time he also began to support Sarah Danby, a recently widowed woman with four children. She bore two of Turner's children and their relationship continued for some years, but he never married her or lived with her. If the erotic drawings he made during this period are anything to go by, Turner's nature had a vigorously sensual side; however, he did not permit any relationship to encroach on his crowded programme of work.

In the spring of 1799, William Beckford, a rich collector of art and one of Turner's patrons, invited the public to his house to study a pair of famous paintings by the great French artist Claude Lorrain. These works had a decisive impact on Turner, who immediately decided to paint historical pictures on the same grand scale. It was a

A magic touch
This painting by C.W. Cope offers a convincing portrait of Turner's stocky figure, and it is equally successful in suggesting his absorption in his art as he touches up a painting, as well as his rather curmugeonly nature. The spectators appear to be struck with amazement by what they are witnessing, but as far as the painter is concerned they hardly exist.

Lord Egremont of Petworth

After the death of his father, Turner found solace in frequent visits to Petworth, the ancestral home of the kindly eccentric Lord Egremont, a patron of the arts. Between 1831 and the peer's death in 1837, Turner often lived for months at a time in the casual elegance of his Sussex estate.

Lord Egremont was renowned for his easy-going hospitality, his generosity and his innumerable mistresses. Petworth was often filled with aristocratic house guests, but amid the well-heeled gaiety the reclusive artist was free to keep himself to himself. He had his own studio at the top of the mansion where he could work in isolation.

A patron of the arts
George O'Brien, 3rd Earl of Egremont, was a keen collector of the art of both the past and of his own time. His frequent guest, Turner, painted The Square Dining Room at Petworth *(right).*

Snowstorm, Mount Cenis
When Turner attempted to cross the snow-laden Alps on his way back from Italy in January 1820, his stagecoach overturned on the summit of Mount Cenis. Turner had to make the long descent by foot. He recorded the incident the same year in this watercolour.

typical reaction: instead of being overawed by the Old Masters, Turner instinctively responded by trying to imitate, compete with and, if possible, surpass them. Throughout his life he was well known for his fiercely competitive attitude towards his fellow artists.

In 1802, when Turner was still only 26, he was elected a full member of the RA. Despite periodic disagreements with his colleagues and occasional absences from its exhibitions, he made the Academy his professional and emotional home for the rest of his life. He always remained loyal to the RA, seeing it almost as his 'mother' – just as he saw his paintings as his 'children'.

PROFESSOR AT THE ACADEMY

In 1807, at the age of 32, Turner was appointed professor of perspective at the RA; but although his pupils regularly attended his classes, they learned little. Turner would spend the whole time mumbling to his assistant, and no one could hear a thing.

Turner made his first trip to the Continent in 1802, soon after the treaty of Amiens between England and France created a brief period of peace in the long Napoleonic wars and made such travel possible. Having looted many of the great art collections during his conquest of Europe, Napoleon decided to put his treasures on show at the Louvre, and Turner was one of the first painters to cross the Channel to see them. He landed at Calais in a high gale which, typically, he sketched on the spot, adding the note 'nearly swampt'.

Before going to Paris he fulfilled a long-held ambition by travelling to Switzerland. To save money he bought his own small carriage. The

Riverside retreat
Turner had Sandycombe Lodge built beside the Thames at Twickenham in 1811. At first he called the place Solus Lodge, indicating his desire to be alone.

The glamour of Venice
Turner's Venice from the Canale della Giudecca *(1840) exemplifies the city's light-saturated beauty.*

him, but nothing affected him more profoundly than the Italian light. In only two months he made nearly 1,500 pencil sketches in and around Rome, and he was able to watch and draw a timely eruption of Vesuvius, a spectacle much to his taste.

From now onwards Turner was determined to express his own vision of light and its power. No other artist before him had brought the same intensity to the treatment of light as pure colour. He made no dramatic break with the past, but there was a noticeable division between work he did to maintain his income and experimental paintings in which his originality was fully realized.

He continued to travel and to accept commissions. Among these was a royal commission to

journey was hard and exhausting, and later he talked slightingly of the country, but he made over 400 small drawings in his sketchbooks, and the Swiss Alps were among the subjects he returned to most often in his painting. Back in Paris ten weeks later, he devoted himself to a thorough study of more than 30 paintings in the Louvre.

Turner's financial position continued to improve, and in 1804 he felt confident enough to extend his house in Harley Street by building a large exhibition gallery in which he held his own one-man shows – a startling novelty. In the course of his life Turner became increasingly concerned that his work should be seen and understood as a whole.

For the next 15 years, during most of which Europe was closed to the British by the Napoleonic 'Continental Blockade', Turner confined his travels to Britain, visiting the homes and estates of his patrons and making studies of landscape and architecture. His passion for ships, the sea and rivers never diminished. He sketched HMS *Victory* when she entered the Medway in 1805, still carrying the body of Nelson on deck.

After living in Hammersmith for a time, he moved up the river to Isleworth, where he supervised the building of a new house on land at Twickenham which he now owned. Here he was joined by his father, who took charge of his business affairs and acted as his studio assistant.

As his career progressed, Turner slowly became recognized as one of the country's leading painters. Despite the violent hostility of Sir George Beaumont, one of Constable's patrons, Turner's importance became undeniable in 1819, when two major exhibitions included his work.

FIRST VISIT TO ITALY

This year proved to be a turning-point in his life, for during it he made his first visit to Italy. Turner was now 44 and at the height of his powers. Every aspect of Italy and its art seems to have impressed

Turner's Secret Life

Turner was exceptionally secretive, especially over women. He kept a mistress first in Margate, then London, and assumed her surname – Booth.

The mystery which surrounds Turner's private life was increased when the art critic John Ruskin destroyed many of his dead hero's erotic pictures. These were said to have been executed during weekends of drunken debauchery in the dockside taverns of Wapping, East London.

Erotic secrets
One of Turner's erotic sketches. Many such 'lewd' pictures were destroyed after the critic John Ruskin discovered them in the Turner bequest in the National Gallery vaults: he felt that they tainted his idol's memory.

Puggy Booth
To maintain secrecy during his life with Mrs Booth, Turner adopted her surname. His physique earned him the unfortunate nickname 'Puggy' Booth. Even in silhouette his beaky nose and stout figure are easily recognizable.

Turner's East End pub
(right) Taverns were popular and lucrative in the dockside areas of Turner's London. So when the artist inherited property in Wapping, he decided to make it earn money for him by converting his two cottages into a pub.

portray the battle of Trafalgar, into which he tried to put his undoubted patriotism and his love of the sea, while also preserving strict nautical accuracy. To his great disappointment the picture was not well received at court.

In 1828 Turner was back in Rome, and a new explosive intensity of colour began to appear in his paintings. But in the following year the death of his father at the age of 85 was a tremendous blow. Indeed a friend later said that 'Turner never appeared the same man after his father's death; his family was broken up.' Visits to Petworth house as the guest of Lord Egremont brought some solace and gave rise to a series of dazzling interiors.

Soon afterwards, around 1833, he evidently sought comfort of a more personal kind through his relationship with Sophia Booth, a landlady in Margate. Like Sarah Danby, Mrs Booth was only recently widowed when Turner began to take an interest in her, and she too had independent

Rain, Steam and Speed (1844)

This famous picture shows an early Great Western steam train crossing a bridge in rough weather – which Turner, in his thorough fashion, observed by sticking his head out of the train window for ten minutes. Under his hand, this portent of a new industrial age seems as much a force of nature as the elements which surround it.

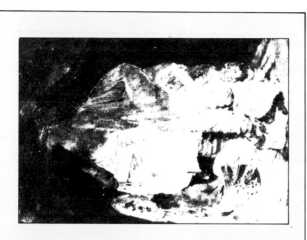

means; in fact she had been married twice before. As usual, mystery cloaks the relationship, but Turner kept her as his companion until he died.

In the early 1830s he began to exhibit views of Venice, and following a visit there in 1835 the city and its extraordinary light became an obsession with him that lasted throughout the remainder of his life. It was an attack on one of his first Venetian pictures that led John Ruskin, then only 17, to write a pamphlet in Turner's defence. This marked the beginning of Ruskin's career as the painter's champion and the greatest critic of his time.

During the last phase of his life Turner painted many of his most famous pictures, including *The Fighting Téméraire*, *Rain, Steam and Speed* and *Peace – Burial at Sea*, his tribute to an old friend and rival, Sir David Wilkie. Turner never lost his zest for painting nature in the raw, on one occasion going so far as to have himself lashed to the mast of a steamboat in order to sketch a storm.

A GALLERY IN CHELSEA

He bought a house at Cheyne Walk, in Chelsea, where he installed Mrs Booth and built a small gallery in the roof. The house faced south and stood on a bend in the river; from his bedroom he could look out on its traffic. He became even more reclusive, calling himself Mr Booth. By now he was over 70 and his health was failing.

With deliberate finality, Turner entitled the last picture he sent for exhibition at the RA *The Visit to the Tomb*. He died on 19 December 1851 in his bedroom overlooking the Thames.

Turner was buried in St Paul's Cathedral. Before the funeral the mourners gathered in his picture gallery and were astonished to see the huge numbers of paintings collected there, many of them rotting in their stretchers and stained by water dripping from a skylight. In his will he left some 300 oil paintings and nearly 20,000 water-colours to the nation, but his request that they should be housed in a special gallery was ignored by an ungrateful government.

The Drama of Nature

**Turner began his career as a precise recorder of picturesque places,
but developed into one of the great painters of the imagination,
conjuring dramatic visions from the full majesty of nature.**

Turner was one of the greatest of all landscape painters – though it would be true to say that by the end of his life he had become a painter not of land, sea and sky, but of light itself. Certainly, few other painters have matched the sheer brilliance of his colours, and none used light to create such powerful and overwhelming images of nature and its impact on human destiny.

A TASTE FOR THE PICTURESQUE

As a young man Turner was gifted with a precocious talent and a driving ambition. Devoted from the first to landscape, he received some training in topography (the detailed depiction of places) and soon became adept at drawing ruined abbeys, crumbling castle walls, decaying villages and other such subjects favoured by the fashionable taste for 'the picturesque'. Turner's visual memory was extremely retentive, but his engravings and watercolours of this early period were based, like almost all his works, on the innumerable sketches he made on his journeys, whether to the Scottish Highlands or the Swiss Alps. He was tirelessly energetic, getting up in time to see the sun rise whenever he could.

Tintern Abbey
Gothic ruins made a strong appeal to Turner's Romantic imagination: he painted many such views in his early career. This watercolour dates from about 1795.

The Thames near Walton Bridges
(below) In 1806-07 Turner made numerous outdoor oil sketches of the Thames. This one, showing a famous beauty spot in Surrey, is painted on a wooden panel.

The Slave Ship (1840)
(detail above) Turner loved the sea and depicted its moods with a violent intensity that no other painter matched. This picture is based on the true story of a ship's captain faced with an epidemic on board: he threw his cargo of slaves overboard, since he could claim insurance on those who drowned, but not on those who died of a disease.

Glacier Valley of Chamonix (1802)
(right) During his first visit to Switzerland, Turner filled six sketchbooks with more than 400 drawings. Like this one, they often show the awesome grandeur of the Alps.

The Parting of Hero and Leander (detail)
(right) Turner often made mythological tales the basis of his landscapes. For some contemporary critics the power of his imagination was too strong: one called this work, dated 1837, 'the dream of a sick genius'.

Once he had taken up oils, he made a name for himself by adapting the styles of other famous landscape painters to the Romantic style of his day. These versions of such masters as Claude, Richard Wilson and Rembrandt were made in a spirit of rivalry rather than homage. Throughout he freely indulged his preference for the melodramatic and catastrophic. Whirlwinds, avalanches, storms at sea and the destruction of great civilizations were typical of his subjects.

Due entirely to his own neglect of them, many of Turner's oil paintings were badly damaged during his lifetime; but fortunately his huge collection of sketches was much better preserved. In 1806-07 he was executing oil sketches directly from nature; as often as not, his subject was the Thames Valley, which he painted while being rowed in a boat. Their vivid grasp of detail and atmosphere anticipates Constable's equally celebrated sketches by almost ten years.

THE ROMANCE OF THE RIVER

Turner associated London and the Thames with other great civilizations – Venice, ancient Rome and Carthage. In one of his Thames sketchbooks, Phoenician ships sweep down the river at Twickenham. Turner was fascinated by every kind of ship and boat, and prided himself on his nautical knowledge. No sooner had HMS *Victory* limped into port after the Battle of Trafalgar than Turner was on board, interviewing the crew and making numerous sketches.

Venice: Moonrise (1840)
The beauty of Venice was irresistible to Turner. This superb watercolour, done on his third visit to the city, shows the expressiveness of his technique. According to an eyewitness, he poured wet paint on to the paper, then 'he tore, he scratched, he scrubbed at it in a kind of frenzy'.

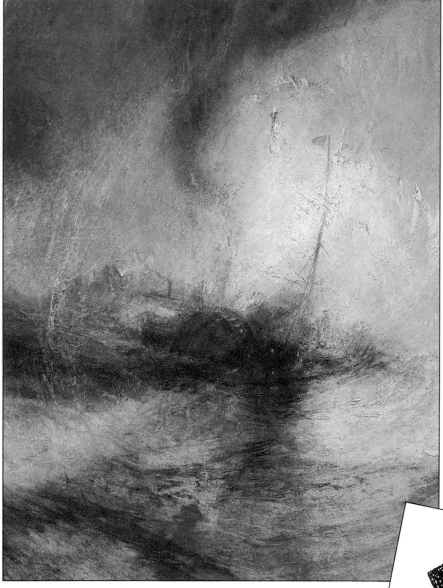

now acquired an almost symbolic significance for him. Jotting down colours in one of his sketchbooks, he wrote 'fire and blood' instead of 'red'.

VIEWS OF VENICE

Turner's tendency towards abstraction did not by any means prevent him from painting pictures which, in their subject matter at least, were very specific. His *Snowstorm*, painted in 1842, carried the subtitle *Steamboat off a Harbour's Mouth Making Signals in Shallow Water and Going by the Lead*, which shows both his love of circumstantial detail and his pride in making his paintings factually accurate. His views of Venice, especially those executed immediately after his visits, are moving just because they combine strict architectural authenticity with an almost magical luminosity of atmosphere. And, as the young lady who followed Turner's example by sticking her head out of the train-carriage window was able to confirm, Turner's observation of such phenomena as trains running through storms (*Rain, Steam and Speed*) was also extremely accurate.

Turner's avalanches and storms expressed his belief in the insignificance of man faced with the overpowering and destructive force of nature; but at the same time his radiant colours and dazzling light testify to nature's life-giving power. It was the tension between these two great contrary visions that made Turner the genius he was. As Ruskin said of him: 'Here and there, once in a couple of centuries, one man will rise past clearness and become dark with excess of light.'

Despite his mastery of oils, Turner never lost his interest in watercolours, which he used both as an aid to his memory in sketches and as a serious medium in its own right. In fact his technique in oils was indebted to his experiments in watercolours, for he devised a method of floating a beautifully subtle film of mother-of-pearl paint over his canvases which gave them a unique delicacy.

By 1805 Turner was applying paint boldly and freely. Later he began to compose his paintings around circular or winding shapes, allowing the eye to be drawn into his receding whorls of colour. This proved especially effective when he came to paint seascapes. Another typical feature is that Turner's viewpoint nearly always looks directly into the sun. In his later masterpieces the immaterial vehicles of colour – steam, smoke, mist, clouds and so on – envelop the forms, which are seen to merge, dissolve and lose themselves in the general blaze of light. Indeed, in some of his most personal works he dispensed with form altogether, relying entirely on the power of colour. Colour

Turner caricatured
This drawing, published in 1846, shows the mockery Turner endured from uncomprehending critics. His Snowstorm (above) was described as 'soapsuds and whitewash'. It is in fact the most spectacular example of his use of whirling, vortex-like compositions to suggest energy and movement. Turner was himself on the boat during the storm, and is said to have had himself tied to the mast to observe it.

JOHN CONSTABLE

1776-1837

John Constable, perhaps the greatest and most original of all British landscape artists, is renowned especially for his views of the Stour Valley in Suffolk, Salisbury Cathedral and Hampstead Heath. He was brought up in the country, and out of his deep love for the English landscape grew a determination to record its beauty: to capture its moistness, light and atmosphere, as well as its shapes and colours.

Today, Constable's genius is acknowledged throughout the world, but during his own lifetime landscape painting was unfashionable, and he was forced to struggle for recognition: he was 39 before he sold his first landscape. And although his magnificent paintings were acclaimed in France, the Royal Academy in London refused him full membership until 1829, only eight years before his death.

A Countryman in London

When he chose art as a profession, Constable left his Suffolk home to live permanently in London. But his bonds with East Anglia remained strong, and he returned each summer to sketch and paint.

John Constable was born in East Bergholt in Suffolk on 11 June 1776; he was the fourth of his parents' six children. His father, Golding Constable, was a prosperous corn merchant who owned wind- and water-mills in East Bergholt and nearby Dedham, together with land in the village and his own small ship, *The Telegraph*, which he moored at Mistley on the Stour estuary and used to transport corn to London. Constable was brought up with all the advantages of a wealthy, happy home.

Most of his 'careless boyhood', as he called it, was spent in and around the Stour valley. After a brief period at a boarding school in Lavenham, where the boys received more beatings than lessons, he was moved to a day school in Dedham. There the schoolmaster indulged Constable's interest in drawing, which was encouraged in a more practical way by the local plumber and glazier, John Dunthorne, who took him on sketching expeditions.

Golding Constable was not enthusiastic about his son's hobby, but gave up the idea of educating him for the church and decided instead to train him as a miller. John spent a year at this work and, though he never took to the family business, he did acquire a thorough knowledge of its technicalities. When his younger brother Abram eventually came to run the business, he often consulted John about repairs to the mill machinery.

FIRST SIGHT OF A MASTERPIECE
Constable's passion for art was decisively stimulated by Sir George Beaumont, an amateur painter and worshipper of art, whom he met in 1795.

The family home
(left) Constable was born in East Bergholt House, near the centre of the small Suffolk village, and lived there until his departure for London at the age of 23. Set on a ridge in several acres of grounds, it overlooked miles of open countryside. Constable's father had the house built in 1774, when the family moved up the hill from nearby Flatford Mill; it was pulled down in the 1840s.

The artist's mother
Ann Constable, the daughter of a London cooper, moved to Suffolk on her marriage at the age of 19. A lively, sociable woman, she helped to run the family business and gave her son much-needed encouragement in the difficult early years.

East Bergholt, Suffolk
(above) An early photograph shows a view down the main street of the village, which nestles in a row of hills above the River Stour. The family home was close to the church, and Constable – after years of waiting – married the rector's granddaughter. He also owned a cottage in the village which he used as a studio during his long summer breaks from London.

Constable at 24
A pencil self-portrait shows the artist soon after he moved to London as a student at the RA.

The artist's father
Golding Constable was a wealthy corn merchant with two water mills and some 90 acres of farmland. He started training John to be a miller, but when a younger son, Abram, showed a flair for the business, he gave the artist an allowance to help him live in London.

Beaumont owned a French masterpiece, *Hagar and the Angel*, by Claude Lorrain, which he took with him wherever he went, packed in a specially-made travelling box. The sight of this picture convinced Constable of his vocation as an artist. Soon afterwards, on a trip to London, he began to take lessons from the painter 'Antiquity Smith', an eccentric character who gave him sound advice and introduced him to the world of professional painting.

By 1799 Golding Constable's reluctance to allow his son to pursue his unprofitable and scarcely respectable career was tempered by the fact that his younger brother Abram was showing promise as a miller and businessman. So Constable was admitted to the Royal Academy school, and his departure was blessed by his father with a small allowance.

In London Constable was a hardworking and committed student who spent his evenings reading and making drawings; but he was homesick for his friends and family in Suffolk, and also for the countryside. For a while he shared rooms with another student, Ramsay Reinagle, who painted his portrait, but Constable became disgusted with his sly copying of Old Masters and his doubtful dealings in the art market. His morale was not improved by the discovery that landscape and landscape painters were held in very low esteem by the Academy, which only respected history and portrait painting.

Letters and baskets of food transported by the family ship kept him in constant contact with East Bergholt, and he spent many of his summer holidays there, using a cottage near his parents' house as a studio. He also did some travelling around England. In 1801 he toured the Peak District in Derbyshire, and two years later he made

109

a short sea voyage from London to Deal in Kent aboard an East Indiaman. He visited the Lake District in 1806, but found the solitude oppressive.

By 1809, when Constable reached the age of 33, he had more or less mastered his craft but had not as yet made a success of his career. He had not been elected an Associate of the Academy – let alone a full Member – and could not live independently on his meagre earnings from a few portrait and altarpiece commissions. However, it was at this unpromising point in his life that he fell in love with Maria Bicknell. She was 12 years younger than him and the daughter of a senior civil servant. More significantly, she was the granddaughter of Dr Rhudde, rector of East Bergholt and a formidable old man who was believed by his family to be very rich. When Constable announced his desire to marry Maria, Dr Rhudde promptly threatened to disinherit her.

THE LONG COURTSHIP

During the next seven years the unhappy couple were often parted and sometimes forbidden even to write; but throughout their long, frustrating courtship they remained loyal to each other. Constable, who felt badly isolated in London, was sustained by his family, all of whom wished to see him married to Maria, and by one of his earliest patrons, the Revd John Fisher, a nephew of the Bishop of Salisbury.

Without a strong vein of obstinacy Constable would not have remained creative through these difficult years, which did, however, aggravate his tendency towards depression and moodiness. He gained a reputation for being hostile, arrogant and sarcastic in his professional dealings, which did not help to sell his pictures. On the other hand, with his family and close friends he was unfailingly generous and affectionate. In fact, his make-up was in many ways contradictory. He

was, for example, a die-hard reactionary in his politics, viewing the prospect of reform with alarm, but distinctly radical in his art.

While courting Maria, Constable adopted a regular pattern of work. He would spend the late autumn, winter and early spring in London, working up his sketches from nature and preparing his paintings for the Royal Academy exhibition, which opened each May. Then he would go down to East Bergholt for the summer and early autumn, escaping from the city with relief.

The death of Mrs Constable in 1815 was a blow which the painter felt deeply. Then, not long afterwards, Maria's mother died too. These events seem to have strengthened the couple's resolve, and by the February of 1816 they had made up

A Lifelong Romance

Constable's love for Maria Bicknell (right) was a guiding passion in his life. He had known her since childhood, and the sketch below is thought to be a portrait of Maria as a young girl. When they fell in love in 1809, Constable's income was meagre, and Maria's family opposed their engagement. The lovers were forced to wait seven years until he could afford to support them both. And while the marriage was happy, it was doomed to be short. At the age of 40, Maria died of TB, leaving a heartbroken husband to bring up their seven young children.

(right) Maria in 1816, just before their marriage.
(below) 'Girl in a Fox Fur' may be Maria, aged 12.

Regency Brighton
The Constable family spent several summers in Brighton after Maria developed TB in 1824. The South Coast resort had been made fashionable by the Prince Regent, for whom Nash designed the exotic Pavilion. But • Constable disliked the *town intensely and described it as 'Piccadilly by the sea'. However, from the beach he could paint seascapes – otherwise rare in his work – including* **Chain Pier** *(right) of 1827.*

their minds to marry in defiance of all opposition. But in May, Constable's father died, sitting peacefully in his chair; and according to his will, Abram was to take over the firm and pay John a share of some £200 a year. Added to his allowance and his earnings from painting, this made marriage possible at last.

Constable wrote to Dr Rhudde, seeking his consent for the last time. The Rector did not reply, but confined himself to a frosty bow from his coach, which was reinforced by a huge grin of congratulation on the face of his coachman above. At the last moment Constable astounded Maria by trying to delay the wedding while he worked on a painting, but on 2 October they were married in St Martin-in-the-Fields by his friend Fisher, now an archdeacon. None of the Bicknell family attended.

John and Maria enjoyed a long and happy honeymoon, returning to London in December. By the spring of the next year Maria, who had already suffered a miscarriage, was pregnant

again, and Constable arranged for them to move into more spacious lodgings. He chose a house in Keppel Street in Bloomsbury, which appealed to him because it overlooked fields and ponds. There was even a pig farm near the British Museum to remind them of Suffolk. In these rustic surroundings their first son was born in 1817.

Marriage and fatherhood seemed to release new creative powers in Constable, and he was soon at work on his 'six-footers', the large scenes of the River Stour which were to become his best-loved masterpieces. The family now enjoyed a settled way of life, dominated each spring by the exhibition of these big canvases, which slowly built up his reputation.

SKETCHES FOR THE HAY WAIN

In 1820 he began his oil sketch for the picture that was to be *The Hay Wain*. The wain itself gave him much trouble, and he finally had to ask Johnny Dunthorne, the son of his old friend, to supply him with an accurate drawing. He finished work

Constable and Turner – rivals at the RA

England's two greatest artists, Constable and Turner, were students together at the RA, but never close friends. Turner easily outpaced Constable in professional success: he was elected a full member of the Academy at 26, while Constable was denied the accolade until the age of 52, just eight years before his death.

At that time the RA had a virtual monopoly in the picture market, and Constable's failure cost him dearly. He was 39 before he sold his first landscape, and in his entire life he sold less than 20 paintings in England.

The summer exhibition
The Royal Academy exhibition was a society event which drew large crowds each year. It was the main showcase for artists to display their work, and they competed fiercely to have their pictures hung in prominent positions. Constable chose the large format of his 'six-foot' canvases to make his paintings stand out and catch the eye of potential purchasers.

Constable teaching
Constable's election to the RA came too late to influence his career – his most creative years had already passed, and the death of his wife Maria had plunged him into melancholy. But he enjoyed teaching, and his new status as an Academician gave him the opportunity to champion landscape painting.

on the painting in April of the following year, soon after his second son was born. It has become his most famous picture, although it made little impact in England when it was first exhibited, and was eventually bought by a French dealer.

Maria's health had always been delicate, and in 1821 Constable settled his family in a house at Hampstead, where the air was cleaner. For his own use he rented a room and a little shed from the village glazier. Standing some 400 feet above the smoke of London, Hampstead was at that time a farming area, with sand and gravel workings. Along with the Stour valley and Salisbury, it became one of the few landscapes to which Constable responded creatively.

In 1824 the king of France awarded Constable, in his absence, a gold medal for *The Hay Wain*. And for the first time his six-footer of the season, *The Lock*, was bought for the asking price while on exhibition at the Royal Academy.

MARIA'S TRAGIC ILLNESS

Tragically, just as it looked as if he was achieving professional independence, the first signs of his wife's pulmonary tuberculosis showed themselves. Hoping to restore her health, he sent Maria and their four young children to Brighton for the summer. Constable joined them for a few weeks and painted a number of marine scenes.

The next two years saw the birth of two more children, but no improvement in Maria's health. Then, in January 1828, the birth of her seventh child weakened Maria badly. In March her father died, leaving her £20,000 and at last putting an end to their money worries. But Maria's coughing worsened, she grew feverish at nights and throughout the summer she wasted away. She died on 23 November 1828 and was buried in Hampstead.

Constable told his brother Golding, 'I shall never feel again as I have felt, the face of the world is totally changed to me.' The marriage for which

he had waited so long had lasted only 12 years.

Constable slowly picked up the threads of his professional life. Ironically, he was elected a full Academician the following February, although by only one vote. His great rival Turner brought the news, and stayed talking with him late into the night. In time, new projects began to interest him, notably the publication of engravings taken from his paintings and oil sketches. But the period of his greatest achievements was over.

In 1835 Constable painted *The Valley Farm*, a view of Willie Lott's cottage in Flatford, which also appears in the *Hay Wain*. This was his last major picture of Suffolk. The buyer wanted to know if it had been painted for anyone in particular. 'Yes sir', Constable told him. 'It is painted for a very particular person – the person for whom I have all my life painted.' He died at night on 31 March 1837 and was buried beside Maria in Hampstead.

Constable's Hampstead
In Constable's day still a village outside London, Hampstead was the painter's home from 1827, inspiring such fresh, vigorous pictures as The Admiral's House *(1820-25, above). The Constables and their eldest son are buried together in Hampstead Parish Churchyard (left).*

Scenes of the Stour Valley

Constable's most vital inspiration came from the scenes of his boyhood, which he said 'made me a painter'. These few square miles of Suffolk are now known as 'Constable country'.

Constable is often described as the greatest painter of the English landscape; but it is truer to call him the painter of Suffolk, or rather the Stour valley – the 12 square miles around his birthplace in East Bergholt, which even in his own day became known as Constable country. He could never bring his extraordinary gifts to bear on a landscape which held no personal meaning for him. Apart from Suffolk, only Hampstead, Salisbury and to a lesser extent Brighton stimulated the intense observation and passionate feeling which are the hallmarks of his best paintings.

Constable seems to have realized where his genius lay in 1802, while studying at the Royal Academy in London. He wrote to his old sketching companion John Dunthorne, the village glazier, that he was determined to come home and study nature, the source of all originality in art. His

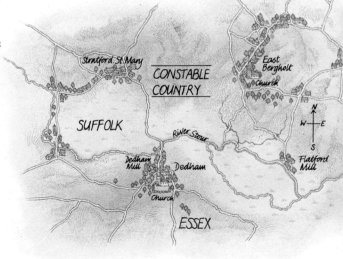

Constable on Suffolk

'Tis a most delightful country for a landscape painter; I fancy I see Gainsborough in every hedge and hollow tree.'

'The sound of water escaping from mill dams, willows, old rotten banks, slimy posts and brickwork – I shall never cease to paint such places.'

'I even love every stile and stump, and every lane in the village, so deeply rooted are early impressions.'

Stratford St Mary
(left) This pencil and wash sketch shows the house once known as Old Valley Farm, on the road towards Dedham from Stratford St Mary. Constable sketched the house twice in 1827.

Constable Country
Most of Constable's Suffolk pictures show scenes within walking distance of his home in the Stour valley.

East Bergholt
(right) A detail from
Golding Constable's
Flower Garden *(1815)*
shows a view from the back
of the family house.
Constable was the first
English artist to lavish
such attention on barns
and outhouses.

plan was to make a 'pure and unaffected representation' of the scenes of his childhood. With this end in mind, he not only spent that summer and autumn in East Bergholt, but also bought a cottage in the village to use as a permanent studio.

THE SUMMER SKETCHBOOKS

Almost every summer for more than 15 years he returned to the village to make detailed records in his sketchbooks of every object, activity or view that caught his interest. The summer of 1813 was particularly valuable. The weather was magnificent, and Constable walked daily in the Stour valley, sketching obsessively. 'I almost put my eyes out with that practice', he wrote later.

His sketchbook for that year has fortunately been preserved, and clearly shows his working methods. The tiny drawings measure no more than 3½″ × 4¾″, but cover an extraordinary range of subjects: the river and its barges, sheep

The Hay Wain (1821)
Constable's most famous
painting (above) shows
Flatford Mill in early
summer, disturbed only
by an empty wagon being
pulled across the Stour.

Flatford Mill
(right) This oil sketch for
The Mill Stream, *painted*
around 1812, shows the
same scene as The Hay
Wain, *with Willie Lott's*
cottage on the left. Such
sketches, made rapidly in
the open air, served as
notes for the full-size
paintings.

Farmland views
Two tiny pencil sketches
show the fields near East
Bergholt: the first looks
north to his father's
windmill; the second looks
west beyond Stratford St
Mary. Constable made
hundreds of such sketches
in the fine summers of
1812-13.

sheltering from the heat under a tree, cottages, farms and churches, mooring posts and water lilies, ploughmen and their horses, and dozens of little details, including the cuff of a jacket.

These scenes, Constable said, made him a painter, and his feeling for their visual beauty was enhanced by his understanding of the work being done around the locks, towpaths, boatyard and meadows. His apprenticeship in his father's mills had taught him not to look only at the buildings, trees and people. He also watched the sky and the river with the professional eye of a miller, whose livelihood depended on understanding the weather and its ever-shifting moods.

Yet despite Constable's devotion to Suffolk and its countryside, the great majority of the finished works were painted not in East Bergholt, but in London, with the sketchbooks and some small oil-

The Leaping Horse (1825)

A detail from this famous painting (below) shows Constable's characteristic use of small areas of brilliant red, often against green, and of small blobs of white on brown to convey the impact of light. Here, the red bridle on the tow horse helps attract the eye to the key element in the picture; and the light shimmering on the wet wooden barrier is captured by the white paint of 'Constable's snow', the derisive name given by hostile critics to this innovative technique.

studies serving as 'notes'. Just one early picture, *Boatbuilding*, was completed in the open air; the other major canvases were painted in his London studio during the winter months.

For the famous 'six footers' exhibited at the Royal Academy, Constable went through one more stage of preparation, painting a full-size oil sketch, to work out the composition and blocks of colour he would finally use. These sketches have also been preserved and are much admired by modern critics for the freedom with which he used his palette knife to apply the paint, capturing the effects of the English weather with all its changes.

THE GREAT CANAL SCENES

But the finished versions of the great canal scenes show Constable's genius at its height. Here, as nowhere else, he captured the atmospheric effects of early summer in the open air, the movement of clouds across the broad Suffolk sky and the impact of sunlight on the waters of his beloved Stour.

To convey on canvas the sun's rays glittering on the river surface and dancing on the foliage of trees

agitated by the wind, Constable abandoned the 'fiddle browns' of traditional landscape painting for the true colours and textures of nature. Restricted by the paints available to him, he used pure yellow and white for the flash of sunlight on dew, and captured the motion of clouds and the racing wind with rapid, nervous brushwork of unsurpassed sensitivity.

THÉODORE GÉRICAULT
1791-1824

A man about town with little formal training as an artist,
Géricault was regarded by many of his contemporaries
as merely a gifted amateur. But although he produced
only a handful of works during his brief life, he changed
the entire course of French art. He was one of the greatest
of all horse painters, even his earliest efforts pulsating
with Romantic energy; but his masterpiece was an epic
of human suffering, sensational in its scale, emotional
impact and daringly modern subject matter.

Gentleman of Genius

Despite his wealthy background and assured social status, Géricault was irresistibly drawn to painting. His artistic achievement was great, but guilty passion and a self-destructive streak turned his life into a tragedy.

Jean-Louis André-Théodore Géricault was born at Rouen in Normandy on 26 September 1791, the only child of Georges-Nicolas Géricault, a lawyer, and Louise-Jeanne-Marie Caruel. Georges-Nicolas gave up his legal work to become a partner in the flourishing Parisian tobacco firm run by his brother-in-law, and consequently the family moved to the capital in the mid-1790s. Georges-Nicolas prospered, and although France was caught up in revolution and war, his son was brought up in extremely comfortable circumstances.

Géricault was sent to boarding school and on to the Imperial Lycée, but his precocious artistic gift seems to have developed independently, almost without effort or tuition. By his teens he had also acquired the passion for horsemanship that was to play such an important – and ultimately fatal – role in his life. When his mother died in 1808, he received an annuity that enabled him to live as he pleased, and immediately left the Lycée. But he continued to live with his father and joined the family firm, working under his uncle.

EARLY MASTERS

This course was probably adopted solely to keep his father happy, for Géricault never seriously attempted to become a successful businessman. Much of his time was spent with Carle Vernet, an older artist who had made his name as a painter of portraits of horses and sporting events. Although immensely popular in England, this was an unusual genre for a French artist to work in, and Géricault's choice of master indicated that one of his main (and lifelong) interests was already well developed.

However, when his business career was finally cast aside and he began his formal training as a painter, Géricault chose to enter the fashionable studio of Pierre-Narcisse Guérin. There he could hope to learn the rigorous disciplines of academic art, and to embark on a conventionally successful career, punctuated by prize- and medal-winning, that would culminate in lucrative state commissions and a place on the Imperial Honours List.

If this was Géricault's intention, he evidently found himself incapable of carrying it out, perhaps alienated by the rather unimaginative routines (for example, copying antique busts) that made up academic training. After about six months he no longer went regularly to Guérin's studio, although he put in occasional appearances for some years to come. Guérin probably tolerated this behaviour

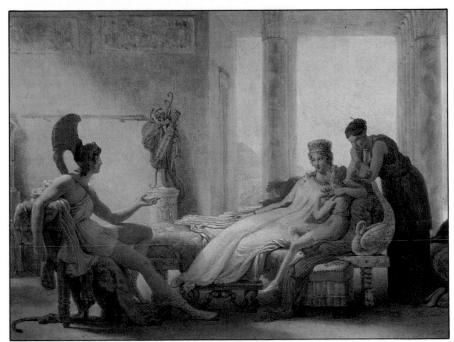

The horse painter
An early influence on Géricault, Carle Vernet was a painter of horses and sporting scenes. His equestrian tastes were apparent even in his battle scenes (top).

Classical master
Aeneas Telling Dido of the Disaster at Troy (*above*), *by Géricault's master, Guérin, is one of the less ponderous examples of the Classical manner.*

because Géricault was a gentleman – which meant a leisured dilettante whose fees were welcome but whose interest in art, however genuine, was bound to be sporadic in view of his social and other commitments. This reputation clung to Géricault for years, apparently confirmed by the relatively small number of his works that were publicly exhibited.

In March 1812 Géricault made another tentative move in the direction of a conventional career, registering to compete for the prestigious Rome Prize, which entitled the winner to a period of state-subsidized study in Italy. Then he changed his mind and decided to take a short cut to fame by exhibiting at the Salon. Held every two years, this great exhibition was virtually the only occasion on which artists could show their work to the general public, and consequently most of the leading figures of the day did so.

For a half-trained novice to put himself in competition with contemporary masters such as Guérin and Gros was an act of some audacity. Moreover he had nothing ready, had little or no experience of oil painting, and did not even have his own studio; and the Salon opened at the beginning of 1812. With one of the extraordinary bursts of energy that he could summon up, Géricault completed his preliminary drawings and sketches, rented a vacant shop on the Boulevard de Montmartre, and set to work on a large equestrian painting. A humble carriage horse was brought to the shop each day to model for a cavalryman's spirited steed, and two of Géricault's friends sat respectively for the rider's head and body. In about three weeks – an astonishingly short time for such a large work – *The Charging*

Chasseur was ready. Rumours of Géricault's feat were already circulating, and the painting aroused a good deal of interest and favourable comment. It was awarded a gold medal, but failed to find a buyer; and there was no recognition that Géricault had injected a new dynamism into equestrian portraiture, eclipsing the efforts of his better-known competitors. This was a good deal to

High society
(above) Wealthy and well-born, Géricault seems for a time to have been torn between his artistic ambitions and the pursuits of a young man about town.

Energy
Despite its large size, Géricault's Charging Chasseur (left) was completed in about three weeks and enjoyed a favourable reception at the prestigious Salon. The artist succeeded in making this a prime Romantic evocation of physical energy.

Conflict
Wounded Cuirassier Leaving the Field of Battle (right) is less successful than the Chasseur, but more original. Instead of showing rider and steed acting proudly in unison, Géricault chooses a tense, cheerless moment in which a wounded man struggles to drag away his frightened horse.

expect, but Géricault – probably suffering from a nervous reaction after his labours – was disappointed and discouraged.

ART AND WAR

Despite an artistic preoccupation with soldiers and horses that lasted for years, Géricault remained curiously aloof from the actual military events of his time. In 1811, when he became liable for conscription, his father paid the substantial sum of 4,000 francs to provide a substitute who would serve in his place. Napoleon's empire began to crumble after the disastrous retreat from Moscow in 1812, but although levies of increasingly young men were called up in 1813-14, Géricault was not among them.

It is possible, though by no means certain, that Géricault shared his father's royalist views, hoping that Napoleon would fall and that the old Bourbon monarchy would be restored. When this did happen, in 1814, Géricault applied for membership of the Grey Musketeers, an élite company of household cavalry that was being formed to serve the newly returned Louis XVIII. However, with Napoleon gone and Europe at peace for the first

Roman prize
The Villa Medici (above) was home to those French artists who were awarded the Rome Prize, which enabled them to study in the Eternal City, still regarded as the source of the main artistic tradition. Géricault too went to Italy, but without official backing.

time in years, Géricault may have been less concerned with a military career than with belonging to a smart, exclusive group that would put him among the most fashionable young men in Paris. It is hard to believe that he expected to combine this with a career as a painter, although while waiting for his commission to come through he dashed off another large equestrian picture for the Salon of 1814. *Wounded Cuirassier Leaving the Field of Battle* was exhibited beside the earlier *Charging Chasseur*, so that – intentionally or otherwise – they summed up the immediate past, evoking the glorious energy and ultimate breaking of the Imperial army. Since the rest of the Salon was devoted to the theme of peace, Géricault's uncomfortable reminders of the Napoleonic era were received in virtual silence.

Early in 1815 Géricault was accepted into the Grey Musketeers. Then, when he had undergone a few weeks of garrison duty, his new profession

Royal flight
(above) restored to the throne only months earlier, Louis XVIII fled from the Tuileries as most of his troops went over to Napoleon. Géricault helped to escort the King – the closest he ever came to seeing action.

Admiring sculptor
Géricault's inner uncertainty surfaced when the sculptor Pradier (right) admired one of his drawings. Géricault believed that he was being mocked and was ready to fight a duel with him!

The 'Medusa'
Géricault's Raft of the 'Medusa' *(below) was based on an actual shipwreck, so newsworthy that it even inspired theatrical tableaux with music; a print advertising one such performance (right) clearly borrows its general layout from Géricault, while muting its horrors and emphazising the decorous joy of the survivors.*

took on a completely different aspect. Napoleon slipped away from Elba, landed in the south of France with a handful of men, and marched north. Unexpectedly, opposition to 'the flight of the eagle' melted away, and on 19 March Louis XVIII again took refuge in flight. Caught up in the confusion, Géricault experienced his one and only military adventure. 'When I saw the cowardice of all those soldiers who threw down their arms and denied their oaths, I resolved to follow the King.' For six days he was a member of the military escort that accompanied Louis to within sight of the Belgian border; then he returned, disguised as a carter, and lived discreetly in the country.

Discretion was soon unnecessary. On 18 June the French army went down in final defeat at Waterloo. Napoleon abdicated for a second time and Louis XVIII became king again. But we hear no more of Géricault as a Grey Musketeer.

AN ILLICIT AFFAIR

A more crucial event in his life was a love affair that seems to have begun at about this time. Some six years older than Géricault, Alexandrine-Modeste Caruel was his aunt, the mother of two children, and the wife of the much older Jean-Baptiste Caruel, who as head of the Caruel family business had enriched Géricault's father. Alexandrine's affair with Géricault must have been genuinely passionate, for he felt deeply guilty and yet found it agonizing to extricate himself. Eventually he decided to go to Italy, where he could also refine his art, after the custom of the time, by studying the works of the great Renaissance masters. He had already begun an intensive private study of academic techniques, and in March 1816 – perhaps as a symbolic return to respectability – competed in earnest for the Rome Prize. When he failed even to qualify for the final stages of the competition, he decided nevertheless to make the journey south.

Géricault's life is poorly documented, and little

is known about his stay in Italy. His surviving letters suggest that he often felt lonely, perhaps on account of his separation from Alexandrine, or perhaps because, as a gentleman amateur, he was an outsider among the artists of the French colony in Rome. One anecdote conveys the violent fluctuations of feeling to which he was subject. The sculptor Pradier visited Géricault's lodgings and, having studied his drawing of a man taming a bull, exclaimed 'You are a great artist and will be a master!' Géricault was initially flattered but, brooding over the faults of the drawing, finally concluded that he had been cruelly insulted and challenged Pradier to a duel. Pradier eventually convinced Géricault that his remarks had been sincere, and the painter embraced him, exclaiming 'Is it really true, then, that I have talent?'

In September 1817 Géricault decided to leave Italy so abruptly that it seems likely that he was summoned by a message from Alexandrine. At any rate the affair was resumed. This time the consequences were disastrous: she became pregnant. Evidently there was no question of her husband being the father, so a scandal was unavoidable. Géricault's child, a boy, was born on

121

survivors and pulled along by the lifeboats. Soon, however, the sailors became tired of making such slow progress and callously cut the ropes attaching their lifeboats to the raft, which was left to the mercy of the elements. Miraculously the raft was located after 13 days of horrors, including cannibalism, with 15 men still alive. As so often, the government attempted to conceal what had happened, making the scandal all the more sensational and damaging as the survivors fought to make the truth known.

In order to paint this episode, Géricault bought a huge canvas, set it up in a large, specially hired studio, and shut himself away after shaving his head so that he would not be tempted to go out into society. He toiled from dawn to dusk for eight months, working with extraordinary concentration until his masterpiece, *The Raft of the 'Medusa'*, was finished. Exhibited at the Salon in August 1819, it created a furore and divided the critics; and if its greatness was not fully grasped, at least there were many witnesses to its overwhelming emotional impact.

Géricault, however, was deeply dissatisfied with the outcome, and for a time considered giving up painting. He was overwrought after the supreme effort he had just made, and a long summer holiday by the Seine at Féricy failed to restore him. At the end of September 1819 he fell ill, and a few weeks later had a serious breakdown

In the Studio
Portrait of a Young Man in an Artist's Studio *(left, c.1820) is the archtetypal image of the Romantic artist, perhaps representing one of Géricault's assistants.*

Picture show
The Raft of the 'Medusa' *remained so topical that in 1820 Géricault brought it to London, showing it at the Egyptian Hall, Piccadilly (below).*

21 August 1818 and discreetly fostered; Alexandrine was sent into the country in disgrace, and the affair came to an end. Few details are known, but the effect of such a scandal on a close-knit, upper-middle-class family must have been devastating.

THE *MEDUSA*

Coincidentally or otherwise, Géricault now performed an extraordinary, almost penitential act of creative withdrawal. He had long wanted to paint a truly monumental picture, executed in the grand manner, but one that would take a modern event as its subject – a quite revolutionary project that was completely at odds with the ideals of the reigning Classical school. He had tried to do so in Italy, but had failed. Now he discovered what he needed in a sensational incident, dating from July 1816, whose scandalous repercussions were still being felt: the wreck of the *Medusa*, a government ship carrying soldiers and settlers to Senegal. The wreck itself was the result of incompetent seamanship, but worse was to come. There were too few lifeboats, so a raft was constructed for 150 of the

have enjoyed the social and sporting life, and to have made a large circle of friends and acquaintances. But he was also rumoured to have attempted suicide, and when he left the country an English friend dashed off a hasty, underpunctuated but vivid diary entry describing his 'profound and melancholy, sensible, singular life – like that of the savages we read of in America, lying torpid days & weeks then rising to violent exertions riding tearing driving exposing himself to heat cold violence of all sorts . . . fear he is in a bad way'.

After Géricault's return to France his behaviour became even more obviously self-destructive. Short of money, he spent lavishly and plunged and lost on the stock exchange; in poor health, he continued to ride recklessly, suffering a series of accidents during which he first acquired and later burst a large abscess close to the base of his spine. Ironically, it was during this period that he executed his famous series of portraits of the insane. Géricault seems to have come to his senses towards the end of 1822, but although he was able to make a temporary recovery, he was now suffering from a fatal wasting disease caused by a tumour that slowly ate away his spinal column. Bedridden from February 1823, he worked to support himself until his muscles simply gave out. Thirty-two years old, still hoping to recover and meditating ambitious new projects, Théodore Géricault died on the morning of 26 January 1824.

Old Master
Superbly self-portrayed, Jacques-Louis David (above left) was the greatest Neo-Classical painter of his time, much admired by Géricault.

The deathbed
Géricault's death from cancer of the spine (below) was heroically endured. Only 32 years old, by the end he was emaciated and seemingly weightless.

during which he suffered from delusions of persecution. He made a rapid recovery, but from this time onwards neither his health nor his stability could be relied upon.

Once more Géricault looked to travel for a solution to his problems. In April 1820 he went to England with *The Raft of the 'Medusa'*, which he arranged to have put on show by William Bullock at the Egyptian Hall in Piccadilly, London; admission cost a shilling (5p) and a leaflet describing the *Medusa* tragedy was available for sixpence (2½p). The exhibition ran for six months, and 'M. Jerricault' received a handsome sum as his share of the profits.

SELF-DESTRUCTION

Géricault stayed in England until December 1821, except for a break of unknown length during which he visited Jacques-Louis David, the founder of the French Classical school, whose republican and Bonapartist past had condemned him to exile in Brussels. In England, as well as making a superb series of lithographs recording the vigour and brutality of the Regency scene, Géricault seems to

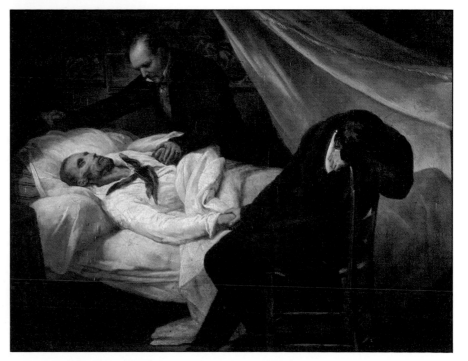

The Power to Shock

Although Géricault exhibited only three paintings during his lifetime, his innovations in content and treatment breached the Classical tradition and marked the beginning of the Romantic movement in French art.

Carnival study
During his stay in Italy, Géricault made his first attempt to produce a modern-subject picture executed on a monumental scale. Powerful drawings and studies (left) survive for the projected Race of the Riderless Horses, *but the final oil painting was never done.*

The Chasseur
In this oil study for The Charging Chasseur *(below) the free handling of the paint gives the picture an energy and vividness that in some respects surpasses that of the more highly finished picture submitted to the Salon.*

Géricault's contemporaries can be forgiven for believing that he was at heart an ardent amateur, working in desultory fashion and showing his paintings only when the impulse seized him. There is even some truth in this, for an artist compelled to earn his own living would certainly have finished and exhibited more paintings in a career lasting almost a dozen years. But the wealth of sketches, studies and finished drawings that Géricault left behind makes it clear that he in fact worked hard and regularly at his art. He was not inhibited by lack of energy or commitment, but by the difficulty of translating his ideas into ambitious paintings of contemporary scenes. During his long stay in Italy, for example, he made elaborate preparations for a *Race of the Riderless Horses*, based on the

spectacular equestrian events held during the Roman Carnival, only to abandon the project after months of work and return to France. Modern taste, schooled by Romanticism, finds the preliminary drawings and studies fascinating in their own right, but Géricault's contemporaries chiefly valued finished works, and above all paintings on the heroic scale. In this sense, then, Géricault failed more often than he succeeded.

Some of the difficulty may have been psychological – a tendency to disperse his artistic energies, and to fall into depression and self-doubt; certainly the raging, relentless intensity with which he attacked his three successfully completed large-scale canvases suggests a man who needed to screw up his determination to an abnormal pitch if he was to carry through the task he had set himself. But a source of objective difficulty also existed in the conventions with which Géricault found himself hedged in. Far more than in Britain or Germany, the arts in France were state controlled through academies which rigidly classified them into genres and prescribed the 'correct' way in which each should be treated. History painting, for example, ranked higher than portraiture, and both were regarded as far more valuable than landscapes. For the most part, 'history' meant the distant past, although while Napoleon ruled France an exception was made for his battles and other exploits, which were consciously equated with the great deeds of antiquity.

Even Géricault's first great exhibition piece, *The Charging Chasseur*, did not fit comfortably into the established categories. He passed it off as a portrait, although spectators must have wondered why he wanted to immortalize the unknown Lieutenant Dieudonné on the same kind of scale as the famous Napoleonic cavalry leader Joachim Murat, whose portrait also hung in the 1812 Salon; and consequently Géricault's picture was praised for its skilful execution but found no buyers. In reality, of course, *The Charging Chasseur* was neither history painting nor portrait, but an evocation of heroic energy as embodied in one of the prime Romantic symbols, the horse. Two years later

Severed head

(left) Géricault's preparatory work for the 'Medusa' included many gruesomely detailed studies of severed heads and limbs.

'Medusa' study

(below) The cursory brushwork and suggestive effects in a study such as this have their own distinct aesthetic appeal.

Géricault gave the picture a historical dimension of sorts by pairing it with his just-completed *Wounded Cuirassier Leaving the Field of Battle*, although neither the glory nor the downfall of the Napoleonic soldier were popular topics at the time. The *Wounded Cuirassier* was not entirely successful as a work of art (the artist himself condemned his rendering of the soldier's 'calf's head with the big, stupid eye'), but it broke new ground in the way it portrayed the relationship between man and beast: instead of the cold, commanding figure in the saddle, Géricault showed a struggle taking place between the weary, dismounted man and his alarmed, rebellious steed.

THE MASTER-WORK

Fine paintings though they are, the *Chasseur* and the *Cuirassier* have lost their power to unsettle. By contrast, *The Raft of the 'Medusa'* still delivers a tremendous emotional shock. Huge, brilliantly structured and organized, and filled with monumental figures, it has many qualities that represent the Classical school at its best; but it is a world away from Classicism in the extreme nature of the subject matter, the way in which details of misery and anguish are dwelt upon, and the livid light in which the scene is bathed. Moreover, it violated one of the principal canons of Classicism, since it applied the grand manner of history painting to a subject that was deemed quite unworthy of it. Without anyone quite realizing it, *The Raft of the 'Medusa'* struck a great blow for the liberation of French art, because it demonstrated that a modern subject, too, could be treated with the high seriousness accorded to Classical themes.

However, the first spectators to view the painting were probably more interested in its current relevance and accuracy, which had certainly also concerned Géricault himself. In his quest for authenticity he studied the dead and dying in a local hospital, made brilliant studies of severed limbs and heads, and brought in some of the better-known survivors of the shipwreck to serve as models. This aspect of the painting struck contemporaries so forcibly that it was taken by many in Paris as a contentious political statement, and was a money-spinner in London because of its 'news' value. Yet now it is not its realism that is most striking, but the surging Romantic quality of the scene as the eye sweeps across it from left to right, rising up from death and despair to the energy and hope aroused by the sighting of the rescuing ship *Argus* on the horizon.

STUDIO TECHNIQUES

Géricault's virtuoso displays with the brush were preceded by surprisingly laborious preparatory work. His compositions were not devised in a flash of inspiration but by a slow process of development: he made one drawing after another, constantly varying their content and design, so that as a series they resemble the frames of a film. But once the preliminaries were over he painted with extraordinary speed and certainty. The most common method of painting on any scale was to work from a large study of the final picture which had been 'squared up' by having a grid pattern superimposed on it. But Géricault drew an outline of his composition directly on to the canvas and then painted each figure from a model who was brought into the studio and posed exactly as he or she would appear in the picture. Several eyewitnesses to the painting of the *Medusa* tell much the same story as Géricault's friend and disciple Montfort: 'His manner of working astonished me as much as his intense industry. He painted directly on to the white canvas, without a rough sketch or preparation of any sort, except for the firmly traced contours, and yet the solidity of the work was none the worse for it. I was struck by the keen attention with which he examined the model before applying brush to canvas. He seemed to proceed slowly, yet in reality he got on very rapidly, placing one touch after another in place and rarely needing to go back over the work.'

Géricault was also a master of lithography, a printing technique which had been introduced just a few years after his birth. The artist drew on a special kind of stone with a water-repellent crayon; when the stone was wetted and covered with a greasy, water-repellent ink, the ink would only 'take' on the drawn areas, from which prints could then be made. Géricault had made a number of lithographs of Napoleonic subjects just before undertaking *The Raft of the 'Medusa'*, but his masterpieces in the medium were executed in England, evoking a rough, sordid but intensely vital Regency society that had not yet been tamed by the imposition of Victorian values.

In 1822-23 Géricault painted his last great works. These portraits of monomaniacs remained unknown for years after his death, but are now considered to be among the finest 19th-century portraits. Originally a group of ten paintings (of which five still survive), they seem to have been executed for Géricault's friend Dr Georget, of the Salpetrière asylum in Paris, probably to assist in attempts to classify types of insanity in terms of physionomy. Géricault was undoubtedly touched by the morbid side of Romanticism, but here the treatment is all the more effective for its sobriety. *The Kleptomaniac* and *The Woman suffering from Obsessive Envy* are almost everyday, 'normal' individuals – too much so for comfort.

One of the models Géricault employed while painting *The Raft of the 'Medusa'* was a young man named Eugène Delacroix, who lies face down in the centre foreground of the picture with his left arm flung out over a beam. With singular appropriateness Géricault befriended Delacroix, even passing on a state commission to the needy younger artist. In his turn Delacroix would take up the cause left leaderless by Géricault's untimely death, painting modern subjects such as *Liberty Leading the People* and raising high the standard of Romantic revolt.

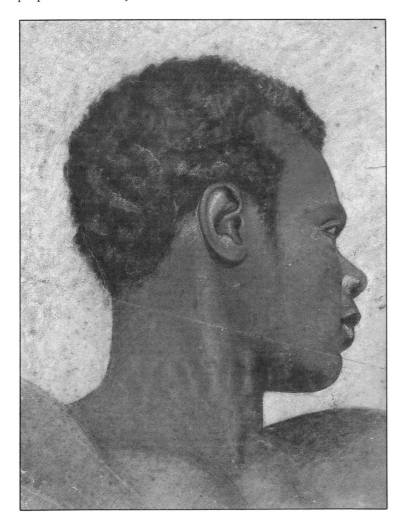

Portraits of the insane
The Woman suffering from Gambling Mania *(above) is one of the group of portraits of monomaniacs that were probably painted c.1820-22.*

Head of a Negro
(left) This is a striking example of Géricault's mastery of lithography, a printmaking technique introduced by Alois Senefelder in 1798.

FRANZ SCHUBERT

1797-1828

Like so many Romantics, Schubert had a brief, unhappy but immensely creative life that belied his rather mundane appearance. Dying at 31, he left a legacy of splendid symphonies and wonderful songs.

A much-tried man
Schubert transcended the trials of his often unhappy life to compose ethereal, sparkling music that, in its wit, charm and range of feeling, reflected his humanity and genius.

Few composers have written music so endearingly human as Franz Peter Schubert. Mozart's music is magical, but gives little impression of the man; Haydn's shows a craftsman at work; Beethoven is a titan. But with Schubert it is as if we were standing at his shoulder, watching him at work and sharing his innermost thoughts.

The first thing we learn about Schubert from the writings and letters of his friends and acquaintances is that, as we might expect from his music, he was greatly loved by those who knew him. All his friends were fiercely loyal, although he sometimes failed to realize it. The playwright Eduard von Bauernfeld, a close friend, remembered him as 'the most honest soul and the most faithful friend'. Later, in an obituary poem, he wrote:

So true and honest, not of common clay,
So free from artifice, so skilled in art.
A single mind his guide through all the days,
Which made him thoughtful, yet did joy impart.

The same writer also tells us, however, that Schubert was 'more taciturn than other mortals'. It seems that the composer had a warm, friendly nature that had to be discovered behind a natural shyness and reticence. His artist friend Moritz von Schwind remarked in retrospect: 'The more I realize now what he was like, the more I see what he has suffered.' From these and similar comments we get a picture of a man who

127

Understanding father
*Franz Theodor Schubert
(left), the composer's father,
loved music and fostered his
son's talent. They often
spent musical evenings
together at which young
Franz would gently correct
Papa's mistakes.*

was dominated, sometimes unwillingly, by the force
of his genius and yet desperately unable to make the
best use of his gifts – at least in a worldly way. The
warmth of his nature is reflected in his music, but the
shyness that came partly from his humble origins
made him too timid to challenge the musical
establishment, so that throughout his life Schubert
saw lesser men gaining all the honours.

His friends found him very stubborn at times. He
would fall out with those who were willing and able
to help him, squandering many chances that were
put his way. This partly accounted for his poor
success in the competitive world of the theatre. Lack
of effort is hardly the right description of one who
wrote so much in a comparatively short life, yet he
did leave many works unfinished, and several have
movements half sketched out but never completed.

Very little is known about Schubert's working
hours, for he spent them very much alone. In the
evenings, in coffee houses and taverns, he became
cheerful and outgoing. But there is little doubt that he
was a depressive, rarely able to escape from himself
without the help of alcohol. When he did so he would
over-indulge, refusing to dilute his wine with water
after the Viennese fashion, and often becoming

Prestigious schooling
*The Imperial and Royal
School in Vienna (right),
where young Schubert was a
choirboy and pupil between
1808 and 1813. By the time
he went to the school at the
age of 11, he was already a
prolific composer and a
talented pianist and
violinist. Teachers found
that there was little they
could teach him about
music.*

Salieri
While at the Imperial and Royal School, Schubert made a great impression on the eminent composer Antonio Salieri (above), who gave him lessons in composition. Unfairly, Salieri is now mainly remembered as the supposed poisoner of his brilliant young rival, Mozart!

boisterous and even violent, and, in the final stages, morose and brooding. Schwind believed that Schubert damaged his health by his heavy drinking and hastened his death. There were many embarrassing scenes before his friends helped him back to his room in the small hours of the morning. Having slept it off, he would work in solitude all the next day and then emerge again for yet another riotous evening.

Physically, Schubert was not well endowed. He was very short, about five-foot-one, and so plumply built that his friends nicknamed him *Schwammerl* – 'the little mushroom', or, in English schoolboy terms, 'Tubby'. He had a round, fat face, a short neck and none too high a forehead. Those eager to mention some more attractive features speak of his well-shaped (though thickish) lips and a dimpled chin. According to his friend Sonnleithner, Schubert had 'a mass of brown and naturally curly hair, round shoulders and back, chubby arms and hands with short fingers – and, if I remember rightly, grey-blue eyes'. He walked in a hunched-up fashion and his expression was 'generally obtuse and inclined to be sullen'. However, most witnesses agree that when he was interested in a conversation or listening to music his face came alive and he had a sweet-natured smile.

We have the benefit of several portraits of Schubert painted by friends during his lifetime, and although they do not entirely agree (and some cannot resist the obvious temptation to romanticize), there is no mistaking the short stumpy nose and the short-sighted eyes (Schubert's sight was bad from boyhood) peering from behind the ill-fitting spectacles which are still kept in the Schubert museum in Vienna. In later years, when Moritz von Schwind was asked to sum up his appearance, he described Schubert as 'a drunken cabby'. Others have added their mite of depreciation by describing him as 'a

Bavarian peasant' and 'undistinguished'.

In the end, of course, these things matter very little. They all loved their small, shy, gentle friend; and posterity does not demand that those who write like angels should necessarily look like them.

EARLY YEARS IN VIENNA

Of all the great composers whom we think of as Viennese, Mozart and Beethoven among them, only Schubert was actually born there. He was the son of a poverty-stricken teacher, who ran a private school in a Viennese suburb, and an erstwhile cook. Living in inadequate conditions and rarely well fed, his parents had attempted to raise no less than 11 children before Franz Peter came on to the scene. Of these only the first, Ignaz, and the last two, Ferdinand and Franz Karl, survived into adulthood.

Franz Peter Schubert was born on 31 January 1797, in a small room used as a kitchen, and was duly baptized as a Catholic. Little is known of his early childhood, but we imagine a stocky but unathletic child, short-sighted and intellectually inclined, who studied at his father's school from around 1803. Father Franz did all he could to interest his children in music, and the oldest brother, Ignaz, by then about 17 and teaching at the school, attempted to nurture Schubert's obvious gifts. He soon admitted that his pupil had natural abilities that went far beyond his own, and that he could teach him nothing. Schubert began writing compositions for the family, and by the age of ten he was the leading singer in the choir of the local church, and was writing music to be performed there.

In 1808 Schubert was admitted to the Court Chapel choir at the Imperial and Royal School. If he felt some initial excitement at donning the military-style uniform, he must also have come to terms with

Music alfresco
Despite his reticence, Schubert's presence was much valued on social occasions and it is not surprising to see pictures of him at a picnic – an open-air 'Schubertiad' – with his friends (right).

The interpreter of the songs
The famous baritone Johann Michael Vogl befriended Schubert and interpreted his songs, giving them such public prominence as they achieved during the composer's lifetime. Schubert often accompanied Vogl (above).

the rather bleak regime that it represented. It was very much a round of hard work, with school lessons all day, music lessons in the evening, and very few weekends in which he was not obliged to take part in some concert or service. Visits from his family were rare. Schubert sent many typical schoolboy notes asking for a little more pocket money and some food with which to enhance a meagre diet: 'After a so-so lunch we've to wait eight and a half hours for a rotten supper.'

He did reasonably well at his general work, and of course found the musical studies no trouble at all. 'A very special musical talent' noted his report at the end of the second term. The grounding and opportunities he received were incomparable. As well as singing in the choir, Schubert played in the school orchestra and became familiar with the music of composers such as Haydn and Mozart, with occasional sorties into the work of 'moderns' such as Beethoven. Fellow pupils remembered Schubert as 'shy and uncommunicative'; he spent most of his spare time composing and practising in a deserted room.

Schubert's father had some doubts about the wisdom of young Franz making a musical career, and would have preferred his son to follow his own calling as a teacher. Schubert's mother died in May 1812, and after this, father and son were drawn much closer together. When Schubert's voice broke in July he had to leave the choir, but his father agreed that he could stay at the school for another year if he worked hard at his academic studies as well as music. It was to be a fruitful year. Schubert was taken on by Kapellmeister Antonio Salieri as his special pupil in harmony and counterpoint, and they got on well. Schubert was always proud to call himself 'a pupil of Salieri'; while the master, like everyone else, simply declared that Schubert 'knew everything there was to know about music' without much help from him.

A RELUCTANT SCHOOLMASTER
At this time Schubert was offered a scholarship by the Emperor, but since music was given the lowest priority in the course of studies offered, he declined it and decided to humour his father by joining the

Lost love
Schubert fell in love with Therese Grob (above) and would have married her had his poverty not made the match impossible: her parents insisted on her marrying a wealthy baker.

family school as a junior master. There was much family rejoicing, but Schubert loathed the work. It was not at all easy for a man of his temperament, as well as being very poorly paid. Schubert's father had remarried, and Franz got on well with his step-mother, who helped him with money. He stayed at the school until 1816, and in spite of its demands his three years as a teacher proved to be fruitful ones. During this period he wrote about 400 compositions including his first three symphonies, some of his early attempts at opera, string quartets, masses, and some 350 songs in which he gradually found his true style. He had his first considerable success with a song, *Gretchen am Spinnrade* ('Gretchen at the spinning-wheel'), a setting of words by the poet Goethe which was passed round among his friends and sung at many amateur concerts.

Schubert made the acquaintance of a brilliant young pianist, Mme Jenny, and his thoughts at this time were occasionally directed toward the fair sex. He fell in love with Therese Grob, the young daughter of a friend of the family who had sung in his Mass in F at the local church. The affair continued for a while, but as an impoverished schoolmaster, Schubert was in no position to marry, and she eventually wedded a wealthy baker.

By early 1816 Schubert had grown thoroughly tired of coping with unwilling pupils, and decided to gain his freedom. He wrote for the vacant post of Music Director at Laibach, giving Salieri as a reference. However, Salieri was not entirely to be trusted. He recommended another pupil, and Schubert was turned down. Throughout his life he was to find similar difficulty in obtaining official support, and it made him ever more reluctant to seek it. However, Schubert buried his resentment and wrote a cantata to celebrate Salieri's 50th birthday.

In his diaries Schubert ruefully remarked that 'Man is the plaything of chance and passion – to some it is given and others have to struggle'. With Therese in mind he found 'the idea of marriage full of terror for the single man'. He continued to take his daily walks in the country and to refresh his mind with its beauties. And he proudly noted, on 17 June 1816: 'I composed today for the first time for money. Namely a cantata for Professor Watteroth's name day to words by Dräxler. The fee is 100 Viennese florins.'

THE YOUNG COMPOSER
And so Schubert stepped out into the world to become a composer. Leaving home, he lodged for a while with his friend Josef Spaun. Through him he now met a medical student, Franz von Schober, whose rich Viennese family were keen patrons of the arts and lived an unconventional Bohemian life. In the autumn Schober persuaded Schubert to move into the family home, and tried to help him in every way. It was there that the composer met the famous singer Michael Vogl (whom he had heard singing Gluck) and diffidently showed him one of his songs. Vogl declared that it was not bad, but secretly he was greatly impressed and soon became a great champion of Schubert's music. His performances of the songs did a great deal to make Schubert known in Vienna.

By 1817 Schubert had written some of his most attractive songs, including *Die Forelle* ('The Trout') and *An die Musik* ('To Music'), so essentially Schubertian in their melodic grace and flow, and also dramatic pieces such as *Der Tod und das Mädchen* ('Death and the Maiden'). He worked on his Fourth Symphony, which had a definite flavour and style of Beethoven about it, and composed the carefree Fifth Symphony, infused with the spirit of Mozart. Although his music was still considered daring and unconventional he was gradually being taken up by the fashionable 'Biedermeier' society of the day: the

Life supports
Schubert's friends were very important to him, as companions and also because they did everything they could to promote his music. He is pictured above with Anselm Hüttenbrenner and Johann Jenger.

drawing-room society people who lived their cultural and intellectual lives in a cosy unawareness of the political and revolutionary stirrings of the period.

Schubert often grew tired of the endless socializing in these circles, and he was glad to be offered employment for the summer of 1818 as music tutor to the two young daughters of Count Esterházy at Zsetiz, a hundred miles from Vienna. It was his first long journey, and once there he enjoyed the leisurely life as well as a mild flirtation with a pretty lady's maid called Pepi. But even this began to pall, and Schubert was glad to return to Vienna for the winter. Through influential friends he now received his first commission for a one-act opera, for which he was paid a wretchedly small fee.

In the summer of 1819 Schubert went for a trip into the Austrian countryside with Michael Vogl. It was one of the happiest periods of his life and, while staying with an old friend, Albert Stadler, he wrote a sparkling piano quintet for the local musical society with a variation movement based on his *Die Forelle* – the happily inspired 'Trout' quintet. Back in Vienna for the winter of 1819-20 he was involved in an unpleasant brush with the authorities when he attended a gathering that the police believed (probably wrongly) to be politically subversive. His friend Johann Senn was arrested and spent a year in prison, but Schubert was allowed to go free.

By 1821 he was becoming reasonably well known as a composer and was given a job at the Court Theatre, but his unpunctuality and lack of cooperation soon put an end to it. Schubert's income mainly came from the modest fees that he could command for his drawing-room appearances. At these he would perform his duties well enough, but he refused to socialize and detested the praises and speech-making at the end. He was happy to be left to improvise at the piano while the young people danced.

Meanwhile his work had still not been published, and some of his friends thought it high time that it was. Sonnleithner, Josef Hüttenbrenner and others

'The Trout'
In 1817 Schubert set to music Die Forelle (The Trout, *left*), *a poem by his near-namesake C.F.D. Schubart. The song won immediate popularity, and Schubert used its melody again two years later, as the theme of his piano quintet in A major, better known as the Trout Quintet.*

persuaded the publisher Diabelli to put out some of Schubert's best songs on a sale or return basis. The first was *Erlkönig* in April 1821, and others quickly followed. As a result Schubert earned a small but regular income from his music at last.

ILLNESS AND DESPAIR
In 1822, probably after one of his usual hard-drinking evenings, Schubert was persuaded by some of his boon companions to visit a brothel. It was typical of his malign destiny that he was the only one to suffer, contracting a syphilitic infection that was to have tragic consequences. The disease, and the painful mercury treatment prescribed for it, made him desperately ill, and he spent the early part of 1823 in hospital. All this weakened an already unstable

Contrasting views
Rich and mysterious, Gustav Klimt's painting of Schubert at the piano (detail, left) makes no pretence of literal accuracy, but evokes the composer's music in its gentlest vein. By contrast, Schubert's painter friend Moritz von Schwind offered a wild romantic vision of the Erl King (right), a famous song based on Goethe's chilling verse tale of the supernatural. In this, a father races at breakneck speed through the night, his terrified child in his arms, as he tries to escape the ghostly Erl King.

constitution, and he was a long while recovering. It was at this time that he wrote: 'There is no man in the world as wretched and unhappy as I'; it was a bleak time after what had seemed a hopeful period. His 'Unfinished' Symphony, written at the end of 1822, seems to have been born from the depths of his personal tragedy.

By this time even the Schubertiads – the merry evenings he spent with his friends – were beginning to disintegrate. From now on he lived a life that alternated between occasional moments of hope and happiness and deep depression. His friends scattered; even his great ally Vogl retired. He kept in touch sporadically, writing in 1824 to the painter Kupelwieser:

Imagine someone whose health will never be right again, and whose sheer despair makes things ever worse rather than trying to improve matters; imagine someone whose highest hopes have been dashed and to whom the happiness of love and friendship brings only pain; whose enthusiasm for all things beautiful threatens to forsake him – and I ask you if such a one is not a wretched and unhappy being? Each evening when I retire to bed I hope I may not wake again; and each morning brings back yesterday's grief.

Yet despite his doubtful health and moods of gloom and despondency, Schubert's friends would often find him busy and wrapped up in his work. He composed the sunny Octet and, probably in the summer of 1825, wrote the great and glorious C major Symphony. In that summer of 1825 he went to Hungary with Vogl and repeated some of the pleasures they had experienced on their first trip together. In 1826 his friends again made efforts to procure an official post for him, but all of them failed.

A TRAGIC END

In the darkest of moods Schubert sat down and wrote his song-cycle *Winterreise* ('Winter Journey'). He warned his friends that they would be shaken by it; and they were. The bitterness and sense of despair in the songs made even the optimistic Schober feel gloomy. Yet, in all his grief, Schubert was still to write some of his most beautiful and profound music, including the two glorious Piano Trios and the great String Quintet; and various offers from publishers induced a certain optimism again. Schubert revised the score of the C major Symphony for the *Musikverein*, but they found it too difficult to play and it was not performed until 1839. There was a very special pleasure for him in a concert of his music on 26 March 1828, when the E flat Piano Trio was played. Yet even this was marred by the public attention devoted to the magical playing of the great violinist Paganini, who had given his first concert in Vienna shortly before. The papers were so full of the Italian 'comet' that there was no room for any mention of Schubert's music.

That year, Schubert had been studying Handel's music, and consequently decided to arrange lessons in counterpoint. 'Now for the first time I see what I lack.' But before he could start the lessons he fell seriously ill again and moved into his brother Ferdinand's house so that he could be looked after. In October 1828 he went for a short holiday to Eisenstadt, where he brooded for a long time over the grave of Haydn. Returning to Vienna he grew worse, but he managed to go for walks and to work a little until 11 November, when he took to his bed. He tried hard to regain his strength, but on the 16th his condition suddenly deteriorated and a nervous fever was diagnosed. On the afternoon of the 19th, with Ferdinand and the doctor at his side, Schubert suddenly grasped at the wall, murmured 'This is my end', and died.

Attended by his friends and family, Schubert's body was taken to the cemetery at Wahring and buried in a grave next to Beethoven's. An epitaph by Grillparzer, a contemporary poet, was engraved on his tombstone: 'The art of music here entombed a fair possession, but even fairer hopes.'

Schubert's Symphonies nos. 5 and 8

Schubert composed his Fifth Symphony at the age of 19, and it positively bubbles over with youthful gaiety. The 'Unfinished', no. 8, is a relatively mature work of exquisite lyrical beauty and intensity.

Schubert at 16
(above), in the year he composed his First Symphony. Over the next three years music poured from his pen, culminating in the delightful Fifth Symphony.

Symphony no. 5

Luckily for us, Franz Schubert began to compose symphonies at a remarkably early age, and had consequently produced nine by 1828, the year of his tragically untimely death at 31. Like his beloved Mozart – but unlike Brahms or Bruckner, who were slow starters – Schubert took to symphonic writing with no apparent effort. His First Symphony was played by the Imperial Choir School orchestra in Vienna during, or soon after, the month in which he left school, October 1813. Having written one symphony, the youthful genius seems to have taken to the form at once, composing with typical haste and lack of inhibitions. He produced a symphony in each of the following years, 1814 and 1815, while in

In the spirit of Mozart
In its youthful spontaneity and enchanting melodies, Schubert's Fifth Symphony conjures up the light, pastoral world of the 18th century. Describing it as 'Mozartian' is, one critic suggests, a compliment to Mozart (below).

1816 he composed no less than two. The Fifth Symphony was completed in September 1816, although it was not performed until 13 years after his death.

A YOUTHFUL SYMPHONIC MASTERPIECE
Schubert was 19 when he composed his Fifth Symphony, and the music reveals the fact. Not in any lack of skill – this young man was already highly experienced – but in its essentially youthful gaiety.

However, the year or so that led up to the writing of the Fifth Symphony was of some artistic importance. In his book on Schubert, Alfred Einstein calls it a 'year of indecision'. Schubert was well acquainted with the symphonies of two very different composers, Mozart and Beethoven. His early symphonies had clearly been modelled on those of these masters, and were successful compositions as such. But Schubert now needed to discover his own individual style as a symphonist. He had already done so in other areas of music – for example as a composer of songs, producing such wholly personal masterworks as *Gretchen am Spinnrade* ('Gretchen at the Spinning Wheel') and *Erlkönig* ('The Erl King'). But by 1816 he had not yet found a way to be entirely himself in a large-scale work.

Schubert himself probably realized this, for after his Beethoven-like Fourth Symphony in April 1816, he seems to have decided that his own path lay in a very different direction. For it is Mozart, above all, whose spirit seems to preside over the Fifth Symphony, which Schubert began as soon as he had done with the Fourth. He finished it three months later. But this is Mozart as reinterpreted and filtered through Schubert's temperament to create an original composition. The paradox is illustrated by the fact that the very places in the symphony which are often said most strikingly to recall Mozart are also the most inspired and the most distinctively Schubertian.

Programme notes

The Fifth is the shortest among Schubert's youthful six symphonies (all written before he was 21) and is scored for a smallish orchestra consisting of one flute, two each of oboes, bassoons and horns, and strings. At one time it used to be called 'the symphony without trumpets and drums', and moreover there are no clarinets in the orchestra either.

FIRST MOVEMENT – ALLEGRO
The first movement has a charm and spontaneity that are typical of Schubert. It begins briskly yet softly: the first theme, introduced by woodwind and a little downward scale on violins, has a gracefully playful, kittenish quality:

Example 1

One commentator, Mosco Carner, asserts that the 'impudence' of this tune comes from the Viennese street songs; and indeed it makes a fitting opening to what has often been described as Schubert's most Viennese symphony. The upward figure is soon turned upside-down in a flute-violins dialogue, and the little downward run also recurs several times. Suddenly the whole orchestra, forte (loudly), plays an upward figure derived from the first theme, and the music proceeds quite purposefully and yet playfully to the second theme. This theme is echoed by the flute and oboe, and the music then bounds along towards the end of the exposition section, which has fulfilled its function of stating the main themes of the movement. The little changes from major to minor – from a light to a slightly darker mood – are typical of Schubert. The exposition ends with two vigorous chords and is then repeated, complete, in the 'classical' symphonic tradition.

Now comes the so-called 'development section'; we hear the music of the opening section once again, yet in a different guise: it is the introduction to the first theme rather than the theme itself which now occupies the composer, as the music moves through various quite remote keys. It is played softly, but leads to louder passages and what appears to be a new tune which derives, however, from the second theme. The music becomes calmer for the recapitulation (restatement

section), and our first theme (Example 1) reappears, this time somewhat unconventionally, in a different key, E flat major. The second theme, although approached differently, is familiar enough when it appears. The coda (closing section) features upward-rushing scales and brings the movement to a bright, boisterous close.

SECOND MOVEMENT – ANDANTE CON MOTO

The Andante con moto is song-like, and, to at least one commentator, suggests 'the peace and beauty of a pastoral summer's evening'. Many critics have mentioned Mozart, but some at least have found features of the harmony – the chord and key sequences – that are wholly typical of Schubert, as are the 'grace and sweetness' of the whole.

The movement begins with the leisurely deployment of a lovely violin melody – at times counterpointed (matched with a similarly contoured

melody) by the flute. Soon, however, comes a strange change of key, to C flat major, that could never have occurred in Mozart: a new tune is introduced here in the form of a dialogue between violins and woodwind. Then, via several changes of key and mood, Schubert gradually leads us back to the main opening theme (strings alone), which is then presented in a florid variation, that is, with extra decorative notes. Finally the first theme returns to bring the movement to a gentle close.

THIRD MOVEMENT – MINUET: ALLEGRO MOLTO

This fresh and vivacious movement is brisk for a minuet, which originally, at least, was a rather stately dance, but in

Old Vienna
The first theme, which in its 'cheekiness' resembles the songs sung in the streets of Vienna (below), makes a fitting opening to Schubert's most 'Viennese' symphony.

other respects it is quite traditional. Its striking and rather stern first theme has tutti (full orchestra) phrases alternating with gentler ones played by the violins. In the second section, flute, oboe, violins and low strings toss back and forth the first couple of bars of the theme over a repeated-chord accompaniment. Each of these two sections of the minuet is repeated. Then comes the trio (central part) of the movement, far gentler and smoother, although its lilting tune may well be derived from the striding opening theme. At one point the flute and oboe imitate the violins' tune at two bars' distance in a leader-and-follower manner. After that comes a da capo (in which the opening two sections are played over again, stopping short at the point where the trio is reached).

FOURTH MOVEMENT – ALLEGRO VIVACE

'Pure Haydn', said Einstein of the finale. Indeed, in this last movement Schubert seems to look affectionately back to the 'classical' 18th century. Like the first movement, it is in sonata form: two themes or 'subjects' are stated (exposition section), developed, and then restated (recapitulation). The dancing first theme ends with a little figure, innocent in itself, which is to play an important part in the music. It instantly gives rise to a second tune, led off by the flute and oboe, before returning to be repeated. A new idea, with alternating long notes and rushing string scales, all played loudly, comes to an end with a brief pause, which is followed by an extremely charming and graceful second theme:

Example 2

This second subject leads, via a passage of triplets (groups of three notes), to the end of the exposition and its subsequent repeat – a repeat which is sometimes omitted in performance. The development continues the busy inventiveness of this playful yet energetic finale. Fragments of the first theme are tossed about in a range of keys. Finally the home key of B flat major is once again reached – note the pause on a full-orchestral chord – and the first theme launches the recapitulation. With some compression we arrive at the second theme, after which all is much as before to bring the symphony to a vivid conclusion.

Romantic affinities

Turner's Norham Castle at Sunrise *(right) evokes the dreamy mood that pervades the second movement of the 'Unfinished'.*

Symphony no. 8 ('Unfinished')

Despite its apparently unpromising name, the 'Unfinished' Symphony in B minor has been a repertory piece since its first performance in 1865. For although it has just two complete movements, they *are* complete, with Schubert's own detailed orchestration; and, moreover, they contain some of his most beautiful and expressive music. Finally, although the work ends in the 'wrong' key of E major, and we know that the composer intended to continue it with a scherzo (and surely a finale too), it does not sound incomplete in the sense that we are not left feeling unsatisfied at the end of a performance.

Programme notes

Schubert completed the two movements of the 'Unfinished' Symphony at the end of October 1822. Then, having composed at his usual speed, he put the manuscript aside to begin work on his *Wanderer Fantasy*. In the following year he gave the score away to his friend Josef Hüttenbrenner. Despite more than a century of research and speculation, nobody knows why he decided to part with an incomplete composition. He certainly worked on his scherzo third movement, reaching the central trio section in a piano sketch and something considerably less than this in orchestrated form. However, when his mind turned once again to symphonic writing, it was another work altogether that emerged: the 'Great' C major Sym-

phony which he composed in the year of his death, 1828.

FIRST MOVEMENT – ALLEGRO MODERATO

The passionately intense first movement begins with eight very soft bars for cellos and basses:

Example 3

These serve as an introduction, and do indeed lead to the first subject, but they are much more important than this suggests, yielding thematic material of great power. The first subject is, nevertheless, the gentle, almost twilight tune that we now hear played by the oboe and clarinet in unison over a rustling string accompaniment. The music builds to a climax until, breaking the flow, it arrives at a long, sustained note on bassoons and horns. Now comes Schubert's masterstroke: an enchanting, warmly expressive melody is played first by the cellos and then by the violins. But after a mere 18 bars it suddenly stops and there is a moment of complete silence. Fierce tutti (full orchestra) chords break in and change the mood, and although after a few bars the second theme resurfaces, it is only at first in fragments, agitated where before all had been smooth. It seems that the latent unrest of the symphony's opening has erupted, and that the calm can now never be fully restored. Nevertheless, five pizzicato (plucked) string notes descend slowly for the repeat of the exposition – all the music that we have heard until now.

The development section begins with the same music that opened the Symphony (Example 3), though now in a new key: E minor. The theme creeps forward mysteriously, building towards a violent climax in which harsh chords, played fortissimo (very loudly), alternate with the offbeat accompanying chords, played piano (softly), of the second subject.

Now the development pursues its stormy way. The mysterious opening bars (Example 3) are thundered out by the whole orchestra, breaking up into fragments thereafter. The strings rush in furiously while wind and timpani play a pounding dotted rhythm. The climax of this development – which has been called a 'symphonic battle' – now occurs.

The wild music soon subsides towards the recapitulation section of the movement. The rustling strings and oboe-clarinet theme are restated, modified only as is needed to give us the second subject – that sublime melody (cellos as before) in a different key, D major. In a brilliant formal stroke it is extended by an extra four bars at the point where, in the exposition, it was interrupted: the extra bars move us into the 'home' key of the symphony, B minor, for the fierce tutti chords. And so, regularly, onwards to the pizzicato, descending strings that mark the end of the recapitulation.

Finally the closing section of the movement, or coda, begins rather like the development, rising fairly swiftly to a fortissimo climax. But this drops at once to its opposite, pianissimo (very softly), as the oboe and clarinet mournfully intone the opening bars of the symphony. They are echoed by the full orchestra, and the music subsides once again briefly before four loud assertive chords bring the movement to a close.

SECOND MOVEMENT – ANDANTE CON MOTO

The slower second movement begins in the key of E major: according to Mosco Carner this is Schubert's key for 'peacefulness, dreamy contemplation, quiet resignation, pastoral feelings'. And the Andante con moto has all the lyrical beauty of the first movement, with perhaps an added poetry and depth. A brief prelude, for horns and bassoons over plucked basses, ushers in the main, wonderfully serene melody. The gentle mood is sustained only for a little while, however. There ensues what has been called 'a fortissimo passage of a processional nature' (wind over march-like strings) whose melody clearly derives from the violins' opening theme, which then quietly reasserts itself.

Now the second main melody is introduced. A quiet repeated-chord accompaniment on the strings supports a plaintive yet caressing tune played by the clarinet, which is then taken over by the oboe. This, like the first theme, has a little pendant:

Example 4

'The torso'
The 'Unfinished' Symphony is often referred to as 'the torso'. For like a Greek torso (above) it is incomplete, yet its beauty is not spoiled.

Suddenly this second melody bursts out fortissimo in the orchestral bass, and the music moves fiercely towards a new key, D major, and an abrupt softening in tone; the cellos and basses play a melodic line deriving from the second (clarinet) theme, while the violins mimic them, loosely, at the distance of a bar. This exquisite passage leads into the recapitulation.

Finally we reach the coda, which is of exceptional beauty. Fragments of the first theme seem to bid us a reluctant and loving farewell; the plucked cellos and basses are still there, and so are the 'lonely' soaring violin lines. The dynamic level is ppp, barely a whisper yet still expressive. On a note of the utmost serenity the symphony sinks into silence.

Was the Symphony 'Unfinished'?

It has been suggested that Schubert's Symphony no. 8 is not incomplete at all, but is simply a work conceived in two movements, like a few of Beethoven's piano sonatas. This is most unlikely, since we have Schubert's sketch of a third movement, a scherzo, with an orchestrated page written on the back of the last page of the Andante con moto. A second theory is that Schubert did in fact complete the symphony, but that the last two movements were either lost or destroyed; but this seems to have been disproved by a discovery of the scholar Dr Christa Landon in Vienna, published in 1969. She found a second page of the composer's orchestral score of the third movement (the Scherzo). The page is incomplete, and it appears certain that Schubert removed it before sending the two-movement symphony to Josef Hüttenbrenner.

Why then did Schubert never complete the work? Maurice Brown suggests that his inability to finish the symphony may have been connected with his illness at the end of 1822. Mosco Carner points out that the key of the 'Unfinished' Symphony, B minor, was in Schubert's time considered 'dark' in character. Its use was rare in a major work, and no symphony by Haydn, Mozart or Beethoven is in that key. He notes that Schubert's songs in the key of B minor have texts expressing longing or grief.

ABANDONED

Perhaps the most convincing line of thought, however, is offered by Hans Gals. He argues that Schubert abandoned the 'Unfinished' Symphony for the same reason that he left many other works incomplete: because difficulties had arisen and he had lost pleasure in the work. Schubert worked happily and at an almost frantic speed, but when he reached a stumbling block he did not have the patience to wait for fresh inspiration. The increasing sparseness of the sketch for the Scherzo suggests a growing reluctance to continue with the symphony. Having written two magnificent movements of extreme beauty, Schubert laid the work aside; and never in his life did he return to an unfinished work. Perhaps with a sense of failure, he gave the manuscript away.

Now, and more briefly, to the known historical facts. The two completed movements of the symphony are dated 30 October 1822. In the following year Schubert sent the score to his friend Anselm Hüttenbrenner, via Hüttenbrenner's

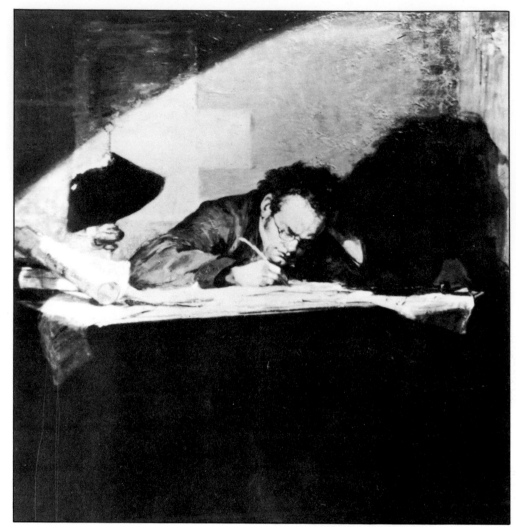

Torrential inspiration
Schubert composed with great rapidity (above), relying on inspiration. Perhaps this was why he never returned to work left unfinished.

brother Josef, so that it could be presented to the Styrian Music Society. Hüttenbrenner was associated with the society, which had just granted Schubert honorary membership in recognition of his services to music. Instead, Hüttenbrenner kept the score to himself for over 40 years; perhaps, being himself a second-rate composer, Anselm had grown jealous of Schubert's success.

Finally, in 1865, the elderly musician was persuaded to hand the score over to Johann Herbeck, the conductor of the Vienna Philharmonic Orchestra. However, Anselm gave up this musical treasure only on condition that one of his works should be performed with it. Herbeck duly performed the works in Vienna on 17 December 1865, and Schubert's symphony was published the following year. It was greeted with rapturous applause by audience and critics alike, while Anselm's work was largely ignored. It was only after another 20 years that the nickname 'Unfinished' became attached to Schubert's masterpiece.

Unreliable friend
Schubert sent the symphony to 'crafty-eyed' Anselm Hüttenbrenner (above), who kept it for over 40 years and was at one time suspected of having destroyed the last two movements.

MARY SHELLEY

1797-1851

Although she was the daughter of distinguished intellectual parents
and the wife of a famous poet, Mary Shelley shrank from public
notice, embracing the obscurity that still clings to her name. Even
now, many people are astonished to learn that as a girl of 19 she wrote
one of the most imaginative and horrific novels of her time:
Frankenstein. Mary's eight years with Shelley were marked by
tragedy, trauma and exile, but they were also years of inspiration that
helped to form her own distinctive powers.

The Shadow of Fame

Drawn into an illustrious circle and a life of extraordinary intensity, Mary Shelley suffered more than her fair share of tragedy. Within a few years of a teenage elopement, she was widowed and alone.

Mary Shelley was born in London on 30 August 1797. Her parents were the pioneer feminist Mary Wollstonecraft and the political philosopher William Godwin. But she was never to know her mother, who died of septicaemia just ten days after giving birth.

Although Mary adored her celebrated but hopelessly impecunious father, he was able to spend little time with her. When he remarried a few years later, Mary took an immediate and not unjustified dislike to her new mother, Mrs Mary Jane Clairmont, an unremarkable but pretentious woman with two children, Charles and Jane. As she grew up, Mary Godwin took refuge in the studies which were to serve as a great consolation throughout her life.

SECRET AFFAIR

In 1812, when Mary was staying with a family friend near Dundee, a young and fervent admirer of Mary's father began to frequent the Godwin household. The visitor was Percy Bysshe Shelley, aristocrat, political radical and poet, who was also highly imaginative, somewhat unstable and, to many women, immensely appealing. He had married at 19 and had a daughter, Eliza Ianthe. However, this did not prevent him from falling in love with the 16-year-old Mary when she finally returned from Scotland in the spring of 1814. Mary was not strikingly attractive, but according to a friend she was 'agreeable, vivacious and sparkling, very pretty, with fair hair and complexion and clear bright white skin' – and she was an intellectual.

For Shelley, now disillusioned with his young wife Harriet, Mary's attraction was all the greater because her parents were William Godwin, whom he venerated as a father figure, and Mary Wollstonecraft. By the end of June – after a clandestine courtship at Mary Wollstonecraft's grave – Shelley and Mary had declared their mutual love.

Godwin was horrified. He tried to persuade Shelley to patch up his relationship with Harriet, who was pregnant again, and insisted that he stopped seeing Mary. But he could not keep the lovers apart, and at the end of July they decided to elope to the Continent. At the last moment they agreed that Mary's step-sister Jane – soon to adopt the name Claire – should come with them. Claire, with her dark hair, olive skin, and exuberant and demanding nature, was in many ways the opposite of Mary, who would soon regret the invitation.

The three young people fled to France and embarked on a journey through a country ravaged by war and famine. Their high spirits carried them through, but by the time they reached Switzerland, these, as well as their finances, had begun to wane. Mary was pregnant, unwell and irritated by Claire's company. Desperately

Mary Shelley
A supposed portrait of the writer when she was 19. By this time Mary had enjoyed a passionate, clandestine love affair with Shelley, who was married to another; had eloped with him against her father's and his family's wishes; had travelled to Switzerland and back with him; had watched him go into hiding to avoid imprisonment for debt; had given birth to a baby daughter by him; and had suffered the anguish of seeing her baby die just two weeks later.

River Tay, Scotland

Frail and unwell, Mary, aged 14, was despatched to her father's friend William Baxter, near Dundee. She spent two happy years there, going for long walks on the Sidlaw hills and along the River Tay (left). As she wrote in her introduction to Frankenstein, *'It was beneath the trees of the grounds belonging to our [the Baxters'] house . . . that my true compositions, the airy flights of my imagination, were born and fostered.'*

short of money, the three decided, quite suddenly, to return home.

However, they were scarcely better off in England. Despite constant visits to banks, lawyers and money-lenders, Shelly had to go into hiding to avoid the bailiffs and the dreaded debtors' prison, leaving a pregnant Mary terrified and alone. Eventually Shelley succeeded in securing a loan, whereupon Mary's father, who was still hostile to the couple, made the first of a series of demands for money that were to plague Mary and Shelley throughout their life together.

Another cause of tension was Shelley's interest in Claire, which Mary increasingly resented, despite the fact that – on Shelley's suggestion – she was developing a close relationship with his best friend, Thomas Jefferson Hogg. Shelley evidently hoped to set up a kind of commune, but the idea collapsed soon after the birth of Mary's first child – a tiny, fragile daughter – in February 1815, when she was seven months pregnant. Two weeks later Mary awoke to find that her baby had died. An entry in her journal reflects the anguish she felt over her loss: 'Dream that my little baby came to life again; that it had only been cold, and that we rubbed it before the fire and it lived.'

Mary gradually began to recover her spirits, no doubt helped by Shelley's agreement that Claire should leave, and by a financial settlement which guaranteed Shelley an annual income of £1000. They moved into a house on Bishopsgate Heath, at the edge of Windsor Forest, and Mary, who was pregnant again, happily settled into a private life with Shelley in which they studied, wrote, walked and rowed on the Thames with friends. She developed from an ill, anxious girl into a confident young woman, and in January 1816 gave birth to a

Illustrious father

(above, left) William Godwin was a radical intellectual who attracted a coterie of distinguished admirers. He had published a seminal work entitled An Enquiry Concerning Political Justice *and challenged contemporary thinking on politics and religion as well as marriage. Mary's relationship with him remained close and intense, despite his burdensome demands for money from Shelley.*

Childhood home

(above) Mary grew up in the modest surroundings of London's Skinner Street in Holborn. It was here, over a bookshop at number 41, that her parents lived, and here that she first set eyes on the ardent young poet and radical, Percy Bysshe Shelley.

received news that Mary's half-sister Fanny had killed herself. Mary, stricken with guilt and grief, was almost expecting the new blow when in December they heard that Shelley's wife Harriet had also committed suicide by drowning herself in the Serpentine in Hyde Park. Shelley, hoping to secure custody of his two children, Ianthe and Charles, decided that he would have a better chance of doing so if he and Mary married. It was against his principles, but the ceremony duly took place in December 1816.

In January, Claire, who was again living with the Shelleys, gave birth to a daughter, Allegra. At the same time the chancery suit for custody of Shelley's children began. The following month Mary realized she was pregnant again, and the Shelleys moved to Marlow in Buckinghamshire, where she settled down to finish *Frankenstein*.

In September she gave birth to a baby daughter, Clara, but immediately succumbed to post-natal depression. At the same time Shelley's health – frequently bad – deteriorated drastically. In the meantime there was a flurry of local speculation about Allegra's origins. Claire had never publicly explained her daughter's parentage, but had always hoped that Byron would give his daughter a privileged upbringing. Gossip now put the Shelleys under pressure to help her.

In March 1818 they set off for Italy. The lively, affectionate Allegra was sent with their nursemaid, Elise, to Venice, and the rest of the party travelled to Tuscany. Meanwhile *Frankenstein* had been published anonymously and an excited Mary was beginning to receive favourable reports about it.

strong, healthy son whom they named William after her father.

Meanwhile Claire had succeeded in 'capturing' no less a figure than the poet Lord Byron. It was a brief affair, but by the time Byron departed for Switzerland, Claire was pregnant. Shelley and Mary, distressed by Godwin's continual demands for money, the public's indifference to Shelley's poems and their own rejection by society, were contemplating a return to the Continent, and Claire easily persuaded them to take her with them to Switzerland. Mary had been introduced to Byron and, while disapproving of his excesses, had found him fascinating and was happy to meet him again. Once more the threesome travelled across the Continent, and in May 1816 they joined Byron on the shores of Lake Geneva. Here the friends rented two adjacent villas and spent much time together, going on boating trips and talking far into the night at Byron's house, the Villa Diodati. The conversation frequently turned to horror, and one evening Byron suggested that each of them should write a ghost story. Only Mary actually did so, drawing on a particularly vivid nightmare to create *Frankenstein*.

Soon relations between the two households became strained, Byron having long lost interest in Claire. As the summer came to an end, Mary and Shelley decided that it was time to leave, and in September they arrived back in England.

UNFORESEEN TRAGEDIES
They settled in Bath, in happy domesticity, until they

Graveside romance
(above) In order to escape the constant wranglings at home, and also to conduct her courtship in secret, Mary began meeting Shelley by her mother's grave in St Pancras Churchyard. It was here that, united in hearts and spirit, they plighted their troth to each other.

In August, Shelley and Claire set out to see Allegra; then, ten days later, Mary received a letter asking her to join them. Her daughter Clara, not yet one year old, was ill, but Mary felt that she must go. So began a nightmare journey across Italy in which Mary had to watch her small daughter visibly failing in her arms. On her arrival in Venice the baby died. In her anguish, Mary blamed Shelley for Clara's death, and it is possible that she never fully forgave him.

A BLEAK WINTER

Mary, Shelley and Claire soon embarked on another period of travel, this time to Rome and Naples. Here they immersed themselves in the study of Italian and classical literature, but it was a bleak winter in which they all felt depressed and homesick. In February 1819 the birth of a girl named Elena Adelaide Shelley was registered in Naples. Her official parents were Mary and Shelley, but her true parentage has remained a matter of speculation to this day. There have been claims that she was the daughter of Shelley and Claire, but it is more likely that the mother was the Shelleys' servant Elise. Whoever the parents were, Elena was left with foster parents when the Shelleys once more returned to Rome.

Rome was Mary's favourite city, but on this occasion she could not shake off a feeling of gloom. Then her beloved son William succumbed to a bout of dysentery. He seemed to rally, but suddenly, just two weeks after the first signs of illness, he died before Mary's and Shelley's despairing eyes.

William's death was a blow that was to mark Mary for life. Unconsoled by the knowledge that she was

Mary Wollstonecraft

Born in London in 1759, Mary Shelley's mother, Mary Wollstonecraft, experienced a difficult childhood. One of three daughters, she had little formal education and often witnessed her drunken father beating her mother. These scenes planted in her a determination to fight for the cause of women, to ensure, among other things, that girls received a decent education, that they had the possibility of supporting themselves and that they were not always physically and economically at the mercy of men. She wrote a book called *Thoughts on the Education of Daughters* and gradually found herself part of a distinguished and radical social circle. In 1792 she published *A Vindication of the Rights of Woman*, a pioneering feminist work which is now a recognized classic.

Her private life was less successful. At 32 she became infatuated with the painter Henry Fuseli and, reeling from this hopeless relationship, she travelled alone to France, where she soon became involved with an American adventurer, Gilbert Imlay, and found herself pregnant by him. By the time their daughter Fanny was born in 1794, Imlay had already begun to tire of her. Mary attempted suicide, first in Paris, then in London, and it was not until she formed a friendship with William Godwin that she found genuine happiness. In March 1797 they married – Mary was pregnant. But their joy was to be short-lived – on 10 September 1797 Mary died a few days after giving birth to a daughter, the future Mary Shelley.

Alpine travels
Claire Clairmont (inset left), Mary's step-sister, joined the young lovers when they eloped to Switzerland and became increasingly unwelcome as their journey progressed. At one point Shelley bought a donkey to help carry the girls. But it was small, sickly and feeble, and Shelley ended up by carrying it clasped to his bosom, with Mary and Claire following, exhausted, at the rear.

Percy Bysshe Shelley
(right) Poet, free-thinker and political radical, Shelley swiftly captured Mary's heart. At 16, months after meeting him, she wrote the verse 'But ah! I feel in this was given/ A blessing never meant for me,/ Thou art too like a dream from heaven/ For earthly love to merit thee!'

Another William

An alert and happy child, little William (named after Mary's father) was his parents' pride and joy. Mary felt specially close to him, but always had a sense of impending doom.

On one occasion, as her son lay sleeping in his cot, she wrote of another – fictional – William 'with sweet laughing blue eyes' whose life is cruelly cut short. Her dark imagination pictured this boy 'rosy with health' strangled by Frankenstein's monster. Her vision of death was prophetic. Three years later her own William fell ill with dysentery and died.

Field House

(right) Situated in the village of Warnham, near Horsham, Sussex, Shelley's family home reflected the wealth into which he was born. Quarrels with his father kept Shelley away from the house for much of his life, and even when his grandfather died, Sir Timothy would not let him in to hear the reading of the will; Shelley reputedly sat on the steps in front of the house reading Milton.

In 1844, after old Sir Timothy's death, Mary's son Percy inherited the baronetcy and moved into the house, reclaiming the place his father had been denied.

pregnant again, she left Rome as quickly as she could and returned with the others to Tuscany. After five years of trouble and tragedy Mary was in the throes of an emotional breakdown. Shelley offered her love and care, but she felt incapable of responding.

In November 1819 Mary bore a son, Percy Florence, but she found it hard to believe that he would live and flourish. It was a difficult time for her. Godwin was demanding money again; Byron was refusing all Claire's pleas to let Allegra spend some time with her; and matters were close to breaking point between the two step-sisters. On top of this, Paolo Foggi, an ex-servant and husband of Elise, was attempting to blackmail them over little Elena Adelaide Shelley, who had recently died.

The only alleviation in Mary's difficulties came when Claire left and Mary was able to establish a happy working routine, writing her third novel, *Valperga*. At the end of October 1820 the Shelleys moved to Pisa and made a number of new friends, including Edward and Jane Williams. Byron joined them a year later, having left Allegra in a convent, and shortly afterwards Edward John Trelawny, a swashbuckling adventurer, also arrived. He stimulated Shelley's love of water and boats with tales of adventures at sea.

'EXPECTATION OF EVIL'

In some ways it was a happy time for Mary, until news came of Allegra's death from typhus. A distraught Claire joined them as they and the Williamses moved to a house on the Bay of Spezia. Mary was pregnant again and unwell, and while Shelley and Edward Williams threw themselves into the enjoyment of sailing their new boat, she began to feel depressed and inexplicably anxious.

In June she suffered a miscarriage. She was still weak from it when Shelley announced that he and Williams were going to sail up the coast to Livorno. Years later she wrote that 'a vague expectation of evil shook me to

Funeral pyre

Edward Trelawny, deeply moved by the death of his friends Shelley and Edward Williams, battled with the Italian authorities for permission to cremate Shelley after the fashion of his beloved Greeks. Having seemingly moved heaven and earth to do so, he was finally successful, and set up a funeral pyre in a wild and beautiful spot on the shore close to Via Reggio, near Florence. In classical Greek fashion, Trelawny procured salt and frankincense to fan the flames, and poured wine and oil over the body. A copy of Keats's last book, which had washed ashore with Shelley, was placed beside his body so that the souls of the two great poets might be merged.

As the flames lapped Shelley's body, Trelawny plunged his hand into the fire and pulled out his friend's heart, struck by all that it symbolized. At Mary's request, the poet's ashes were buried in the English cemetery in Rome beside the body of the Shelleys' beloved little son William.

Byron's Allegra
Born to Claire Clairmont and Byron, Allegra was soon caught in a bitter tug-of-war between them. Byron would not allow Claire to see her, and eventually put her into a convent. Tragically, when Allegra was just five she caught typhoid and died before either Claire or Byron could reach her.

agony' and she tearfully begged him not to go.

Both Mary and Jane Williams, with whom Shelley was now in love, received letters describing Percy and Edward at Livorno. There was a terrible thunderstorm which the wives supposed to have delayed the two men's departure for home. But then they waited – and waited – for their return.

Mary later wrote, 'To tell you all the agony we endured during those 12 days would be to make you conceive a universe of pain – each moment intolerable and giving place to one still worse.' Their fears were finally confirmed when the bodies of Shelley and Williams were washed up on 18 June 1822.

LIFE WITHOUT SHELLEY

In the days that followed, Mary was overwhelmed with despair. She longed to die, but the future of her son depended on her. Consequently she pulled herself together and made plans to stay in Italy and work, in the hope that she would be helped by an allowance from Shelley's family. But when his father wrote that he would maintain her son, Percy, only if she gave him up, she refused and reluctantly returned to England. Here she met Jane Williams again and renewed their friendship, although Jane never shared Mary's increasingly idealized view of Shelley.

Faced with lack of money and dismal lodgings, she struggled to write a new novel, *The Last Man*. It was then that she heard of Byron's death and more than ever saw herself as the 'last man', 'girded, walled in, vaulted over, by seven-fold barriers of loneliness'.

In 1827 Jane Williams went to live with Hogg, with whom she had been having a love affair for some years. Away from Mary she began to gossip about the Shelleys' relationship, poisoning Mary's precious memories. Many of Mary's other old friends were to turn against her in later years. They came to regard her as a cold, conventional woman who had rejected the radical beliefs of her husband in favour of social approval.

Mary sought respectability for the sake of Percy Florence, who became the emotional focus of her life. Intent on giving him a good education, she sent him as a day boy to Harrow at the age of 12. Meanwhile her life remained poverty-stricken and solitary.

LESS TROUBLED DAYS

Mary eventually began to enjoy a middle age in which she travelled on the Continent with Percy and wrote a good deal of non-fiction. And in 1844, when Shelley's father, Sir Timothy, died, leaving his estate and baronetcy to his grandson, her money worries were over. Unfortunately her new status made her vulnerable to blackmail attempts by people who had acquired letters written by her or by Shelley. She fought them off, but the attacks on her privacy took their toll on her health.

Mary had tired of life by the time she met her son's wife-to-be, Jane St John, early in 1848. Jane was a young widow who quickly became a devoted friend. She contributed much to such happiness as Mary enjoyed in the last years of her life. In the winter of 1850 Mary became increasingly paralyzed and, knowing she was dying, passed on to Jane the care of Shelley's papers and reputation. On 1 February 1851 Mary Shelley died.

Dark Imaginings

Inspired by Romantic ideas and personalities, Mary Shelley's grand visionary works often echo the torments of her own life. Her resonant imagination captured the spirit of her age.

The woman who wrote *Frankenstein* had a very modest opinion of her own talents. Years after the novel was published, Mary Shelley remarked despairingly in a private letter that 'I should be happy if anything I ever produced may exalt and soften sorrow . . . But how can I aspire to that?'

Along with this humility went a curious reluctance to discuss herself or her own work. Her letters and journals contain only passing references to her writings: 'I am very averse to bringing myself forward in print', she confessed in her introduction to the 1831 edition of *Frankenstein*. This was the only occasion on which she wrote at any length about how she conceived and composed her books.

Yet even in her lifetime Mary's greatest work had begun to acquire its now almost mythic significance. The story of an obsessed scientist and his monstrous creation, *Frankenstein* established Mary Shelley as a successful writer when she was in her early twenties. Her husband's later fame as a poet makes it easy to forget that during his lifetime she was better known than he was.

Frankenstein triumphed despite a mixed reception from the critics. The *Quarterly Review* raged against the 'tissue of horrible and disgusting absurdity this work presents', prejudiced by its dedication to Mary's father, the notorious radical William Godwin. But Sir Walter Scott warmly praised 'the author's

original genius and happy power of expression', although he and many others assumed that *Frankenstein* had been written by Percy Shelley. When they discover that the author was the poet's very young wife, they were astounded. Their feeling was expressed by *Blackwood's Magazine*: 'For a man it was excellent, but for a woman it was wonderful.'

The public verdict was clear – *Frankenstein* was a best-seller which kept its popularity year after year. When Mary returned from Italy after Shelley's death, she found that a dramatized version of the novel was being performed at the English Opera House – the contemporary equivalent to a film being made from the original. And in the House of Commons,

A model hero
(right) Lord Byron
clearly excited Mary's
imagination as a
romantic figure, for
he appears, thinly
disguised, in
Lodore, Valperga
and The Last Man.
It was his idea that he
and his friends should
each write a ghost
story, a suggestion
that induced Mary to
create Frankenstein.

Villa Diodati
During the summer
of 1816, Mary and
Shelley gravitated to
Byron's house on the
shores of Lake Geneva
(below) near which
they were living. It is
hardly surprising
that the spectacular
lake and mountain
scenery of the area
greatly influenced the
plot and atmosphere
of the book that Mary
began to write there.

'Canning [the foreign secretary] paid a compliment to *Frankenstein* in a manner sufficiently pleasing to me.'

Reticent though she was, Mary Shelley did state her literary creed: 'a fiction must contain no glaring improbabilities, and yet it must never divest itself of a certain idealism, which forms its chief beauty.' 'A certain idealism' evidently meant a significant depth and perhaps a larger-than-life quality incompatible with pedestrian realism. Certainly Mary Shelley tended to avoid everyday settings and events in her fiction.

A NEED TO SELL

Frankenstein, *The Last Man* and a handful of short stories represent Mary Shelley's fantastic and futuristic vein. But she also wrote about the violent and colourful past. Her second published novel was *Valperga* (1823), a tale of medieval Italy 'raked out of fifty old books', according to her husband.

Valperga proved as commercially successful as *Frankenstein*. By the time it was published, Shelley had been drowned and Mary, left to provide for herself and her son, was about to return to England. Unluckily she had assigned all the profits from the book to her perpetually penniless father, so she was now forced to become a professional writer in the full sense, obliged to please the public if she was to survive.

Her third novel, the apocalyptic fantasy *The Last Man* (1826), was as ambitious as *Frankenstein*, but it was received without enthusiasm. Tastes had changed, and this was probably why Mary wrote no more novels in the highly imaginative vein that we value most. *The Last Man* proved to be her last novel (though by no means her last story) of real merit. However, *Lodore* (1835), a society novel, achieved popular success, possibly because it contained many characters and episodes that, as readers very well knew, were drawn from Mary's own life.

PUBLIC SCRUTINY

After *The Last Man*, Mary Shelley published only three novels in 25 years. Her imaginative work was out of fashion and, increasingly anxious for social acceptance, she was painfully conscious that everything she wrote was being read with an eye to its bearing on the scandalous lives of the dead poets Shelley and Byron. This scrutiny seems to have had an inhibiting effect that progressively impaired Mary's creativity. She evidently found it less stressful and emotionally demanding to perform other literary labours – to produce a piously admiring edition of Shelley's poems (1839), and to write *The Lives of the Most Eminent Literary and Scientific Men* and *Rambles in Germany and Italy*. It was an odd literary end for the author of *Frankenstein*.

Readers who looked for autobiographical

Age of discovery
(left) The vogue for
scientific discovery lit
the 19th-century
imagination, as
awesome powers
suddenly seemed to be
within reach. Out of
this atmosphere of
excitement – half
superstitious, half
rational – came Mary
Shelley's fantastic
notion of a creature
assembled in a
laboratory and given
life by a scientist.

Percy Bysshe
It was thought, when
Frankenstein was
published, that
Mary's husband (left)
was the true author,
since such a work was
supposedly beyond a
woman. Shelley was
proud of his young
wife's achievement,
and encouraged her;
for he – unlike Byron
– believed the ideal
wife should be her
husband's intellectual
equal.

references in Mary Shelley's fiction were rarely disappointed. Characters and incidents from the earlier part of her life appear again and again in her work, either in remembered detail or reworked into might-have-been episodes.

Mathilda, written just before *Valperga* but not published until 1959, reflected her passionate attachment to her father, fusing incestuous fantasy about the past with the reality of her own immediate grief as a bereaved parent. Much more of Mary's writing drew on her eight years as Shelley's companion and wife. Their debt-ridden days in London are described in *Lodore*, and in *The Last Man* the Shelley-figure Adrian perishes by drowning, as did the real Shelley.

DEAD HEROES
The images of Shelley and Byron inspired most of the leading male characters in Mary's best novels and stories. Shelley is clearly the model for the devoted Woodville in *Mathilda* and the unworldly, unattached Adrian in *The Last Man*. But these are idealized versions of the real poet, who was more complex, more sensual and less dependable than Mary's fictional heroes. Both as a novelist and an editor Mary worked to make Shelley respectable by turning him into the archetypal 19th-century Romantic poet, whom Matthew Arnold saw as 'a beautiful and ineffectual angel' beating his wings in the void.

By contrast, Mary did justice to both the virtues and the faults of the man she nicknamed 'Albé' – Lord Byron. It is 'the dear, capricious, fascinating Albé' – not Mary's husband – who dominates her fiction. He is clearly the model for Castruccio in *Valperga*, Lodore in the novel of that name, and Lord Raymond in *The Last Man*. His impetuous, heaven-challenging figure evidently had a strong appeal for Mary.

Short stories provided Mary with an important source of income after Shelley's death. Most of the stories were written for gift books

Apocalypse
Scenes of ultimate destruction (above) are one of the hallmarks of Mary's imagination.

such as *The Keepsake*, lavishly produced annuals of a kind which were a popular feature in the early 19th century. Mary Shelley complained that there was not enough space in the annuals to develop an idea properly, but she may well have benefited from the need to make her tales short, and some of them are among her best works. Her brand of fantasy was evidently more acceptable in this form, and she wrote a number of stories on 'science fiction' themes such as seeming-corpses that are brought back to life after a lapse of centuries.

In *The Mortal Immortal*, the immortal narrator remains ever young while his wife grows old and querulous – exactly the situation in which Mary Shelley found herself, although Percy Bysshe Shelley enjoyed eternal youth and immortality in a rather different sense. Mary had something in common with the hero of *The Last Man*, and wrote, as she looked back at the circle of genius she had once known, '*The last man! Yes, I may well describe that solitary being's feelings, feeling myself as the last relic of a beloved race, my companions extinct before me.*'

Gloomy foresight
Preoccupation with death, decay and ghoulishness (below) were not peculiar to Mary – they were a facet of Romanticism. But there was plainly a morbid streak at work in her writing. Did she perhaps feel gloomy intimations of the future? At the age of 44 she revisited the spot where she had written Frankenstein *and, reviewing her life, saw that 'storm and blight and death had . . . destroyed all'.*

EUGÈNE DELACROIX

1798-1863

Eugène Delacroix was the supreme artist of the French Romantic movement. According to rumour he was the illegitimate son of the famous statesman Talleyrand, and as a young painter he received remarkable help from the state – almost as if someone powerful was secretly pulling strings. He moved in fashionable circles where he was in great demand, despite the fiery nature which smouldered beneath his charm.

For most of his distinguished career, Delacroix painted vast canvases for exhibition at the annual Salon. Their uncompromising subject matter often shocked the critics, but several of his paintings were purchased by the government. For the last three decades of his life he devoted his energies to painting giant murals for ceremonial and religious buildings. He died at the age of 65, in self-imposed isolation.

A Tiger in the Salon

Eugène Delacroix had a dual personality: behind his charming exterior lurked an inner violence, revealed only in his paintings. Friends likened him – in his elegance and ferocity – to a tiger.

Ferdinand Victor Eugène Delacroix was born in the Parisian suburb of Charenton Saint Maurice on 26 April 1798. His mother, Victoire, came from an illustrious family of royal cabinetmakers, and her husband, Charles Delacroix, was a member of the revolutionary government, who had voted for the execution of Louis XVI in 1793. Charles had also been Minister of Foreign Affairs, but in 1797 he was demoted to become Ambassador of the French Republic in Holland. He was abroad when Eugène was born, and modern research has revealed doubts about the boy's true parentage.

Although Delacroix seems never to have been aware of them himself, rumours circulated that his real father was a far more powerful figure. For Charles had been replaced as Foreign Minister by Talleyrand, a friend of the family and one of the most able diplomats of his time. And the great Talleyrand, it seems, took not only Charles Delacroix's job, but also – for a while – his wife.

After his return from Holland, Charles was appointed Prefect of the Gironde region, and the family moved to Bordeaux. The provincial city was quiet compared with Paris, but Eugène's childhood was not uneventful. 'By the age of three',

The artist at 20
Delacroix was uneasy about this revealing portrait of him, painted by Théodore Géricault in 1818: 'The wickedness of my expression almost frightens me', he said. The artist always sought to suppress his wild side.

according to his novelist friend Alexandre Dumas, 'he had been hanged, burned, drowned, poisoned and choked.' Hanged when he caught his head in a horse's forage bag, burned when the mosquito net over his bed caught fire, drowned when the servant accidentally dropped him in the harbour at Bordeaux, poisoned when he ate some verdigris and choked when he swallowed a grape.

School life in Bordeaux was rather less exciting. Delacroix had shown an aptitude for music, and the town organist, who had known Mozart, encouraged him to become a violinist. But in 1805, when Eugène was seven years old, his father died, and a few months later the family moved back to Paris. Eugène entered the Lycée Impérial, where he did well without shining, and showed an enthusiasm for literature. Holidays were spent in Normandy at an old Gothic abbey owned by a cousin, where the picturesque ruins made a powerful impression on him. He took up sketching and was encouraged by his uncle Henri Riesener, who was himself a talented painter. Together they made occasional visits to the studio

A powerful father
(above and left) Delacroix was born during Napoleon's rise to power, nominally the son of Charles Delacroix, a member of France's revolutionary government. But rumours suggested that his real father was a family friend – the brilliant statesman Talleyrand, who was present at Napoleon's coronation in 1804. A detail from the commemorative painting shows the similarity of their features.

In 1818 Delacroix watched Géricault working on his huge dramatic painting of a contemporary shipwreck, *The Raft of the 'Medusa'*. He was so excited, he later recalled, that when he left Géricault's studio he 'started running like a madman', not stopping until he reached his room.

The results of this encounter were seen in 1822, when Delacroix completed his first major painting and submitted it to the official Salon. At that time success at this annual public exhibition was crucial to a young artist's career, and Delacroix responded by producing a very large painting of an unconventional subject, *The Barque of Dante*, drawn from a medieval poem, Dante's *Inferno*, rather than the conventional Greek and Roman myths. It caused a sensation. Baron Gros, one of Napoleon's favourite painters, had it framed at his own expense and the picture was bought by the state and hung in the Luxembourg Palace galleries.

Teenage passion
In his teens, Delacroix became infatuated with his sister's English maid, Elisabeth Salter, but his love letters – in appalling English: 'O my lips are arid since had been cooled so deliciously' – failed to impress her.

Visits to the zoo
Delacroix often visited the Paris zoo, and wrote about its 'extraordinary animals' in his journal. Exotic beasts were a major source of inspiration for his paintings.

of Pierre Narcisse Guérin, a leading academic painter and teacher.

In 1814 Delacroix's mother died, leaving him inconsolable. He immediately moved in with his sister, Henriette, but his problems increased when she embroiled the family in disastrously expensive legal proceedings which impoverished them all. A year later, showing the determination that proved one of his most striking characteristics, he enrolled as an art student at Guérin's studio.

A CLASSICAL TRAINING

In 1816 Delacroix moved to the Ecole des Beaux Arts, then dominated by Neo-Classical painters who promoted a rigidly formal teaching programme of study from plaster-casts of Greek and Roman sculpture, and life drawing from the nude model. Careful drawing and morally uplifting subjects from ancient history or mythology were the order of the day.

But one of the students was a young man called Théodore Géricault, who was interested in a completely individual form of artistic expression.

Delacroix left the Ecole des Beaux Arts in triumph: 24 years old, bursting with ambition and confident in his own ability. He began to keep a journal, self-consciously forcing himself to examine his motives, experiences and ideas. He was now involved in the burning artistic debates of the day and was drawn towards the circle of Romantic writers and artists who had turned away from academic tradition and correctness and sought truth in their personal emotional response to the world and human experience. Delacroix's second major Salon painting, *The Massacre of Chios*, reflected these new concerns, for it showed a bloody incident which had recently occurred in the Greek War of Independence. Gros now turned against his protégé and called his work 'the

massacre of painting'. But Delacroix had his supporters too, and his prominence among the younger generation of French painters was now undeniable.

For the next few years Romanticism was in full flower and Delacroix was recognized as the movement's outstanding painter, although he consistently refused to accept that he was in any sense the leader of a school. Nevertheless, for a time he threw himself into the social and artistic whirl, reading Byron's poems and applauding the performances of Shakespeare's *Hamlet* that thrilled Paris in 1827. Among the audience he was likely to find such fellow-Romantics as the composer Hector Berlioz and the poet Victor Hugo. Delacroix was friendly with Hugo for a time, producing the

The July Uprising
In July 1830, Parisians took to the streets in revolt against the reactionary King Charles X, forcing his abdication. Delacroix watched the fighting, but took no active role.

Faithful servant
(right) For the last 30 years of his life, Delacroix was cared for, cosseted and controlled by his devoted housekeeper Jenny le Guillou. Fiercely possessive, she encouraged his increasing isolation from society.

The Moroccan Adventure

On New Year's Day 1832, Delacroix left Paris on the journey of a lifetime. A young diplomat, Count Charles de Mornay, was going on an ambassadorial visit to the Sultan of Morocco, and had invited him along to record the trip. The artist was overwhelmed by what he saw – his Oriental imaginings made real.

Six weeks in Tangier were followed by a 200-mile trek to the Sultan's Palace at Meknes, where the French party was given exotic gifts: a lion, a tiger, Arab stallions and gazelles. Delacroix later enjoyed the delights of the 'lovely human gazelles' in a harem in Algiers. The experiences of this six-month trip inspired him for the next 30 years.

The light of Tangier
(above) The bustling streets of Tangier were exhausting as well as exciting. Delacroix wrote that the blazing sun's reflections from the whitewashed walls 'tire me excessively'.

The Sultan's city
(right) Delacroix made numerous sketches during his trip. He filled seven notebooks with drawings and watercolours like these studies made around the walls at Meknes in Morocco.

costume designs for his play *Amy Robsart*, but within a few years their friendship cooled. Hugo described Delacroix as 'a revolutionary in his studio' but 'a conservative in the drawing-rooms'.

Indeed, according to many contemporaries Delacroix had a disturbingly dual nature. In the brilliant society in which he moved he was generally regarded as elegant, highly cultivated, witty, yet aloof. One writer reported that 'He was easy, velvety and winning, like one of those tigers whose supple, formidable grace he excelled at rendering, and in the drawing rooms everybody used to say: "What a pity so charming a man should paint such pictures".' Yet behind the impeccable façade, 'the tiger' had a violent, passionate nature and a streak of savagery. The

Romantic ruins
Delacroix spent many summers at Valmont, a magnificent estate that belonged to his cousins in Normandy. Their manor house was attached to a ruined abbey, and it was in this picturesque setting that he began a love affair with his cousin Joséphine which spanned three decades.

poet Charles Baudelaire described him as 'a volcanic crater artistically concealed beneath bouquets of flowers'.

Among Delacroix's acquaintances was the English painter Richard Parkes Bonington, whose use of clear, brilliant colour for depicting episodes from medieval history he greatly admired. Sir Walter Scott was one of his favourite authors: the British influence in general was strong. In 1825 Delacroix had spent a few months in England, visiting painters such as Sir Thomas Lawrence and David Wilkie. His journal describes an ecstatic boat trip on the Thames, drifting through the lush English countryside. The works of John Constable impressed him deeply, although not sufficiently for him to turn often to landscape as a subject.

THE SPIRIT OF ROMANTICISM

In 1827 Delacroix exhibited his third important Salon picture, which more than any other expresses the darker side of Romanticism in which death and sex are strangely mingled. The idea for *The Death of Sardanapalus* came from one of Byron's poems, but the violence and voluptuous eroticism are all Delacroix's own. The critics were horrified and urged the young painter to take a grip on his talent and not squander it on such excesses. Even Delacroix was taken aback by what the painting revealed of his own suppressed sensuality, for consciously he was always appalled by any lack of restraint or control.

Perhaps Delacroix had become obsessed with his own sensual experiences. In his youth he had had a number of love affairs, notably with Elisabeth Salter, an English girl who was his sister's maid, and with his cousin Joséphine de Forget (an attachment which lasted nearly 30 years). But as he grew older, his relationships with women were more often earnest friendships, devoid of sex. Slowly, he became more solitary, more preoccupied with work. His health became a major problem. From as early as 1820 he had been subject to fevers that sometimes laid him low for days, and throughout his life he suffered from attacks of laryngitis that could become quite serious and leave him weak and listless. For such an energetic man he was small and frail, and his

Delacroix the dandy
Elegantly dresssed, witty and charming, Delacroix was a popular figure in society drawing rooms.

The artist's studio
Delacroix lived at this studio on Paris's Right Bank for 12 years fom 1845.

A Lasting Friendship

When he was in his mid-forties, the normally solitary Delacroix developed a close friendship with one of the most illustrious couples in France – the composer Fryderyk Chopin and his mistress, the novelist George Sand. Chopin was unimpressed by Delacroix's painting, but the artist adored his music and had a piano installed in his Paris studio, so that Chopin could play whenever he dropped by.

Delacroix spent three summers with the couple at Sand's country home, amid a happy family atmosphere. He was particularly devoted to the composer and treated him as a younger brother; when Chopin died in 1849, Delacroix was devastated.

bouts of intensive work often had to be followed by periods of rest.

At the 1831 Salon Delacroix exhibited *Liberty Leading the People*, now – in France, at least – his best-known picture. He had painted it enthusiastically to glorify and commemorate the revolution of the previous year, which destroyed the reactionary Bourbon monarchy and swept 'the citizen king' Louis Philippe to power. It was a huge success, and confirmed his pre-eminence among painters opposed to the insipid productions of the Ecole des Beaux Arts and the severe classicism advocated by his rival Jean Dominique Ingres, the one truly great exponent of 'official' painting.

At this juncture Delacroix benefited from an extraordinary stroke of luck that was to transform his art. Thanks to the influence of friends, he was chosen to accompany Count Charles de Mornay on an official visit to the Sultan of Morocco. In January 1832 the party set off for Tangier and Meknes, also visiting Spain and Algiers.

After years of feeling – at a distance – the Romantic love of all things oriental, Delacroix was overjoyed. The brilliant light and rich colours of North Africa swept him away. He witnessed in person scenes that the Romantics had been conjuring up from their imaginations – fighting horses, fierce and noble warriors from the desert, women secluded in the harem, Dervishes whirling in the streets. He was struck even more forcibly by the simple dignity he found in Islam, which he compared to the heroism of the Greeks. 'In this short time', he wrote, 'I have lived through 20 times as much as in months spent in Paris.' His vivid memories and his hundreds of notes and sketches were to provide inspiration for the rest of his career.

GOVERNMENT COMMISSIONS

On his return the government began to shower Delacroix with monumental commissions. While he continued to paint smaller easel pictures with increasing facility and freedom, these major decorative schemes absorbed the greater part of his energies for the rest of his life. From 1833 to 1837 he decorated the Salon du Roi in the Bourbon Palace. Then came nine years (1838-47) spent on the Library of the Bourbon Palace, and seven years on the Library of the Luxembourg Palace (1840-47). From 1850 to 1851 Delacroix worked on the Galerie d'Apollon in the Louvre, after which he painted murals in the Hôtel de Ville; they were destroyed, along with the Hôtel de Ville, during the suppression of the revolutionary Commune in 1871. Meanwhile, from 1849 to 1861, he was working even more ambitiously at the Chapelle des Saintes Anges at the great church of St Sulpice.

It would be hard to exaggerate the magnitude of the tasks Delacroix set himself, labouring for months at a stretch to cover huge areas of wall and ceiling, working on preparatory designs, doing endless sketches, and marshalling assistants. A friend wrote: 'To conceive of what such labour was like, you had to have seen him at the end of the day . . . pale, tired out, hardly able to talk, dragging himself along as if he'd just escaped from torture.'

Chopin and Sand
*(left and right) Delacroix
met Chopin through his
mistress George Sand, a
prolific, unconventional
novelist with a legendary
penchant for smoking
cigars and wearing men's
clothing. The Chopin-
Sand affair lasted nine
years, until Chopin's
illness and Sand's family
problems drove them
apart. They separated in
1847, two years before
Chopin's death.*

And while this was going on, he was patiently writing his journal, contributing numerous articles to papers and magazines, working on an unpublished dictionary of the arts, and painting literally hundreds of smaller pictures largely drawn from his North African travels.

As a distraction Delacroix would attend the private salons of rich patrons of the arts in the mornings, where his wit and intelligence were in great demand. It was said that he had 20 different intonations for a simple polite greeting, ranging from the genuinely cordial to the openly contemptuous. He had only a handful of real friends – among them the formidable woman novelist George Sand and her lover, the composer Chopin – but his enemies kept clear.

A JEALOUS GUARDIAN

As he reached middle age, Delacroix was seen less and less in society. His work demanded too much time. His trusted housekeeper, a Breton peasant woman called Jenny le Guillou, guarded him jealously in increasing seclusion. And from 1844 he rented a house at Champrosay in the forest near Fontainebleau to recover from the illness and exhaustion that resulted from his labours. From here he commuted to his Paris studio in the Rue Notre Dame de Lorette.

In 1855, when the artist was well into his fifties, a major retrospective exhibition of his paintings was held and won considerable acclaim. Delacroix was awarded the Grande Médaille d'Honneur and created Commander of the Legion d'Honneur. In 1857 he was elected a member of the Academie des Beaux Arts, a major honour. Then, in 1859, he sent his last pictures to the Salon. They were foolishly attacked by critics, and Delacroix resolved to have nothing more to do with the public exhibition at which so much of his early output had been seen.

Delacroix now moved to an apartment in Paris, though he still spent a good deal of his time in the country. Hardly anyone seemed to notice when, after a few rare months of good health, he completed the paintings in St Sulpice. He retired to Champrosay bitterly disappointed, his life almost over. Death came on 13 August 1863, in his Paris apartment, after a final bout of his recurring throat complaint.

Murals for a church
*(left) Delacroix devoted the
second half of his life to
painting monumental
decorative schemes in the
churches and government
buildings of Paris. The
dramatic murals at St
Sulpice were his crowning
achievement of this kind.*

Boldness and Colour

A true Romantic, Delacroix favoured themes of violence, passion and bloodshed. He approached his subjects with startling boldness, electrifying them with the brilliance of his colours.

In his will, Delacroix left a few paintings to relatives and friends, but asked for the great majority of his works to be sold. When the executors arrived, they made a staggering discovery: the artist's studio contained no fewer than 9,140 separate items. There were 853 paintings, 1,525 pastels, 6,629 drawings and an assortment of engravings, lithographs and sketchbooks. This demonstrates not only what an energetic and productive man Delacroix was, but also how important drawing was to his working method. For every full-scale picture there might be hundreds of prepatory studies.

Delacroix learned to work in this way at the Ecole des Beaux Arts, where he was trained in the academic method. In part, his teaching consisted of close study of Greek and Roman art, together with the paintings of the Old Masters, particularly Michelangelo and Raphael from the High Renaissance and Poussin and Rubens from the 17th

The Giaour and the Pasha (1827)
(below) Some of Delacroix's most exciting works were inspired by Byron's poems, especially The Giaour, *about a Venetian warrior and his love for the Pasha's concubine.*

Pastel sketches
(above) The exquisite sketches for The Death of Sardanapalus *show how important preliminary studies were as part of Delacroix's working method. He made many drawings for this painting.*

century. By the time he came to work on his own large-scale pictures, he had a thorough knowledge of what had gone before, so that he could both draw on the art of the past and also emulate its grandest achievements. Essentially, Delacroix was trained to be a studio painter, like almost all artists of his time. While he might keenly observe what he saw in the countryside or city streets, he regarded a painting as something to be constructed from the imagination in a studio.

WORK IN PROGRESS

When working on one of his Salon pictures, Delacroix first sketched the general composition as it appeared in the mind's eye, perhaps varying the viewpoint or the positions of particular figures. When satisfied with his overall scheme, he would hire professional models and sketch them in the poses of his figures. Then he would concentrate on details, drawing a foot, a sword-hilt or a horse's head. His sketches were put down on paper very quickly; late in his life, he wrote: 'If you are not skilful enough to sketch a man falling out of a window during the time it takes him to get from the fifth storey to the ground, then you will never be able to produce monumental work.'

As colour came to be of prime importance in Delacroix's art, he would use pastels for some of the more developed drawings. Oil sketches would follow, perhaps a rough tone and colour scheme for the whole composition, perhaps more finished

Dramatic water-colours

(above) Delacroix's early watercolours demonstrate his mastery of tonal effects. In Horse Attacked by a Tiger (1825) the violence of the conflict is intensified by the skilful modulation of light and shade across the muscular bodies of the animals.

Lion Hunt (1855)

(detail, left) Following the example of the great Flemish master Rubens, Delacroix painted several pictures of lion hunts. In these he transformed the studies of caged animals he had made at the zoo into fantastic compositions of wild lions engaged in ferocious combat. 'I have no love of reasonable painting', he once wrote. 'There is in me some black depth which must be appeased.'

Grand designs

(above) Delacroix devoted much of his career to painting large decorative schemes. This is a working sketch for the ceiling of the Galerie d'Apollon (1850-51.)

studies of particular figures. Throughout the months of work he would go off to the galleries to discover solutions to the particular problems of the moment.

While the careful construction of his compositions reflected the training he had received, Delacroix completely rejected the Neo-Classical style favoured by less adventurous contemporaries. Although he resisted the labels of the critics, he was a Romantic, seeking truth to nature in the free play of his imagination and emotions. He believed that painting should express not just the nobility, heroism and grand tragedy of Classical mythology, but also fear, melancholy, passion and eroticism – every facet of heightened emotional experience.

Accordingly Delacroix turned to the new subject matter of the Romantic movement. Orientalism was one aspect, and he sketched eastern costumes and weapons in a friend's collection. Music and poetry also inspired him. He made friends with Chopin and arranged for the composer to play for him in his studio, while in his journal he wrote: 'To fire your imagination always remember certain passages from Byron.' The zoo also provided him with ideas, and he often went there to study the wild animals.

THE POWER OF COLOUR

Colour was his single greatest obsession. For Delacroix it held far greater possibilities than the accurate draughtsmanship taught by the acad-emies, and it was the means through which he expressed the full scope of his vision. He first discovered the power of colour relationships while working on *The Execution of Doge Marino Faliero*. Frustrated because the gold cloaks would not glimmer warmly, Delacroix resolved to go to the Louvre to examine the paintings of Rubens. As he was getting into a cab, he saw a shaft of sunlight lighting up the gravel underfoot, casting violet shadows. Suddenly the yellow of the cab glowed with greater intensity, and he realized that by juxtaposing complementary colours their richness would be intensified.

Increasingly Delacroix inclined to leave black out of his palette, relying on reflected violet and green in the shadows to make the highlights of his flesh tones stand forward. His experience of the light and colour of Morocco encouraged him in this direction, and at about the same time he came across the theoretical writings of the chemist Eugène Chevreul, who observed that pure colours actually create in the eye an illusion that each is surrounded by its complementary – yellow by violet, blue by orange, red by green.

Delacroix's writings show him much concerned with theories of art as part of his search for intellectual formulae that might be employed to explain and justify the nature of his creative vision. His practice, however, is best summed up by a more personal dictum: 'One must be bold to extremity; without daring, and even extreme daring, there is no beauty.'

Women of Algiers (1834)

(above) In this beautiful harem scene Delacroix used primary and complementary colours to create a vibrant colour harmony. In the turban of the negro woman, for example, a brilliant strand of green brings out the intensity of the red in the material. Even in small details like her necklace, red and green beads alternate.

158

VICTOR HUGO
1802-1885

Endowed with prodigious vitality, Victor Hugo dominated the
French literary scene for over 50 years. He became his country's
greatest poet, engineered the triumph of Romanticism in the theatre,
and wrote *Les Misérables* and other novels of epic scope and power.
Hugo's demanding ego made his private life tempestuous, and also
thrust him into the political arena, where he became successively a
peer of France, an exile in the cause of liberty and, in his venerable
old age, a pillar of the Republic.

The Romantic Egoist

Hero and victim, passionate lover and compulsive sensualist, deputy and exile, social climber and people's champion – Hugo was himself a figure of romance, carrying all before him with his mighty pen.

Victor Marie Hugo was born on 26 February 1802 at Besançon in eastern France. He was the third son of a mismatched couple, Major Léopold Hugo and his wife Sophie Trébuchet, each of whom was already becoming involved with someone else; in Sophie's case this was General Victor Lahorie, Victor Hugo's godfather, after whom the poet was named. The child was sickly, but unexpectedly survived, developing a huge head that remained a striking physical characteristic well into adult life.

As a soldier's son Victor Hugo had a highly suitable childhood for a great French Romantic, touched by the splendours and miseries of the Napoleonic era. His early years were mainly spent in Paris, but his father was rising fast in the service of Napoleon's brother, Joseph Bonaparte, and in 1807 Sophie and the children joined him at Naples. There was no reconciliation, but in 1811 the family was nonetheless reunited again in Spain, where Joseph had become king of a rebellious people. Victor Hugo never forgot the long stagecoach journeys he made as a child, the martial bustle and marble palaces, and above all the vivid strangeness of Spain,

Remarkable parents
Leopold Hugo, the writer's father (below), was a carpenter's son from Nancy who made a distinguished career in the Revolutionary and Napoleonic armies, eventually becoming a general. Passionate and impetuous, at 24 he married Sophie Trébuchet (below, right), a sea-captain's daughter who was 25. A cool, strong-willed woman, Sophie quickly tired of Leopold.

Born on the move
The son of an officer on active service, Hugo was conceived in a moment of ardour at Donon, the highest point of the Vosges mountains, and born at Beşancon (above).

which his writings would help to make the archetypal land of exotic passion in the eyes of French Romantics.

Relations between husband and wife grew steadily worse, and Sophie left Spain in 1812, taking with her the two younger children, Eugène and Victor. Napoleon's empire was now crumbling fast, but Léopold, while distinguishing himself in the final, desperate events of 1814-15, found time to exert his parental authority and board the boys at a Parisian school, the Pension Cordier. Showing their mettle early, Victor and Eugène became the school's 'kings', each lording it over a faction of their fellow-boarders.

While admiring their father from a distance, the boys adored their mother and rebelled when Léopold tried to place an aunt in authority over them. For her part, Sophie, whose lover had been executed after attempting to overthrow Napoleon, showed equal single-mindedness in her devotion to her children. In 1818, when she and Léopold were legally separated, she gained custody, Victor and Eugène came to live with her, and although both were enrolled as law students, she made no attempt to make them work at anything but literature.

LOVE AND FAME
However, Sophie soon had a rival. The Foucher family had been close friends of the Hugos for years, and as a child Victor had played with little Adèle Foucher. By 1819 the 16-year-old Adèle had become a dark beauty; and one day, in the Fouchers' garden, she said to Victor, 'Tell me your great secret and I'll tell you mine.'

responsible for the fate of his brother, whom he had overreached in poetry and love, and brotherly strife would often figure in his subsequent writings.

Despite this tragedy, Hugo was a happy and successful man in the 1820s. Generous royal pensions and his own inexhaustible productivity ensured that he could support his growing family in style. His first child lived for only a few months, but by 1830 Adèle had borne him two boys and two girls. And he was surrounded by an admiring circle of writers and artists who enlivened his leisure hours and fed his undoubtedly growing sense of self-importance.

Hugo's attempts to conquer the stage with Romantic costume dramas met with stiffer opposition, including a brush with the censorship. Undeterred, he wrote *Hernani* in less than a month. A melodrama that defied all the established conventions, it came to be regarded as the moment of truth in the struggle between Classicism and Romanticism. Hugo's friends recruited supporters from the Latin Quarter to applaud it, while equally determined opponents organized to drown the performances in laughter. On 25 February 1830 the 'battle of *Hernani*' took place, and was repeated almost every night for the four months of the play's run. By its end Romanticism was victorious and Hugo had emerged as the leading French writer of his generation.

The literary revolution was followed in July 1830 by a political revolution which overthrew the Bourbon King Charles X in favour of a more liberal regime headed by King Louis Philippe. Hugo's Catholic and royalist convictions had steadily waned, so he was able to hail the new dispensation – and remain in high favour. In 1831, with the play *Marion Delorme* and the novel *Notre-Dame de Paris*, he reached new heights of popularity.

Hugo's pleasure in these public successes was diminished by painful private disillusions. Worn out by childbearing – and perhaps by her husband's immense sexual vitality – Adèle ended their physical relations. Caught up in the world of the theatre, Hugo himself had become a less domestic creature; but he suffered intensely when Adèle turned to another man, the critic Sainte-Beuve, with whom she seems to have remained in love until the mid-1830s.

A ROMANTIC AFFAIR

The Hugos' marriage, and much of their mutual affection and respect, survived. But the end of their

'My great secret is that I love you', he declared. To which Adèle replied, 'And my great secret is that I love you.' But although they vowed to marry, there were formidable obstacles, not the least being Victor's lack of position and the inflexible opposition of Sophie, whose word was still law to her sons.

Over the next few years Hugo proved himself, publishing scores of articles, his first book of verse, and a novel, *Han d'Islande*, in the Gothic horror vein. In June 1822 Sophie died, aged only 49, and General Hugo gave his consent to Victor's marriage, which took place in Paris, at the church of St Sulpice, on 12 October 1822. The following day the happy couple learned that Eugène Hugo, who also loved Adèle, had become insane. This was the first of the family tragedies that were to darken Victor Hugo's life; in this instance he felt

Adèle
Victor Hugo won the love of his childhood friend Adèle Foucher (above), but had to make his way in the world before they were allowed to marry.

Hernani
The staging of Hugo's drama became 'the battle of Hernani' – a much-caricatured faction-fight between Classicists and Romantics (right).

Man of the theatre
With his massive brow and transparent egoism, Hugo was a gift to the cartoonists (left). In his late twenties he set out to conquer the theatre, becoming the leader of the Romantic school with Hernani, Marion Delorme *and* Ruy Blas. *After a dozen years of success he had a resounding failure with* Les Burgraves (1843) *and gave up writing for the stage. It was almost 30 years before his plays came back into fashion.*

romantic and sexual relationship released Hugo's powerful sensuality, and he now embarked on a remarkable amorous career that carried on into extreme old age. However, its first landmark was an affair in high Romantic style. In 1833 Hugo began a passionate relationship with the beautiful actress Juliette Drouet. Besotted with the poet, she agreed that she must redeem her rather colourful past – and assuage his jealousy – by living in complete seclusion; she received only him, and for the next 12 years never went out on foot unless he accompanied her. Her theatrical career faded away, and Juliette devoted herself entirely to the Master, copying his manuscripts, learning his works by heart and even mending his clothes.

She had Hugo all to herself for only a few weeks each summer, when the lovers travelled to France, Belgium or the Rhineland. The Rhine and its castles, with their dark medieval past, obsessed Hugo, inspiring some of his best drawings and also the play *Les Burgraves*; but when this was performed in March 1843 it was received with mounting hostility and soon taken off. Classicism was back in vogue, and after this, 'the Waterloo of the Romantic drama', Hugo wrote no more for the stage.

In reality his arrogance and egoism, fuelled by Juliette's adoration, had become hard for independent minds to tolerate, and were at least partly to blame for the play's failure. Hugo had alienated many former friends and now had a growing band of ill-wishers. Nevertheless he pressed on, evidently determined to play a role in politics. He cultivated the new royal family. In 1841, at his fifth attempt and after energetic lobbying, he was elected to the Académie Française, the exclusive society of literary 'immortals'. And having obtained this indispensable qualification, he was finally made a peer of France – Viscount Hugo – in 1845.

During these years tragedy and farce mingled in Hugo's private life. His beloved daughter Léopoldine married in February 1843; in September Hugo and Juliette, returning from a holiday in Spain, read in a newspaper that 'Didine' and her husband had drowned in a boating accident. Grief-stricken, Hugo consoled himself with work, sex and politics. He took another

Faithful Juliette
Painted in 1883, the year of her death, this portrait (right) shows Juliette Drouet as she was after a lifetime of devoted service to Hugo. Half a century earlier, as a young and lovely actress, she had fallen in love with him, and she remained steadfast, tolerating his infidelities and eventually sharing his long exile from France.

Revolution, 1830
The revolution of 1830 was celebrated with stirring symbolism by Eugène Delacroix in his painting Liberty Leading the People *(1830, right). The Bourbon monarchy, restored after the fall of Napoleon, was driven from the throne and replaced by the more liberal-minded Orléans dynasty in the person of King Louis Philippe. Hugo, who welcomed the change, remained in high favour.*

mistress, a painter's wife named Léonie Biard. He intrigued and became a peer. And three months later, before he had had a chance to make his maiden speech, the outraged husband and police officials broke into a Parisian apartment and discovered the poet and Léonie in undeniably compromising circumstances. As a peer Hugo could not be arrested, and the ensuing scandal, although immense, could be lived down by ignoring it. But for the time being the poet's political ambitions and pronouncements became distinctly muted.

This relative obscurity was probably to Hugo's advantage, for in February 1848 revolution broke out again in Paris. Louis Philippe fled, a republic was proclaimed, and all peerages – including Hugo's – were abolished. But he remained determined to influence events. He was elected as a deputy to the National Assembly, and reached a wider audience through his sons' journal, *L'Évènement*.

Despite his shifts of allegiance, Hugo remained true to a number of admirable libertarian ideas, and felt a lifelong sympathy for the poor. Since he proved to be politically inept, he never seemed likely to hold high office; but he did get into serious trouble. In the presidential elections he supported the candidature of Louis-Napoleon Bonaparte, who took good care to flatter the poet, as well as appearing to share his vaguely socialistic ideas. Though himself an unknown quantity, Louis-Napoleon was the nephew of the emperor whom Hugo's father had served, and his name alone was worth many thousands of votes. After he had duly been elected, Hugo quickly became disenchanted – perhaps because he had not been offered a ministry, but also because the new regime sought to stifle working-class

Hugo the artist
A gifted artist whose paintings and drawings were often closely related to his poetic preoccupations, Hugo achieved particularly striking and sinister results in Gothic subjects such as castles (right).

Beloved daughter
Family tragedies haunted Hugo; one of the worst was the drowning of his daughter Léopoldine (left).

discontent by reactionary education and press laws, and by deporting political offenders. Hugo was loud in his opposition, but it was his sons, as editors of *L'Évènement*, who suffered imprisonment under the new laws. The writer's response was to attack the new president at his weakest point, asking 'Because we have had Napoleon the Great, must we have Napoleon the Little?'

Meanwhile Juliette Drouet learned of Hugo's long-standing liaison with Léonie Biard, who deliberately brought about the crisis by sending the poet's love letters to her ageing rival. As ever, Juliette was ready to sacrifice herself; but Hugo wavered, since he was genuinely attached to her . . . but also to Léonie. The bizarre outcome was that the trio agreed to go on as they were for a trial period of several months, after which

Second Empire
Louis Napoleon was Napoleon Bonaparte's nephew, and his early career was based on exploiting his famous uncle's name. After the 1848 revolution he was elected president of the French Republic, at first supported but later bitterly opposed by Victor Hugo. In December 1851 Louis Napoleon launched a coup that eventually enabled him to set up the Second Empire, with himself as the Emperor Napoleon III. Hugo went into exile, returning to France only after the collapse of the Empire in 1870.

for longer or shorter periods abroad; but the ever-devoted Juliette remained at hand, happy because exile had brought her back into the centre of her lover's life. Apart from a monthly dinner given for the poor children of the island, Hugo remained aloof from the ordinary life of Guernsey, seeing himself as a symbolic hero and martyr. When Napoleon offered an amnesty to political exiles, the poet rejected it with scorn: 'When freedom returns, I shall return!'

Hugo had begun his new life in relative poverty, but in 1856 a collection of poems, *Les Contemplations*, enjoyed an extraordinary success and earned enough for him to buy a fine mansion on the island; he baptized it Hauteville House, and spent years turning it into a fantastic Gothic-Oriental retreat. Prolific as ever, he published collections of unsurpassed lyrical, religious and philosophical poetry and, in the novel *Les Misérables* (1862), his great 'epic of poverty'.

In 1870 Hugo's exile came to an unexpectedly abrupt end. War broke out between France and Prussia, the French army suffered a series of humiliating defeats, Napoleon was captured and his apparently secure regime fell to pieces. France became a republic again. Hugo received a hero's welcome when he returned to Paris, and readings from his poems raised enough money to buy three guns for the defence of the capital. Nonetheless the republic was forced to seek terms from the victorious Prussians, and Hugo served briefly as a deputy in the new republican Assembly. The sudden death of his son Charles distracted him from politics, and he took no part in the bloody establishment, and still more bloody supression by the French government, of a 'Red' Commune in Paris. But his openly expressed

Guernsey home
During his long exile in the Channel Islands, Victor Hugo made a small fortune from his poetry collection Les Contemplations. *He used the money to build Hauteville House on Guernsey; the rich, bizarre decoration of the interior is suggested in this painting by Charles Hugo (right).*

Hugo would choose between his two loves.

The issue remained in doubt until events took the decision out of Hugo's hands. On 2 December 1851 Louis-Napoleon staged a carefully planned *coup d'état*, the first step on the road that led to him assuming the title of Napoleon III in 1852. After an unsuccessful attempt to organize resistance, Hugo went into hiding, helped by Juliette, whose courage and loyalty in the crisis ensured that she would always retain his love and protection, if not his sexual fidelity.

EXILE AND TRIUMPH
On 11 December, disguised as a workman, Hugo fled to Brussels, where he was joined by Juliette. His pamphlet *Napoleon the Little* made France unsafe for his family, and by August 1852 they were all installed at Marine Terrace, St Helier, on the island of Jersey, with Juliette, as ever, living not far away.

In the event, Hugo's exile lasted for 18 years. In 1855, having joined in a protest against Queen Victoria's visit to Napoleon III, he was expelled from Jersey and settled on the still smaller island of Guernsey. There, although visited by fellow-exiles and admirers from abroad, his social life was a far cry from the days of his Parisian greatness; yet he seemed to thrive on it.¹ Exile wore down his family, whom he grudgingly allowed to stay

Paris at bay
Prussia's victory over Napoleon III in 1870 enabled Hugo to return to France; but for Paris the war was a traumatic event. Besieged and taken by the Prussians, it was subsequently proclaimed a revolutionary commune – a semi-socialist 'state' in conflict with the French government established at Versailles. Government forces invested the city, which was captured amid destruction (right) and mass executions of Communards. Hugo's sympathy for the victims made him extremely unpopular for a time.

sympathy for Communard refugees was enough to ensure his expulsion from Belgium, where he had been trying to settle Charles's affairs.

In France too there was a conservative reaction in the wake of the Commune, and Hugo was defeated in the 1872 elections. But certain patterns remained unbroken. His writings were as popular as ever. Family tragedies continued to haunt him: in 1872 his daughter Adèle became insane, while in the following year his remaining son, François Victor, died. And at 70, Hugo's emotional and sexual life was as tangled as ever. Adèle Hugo had died in 1868 and Léonie Biard was merely a memory. Juliette, now an ailing old lady, still adored him; but in Paris his fame drew countless women to him, including the ravishing Judith Gautier, and Hugo was still incapable of resisting temptation, despite the fact that he was rapidly becoming a national institution.

By the mid-1870s political reconciliation and the respect due to age were working in Hugo's favour. In 1876 he entered the French Senate. In 1877 he published *The Art of Being a Grandfather*, a collection of poems inspired by his grandchildren Georges and Jean, which presented Hugo in his most venerable guise. The 27 February 1881, when the poet entered his eightieth year, was declared a national holiday and celebrated with pomp and ceremony. Juliette died in 1883, and at last Victor Hugo followed her on 18 May 1885. In his will he left 50,000 francs to the poor and asked to be taken to the cemetery in a pauper's hearse. Instead his funeral became one of the great public events of the century, and his remains were interred in the Panthéon with those of Jean-Jacques Rousseau and others who had served France well.

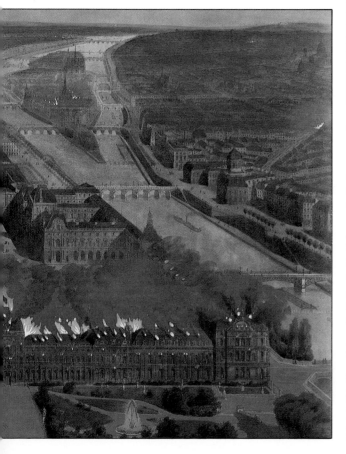

'The Divine Sarah'
The most famous actress of her day, Sarah Bernhardt (above) was also adept at dramatic self-advertisement, as this picture demonstrates. In 1872, playing the Queen of Spain in a revival of Hugo's Ruy Blas, she scored an immense success that consolidated the writer's reputation in post-Commune France. Bernhardt and Hugo may well have been lovers at about this time, despite Hugo's advanced age.

Hugo's apotheosis
Victor Hugo's funeral was a national spectacle, with an immense procession, tricolour flags draped in black crêpe, and mountains of flowers. His coffin lay in state under the Arc de Triomphe (right).

Parisian Epics

Victor Hugo's contemporaries were overwhelmed by the passion, colour and rhetorical splendours of his writing. And although some of it has dated, his poems and the sombre power of his novels still move modern readers.

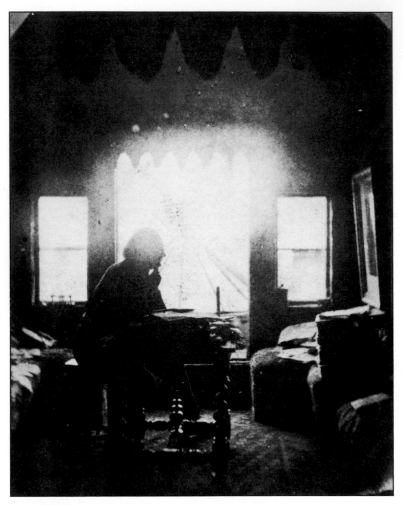

Energetic genius
Victor Hugo seems to have been able to work anywhere and in almost any circumstances. Exiled from France, he continued his angry paper onslaughts on Louis Napoleon (below), rejecting any possibility of returning while the dictator remained in power. He eventually settled on Guernsey at Hauteville House, working in a study (left) furnished in typical Victorian style. His tools of the trade were the traditional quill pens (below, left), which had to be regularly sharpened; for a major project such as Les Misérables, *Hugo evidently needed a large supply.*

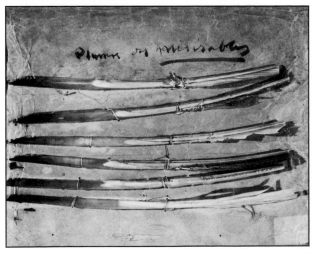

In Victor Hugo, great literary gifts were allied to a huge appetite for work. Most poets have written relatively slowly, but Hugo published volumes of verse in even greater numbers than the plays, novels, essays and travel books that flowed from his pen. His drawers were always filled with a backlog of unpublished writings, and he was not above arranging poems composed over years or decades into a collection, redating them so that they appeared to be inspired by a single event or theme, such as the anniversary of his daughter's death or his love for his grand-children – a self-serving but perhaps artistically justifiable practice that shocked Hugo scholars when they examined the original manuscripts. Even after so much energetic book-manufacturing, volumes of unpublished work by Hugo continued to appear for years after his death in 1885.

To accomplish so much, Hugo was some-times driven to extremes. To finish his novel *Notre-Dame de Paris* by the stipulated date, he put on a long, monk-like robe, locked up his clothes so that he would not be tempted to go out, and shut himself away until the book was done. But for most of his life Hugo found time for work, sex, society and politics because of his ability to follow a routine and to produce with an almost machine-like regularity. 'What a manufacturer! How he calculates his pro-duction!' wrote a Romantic-minded contem-porary in comic dismay. Hugo rose at dawn every day, swallowed two raw eggs and a cup of coffee, and set to work. He wrote a hundred lines of poetry or twenty pages of prose, casually dropping each completed page on to the floor for his valet to collect. When Juliette Drouet had fair-copied them, they were ready for the printer.

HUGO – ALAS!

When one of France's finest modern writers, André Gide, was asked whom he considered the greatest French poet, he replied 'Victor Hugo – alas!' This wittily captured the ambi-guous response of subsequent, cooler-tempered generations of French readers, embarrassed by some of Hugo's high-flown sentiments and Romantic raptures, and by bombastic passages of verse and prose in which the poet's unsurpassed musicality failed to conceal an absence of thought or even meaning. But in the last analysis they too were

Best seller
Victor Hugo's novels represent the Romantic movement at its most sensational, with a strong likeness to the 'Gothick' novels of terror which had been popular since the late 18th century. As the advertisement for Les Misérables *(left) and the cover for* Notre-Dame de Paris *(below) suggest, publishers were quick to exploit this appeal.*

won over by his command of language, his supreme technical skill, and the universal mastery which enabled him to compose the most tender lyrics, scorching political satires, religious meditations and majestic visions of entire historical epochs.

For most non-French readers Hugo is above all the novelist who wrote *Notre-Dame de Paris* (1831) and *Les Misérables* (1862). These are far removed from the careful realism of most English 19th-century novels, although they have features in common with the works of Charles Dickens, including an obsession with violence and a profound sympathy with the poor and oppressed. Hugo's scenes are painted in the strongest possible colours, the characters are either sublimely heroic or unrelievedly evil, and the action is always melodramatic and often implausible. But, as in his poems, Hugo's imaginative energy and narrative drive convince and compel the reader from beginning to end.

With the assistance of cinematic adaptations as *The Hunchback of Notre-Dame,* Hugo's *Notre-Dame de Paris* has acquired a near-mythic status; almost everybody knows the scene in which Quasimodo, the hideously malformed bellringer, swings down from the cathedral belfry and rescues the gypsy girl Esmeralda from the scaffold. It was a stroke of genius on

Hugo's part to make Quasimodo the real hero of the novel, his love and loyalty standing out in vivid contrast with the shallowness of Captain Phoebus, Esmeralda's handsome seducer, and the inner corruption of Quasimodo's master, the apparently saintly Frollo, whose lust and jealousy lead him to murder Phoebus and allow the girl to die for the crime. The swarming population of 15th-century Paris and the brooding presence of Notre-Dame itself are felt throughout the book. They come together in a great set-piece during which an army of beggars, thieves and gypsies tries to rescue Esmeralda by storming the cathedral, only to be driven off in a display of demonic energy by Quasimodo, who hurls beams and molten lead down upon them.

Notre-Dame de Paris ends in tragedy and pathos, uniting Quasimodo and Esmeralda in the darkness of the charnel-house. Doubtless Hugo's version of the Middle Ages was largely a product of his dark imaginings, comparable in atmosphere to his many remarkable, crepuscular and sinister paintings and drawings. But like other works of the imagination, the novel had a significant effect on the real world: more than any other single influence it made Frenchmen aware of their medieval past, and inspired the earliest campaigns to preserve the country's ancient monuments.

Gothic line
The Gothic quality of Hugo's imagination is apparent in many of his very skilful drawings.

LES MISÉRABLES

Les Misérables, widely regarded as Hugo's greatest novel, resembles *Notre-Dame de Paris* in being centred on Paris and vitally concerned with the underworld. But it is set in the recent past, the main events taking place between the fall of Napoleon in 1815 and the July Revolution of 1830. Unusually, Hugo worked intermittently on the tale from some time in the 1840s, although the final version was dashed off with his accustomed speed in the May and June of 1861. Written by an exile, *Les Misérables* enjoyed an enormous success that mildly embarrassed the French government and caused rejoicing among Hugo's fellow-republican exiles. However, the novel was not a political act so much as a blow against social and legal oppression, proclaiming the indomitable spirit of humanity. This is embodied in Jean Valjean, an ex-convict whose crime was to have stolen a loaf of bread. Determined to reform, he nevertheless becomes entangled with the law again, and is obsessively pursued by the police agent Javert. More than once Valjean makes a new life for himself, only to be unmasked and forced to fly from his adversary. In the course of his adventures he takes charge of a young girl, Cosette, brings her up, and ensures her happiness – but not his own – by rescuing her lover, who has been wounded during the July Revolution, and carrying him to safety through the sewers of Paris. A huge, sometimes clumsy book, *Les Misérables* represents a concession to the spirit of the 1860s, part-Romantic and part-Realist; but as so often with Hugo's work, it triumphs by reason of its epic sweep, carrying the reader along on a tumultuous journey from the battlefield of Waterloo to the barricades of 1830.

Hugo's other, less widely-read novels include *The Toilers of the Sea*, a magisterial ocean-epic, inspired by his island exile, which some critics have called his finest work of fiction. His costumed dramas are probably the least acceptable of all his works to present-day tastes, their implausible motives and relentlessly noble attitudes being of a kind now tolerated only in opera; and in fact *Hernani* and *Le Roi s'amuse* are now mainly remembered as the inspirations for Verdi's *Ernani* and *Rigoletto*. Hugo's *Hernani* (1833) remains of some interest as a landmark in the history of French Romanticism, and also because, along with *Ruy Blas* (1838), it exemplifies his enduring fascination with Spain as a land of passion, violence and honour. In *Marion Delorme* (1831) Hugo dealt with a theme that became a staple of French Romanticism: the redemption of a courtesan by love. Its fame was later eclipsed by Alexandre Dumas the younger's *Dame aux Camélias*, but Hugo had already played out the drama in reality with Juliette Drouet, whose life even conformed to the unwritten literary rule that a 'fallen' heroine might be ennobled by love but could not be permitted to achieve happiness.

Hugo seems to have felt the need to capture his every feeling and experience on paper. He carried a notebook wherever he went, recording the life of the street, revolutionary crowds, coronations and executions. Published as *Things Seen*, these notes are vivid and realistic, emphasizing the commitment to his own time that he expressed fictionally in *Les Misérables* and such lesser works as the harrowing *Last Day of a Condemned Man*. In spite of his Romantic taste for violence, Hugo was a lifelong opponent of the death penalty and an advocate of mercy, political as well as legal. For all his faults as a man and his purple literary passions, he was one of the progressive figures of his age. Explaining the purpose of *Les Misérables* in a letter to a friend, he made a declaration which, if not free from his characteristic egoism, illuminates the noblest side of his life's work:

'A society which admits poverty, a religion which admits hell, a humanity which sanctions war, seem to me an inferior society, an inferior religion and humanity, and it is towards the higher society, the higher humanity and religion that I turn.'

Aspects of Hugo
Much of Victor Hugo's literary life was spent in the heady atmosphere of the theatre. He became the leader of the Romantic school, which rejected the established Classical rules. However, a reading in the green room of the Théâtre Français (above) was a decorous affair, and Hugo (fourth from the right) and his fellow-Romantics look appropiately solemn. By contrast, in his old age Hugo openly adored his grandchildren (right), and – characteristically – published a book about them.

HECTOR BERLIOZ
1803-1869

Throughout his stormy, uneasy life he was labelled a genius by
some, reviled as an untalented freak by others. Possibly the most
original Romantic composer, Hector Berlioz was driven by a unique
musical vision that went far beyond his time.

A solid background

Born into a pious, respectable country family, Berlioz showed his extraordinary temperament at an early age. At 12 he fell in love with Estelle, a girl of 18, becoming so obsessed with her that, whenever she was near, he felt physically ill. He learned to play three instruments and, by 16 (right), was sending his compositions to Parisian publishers. But his father (above), a doctor, refused to let him study music; at 18 he was sent away to medical school in Paris.

To Hector Berlioz, possibly the most original of Romantic composers and conductors, music was 'a heavenly art'. He declared that: 'Nothing surpasses it but true love. The one will always make me as unhappy as the other, but at least I shall have lived.'

The way he lived, with a fiery temperament and perverse delight in provocation, alienated many of his contemporaries. Mendelssohn thought him 'a total freak, without a vestige of talent'. Others, like his close friend Liszt, were entranced by his enthusiasm and unpredictability. They found him delightful, even child-like, and revelled in his devilish sense of humour. Much impressed, the German poet Heine called Berlioz 'an immense nightingale; a lark as great as an eagle'.

All his life Berlioz struggled against bankruptcy, being forced to work as a music journalist for a living. Public opposition to his works and personality in his native France meant that he went largely un-appreciated, despite having such a profound influence in other countries that he is often considered the father of modern orchestration.

Berlioz would whip himself into emotional frenzies in which he was at one moment unable to work, and at another capable of composing and studying tirelessly. His violent swings of mood, combined with rejections and material difficulties, produced an unprecedented directness of passion in his music, but left him an embittered old man, chronically ill, who died alone.

Yet this excessively Romantic figure was also a professional who demanded exacting standards of himself in all that he did. One of the greatest musical innovators, he was grandiloquent, unclassifiable and eccentric: a true maverick of his time.

THE SERIOUS CHILD

Louis Hector Berlioz was born on 11 December 1803 at La Côte St André, in the district of Dauphiné. His father was a much-loved country doctor and his mother a pious, orthodox Roman Catholic. This religion, which Berlioz described as 'so attractive, since it gave up burning people', kept its place in his affections even though he publicly mocked it for most of his life. During Berlioz's childhood his father was his principal teacher, instructing him in Latin, classical literature and the rudiments of medicine, the profession he hoped his son would follow. The boy was encouraged to take up music, but only as a hobby. He played the flute, guitar and recorder rather well, but at this stage showed little interest in the piano. Berlioz seems to have been a rather sensitive and impressionable child; in his highly entertaining *Memoirs* he recalls that, at the age of seven, when translating a passage from Virgil's *Aeneid*, he was overcome by a shudder of nervous excitement. At 12 he discovered his two splendid and fateful passions:

Leaving home

Berlioz's childhood home (left) was a stable, comfortable environment that nurtured his many talents. But Paris, a mecca for artists and musicians, was his true milieu. He soon became known for his fiery personality and strange, intense appearance. His friend Legouve described him at the time; 'his eyes blazing . . . and a head of hair like an immense umbrella or movable canopy overhanging the beak of a bird of prey . . . at once comical and diabolical!'

music and love. Estelle, a neighbour's niece, was 18. The moment Berlioz set eyes on her, he later wrote, he felt an electric shock, and then 'suffered acutely and spent my nights in sleepless anguish'. Each subsequent encounter left him feeling worse, and he never forgot the powerful impression made by his first love.

He began composing in the same period, and by 16 he was offering his works, unsuccessfully, to Paris publishers. But his father refused to believe that Hector was serious about music, and eventually packed him off to Paris to study medicine.

A MUSICAL VOCATION

To the young Berlioz, the Paris of the 1820s was an artistic and musical paradise that made medical school even less appealing. At first, horrified by the sight of the dissecting room, he jumped out of the window and fled. Later he developed a bored detachment from it, amusing himself by feeding pieces of cadavers to the birds. Respecting his father's wishes (and dependent on his money), Berlioz kept up his studies for several years, but his musical bent gradually took complete control of him. He became a regular at the Paris Opéra, and there, seized by the

music of Gluck, he felt that short of fainting he could have had no greater response to the experience. He read and copied Gluck's scores in the library: 'An ecstasy possessed me . . . I went without sleep because of them, and forgot to eat or drink', he wrote. He abandoned the dissecting room and, on submitting some compositions to the composer Lesueur, was accepted as a private pupil.

Berlioz's father, though indulgent, expressed his belief that the new enthusiasm would be short-lived, while the devout Mme Berlioz feared that her boy would be led into raffishly undesirable company.

In fury, Berlioz wrote to them that 'I would rather be Gluck or Méhul dead than what I am in the flower of my manhood . . .' His father relented, allowing him to study music for a trial period; if he failed he was to return to medicine or take up some other respectable profession.

In 1826 the Paris Conservatoire admitted Berlioz, who by then was 23. He composed an opera, then a Mass which, as no one else would perform it, he himself staged with borrowed money. Desperate to pay back the loan, he gave music lessons but was unable to earn enough. Unfortunately his father heard of the affair and was outraged by such

Romantic drama

Bored by medical school, Berlioz began to spend his time at concerts, the opera and the theatre, drawing inspiration from such great artists as Shakespeare, Beethoven and Gluck. Romantic theatre usually portrayed its characters in the grip of uncontrolled passions (left), and Berlioz was cast in the same mould.

extravagance. He settled the debt on Berlioz's behalf, as a matter of honour, but then cut off his son's allowance altogether. Berlioz, more certain than ever of his vocation following his teacher's approval of the Mass, decided to go it alone. But with the coming of winter in 1825, he found himself cold and his clothes threadbare. Needing extra income, he became a singer in the vaudeville chorus of the Théâtre des Nouveautés. Although the inanity of the music he had to perform almost drove him mad, Berlioz coped with this, and the strains of overwork, until his father finally agreed to support him again.

PARIS AND ROME

The years 1827-30 were certainly the most formative in Berlioz's life. He fell hopelessly in love – twice. His work began to receive critical acclaim. And, on the fourth attempt, he won the coveted music scholarship, the Prix de Rome.

Berlioz adored Shakespeare, and eagerly went to see a season of plays presented in Paris in 1827 by the English actor Charles Kemble. Appearing in *Hamlet*, as Ophelia, was the Irish actress Harriet Smithson. Her performance enraptured most of theatre-going Paris; Berlioz himself was overcome, as maddened by her beauty as he had been by Estelle's. He bombarded her with love letters, but she was so frightened by his unrestrained passion that she finally refused to receive any more. Berlioz despaired.

Lacerated by his feelings for Harriet, he plunged into composing the *Symphonie Fantastique*, a musical dramatization of his wild emotions. Despite offend-

ing some critics with its bizarre death sequence, the piece was fairly well received when it was first performed in December 1830. For a time the composition seemed to get Harriet out of Berlioz's system. He wrote to his friend Humbert Ferrand: 'I am no longer in danger from that quarter . . . I pity and despise her.' Later in the same year he fell in love with Camille Moke, a very gifted young pianist.

Inspired, like so many composers of this period, by the German poet Goethe, Berlioz composed *Eight Scenes from Faust*. He sent a copy of the score to the master, along with an effusive letter. But Goethe did not reply: his musical adviser reported scathingly that *Faust* was a work of 'coughs, snores, croakings and expectorations'.

The first pieces submitted by Berlioz for the Prix de Rome met a similar reaction from the judges, but his final attempt, *The Death of Sardanapalus*, based on Delacroix's painting, won him the award by a unanimous verdict.

This proved a mixed blessing, since it included a period of compulsory study in Rome. Berlioz left Paris unwillingly, for, after overcoming strong parental opposition, he had just become engaged to Camille. Rome precipitated another emotional crisis; within weeks, having heard nothing from his fiancée, he started to travel back to Paris; but before he reached the French border, a letter from Camille's mother told him that she had married someone else. Spurned in love once again, Berlioz records in his *Memoirs* his reaction to this 'odious crime'. He would return to Paris disguised as a lady's maid, carrying a pair of pistols and bottles of strychnine and laudanum. Having murdered Camille and her mother, he would then kill himself. However, stopping en route in Nice for a meal, his mood abruptly changed. He stayed there, composed the overture to *King Lear*, and then went back to Italy. For

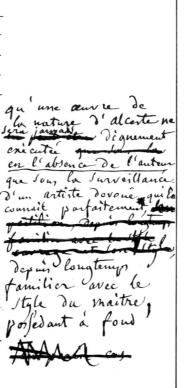

C'est seulement ainsi que les grandes compositions complexes de l'art musical peuvent être sauvées et garanties de la morsure des rats qui grouillent dans les théâtres, dans les théâtres de France, d'Angleterre, d'Italie, d'Allemagne même, de partout. Car il ne faut pas se faire illusion, les théâtres lyriques sont tous les mêmes ; ce sont les mauvais lieux de la musique, et la chaste muse qu'on y traîne ne peut y entrer qu'en frémissant. Pourquoi cela? Oh! nous le savons trop, on l'a trop souvent dit, il n'y a nul besoin de le redire. Répétons seulement ici, pour la vingtième fois au moins, et à propos de la récente reproduction de la Vestale à l'Opéra, qu'une œuvre pareille ne pourra une dignement exécutée, l'absence de l'auteur, sous la surveillance d'un artiste dévoué, parfaitement maître de toutes les questions qui se rattachent à la musique et aux études musicales, profondément pénétré de tout ce qu'il y a de grand et de beau dans l'art, et qui, jouissant d'une autorité justifiée par son caractère, ses connaissances spéciales et l'élévation de ses vues, l'exercerait tantôt avec douceur, tantôt avec une rigidité absolue ; qui ne connaîtrait ni amis ni ennemis ; un Brutus l'ancien qui, une fois ses ordres donnés et les voyant transgressés, est toujours prêt à dire : *I lictor, liga ad palum!* « Va, licteur, lie au poteau le coupable! » — Mais c'est M. ***, c'est Mlle ***, c'est Mme ***. — *I lictor!* » Vous demandez l'établissement du despotisme dans les théâtres? me dira-t-on. Et je répondrai: Oui, dans les théâtres lyriques surtout, et dans les établissemens qui ont pour objet d'obtenir un beau résultat musical au moyen d'un personnel nombreux d'exécutans de divers ordres, obligés de concourir à un seul et même but, il faut le despotisme, souverainement intelligent sans doute, mais le despotisme enfin, le despotisme militaire, le despotisme d'un général en chef, d'un amiral en temps de guerre. Hors de là il n'y a que résultats incomplets, contre-sens, désordre et cacophonie.

the next 12 months he did little except acquire a love of the Italian countryside which later inspired his *Harold in Italy*.

During his stay he met Mendelssohn, and together they explored the local ruins. Mendelssohn was religious, and Berlioz taunted him mercilessly. On one occasion both of them stood poised on a steep ruined staircase, and Berlioz made some sceptical remarks; then Mendelssohn lost his footing, and fell to the ground below. Helping Mendelssohn up, Berlioz declared: 'There's an example of divine justice for you. I blaspheme, you fall!'

'MY THIRTY YEARS WAR'
Back in Paris in 1832, Berlioz found himself still penniless, facing strong opposition and a battle to consolidate his reputation. Harriet was back too, this time running a theatrical company that soon fell into debt. After a performance of the now revised *Symphonie Fantastique*, the two met. Berlioz's re-awakened passion for her was reciprocated, and they had a stormy affair. At one time Harriet accused him of not loving her; exasperated, he decided to make her regret it by taking poison in front of her. In a letter to his friend Humbert he described her reaction to this macabre piece of melodrama:

Dreadful cries . . . (her despair was sublime) – fiendish laughter on my part – desire to live again on seeing her protestation of love – emetics . . . vomiting for two hours . . . I was ill for three days but I survived.

Student and critic
Despite his parents' opposition, Berlioz won a scholarship to study music in Rome. He hated the city, but the surrounding villages (right) and countryside later became an inspiration. Back in Paris and short of money, he was forced to make a living as a music critic. In his Memoirs *he describes what he went through to deliver a piece of copy (above). 'I . . . do anything to fight off the boredom and fatigue . . . It can take eight or nine attempts before I am rid of an article . . . And then the blots and the scratchings-out! The first draft looks like a battlefield.'*

Subject for satire
Berlioz continued to compose and conduct, but his unorthodox style made him a sitting target for the cartoonists (above left).

Berlioz's idée fixe
Playing Ophelia in Hamlet, *Harriet Smithson made an overwhelming impression on him: the moment he saw her he fell hopelessly in love with her.*

They married on 3 October 1833 and had a son, Louis, ten months later. Berlioz later described the subsequent period until his retirement as 'My thirty years war against . . . academics and the deaf'. Although *Harold* was received quite well, and in 1837 the government commissioned his *Requiem*, Berlioz's opera *Benvenuto Cellini* was reviled and the cost of its production put him further into debt. He was saved by a gift of 20,000 francs, probably from the virtuoso violinist Paganini, himself a notorious eccentric. Berlioz used the money to compose *Romeo and Juliet*, which proved highly successful.

Despite incessant work, however, Berlioz's earnings from 1832 to 1842 were pitifully small. He needed a professorship or major conductorship such as other composers had been appointed to; but these were denied him. The Paris Opera, which paid extraordinarily high royalties to composers, consistently rejected his works. So music criticism for the *Journal des Débats* remained his mainstay, depriving him of valuable time for composition. True to form, Berlioz was a caustic, provocative writer whose pieces won him a select following. But they also show just how out of sympathy he was with the prevailing musical standards. He fought an uphill battle with his contemporaries, and his reputation in France began to decline. Nonetheless, throughout his thirties he

composed prolifically, became a figure of European repute and lost none of his youthful fire and panache. A contemporary account describes a performance of his *Symphonie Funèbre et Triomphale* in the open air. Confronted by a full orchestra and brass band of 200, Berlioz conducted with a drawn sword, collapsing at the end across the kettle drums, weeping.

By this time Harriet was weeping too. After six years their marriage was in ruins. When Berlioz went to Germany two years later he had a lover, the singer and actress Marie Recio. Two years after that he left Harriett for good.

Subsequent trips throughout Europe were enormously successful for Berlioz; acclaimed and materially provided for by his hosts, he was to keep travelling for the next 25 years. In London, in 1846, he accepted an invitation to conduct opera at the Drury Lane Theatre, but unfortunately the concert manager ran off with the funds and Berlioz was forced back to Paris. The city, in the throes of the 1848 uprising, was not a welcoming musical environment, so Berlioz soon returned to London for the Great Exhibition of 1851. His music continued to provoke mixed reactions, but during the 1840s and '50s Berlioz established himself as an author of repute. He published his *Treatise on Modern Instrumentation and Orchestration*, the first book of its kind and one which remains a

The Trojans
Berlioz was never really accepted in France, but became an acclaimed musical figure in England and throughout the rest of Europe in the 1840s and '50s. Most of his works were composed during this time, but it was towards the end of his life that he wrote The Trojans, *based on Virgil's heroic tale of Dido and Aeneas (above). He had wrestled all his life with how best to pay tribute to it in music, and for him it was his greatest work. But the opera companies of Europe refused to stage it except in a truncated form. Berlioz felt humiliated by this, and became deeply depressed.*

standard text today, and he also began his *Memoirs* and issued a collection of his journalism.

AGE AND DESPAIR

Despite his successes and international standing, Berlioz did not win his self-proclaimed campaign against the French musical establishment. After his 50th year a series of losses and setbacks slowly wore him down, taming his once fiery spirit. The first loss was Harriet's death in 1854; despite their separation Berlioz grieved deeply. He married Marie soon afterwards and finished his *Memoirs*, but his health started to fail and within three years he was suffering from an acutely painful intestinal disorder.

In 1856 Berlioz started a monumental work, *The Trojans*, based on the Latin classic the *Aeneid*, which took less than two years to finish. Then no one would perform it, except in a drastically cut version in 1863. Ironically this brought Berlioz accolades, enthusiastic reviews and money, and at first he was pleased; but further mutilations utterly disillusioned him. He completed his last work, *Beatrice and Benedict*, but after Marie's death decided to compose no more. Also resigning his post on the *Journal des Débats*, he wrote, 'I say hourly to death: "When you will." '

In an attempt to renew himself emotionally, Berlioz sought out his first love, Estelle. By then a 67-year-old widow, she was bewildered by this intense old man who said he had loved her for 50 years, but she did eventually agree to write to him. Apart from this single contact, a prematurely aged and deeply depressed Berlioz withdrew from the world. Tormented by the increasing pain in his bowels, he took larger and larger doses of laudanum, which left him dazed and stupid. Then, in 1865, his son Louis died of yellow fever in Havana. He found one last pleasure in a conducting trip to Russia, where he left a lasting impression on Rimsky-Korsakov.

After his return to Paris, the death of his lifelong friend Humbert proved the final blow. Berlioz himself died on 8 March 1869. According to accounts by his friends, he died tragically, believing that his genius had been an illusion, and that in death his name and works would disappear forever. In this, fortunately, he was to be proved quite wrong.

Bitter old age
The rejection of The Trojans *and a chronic illness turned Berlioz (below right) into a bitter, unhappy old man who wished only to die as soon as possible. After the death of his wife Harriet he married Marie Recio (above right). But when she too died Berlioz gave up composing and shut himself away. In his despair he reached out to his first love, Estelle, now an old woman whom he had not seen for many years. The letters that she subsequently wrote to him, and a trip to Moscow (above) where he was idolized by young composers, were the only pleasures of his last years. He died in 1869, aged 66, believing that his whole life had been a mistake.*

Symphonie Fantastique, op. 14

Unrequited love, opium, suicide, the guillotine and a monstrous Witches' Sabbath, are some of the lurid ingredients of Berlioz's *Symphonie Fantastique*, a work of vast imagination and originality.

Year of the symphony
The earliest authenticated portrait of Berlioz (above), signed and dated 1830.

'*Episode in the Life of an Artist.*' This is the title given by Berlioz to his *Symphonie Fantastique*, and there is no doubt that the artist concerned is meant to be the composer himself, and the episode a fanciful extension of his own experiences.

In 1827 Berlioz had discovered 'the madness and melancholy' of *Hamlet* and the charms of Harriet Smithson in the role of Ophelia. And if the play appealed to his dramatic sensibilities, the actress 'wrought havoc' in his heart. But whereas he could go to see as much Shakespeare as he pleased, his access to Miss Smithson – whose moving performances were the talk of Paris – was non-existent, since all his addresses to her went unheeded. To be fair to the lady, Berlioz's letters expressing his admiration and undying love comprised only a fraction of the proposals – honourable and otherwise – that she received, and she could not have known that this 24-year-old composer was so earnest and persistent that he would eventually become her husband. Even his attempt to interest her by mounting a concert of his own music (and at his own expense) was unsuccessful.

To have any contact with her in real life therefore appeared impossible; so, since

Berlioz was bursting with frustration, he determined to make contact with her in music. In February 1830 he concocted a romantic tale of his unreciprocated love and its tragic consequences for the lady and for himself, and within two months the *Symphonie Fantastique* was substantially complete. Its programme is melodramatic in the extreme, but there can be no denying the immense skill and imagination with which the young Berlioz carried it out.

The work was first performed on 5 December 1830 at the Paris Conservatoire of Music under the bâton of François Antoine Habeneck. Parisian gossip soon identified Harriet Smithson as the *idée fixe*, and the relatively unknown composer's treatment of the popular favourite must have intrigued the concert-going public. Furthermore, the programme was handed out to the audience, leaving room for doubt only in the most obtuse listener. The symphony was a great success. Its March was encored, there was prolonged applause at the end, and reviews the following day were favourable. 'Bizarre' and 'monstrous' wrote *Figaro*, which was not only nothing less than the truth but also described precisely the qualities the public craved.

Before we examine the programme, a number of facts about it need to be understood. First, the *Symphonie Fantastique* as Berlioz conceived it is only half a work. The audience was intended to sit in a theatre for some 50 minutes with the curtain down while the symphony was played; then the curtain would rise and its sequel, *Lélio*, would be performed by the orchestra with vocalists, chorus and narrator. The impractical nature of such a presentation means that today the *Symphonie Fantastique* is always given on its own.

Second, the programme devised for the symphony was something quite new in its day. Love invariably found its way on to the operatic stage, but to write a symphony dealing so explicitly with a man's feelings for a woman was unusual.

Third, the events depicted are supposed to take place in an opium-inspired dream.

Fourth, this is the first symphony by a prominent composer to employ an *idée*

fixe, or fixed idea, in every movement. It is an easily-recognized melody representing the composer's beloved, but it is modified on each occasion to fit each new context.

Finally, although the end of the symphony is calculated to elicit cheers from the audience, it will be seen from the composer's programme that it does not represent the time-honoured happy ending. Far from it! That requirement was taken care of in *Lélio*, subtitled 'A Return to Life'. It is worth stating that in Berlioz's original sketch of the programme for this work, the finale was to be 'a vision of a night of revelry'. There was no mention of witches; only when he temporarily turned against Harriet did Berlioz make it a Witches' Sabbath.

Our description of each movement is prefaced with an abbreviated version of Berlioz's own programme note.

Programme notes

FIRST MOVEMENT: LARGO-ALLEGRO AGITATO E APPASSIONATO ASSAI

Reveries – Passions. I take as my subject an artist blest with sensibility and a lively imagination . . . who meets a woman who awakens in him for the first time his heart's desire. He falls desperately in love with her. Curiously, the image of his beloved is linked inseparably with a musical idea representing her graceful and noble character. This idée fixe *haunts him throughout the symphony.*

The slow Largo ('broad') introduction begins with one flute and one clarinet. Other woodwind quickly join in and, together with four horns, play a quiet chord which seems to presage a halt. But the violins, muted, play a wistful, hesitant melody which gradually gains in power. At a minor climax, the cellos contribute a disturbed oscillating phrase, and then pizzicato (plucked) double basses sound a word of warning. Suddenly the violins flare into action, and the rest of the strings, plus horns and bassoons, bring about a more intense climax. This quickly evaporates. Berlioz's reveries are indeed disturbed: as the violin theme, now unmuted, develops under agitated woodwind figures, a strange atmosphere of foreboding sweeps mistily around the music. But gradually these doubts are dispelled. A romantic solo horn melody becomes a yearning horn duet, before woodwind and horn chords and trembling strings swell, then recede and swell again, to give way to the fast section.

Marked *Allegro agitato e appassionato assai* (fast, agitated and extremely passionate), this commences with punctuating chords that prepare the way for the *idée fixe*, a melody no less than 40 bars in length on the flute and first violins in unison. This noble theme begins:

Beloved image
Throughout the symphony, the artist, under the influence of an opium-inspired dream, is haunted by an image of his beloved (the actress Harriet Smithson, with whom Berlioz was infatuated). She becomes inextricably associated with a musical melody, an idée fixe, *which appears to torment the artist in every movement. A comparably intense, idealized image of the beloved appears in D.G. Rosselli's famous* Beata Beatrix (*left), for which the artist's wife, Lizzie Siddal, posed.*

Example 1.

A passionate outburst ensues, during which this vitally important melody is referred to several times on violins alternating with woodwind. At one point the woodwind return briefly to the pulsating figure heard earlier on lower strings.

But a phrase (b) growing out of the first two bars (a) of Example 1 presses the music urgently forward:

Example 2

Because of it brevity, the exposition section is repeated.

At the start of the development section, the lower strings take (a) and repeat it over and over as it gradually rises in pitch, while woodwind cry out passionately. A fierce rhythmic figure for strings releases the woodwind's cry of (b), immediately echoed by strings. There

follows another slowly rising figure of pounding strings under further anguished cries from woodwind, now joined by horns. This reaches an abrupt halt, followed by three complete bars of total silence.

Now, over a disturbed accompaniment, the *idée fixe* returns complete: the recapitulation section has arrived. This covers much the same ground as before, but with radical differences in orchestration and thematic detail, including a brief engagement with fugato (several overlapping statements) of (b). Soon the music becomes quieter, and over a soft drum roll played with sponge-headed sticks (one of several novel instrumental effects introduced in the work by Berlioz), the music meditates on what has gone before. Perhaps Berlioz reflected that the exposition had contained no real second subject, for he made amends now with a soulful and extended oboe melody, very nearly as long as the *idée fixe* itself and clearly its close relation.

However, this melody is soon engulfed by a rising tide of passion, and the *idée fixe* returns, coarsened by its transfer to a cornet (no one had used this instrument in a symphony before). This reaches a tortured double climax amid off-beat timpani and swirling strings. In the coda there is still no escape from the *idée fixe*; finally the artist seems to turn for consolation to the Church.

SECOND MOVEMENT: VALSE – ALLEGRO NON TROPPO

A Ball. The artist attends a ball, but the gaiety and festive tumult fail to distract him. The idée fixe *returns to torture him further.*

The rustle of gowns, the carefree chatter and glitter of the occasion – all are skilfully suggested at the start by Berlioz's adroit scoring, which includes four harps (the first time the harp had been used in a symphony). The waltz begins gracefully and with a feeling of total ease and decorum. The artist takes a partner and joins in, lost for a moment in the magic of the dance.

All at once his heart sinks. There, across the hall, he spies his unattainable beloved. She rises to take the floor with another. How smoothly she moves! How gracefully she dances! Then she is lost in the swirl of dancers and the artist must show to his present partner an attentiveness he does not feel.

At length the waltz builds to its climax, but its rush is arrested for the artist by the persistent thought of his beloved, and the end of the dance is ruined for him. It turns into a frenetic scurry and ends with a jagged chord.

THIRD MOVEMENT: ADAGIO

Scene in the country. Alone in the country on a summer's evening, the artist hears two distant herdsmen calling to each other in a ranz des vaches *(an alphorn melody of the Swiss Alps). Their pastoral duet, the rustle of wind in the trees, and the hope that his beloved might yet be his, all lull him into a reverie, but the* idée fixe *returns in his dreams. His heart palpitates and he experiences dread premonitions.*

The sun sets, there is thunder in the distance, then solitude and silence.

For his two Swiss 'alphorn' players, Berlioz chose a cor anglais and an oboe. The lonely call of the cor anglais is echoed from a distance by the oboe, and the two spend a leisurely few moments serenading each other, gradually developing the cor anglais' opening idea. The artist dozes. A melody emerges on the violins and the flute. His sleep becomes increasingly disturbed as the theme is repeated against solemn horn calls and eventually builds into a noble statement. Under an insistent violin figure, the *idée fixe* is heard again on cellos and violas, while the song of the quail on woodwind and horn re-establishes the pastoral atmosphere.

Suddenly roused from his reveries, the artist quickly drifts off again, only to be disturbed by a powerful figure on the cellos and basses. The *idée fixe* (oboe and flute) alternates with this menacing figure, and there is an intense climax, at the height of which timpani enter, fortissimo, now with wooden-headed sticks, creating a harsh effect. A clarinet melody over pizzicato violins brings relative peace to the scene, but soon angry rhythms on lower strings indicate another moment of frustrated desire, and a return to the *idée*

fixe – and to distant thunder. As the sky darkens, the first herdsman (cor anglais) calls again across the valley, but for answer he receives only the sound of threatening thunder (four timpani, played with sponge-headed sticks). Six times he calls, until he realizes that it is futile to go on, and makes his sad way home.

Berlioz spares us a musical description of the next stage of the story, involving a drug-induced trance and murder, for he has even more frightful horrors in store.

FOURTH MOVEMENT: ALLEGRETTO NON TROPPO

March to the guillotine. In despair the artist attempts to commit suicide by taking an overdose of opium, but the drug, too weak to prove fatal, instead induces fearsome dreams. He dreams that he has killed his beloved, is condemned to death, and is being taken for execution. The idée fixe *floats into his mind, only to be terminated by the fall of the blade.*

This grotesque march was rescued by the composer from an unsuccessful opera, and is yet another of Berlioz's symphonic novelties. Timpani, at first struck with sponge, then with wooden sticks, take an important role, contributing to the night-mare aspect of the gruesome ceremony. Two cornets are called for, and also two ophicleides, which today are usually replaced by tubas. (The ophicleide, named from the greek ophis + kleides = 'keyed serpent', is a bass wind instrument made of brass; because of its extraordinary tone it was once nicknamed the 'chromatic bullock'.)

Drums strike up the march, and are answered by a syncopated horn rhythm. There is a rapid timpani crescendo, and the descending melody of the march appears. On its second appearance there is an irreverent countertheme on the bassoon. Then come the drums again, inexorable, diabolically jubilant. Violins take up the march theme, punctuated by a jagged chord on woodwind and brass, fortissimo. Bassoons enter again with a busy theme over pizzicato strings, but they are swallowed up in the second theme of the march – a typically French melody that has something in common with the *Marseillaise*, so often heard in the revolutionary times that led up to the first performance of the *Symphonie Fantastique* in December 1830.

After the repeat of this entire first section, the French march is continued through the middle section with the lead taken by blaring brass accompanied by ever more elaborate and feverish contributions from the other instruments, especially the drums. With a hideous jeering laugh, woodwind and middle strings reintroduce the drooping march theme, now driven forward by bizarre embellishments. At one point it is turned upside-down. The whole grisly assembly joins in the final terrifying statement, bass drum and cymbals marking the off-beats, brass, woodwind and timpani emphasizing the rhythm, and strings playing the part of the exultant crowd thirsting for blood.

An instant of quiet as the victim mounts the steps, and then the crowd roars its delight. The neck is laid on the slot and the watchers hold their breath. On solo clarinet the *idée fixe* passes through the terrified artist's mind; then his head is severed from his body (fortissimo chord) and falls into the basket (pizzicato strings). Cheers from the satisfied rabble.

Carnival of horrors
The terrifying final movement is vividly evoked by Goya's painting of a Witches' Sabbath. *Here the witches, their forms hideously misshapen and degraded, wait with gleeful anticipation to be presented to their master, the horned Devil.*

all the whole company is whirling in abandoned glee, but with a judder the dance is arrested and a dramatic passage on bassoons, cellos and double basses plunges down to the lower regions.

Baleful funeral bells sound in the distance, demanding sobriety. The dancers twice attempt to restart their cavorting, only to be crushed by savage chords. As the bells continue their mournful tolling, the *Dies Irae* sounds out on two bassoons and two tubas at a deliberate pace. This is repeated at twice the speed by horns and trombones, and then again, faster still and with scant reverence, by high woodwind and pizzicato strings to represent the acclamation of the dancers. They end their version with a hideous shriek. A variation of the *Dies Irae* is given the same three-fold treatment; then again, like some sombre judgement from which there is no appeal, the original version is thrice repeated.

But the dancers' energy will not be denied. Amid stern warnings from the brass, they begin again their convulsive dance. To convey the confused aspect of the scene as various groups prance about, Berlioz constructs a fugue (in which the subject is given out by one section of the orchestra and 'answered' by another) against which the warning brass chords, disorientated by the throng, stab through like forked tongues. The eerie dance runs its length until the warning brass gather for a renewed attack and the dance disintegrates, the woodwind crying out in drooping two-note phrases. Two horns utter an invitation to continue the dance. It is accepted spasmodically by bassoons and lower strings, but they become intertwined with the *Dies Irae* before building in strength and terror over a crescendo bass drum roll.

At last the *Dies Irae*, on oboes, clarinets, bassoons, horns, cornets, trombones and tuba, and the dance on strings, piccolo and flute, combine in an amazing sequence of deliberation and abandon. The tension is increased still further by the violins in an ascending repetition of the disorientated brass chords; then, perhaps to imitate the dry rattle of dancing skeletons, the violins and violas reverse their bows and play a rhythm on their strings with the wood. Over this, woodwind continue the dance, but they are suddenly left alone and quickly tumble into chaos. Orchestral chords round them up, and they squeal their acknowledgement. Disruptive rhythms now take charge; the *Dies Irae*, its three diminishing statements telescoped together, now precipitates a final hectic climax. The soul of the doomed artist is claimed by a triumphant Satan.

FIFTH MOVEMENT: LARGHETTO-ALLEGRO-ALLEGRO ASSAI

Dream of a Witches' Sabbath. The artist at a Witches' Sabbath hears again the idée fixe, *but now transformed into a brazen and trivial dance. She has come to witness his burial! Later comes a monstrous parody of the* Dies Irae *('Day of Wrath', from the Latin* Mass for the Dead*). The dance of the witches is combined with the* Dies Irae.

The composer's drugged nightmare continues beyond even the guillotine. Weird, half-formed shapes meet him, and an echo of the jeering laugh heard in the march is his only welcome to a scene of darkness and demons. An ugly cackle is heard on flutes and oboe. It is perhaps a recollection of the very first notes of the symphony, as if the artist, looking back, regrets having ever set out on his adventure. It is echoed by muted horn over a menacing roll on the bass drum. These creepy effects pass before the artist once

more as if in some inescapable and malevolent circular cortege. Then comes the most chilling figure of all: the *idée fixe* enters on solo clarinet in a gawky and distorted dance accompanied only by two timpani. The beloved herself is present and prepares to lead the witches in a dance:

Example 3

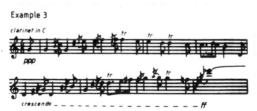

At that last high note the whole gathering of demons and witches screams its approval, then moves in close to prepare for the orgy. Again the *idée fixe* is heard, this time on a clarinet in E flat, an instrument of piercing and unlovely tone, and accompanied now by other harsh woodwind, with four bassoons adding rapid ascending phrases, like bubbles rising in a boiling cauldron. In no time at

SAMUEL PALMER

1805-1881

At his best, Samuel Palmer was an artist of intense
visionary power, creating landscapes in which the
English scene took on a timeless, Biblical quality.
Palmer reached creative maturity in early manhood, but
subsequently found domestic and financial
responsibilities so burdensome that his inspiration
flagged, and only in old age did he recover his youthful
touch. His work was largely forgotten after his death,
but the 20th century has done full justice to his greatness
as a Romantic artist.

feeling 'as if I alone of all mankind were fated to get no bread by the sweat of my brow'. Adding to his worries were his father's flights of fancy and the more serious derelictions of Samuel's ne'er-do-well brother William, who managed to lose £500 – everything he possessed – at billiards; by a grim irony, he was fleeced by one of the Ancients, Welby Sherman, who had turned out a rather shady character and was never seen again!

Samuel Palmer and Hannah Linnell were finally married at the Court House, Marylebone, on 30 September 1837. Given Palmer's known inability to make a pot of tea or a piece of toast, it is tempting to speculate that the death of Mary Ward a few months earlier had helped to make up his mind for him; if so, he must have been sadly disappointed, for Hannah, trained to assist her father, had little or no housekeeping experience. Thanks to generous help from John Linnell, the couple went to Italy for their honeymoon, accompanying George Richmond and his wife. The trip was also intended as a professional venture, and Palmer made sketches as they travelled, hoping to work them up later into saleable pictures. Enchanted by the beauty of Italy,

George Richmond
(left, self-portrait)
Palmer's early friendship with George Richmond was cemented when he lent his fellow-artist £40 with which to elope to Gretna Green. Like most of Palmer's idealistic circle, Richmond ended by compromising with the world, becoming a fashionable portraitist. The difference between the two men was apparent by 1837, when the Palmers and the Richmonds went to Italy together: Richmond made many useful contacts, whereas the unworldly Palmer made none. However, their friendship endured, and Richmond was present at Palmer's deathbed.

he and Hannah visited Milan, Florence, Rome and Naples, then returned to Rome, where most of the wealthy patrons were to be found. But whereas Richmond, now well on his way to becoming a fashionable portraitist, was received everywhere, the eccentric Palmer failed to make useful social contacts, secured only a single watercolour commission, and sold none of the paintings he exhibited.

To make matters worse, he and Hannah wore themselves out dutifully making copies which John Linnell had commissioned from them to help him in his engraving work. Typically, neither Samuel nor Hannah told Linnell outright that the work was much more burdensome than he or they had anticipated. Distance multiplied the mis-

Italian honeymoon
Three days after their wedding the Palmers left for Italy, which Samuel had always longed to visit. They travelled for over a year with the Richmonds, parting with them at Tivoli (above).
Professionally the trip was a disaster, but Palmer loved the light and warmth of Italy, and only returned to London, with reluctance, after two years away.

understandings between Palmer and his father-in-law, and their relations became increasingly strained, especially when, month after month, the Palmers failed to return. Despite their professional failures, Palmer disliked the idea of 'coming back to filthy smoke and black chimney pots', and the 'honeymoon' lasted for two years before he and Hannah left Italy. His hopes of some day seeing the country again were never to be realized.

DISAPPOINTMENTS AND TRAGEDIES

Back at Lisson Grove, the Palmers found that Samuel's brother William had failed to let any of the rooms in the house over the previous two years, and had pawned all the pictures left in his care. Consequently their London married life began impecuniously; but both of them settled down to painting in oils, hoping to establish themselves in this medium, so much more prestigious and profitable than the watercolours and drawings which Samuel had previously concentrated on. But there were still no buyers, and he began to work as an art teacher, taking private pupils. This soon became his chief source of income, and the arrival of children – Thomas More in 1842, Mary in 1843 – ensured that he would have to go on with it, sacrificing time that might have been spent on his own work.

By 1843 Palmer had returned to watercolours as the medium in which he was most likely to achieve some measure of success, although over the following decade he sold only 45 pictures, which brought him about £700 in total. Occasional opportunities did present themselves, as when he was commissioned to execute four illustrations for *Pictures from Italy* by the enormously popular Charles Dickens. But Palmer was fatally incapable

mers had another child, Alfred Herbert, in 1853. But their great consolation was their eldest son, Thomas More Palmer, who developed into an accomplished scholar with a brilliant prospective career at Oxford. Then, early in 1861, his health began to fail, and by July he was dead of a stroke. Overwork may have been a contributory factor, and Palmer always blamed himself for driving the boy too hard. For him, More's death was always 'the catastrophe of my life', and he and Hannah turned in on themselves still more, making a cult of the dead boy.

Again they fled from the place of death, settling at Redhill in Surrey, close to John Linnell. This suited Hannah, whose loyalties were now concentrated on her father rather than her husband, but it was too far from London to allow Palmer to go on teaching. Never a strong character, Palmer seems by this time to have given up the struggle completely, calling Hannah 'the Head of the Household', and himself 'a crushed worm'. The Palmers became largely dependent on subsidies from John Linnell, a situation all the more humiliating in that the two former friends were now on very distant terms.

Palmer's old age makes sad reading. Yet in spite of neglect and disillusion, working in a single cramped room, he miraculously recaptured something of his youthful inspiration, producing a series of masterly watercolours and etchings inspired by the poetry of Virgil and Milton. As so often in Palmer's life, they brought him little in the way of money or reputation. Only a few critics such as John Ruskin had any idea of his achievement, and when Palmer died on 24 May 1881, it was with no certainty that posterity would remember his name.

Respectability

After his return from Italy, Palmer found it easier to support his family by his teaching than by creative work. Hannah became increasingly conventional, and after the death of their daughter Mary the Palmers moved to Kensington (above). By 1851 they were living in a semi-detached house at Douro Place and keeping two servants. Yet Palmer's earnings were still no more than adequate, and sales of his work remained poor.

of following up such openings, and the connection with Dickens lapsed.

After the death of little Mary Palmer in December 1847, her parents no longer wanted to live at Lisson Grove. They moved to Kensington, eventually settling in a small but pretentious semi-detached house. This was done to please Hannah, who had lost her faith in Samuel's ideals and had become increasingly conventional in outlook. Although Palmer was earning a reasonable amount by teaching, the expense of the house and two hired servants kept him short of money. By now he was bitterly conscious of failure, describing himself as 'living somewhere in the environs of London, old and neglected, isolated and laughing at the delusions under which he trimmed the midnight lamp and cherished the romance of the good and beautiful'.

Despite their growing estrangement the Pal-

Late flowering

Neglected by the public, scorned by his wife and devastated by the death of his son More, Palmer nevertheless experienced an extraordinary artistic renewal in his old age. Always fired by poetry, he produced superb etchings and watercolours inspired by Virgil and Milton. His series of Miltonic watercolours, including the lovely Brothers under the Vine *(left), was commissioned by one of Palmer's rare patrons, the solicitor Leonard Rowe Valpy; characteristically, Palmer spent so much time and labour on the commission that he made no money from it.*

A Vision of Eden

Although not always able to call up his full creative powers, Samuel Palmer was a true original. In his hands the English countryside became another Eden, gloriously abundant and untouched by evil.

As a talented youngster Palmer enjoyed some encouraging early successes, but the first evidence that he was capable of developing a distinctive vision of the world is found in his 1824 sketchbook, which contains written notes as well as drawings. There are, significantly, admiring references to the opinions of 'Mr B.' – William Blake, whom Palmer met, and hero-worshipped, in the October of that year. Blake undoubtedly completed John Linnell's work in plucking the young artist from 'the pit of modern art', and his example confirmed Palmer in the belief that a true artist must draw aside 'the fleshly curtain' in order to reveal the deeper, richer meanings that lay behind it.

Understandably, Palmer and the other 'Ancients' who sat at Blake's feet have often been described as his followers. But although the young Palmer did occasionally adapt Blake's compositions to his own needs, the rapidity with which he developed a style of his own indicated that the two men were kindred spirits

rather than master and disciple. Blake's example showed that, despite the predominant artistic literalism, it was still possible to develop and persist in a more visionary style. Furthermore, the common religious elements in the works of Blake and Palmer obscured the fact that they were fundamentally different in feeling and intention. Blake's art was combative and intellectual, each picture carrying a specific 'message' that could in principle be 'read' and understood, however elusive the code might be in practice. And as both poet and artist Blake revelled in 'mental strife'. By contrast, even in 1824 Palmer was creating an arcadian England from which conflict was absent, fashioning images that worked directly on the emotions and could not be reduced to verbal propositions. Where Blake argues and fights, Palmer praises and gives thanks; and so it was hardly an accident that Blake embraced religious and political radicalism, whereas Palmer was a High Church Tory, outraged by signs of unrest among the rustics whom

he always depicted as inhabitants of a timeless earthly paradise.

A BIBLICAL RICHNESS

In retrospect, it seems as though his vision was never more serene and certain than during his years at Shoreham. Palmer's own jottings contradict this impression, often voicing his bafflement and despair, for 'if my aspirations are very high, my depressions are very deep', and he was tormented by the difficulty of reconciling nature and art. But this could hardly be guessed from the works he produced at Shoreham, which are suffused with a kind of Biblical richness and bathed in the blessed light of the sun or moon.

Palmer gave Biblical titles to some of his Shoreham drawings and paintings, notably *The Repose of the Holy Family* and *Ruth Returned from Gleaning*. But in most instances neither the subjects nor the titles suggest that the scenes represented are of any special significance; and in fact the only justification for using terms such as 'Biblical' or 'visionary' to describe them is that their magically suggestive power somehow puts such notions into the spectator's mind.

Early Morning (1825)
In this ink and sepia drawing, the entire scene appears to thrust out towards the spectator, giving it a magical, almost sinister quality.

Moonlight
In Shepherds under a Full Moon *(c.1830, above), a pastoral night scene is bathed in the light of a huge moon.*

Twilight
Late Twilight *(above, left) captures a strange end-of-the-day atmosphere, heightened by the inclusion of a favourite Palmer device, a horned moon.*

Sunlight
The blaze of sunlight behind the Young Man Yoking an Ox *(c.1832, left) somehow imbues the scene with a timeless Biblical quality.*

However, it is possible to identify a few of the devices used (consciously or otherwise) by Palmer, although they hardly account for the full impact of the works. Often the entire scene is rendered as if it existed in the foreground of the picture, its close-up quality and density of detail making it seem to thrust out towards the viewer like a dream landscape; this is particularly apparent in a group of wonderful ink and sepia drawings, including *A Rustic Scene* and *Early Morning*, made by

Palmer in 1825. A sense of strangeness and mystery also arises from the way in which the landscape is often bathed in light, especially from a huge sun or moon, as in *A Young Man Yoking an Ox* and *Shepherds under a Full Moon*. Palmer had a strong feeling for both the night and the often out-of-the-ordinary atmosphere at the end of a day, conveyed for example in *Late Twilight*, which also features another favoured element, a horned moon. Something of what the moon meant to him can

be gathered from his statement that it would 'not only thrill the optic nerve, but shed a mild, a grateful, an unearthly lustre into the inmost spirits, and seem the interchanging twilight of that peaceful country where there is no sorrow and no night'.

Browsing and slumbering sheep and cattle, burgeoning plant life, fat sheaves of corn, timid rabbits and birds – the conventional properties of pastoral idylls all contribute to the creation of a sense of timelessness. That his effects were quite consciously pursued is apparent even before the Shoreham period. In his 1824 sketchbook he noted that 'considering Dulwich as the gate into the world of vision, one must try behind the hills to bring up a mystic glimmer like that which lights our dreams. And those same hills . . . should give us promise that the country beyond them is Paradise'. This might easily be a direct description of a picture such as *A Young Man Yoking an Ox*. Significantly, the inspiration given by Shoreham was rarely translated into a representation of a single identifiable spot: at this point in his life, Palmer's scenes are aspects of a universal Eden.

His relative lack of formal training may have been positively beneficial in keeping Palmer free from academic inhibitions. As a result he was often inventive in the technical means he used to express his vision, bringing together normally separate elements in the same work – a 'mixed media' procedure usually regarded as a distinctively 20th century audacity. *Early Morning* belongs to a group of drawings which are highly innovative, being executed with a pen and dark brown ink and a brush in sepia mixed with gum, after which the drawing was varnished. Palmer

Pastoral
Palmer often worked in the pastoral convention, exploiting the rich web of associations around shepherds and their flocks. In Pastoral with a Horse-Chestnut Tree *(1832, left) the tree is an important protective presence, adding to the sense of harmony and contentment.*

Etching
The Lonely Tower *(right, 1879) is Palmer's masterpiece in a medium that he began to employ in his mid-forties – etching, a form of printmaking that lent itself to finely detailed work and night scenes. This example was inspired by Milton's poem* Il Penseroso, *which describes a 'lamp at midnight hour . . . seen in some high lonely tower'.*

may have served as a substitute for vision, but an even more important consideration may have been that 'photographic' art was saleable whereas intimations of paradise were not. Palmer had once written to his friend George Richmond: 'By God's help I will not sell away His gift of art for money; no, nor for fame neither, which is far better.' But financial and personal pressures, including the prospect of marriage, helped to change his attitude, and for three decades he would strive – with painful lack of success – to achieve recognition by conventional means.

Palmer's two-year stay in Italy accentuated this tendency. Like so many Northerners he was deeply impressed by the art and landscape of the Mediterranean, and in many of his subsequent works he attempted to emulate the brilliant colours of the South. Working against the grain of his temperament and in material and psychological difficulties, his output during the long middle years of his life was, at best, uneven.

CREATIVE OLD AGE

It would be hard to find a parallel to Palmer's career, in which the long-forgotten achievements of youth find an echo in a creative recovery in old age. Paradoxically this may have become possible because Palmer had finally given up all his worldly hopes: his son was dead, he could no longer teach, and he was a barely tolerated outsider in his own home. He was driven back on himself and, in a sense, was free again. By a well-timed stroke of fortune, early in his Redhill 'exile' he received a commission from the solicitor John Rowe Valpy for a series of watercolours based on Milton's poetry. This was not financially important, since Palmer was as hopelessly impractical as ever, investing far too much time and effort in the project; but it helped to impel him into a new phase, and artistically the result was completely justified.

Later still, Palmer used his Milton watercolours as the inspiration for his two masterpieces in the very different medium of etching, which he had taken up in the 1850s. Starkly black and white, and lending itself to the elaboration of delicate detail, etching provided a superb vehicle for night and twilight visions. *The Bellman* and *The Lonely Tower* derive from a single passage in Milton's *Il Penseroso*, referring to 'the Bellman's drowsy charm' and the 'lamp at midnight hour . . . seen in some high lonely tower'. But the setting, as Palmer himself stated, harked back to his earliest glimpse of paradise. It was the village of Shoreham.

painted in oils and also experimented with combinations of oils, tempera and watercolours; but it is as a watercolourist that he is best remembered. However, in major works such as the lovely *Pastoral with a Horse-Chestnut Tree*, he habitually employed watercolours in conjunction with a thickened form of the colours (body colours), achieving a sense of solidity rather than the airy, sketchy quality normally characteristic of the medium.

At some time during the early 1830s the vision began to fade. Material considera-tions may have been involved, but the fact that Palmer felt the need to make working expeditions further afield suggests that Shoreham was losing its power to stimulate him. However, his West Country and Welsh scenes, although still of high quality, notably lacked the intensity of his earlier works.

They were also much more concerned with visual and topographical accuracy, reproducing what the eye – rather than 'the mind's eye' of the visionary – could see. In Palmer's case, fidelity to nature

FELIX MENDELSSOHN

1809-1847

A child prodigy, remarkable for his depth and sensitivity as well as his precocity, Mendelssohn flowered into one of the most celebrated – and best-loved – composers of his time.

Felix Mendelssohn was nothing like the popular idea of a Romantic composer. He did not write by the guttering flame of a candle in an unheated garret, or die, unrecognized, in poverty. He was born into a wealthy and cultured family who did all they could to encourage his prodigious musical talents. By the age of nine he was an acclaimed performer; at 16 he had proved his genius as a composer. Artist, poet, traveller and even mountaineer, he was a man of great sensitivity and charm who numbered among his friends the great, the famous, and the literary and musical giants of his day.

As a boy Mendelssohn won the heart of Goethe; in his prime he captivated Queen Victoria. When he died – at only 37 – two nations went into mourning, for the composer and for the man. Although there can be little doubt that Mendelssohn had much music still to give, he had already won a secure place, both as a composer and as an enormously influential promoter of 'music for the people'.

A CULTURED BACKGROUND

The influence of Mendelssohn's family on his life and works starts with his grandfather, Moses Mendelssohn. Born in Dessau, into poverty and under the severe restrictions imposed on Jews by 18th-century Prussia, Moses took his destiny into his own hands. At the age of 14 he walked 80 miles to Berlin, where he taught himself languages, mathematics and philosophy. He became one of the great thinkers and teachers of the Enlightenment period, and his writings were translated into 30 languages. He was a champion of religious tolerance and fought in particular for Jewish emancipation. Both his philosophical ideals and his talent for making money were passed on to his son Abraham, who became a banker and married the musical and highly educated Lea Salomon.

The young couple settled in Hamburg, where their eldest child, Mendelssohn's beloved sister, Fanny, was born in 1805. Lea noted with uncanny foresight that the baby had 'Bach fugue fingers' – and indeed, had the convention of the time allowed, there is little doubt that Fanny would have become a composer of distinction. As it was, she contented herself with writing songs and performing recitals of other people's music. The composer of the family was to be Felix, born in February 1809. Two more children, Rebekka and Paul, followed in due course.

Two years after the birth of Felix, the family left Hamburg. Abraham, like many other bankers and merchants in the city, had managed to evade Napoleon's trade restrictions and had become very

Mendelssohn at 20, *newly arrived in London. Charming, gracious and debonair, he immediately won the hearts of the English. They were not only moved by the warmth and sentiment of his music, but also found him to be the perfect gentleman.*

Grandfather Moses
The happy, comfortable and enlightened environment in which the young Mendelssohn grew up was made possible by the courage and determination of his grandfather, Moses (right). As a boy, Moses, a poor hunchbacked Jew, had walked the 80 miles to Berlin in the hope of making a better life for himself. There, against a background of prejudice, he prospered, making a name for himself as a philosopher and champion of Jewish emancipation.

Mendelssohn at 12
(below), a brilliant child who captivated everyone.

rich indeed. Like them, he was now faced with a more direct threat from occupying French troops, and consequently the Mendelssohns fled to Berlin.

In Berlin, Abraham made a significant contribution to the defence of Prussia by equipping volunteer soldiers and financing a military hospital. After the victory over Napoleon he was rewarded with a position on Berlin's Municipal Council and an elevated status not usually accorded to a Jew. To cement their new standing, the family converted to Christianity and added the name Bartholdy, already adopted by Abraham's brother, to their own.

MUSICAL BEGINNINGS

In this propitious setting the young boy's genius took root and flourished. He was given a rounded education under Berlin's most prestigious teachers. His principal music tutor was Carl Zelter, a fine teacher, although his coarse behaviour and unconventional dress were more suggestive of his previous occupation as a stonemason than his post as the Director of Berlin's Singakademie.

Zelter's pupil went from strength to strength. At nine he was performing, as a pianist or conductor, before an admiring circle of family and friends, including some of Germany's foremost writers, poets and philosophers; Heine, Hegel, Humboldt and Jakob Grimm were among those who heard him play. At ten Felix began to compose; a young friend witnessed the scene:

I found him on a footstool, before a small table, writing with such earnestness. On my asking what he was about, he replied, gravely, 'I am finishing my new Quartet for piano and stringed instruments.' . . . looking over his shoulder [I] saw as beautiful a score as if it had been written by the most skilled copyist. It was his first Quartet in C minor. Then, forgetting quartets, . . . down we went into the garden, he clearing high hedges with a leap, running, singing and climbing trees like a squirrel.

The boy's energy amazed all who knew him. He studied; he composed without ceasing; at the age of 12 he even started his own newspaper. His mother, with her usual insight, wrote that 'his impulsiveness sometimes makes him work harder than he ought to at his age'. Mendelssohn would always work harder than he ought to, and one day it would kill him.

At the age of 12 Zelter's protégé so impressed him that he proposed to introduce him to Goethe, Germany's foremost poet and sage. When Goethe agreed to see him, his family were thrown into a state of excitement, but Felix was not overawed and reported in a letter home:

He was in the garden and just coming round a hedge. He is very friendly, but I don't think any of the pictures are like him. One would never take him for 73 but 50.

And later he told of their daily routine:

I play here much more than I do at home: rarely less than four hours, sometimes six or even eight. Goethe sits down beside me and when I have finished . . . I ask for a kiss or take one. You cannot imagine how good and kind he is to me.

It was the beginning of a friendship that was to last until Goethe's death and spanned five significant visits. The relationship deepened Mendelssohn's love for good literature, and assured its importance in his music. For his part, Goethe was not only entertained and amused by his young companion, but prompted to a greater appreciation of music, although he never managed to share Mendelssohn's enthusiasm for Beethoven.

After the visit to Goethe, the family, with its entourage of tutors, embarked on a tour of Switzerland. Felix absorbed each new impression eagerly; once awakened, his passion for travelling never left him. As on later journeys, he sketched or painted views whose beauty moved him, and wrote copious letters and poems, often illustrating them with amusing cartoons. He also commented on the native taste in music – yodelling:

This kind of singing sounds harsh and unpleasant when it is heard nearby, or in a room . . . in the valleys, mountains and woods, when you hear it mingling with the answering echoes, it sounds beautiful.

This is early evidence of the critical awareness of the music of others that made him determined to bring good music to the people – to teach musicians to play and the public to listen which was to be one of his major achievements.

Carl Zelter
(left) was an inspired choice as Mendelssohn's music teacher. Something of a rough diamond, he was renowned for his lack of tact, and could be relied upon to lower the tone of a conversation. Yet despite his boorishness Zelter was a man of utter integrity and, in Goethe's words, one of 'subtle and diamantine genius'.

The child prodigy
Mendelssohn plays before the illustrious Goethe at one of the regular Sunday morning musical parties organized by his family (below). The young boy was to strike up a close friendship with the 73-year-old poet and novelist who was then struggling to complete part II of Faust.

The composer-artist
*In addition to his many
talents – composer, poet and
even mountaineer –
Mendelssohn was also an
artist of some ability.
Inspired by the serenity of
the landscape, he painted
this charming view of
Lucerne (above, right) while
on a trip to Switzerland.*

A 'British' friend
*Mendelssohn was lured to
Britain by the enthusiastic
reports of his friend Karl
Klingemann (above), who
was Secretary to the
Hanoverian Legation in
London. Klingemann also
accompanied him on his
memorable trip to Scotland,
where he saw Fingal's Cave
and conceived the* Hebrides
Overture.

Passion renewed
*One of Mendelssohn's
greatest feats was his
rediscovery and revival of
Bach's* St Matthew
Passion *(right). Prior to
this Bach had been regarded
by the public as 'a powdered
wig stuffed with learning'.
Now Mendelssohn created a
whole new wave of interest
in the Baroque composer.
'To think', he exclaimed,
'that . . . a Jew should give
back to the people the
greatest Christian music in
the world.'*

GERMANY'S NEW COMPOSER

Meanwhile, the budding composer delighted his teacher with a one-act opera, *The Uncle from Boston*. After its performance Zelter addressed the audience and congratulated the 14-year-old: 'My dear boy, from this day you are no longer an apprentice, but a full member of the brotherhood of musicians. I hereby proclaim you independent in the name of Mozart, Haydn and old father Bach.'

But Abraham still needed to be convinced that music was the right career for his son. He took him to Paris to see the composer Cherubini, who was Director of the Paris Conservatoire. The verdict was decisive: 'Your boy is talented, he will do well. He has already done well.' Barely a year later, Cherubini was proved right. At the age of 16 Mendelssohn completed his String Octet, op.20, which was partly inspired by lines from Goethe's *Faust*. It is recognized as his first fully mature work, and some critics claim that it is an unparalleled achievement for a 16-year-old; not even Mozart or Schubert produced music of such brilliance so young. Germany had a new composer.

Mendelssohn's next work was another master-piece, his overture to *A Midsummer Night's Dream*. Again the inspiration came from literature, and it has been said that no other music has so successfully captured the essence of Shakespeare. Mendelssohn's friend, the pianist Ignaz Moscheles, declared when he heard it that 'this great and still youthful genius has once again made gigantic steps forward'. Mendelssohn was progressing in other fields too. Having translated Terence's Latin comedy *Andria*, he was awarded a place at the University of Berlin, where he studied aesthetics under the philosopher Hegel.

Mendelssohn next turned his attention to the work of Johann Sebastian Bach, for many years neglected by the listening public. He spent several years working on the score of the *St Matthew Passion*, and when the work was released it caused a considerable stir in the music world. Tickets for the first performance in Berlin were sold out within minutes, and some members of the audience were so moved by the music that they wept openly.

SUCCESS IN BRITAIN

Armed with his now considerable reputation, the 20-year-old set out to conquer more distant lands. Having already made the acquaintance of Sir George Smart, the founder of the Philharmonic Society, Mendelssohn went to stay in London in the hope of being invited to play there. He was introduced to the pleasures of London life by Moscheles and another friend, Klingemann, both of whom had settled there.

After the narrow and stuffy atmosphere of Berlin,

the gaiety and excitement of London turned his head and won his heart: it was the beginning of a lifelong love affair with England. After three days Mendelssohn wrote home: 'I hardly remember the chief events. Things toss and whirl about me as if I were in a vortex, and I'm whirled along with them. Not in the last six months in Berlin have I seen so many contrasts and such variety as in these three days.' He spent his time driving in Hyde Park, delighting in operas, concerts and balls and the charming young ladies he met there, and marvelling at the thickness of the fog and the even greater density of English plum pudding.

When he made his début, it was to deafening applause and the highest critical acclaim. One reviewer noted 'scarcely had he touched the keyboard than something that can only be described as similar to a pleasurable electric shock passed through his hearers and held them spellbound'. He set the seal on his success and established himself as the darling of the British public with a charity concert for the people of Silesia, who had been made homeless by floods. He was fêted everywhere as a musician of transcendent talent and, no less important to the English, a perfect gentleman.

In July, Mendelssohn and Klingemann travelled to Scotland. The young composer was vividly impressed with the romantic scenery of the Highlands: 'When God himself takes to landscape painting, it turns out strangely beautiful . . . everything looks so stern and robust, half-enveloped in mist or smoke or fog . . .' It inspired him to write his 'Scottish Symphony', and also to take out his drawing pad. During a journey to Fingal's cave, already immortalized a decade earlier by Keats, the first bars of the *Hebrides* Overture occurred to him.

Mendelssohn was less impressed with British folk music. He found the sound of bagpipes offensive to his ear, and when he and his friend moved on to Wales he wrote: 'Dear me, a harper sits in the hall of every reputed inn, playing incessantly so-called national melodies; that is to say most infamous, vulgar, out-of-tune trash, with a hurdy-gurdy going on at the same time.'

BROTHERLY LOVE

By the end of August, Mendelssohn was ready to return home. His sister Fanny was to be married, and he wanted to be at the wedding. But he was prevented from going by a carriage accident that injured his knee. From his sickbed he wrote her a desperate letter:

This then is the last letter you'll receive before your marriage. For the last time I address you as Fräulein Fanny Mendelssohn-Bartholdy . . . There's much I would like to say to you, but I'm not really able . . . I feel as if I had lost the reins with which formerly I was able to guide my life. When I think about everything which is now going to change, and take a different shape, everything which I have long taken for granted, then my thoughts become unclear and half wild.

The love between brother and sister had always been passionately strong. Felix inevitably showed his compositions to Fanny before anyone else, and relied on her advice. In his letters he had addressed her ardently. She made him feel 'quite giddy'. He called her his 'angel', his 'darling little sister' and declared, 'My sweet, I love you terribly.' On her side, Fanny

was no less vehemently attached to her brother. When he left Berlin she wrote 'all will be mute and desolate'.

Felix constantly appears in her diary – far more entries are devoted to him than to her fiancé, Wilhelm Hensel. Of him she wrote 'a bridegroom is no more than a man'. Mendelssohn's other sister, Rebekka, reported that Fanny was wont to fall asleep in Hensel's company – she was bored because Felix was not there. On the day of her wedding she wrote to Felix:

London society
Apart from his musical activities in London, Mendelssohn used his many letters of introduction to plunge into high society. Sought after by fashionable hostesses to attend parties and balls (above), he was deeply impressed by the city's splendid houses.

Loving sister
Throughout his life, Mendelssohn shared a deep love and understanding with his sister Fanny (left); there is no doubt that she was the most important single influence on his life. Their correspondence testifies to the intimacy and, sometimes, intensity of their relationship. When Fanny died – she was suddenly felled by a paralytic stroke while playing the piano – Felix was heartbroken. He collapsed on hearing the news of her death, and never fully recovered.

*I have your portrait before me, and ever repeating
your dear name and thinking of you as if you stood
at my side, I weep! Every morning and every moment
of my life I'll love you from the bottom of my heart,
and I'm sure that in doing so I shan't wrong Hensel.*

They must have been well aware that the intensity of their love was not entirely healthy, and that Fanny's marriage was for the best. By the time Mendelssohn returned to Berlin for his parents' silver wedding anniversary – having written an operetta for the occasion – she was Frau Hensel.

In 1830, at the age of just 21, Mendelssohn was offered the chair of music at Berlin University, but he refused. He had just begun to compose his 'Reformation' Symphony, and was totally absorbed by it; he wanted to travel; perhaps he also felt it was a mistake to stay too long in the neighbourhood of Fanny and her new husband. His travels were to take him, via a last visit to Goethe, to Austria, Italy, Switzerland and France. He travelled light, taking with him 'three shirts and Goethe's poems'. He met Chopin, Liszt, Berlioz, Paganini, Meyerbeer, Dorothea von Ertmann, who had been a close friend of Beethoven, and the dramatist Karl Immermann, with whom he intended to collaborate on an opera. His trip to Italy inspired the wonderful 'Italian' Symphony, his Symphony no.4.

LATER ACHIEVEMENTS

In the spring of 1832, deeply saddened by news of the deaths of Goethe and Zelter, Mendelssohn returned to England. Here his performances drew capacity crowds, but he was called back home by his father, who wanted him to apply for Zelter's post as Director of the Singakademie. In the event he was not disappointed when Zelter's deputy got the job – he had further engagements in London and had been

The blue city
Mendelssohn was overjoyed when he was at last able to visit Italy, and painted this pleasing little watercolour of Florence 'at a distance in the valley, the blue city'. But being fleeced by Florence's 'disgusting crooks' rather disillusioned him.

invited to conduct the 1833 Music Festival in Düsseldorf. Here he instituted an important revival of Handel's works besides conducting an impressive series of operas. But neither the audience nor the orchestra lived up to his expectations; moreover administrative difficulties left him no time for composing. Frustrated beyond endurance, he tore the score of Beethoven's *Egmont* in two during a rehearsal, and when, in the summer of 1834, he received an invitation to take over Leipzig's Gewandhaus Orchestra, he accepted with alacrity and relief.

Here, in the cultural capital of Germany, Mendelssohn had a free hand to organize the city's music and plenty of time in which to compose. During his ten-year stay in Leipzig he achieved a great deal. He built a first-rate orchestra out of what began as an undistinguished collection of musicians: no doubt they were as encouraged by the enthusiasm of their conductor as by the handsome salary increase he won for them. As usual his repertoire was wide and varied, and he introduced the public to works that had hitherto been ignored, including Beethoven's Fourth, and later his Ninth. He also premièred Schubert's last symphony; Schumann had unearthed the manuscript in Vienna and saved it from almost certain destruction. Another achievement was to invite the leading soloists of the day to perform at the Gewandhaus. All this contributed to the tremendous success of his concert seasons, bringing about an enormously increased public enthusiasm for music.

SHORT-LIVED HAPPINESS

In 1837 Mendelssohn crowned his happiness by falling in love and marrying. His bride was a captivating girl named Cécile Jeanrenaud. It was eight months before Cécile and Fanny met, and Mendelssohn must have been greatly relieved when Fanny found his wife 'a fresh breeze, so bright and natural'. The marriage was a happy one, and there were five children.

In 1840 the reactionary King of Prussia died, and his successor persuaded Mendelssohn to take up the

The composer's wife
In March 1837 Mendelssohn married Cécile (above), who bore him five children. The marriage was a very happy one – Cécile was 'a fresh breeze, so bright and natural'.

Obituary notice
(above) The portrait and part of the obituary of Mendelssohn which appeared in the Illustrated London News *on 13 November 1847, nine days after the composer's death. Its references to 'a life graced by every private virtue, and illustrated by talents that class him among the greatest of his era' testify to the immense respect and affection felt for Mendelssohn in Britain.*

post of musical director at a new Academy of the Arts in Berlin. The composer left Leipzig with a heavy heart, and his forebodings proved justified. In Berlin he met with bureaucratic obstacles and gradually withdrew from his duties. His next achievement was to found the Leipzig Conservatory, which he built into Germany's foremost academy of music. In the meantime he continued his visits to England, which he always regarded as his second home, and became a firm favourite with Queen Victoria and Prince Albert, who admired his urbanity as well as his compositions. In a typical burst of energy he composed his oratorio *Elijah* in a matter of months for the Birmingham Music Festival of 1846. *The Times* noted its extraordinary reception: 'The last note of *Elijah* was drowned in a long-continuous volley of plaudits, vociferous and deafening . . . Never was there a more complete triumph – never a more thorough and speedy recognition of a great work of art.'

All this tireless activity was taking its toll. Public acclaim for Mendelssohn had never been more tumultuous, but he was driving himself too hard. In May 1847, as he was making his way home from his tenth visit to England, broken and exhausted, he was shattered to learn of the death of his beloved sister, Fanny. He never recovered from the blow. In October he had a slight stroke, and on 4 November he died. He was buried next to his sister. Amidst the public mourning, Cécile was alone. A few days after her husband's death she wrote, with an incoherence that conveys a sharp sense of her grief:

There are corners of my mother-in-law's garden where I must martyr myself to be able to grasp what has happened. Here are the same trees, bower, branches, there is the ruined fountain, and they all still exist. Felix's grave bears a marble cross with his name. Behind it I have planted a lilac and a rosebush. I wanted to keep the mound free and green, but it's always heaped with flowers and wreaths . . . I placed my tributes at his feet.

Six years later Cécile died, utterly inconsolable, at the age of 36.

The Gewandhaus
In the last decade of his life, Mendelssohn focused his activities on the Leipzig Gewandhaus (below). Here, with typical energy and enthusiasm, he built up a distinguished orchestra which became a model for all Europe. Under his leadership they performed many major works that had previously been ignored – including Schubert's last symphony – and were graced with some of the finest soloists of the age. Through such selfless work Mendelssohn created a lasting legacy, enhancing the public's appreciation of music.

Mendelssohn's overtures

In Mendelssohn's hands the overture became high art. Scenes of breezy summer gaiety, the dignity of a Spanish court and heaving stormy seas – all were brilliantly evoked by his masterful music.

The overture in Mendelssohn's hands was essentially what later composers were to call a symphonic, or tone, poem. It was an impressionistic painting in music, usually portraying a natural scene or catching the mood of a literary work. Although Mendelssohn was not the first composer to treat the overture as a self-contained work of this kind, he was an early pioneer in this direction, blazing a trail for such later composers as Brahms, Richard Strauss and Dvořák, as well as giving a considerable impetus to the Romantic movement in general.

An important element in musical Romanticism was the composer's growing awareness of other media. In seeking 'pictorial' inspiration for music, they took account of the parallel efforts of artists and writers. It is not surprising that such major figures as Goethe and Shakespeare became so influential upon the musical Romantic, for they provided him with a repertory of vivid dramatic stories and lyrical inspiration.

Mendelssohn had no more opportunity than the rest of the world to hear most of Schubert's music, which was not fully rediscovered until the second half of the 19th century. But the comparatively few Schubert songs that became known in Mendelssohn's lifetime, together with the flourishing production of Lieder (songs) by lesser musicians must have had a strong influence on a composer who was himself a considerable song-writer.

LITERARY AND MUSICAL INFLUENCES

To Mendelssohn's table therefore came a feast of Shakespeare in the fashionable and accomplished translations by August Schlegel. (The composer was in fact connected to the great translator through his blue-stocking aunt, who married August Schlegel's brother.) As for Goethe, the great German literary genius of the age, Mendelssohn enjoyed a relationship of exceptional mutal approbation with him. He found Goethe 'very kind' and helpful, while Goethe was lavish in his praise of some of Mendelssohn's settings of his songs: a rare accolade, since the great man was not much given to praising musicians.

But probably the greatest practical influence on Mendelssohn was the operatic composer Carl Maria von Weber, who visited Berlin in 1821. Mendelssohn went with his parents to the first performance of *Der Freischütz* and met the composer afterwards. Weber's Romantic innovations filled him with great enthusiasm and led him to write two or three immature

Carl Maria von Weber
The title page from Weber's Der Freischütz, *which strongly influenced Mendelssohn.*

operettas. But deeper than this went the effect of Weber's tight but colourful orchestration, which the young Mendelssohn used as his model. He found particular inspiration in Weber's scherzos (lively movements; literally 'jokes'). Mendelssohn was Weber's true heir, and by a remarkable coincidence he wrote his *Midsummer Night's Dream* overture just two months after Weber's death, using in it a phrase that Weber had used in *Oberon*, which was not heard publicly in Germany until a month or two later. Although Mendelssohn was said to have 'put the fairies to music', full credit must be given to Weber for having pioneered the path to fairyland.

Programme notes

THE HEBRIDES (FINGAL'S CAVE), op. 26

In April 1829 Mendelssohn set off on a visit to London, where his music was enthusiastically received and where he made many new contacts. His close friend Karl Klingemann, a poet, had gone to England earlier and was by now living in Edinburgh, to which he took Mendelssohn in July.

Mendelssohn was greatly impressed by the Scottish scenery. The friends travelled around, Mendelssohn sketching, Klingemann writing accompanying poems, and Mendelssohn conceived the ideas for a 'Scottish' symphony. They visited Sir Walter Scott at Abbotsford, suffered the extremes of Scottish weather and went to the Inner Hebrides. Their destination was a strange natural phenomenon known as Fingal's Cave on the island of Staffa, a weird formation of pillar-like rocks that had been discovered in 1782 and named after a hero of Gaelic mythology. The friends endured a dreadful sea trip from Oban to get there, but it was worth it. Klingemann described the cave as being 'like the inside of an immense organ, black and resonant, utterly without purpose, completely isolated.'

Mendelssohn wrote to tell his family about the visit and enclosed a sketch of the opening bars of the 'Hebrides' overture – 'In order to make you understand how extraordinarily the Hebrides affected me, I send you the following, which came into my head there.' In fact, he had written the insistent little two-bar motive on the journey in anticipation of what he was to see. It took him until December the following year to complete the overture, but he felt dissatisfied with his first version. Following a performance in London in 1831, he thoroughly revised the score. It was not until November 1833, after three such revisions, that he was completely satisfied with the work.

The overture, scored for a normal classical orchestra without trombones, is fairly conventional in form but rich in imagination, a totally dramatic work that must have seemed very daring in its day and later became an inescapable model for any future depictions of moving water. The first motive is a perfect evocation of wave movement, and is brought in right at the beginning by cellos, clarinets and bassoons. Its restless surge is to dominate

Example 1

Fingal's Cave
In spite of his seasickness Mendelssohn was so deeply impressed when he saw the black basalt cavern called Fingal's Cave (left), that he lost no time in elaborating the opening theme of what was to become The Hebrides Overture. *Ten years earlier the poet Keats had been similarly stirred: '. . . the sea' he wrote, 'is continually dashing there . . . For solemnity and grandeur it far surpasses the finest cathedrals.'*

throughout. This is allowed to work on our imaginations, while a skilful touch in the scoring appears in the occasional irregularly placed drum-roll as an extra-strong wave breaks on the rocks. The equally distinctive second subject in D major, with its upward movement, has more of the sea winds about it, and it is presented by cellos, clarinets and bassoons. The waves increase as a third theme, a variation on the original motive, comes in fortissimo (very loudly), still in D, leading to a fanfare for horns and trumpets.

An orchestral storm develops, beginning quietly with the original wave theme played by the lower strings against shimmering violins. There are frequent interruptions by woodwind and brass, and the imagination is free to hear the cries of seabirds, even the bark of a seal. But in fact there are no direct imitations of natural sounds: the effect is achieved simply by ceaseless movement, surges of sound, loud and then quiet, and quick changes of emphasis. The whole is restless and continually moving, the relentless pounding of the waves overlaid with all the smaller effects of sudden wisps of spray, gusts of wind and bird-sounds. The music grows in intensity as the seas get stormier, and there, with us right to the end, is that evocative theme suddenly dying away.

The work was an instant success, even before Mendelssohn made his final amendments. Wagner described the composer as 'a first-class landscape painter'; and Brahms, as ever, wished that he could write something as good. It particularly won the hearts of the British, who were delighted that such great music had been inspired by their island landscape. One writer remarked that 'It brought the perils of the sea straight into the concert hall.'

RUY BLAS, op. 95
When Mendelssohn was asked to write some music, including an overture, for a charity performance of Victor Hugo's tragedy *Ruy Blas*, staged in Leipzig in 1839, he was willing to oblige. He actually disliked the play, a violent and deeply pessimistic piece that found no real response in his nature. 'I intend to call it', he jokingly told his mother, 'not the overture to *Ruy Blas*, but to the Theatrical Pension Fund.'

In *Ruy Blas* Hugo painted a romanticized picture of life and intrigues at the court of Charles II of Spain, taking con-

siderable liberties with historical fact. 'The philosophical motive', Hugo explained, 'is a people aspiring to a higher state; its drama is the love of a servant for a queen.'

Ignoring all this, Mendelssohn wrote a shapely piece of music that belied his opinion of the play as 'detestable and more utterly beneath contempt than you could believe'. Asked for a romance and an overture by the Committee of the Leipzig Theatrical Pension Fund, he found at first only the will to write a song, and asked to be excused from attempting the overture. The Committee knew their man, however, and wrote thanking him for his excellent romance while at the same time expressing the hope that he might be able to write an overture if given longer notice for next year's performance. Proud of his creative facility, Mendelssohn responded by writing the overture in two days in between rehearsals.

By the time he came to write the *Ruy Blas* music the 'elfin' streak that his father urged him to abandon in favour of 'graver things' had been lost. (It was only to return in the pure serenity of the Violin Concerto of 1844.) Mendelssohn was now writing in a vein that seems closer to Berlioz and Liszt, composers he did not particularly admire. His lack of true response to Victor Hugo's work is to be found in the divergence of the overture from the path that the drama took, ending as it does on a fairly optimistic chord of C major, whereas the end of the play is pure tragedy. The rest of the piece, melodramatic and full of foreboding in C minor, is thickly orchestrated with two flutes, two oboes, two clarinets, two bassoons, four horns, two trumpets and three trombones to help it towards a grand Berlioz-like sound.

There is no record of Mendelssohn

Fairyland
William Blake's Oberon, Titania and Puck with Fairies Dancing *(above) is a pictorial equivalent to Mendelssohn's musical* Midsummer Night's Dream.

himself explaining the connection between his music and the drama, and it is generally assumed that there is none, though one commentator, Sir George Macfarren, tied themes to persons with some conviction. What seems more likely is that Mendelssohn, writing in a state of 'amusing excitement', was far more concerned with the music than with its programme meaning. The overture starts with four slow and dignified bars that simply hint at the first theme, with a modified repeat. The principal theme is stated by the first violins and flutes with the other strings accompanying. This we may take to be a description of the nature of *Ruy Blas*. The slow opening is repeated and now hints at the second theme, which is then stated by clarinet, bassoon and cellos, and perhaps represents the queen. This is developed before a third theme, suggesting the raptures of love, appears. The various themes are repeated and woven together before a lively coda ends the overture.

THE TALE OF THE FAIR MELUSINA, op. 32
This overture was written in 1833, by which time Mendelssohn had become a famous composer and travelling conductor. He had gone to Düsseldorf to snatch a respite from his many activities and spend some time composing without any disturbance. He was inspired to write this overture after hearing a dull score for a libretto based on the legend of Melusina.

According to this, Melusina is turned

into a mermaid for one day of each week as a punishment for burying her father inside a mountain, after he had mistreated her mother. Melusina's husband, Lusignan, whom she loves deeply, has promised that he will never investigate the mysterious weekly disappearance of his wife but, overcome by curiosity, he discovers her just on the point of turning into a mermaid. As a result she is doomed to stay in this form for ever.

As usual, Mendelssohn did not try to tell his story literally but rather to catch its mood. It serves as a warning to us not to read too much detail into other works (such as the 'Hebrides' overture) when we learn that Mendelssohn was upset by Robert Schumann's vivid interpretation of the overture. Schumann let his imagination run riot, writing of 'those fables of the life deep down beneath the watery abyss, full of darting fish with golden scales, of pearls in open shells, of buried treasure, of emerald castles towering one above the other'. Originally Mendelssohn called the work *The Mermaid and the Knight*, which gives it a much more earthy aspect.

Marked allegro con moto (lively and brisk), the overture begins with an undulating watery figure for clarinet:

Example 3

Many writers have seen in this theme the inspiration for Richard Wagner's *Rheingold* motive and the opening music of that opera. Here we take it to represent Melusina herself. Mendelssohn develops her character, passing the theme from clarinet to flute and then to the strings. A chord from the woodwind heralds the second section, now in a minor key, which represents the bold knight Lusignan. The actual second theme, introduced by the first violins with a backing of strings and clarinets, is of a distinctly amorous nature, and is developed with passion.

After the two main characters have been presented, the true development begins. First Melusina's theme is restated by the woodwind and then the violins, and combines with Lusignan's theme, both becoming more and more passionate. A coda brings the work to a quiet ending.

There is no obvious adherence to a story line, nor is any attempt made to deal with the story's climax. The overture is simply an evocation, not so much, perhaps, of the human element as of the element that dominates the story – the sea. This was music for which Mendel-ssohn himself had a special affection and he was not pleased to have it overburdened with meaning.

A MIDSUMMER NIGHT'S DREAM, op. 21

This piece of music is probably more representative of the true Mendelssohn, or what we may like to think of as the true Mendelssohn, than anything else he wrote. In the lovely summer months of 1826, he first became acquainted with Shakespeare's comedy *A Midsummer Night's Dream*. He wrote to his sister Fanny: 'I've just finished two piano pieces in the summerhouse – and today or tomorrow I'm going to start dreaming midsummer night's dreams in it; a bit of sheer audacity!' He always recalled with emotion his discovery of Shakespeare, and started to write his music, as he later told a friend, 'in a state of delirium'. Again we must be careful not to read too much summery detail into it, though a friend of the composer tells us that Mendelssohn himself indicated the point where he had depicted a fly buzzing past. Nor is there any direct link with the play's story or characters; it is simply an evocation of its enchanted summer mood.

Mendelssohn showed his first score to his friend Alfred Marx, a brash young intellectual whose advice the young composer took very seriously until the two men quarrelled in 1839.

On this occasion Marx was pleased with the four opening chords of Mendelssohn's overture, but found what followed 'merry, delightfully vivacious, altogether pleasant and altogether lovely' but not good enough to associate with Shakespeare. Mendelssohn was deeply hurt and departed without a farewell. After a few days' sulky silence, Mendelssohn wrote to say that he had to agree, and asked for Marx's help to put things right. Accepting his friend's detailed criticisms he rewrote most of the work, retaining small parts here and there of which Marx had approved.

He completed the final version in August. In November the pianist Moscheles heard Felix and Fanny play a piano duet version and discovered a 'great though still youthful genius'. At Christmas a private performance of the orchestrated work was given at the Mendelssohn house, and in February it was given its first public performance at Stettin under the composer/conductor Karl Loewe. The concert also included Mendelssohn's A flat Concerto for two pianos (played by Loewe and Mendelssohn) and the first performance in that part of Europe of Beethoven's Ninth Symphony, in which Mendelssohn played among the first violins. The overture had a fine reception. 'The bloom of youth lies over it' was Robert Schumann's enthusiastic response.

The overture begins Allegro di molto (very lively) in E major with four long chords played by the woodwind followed by a quiet chord in E minor on the violins and violas. Then follows what has become known as the 'fairy music' played by the violins with pizzicato (plucked) viola accompaniment. An additional theme is added by the full orchestra. A melodious second theme in B major is started by the woodwind. This is followed by several smaller themes, which were later connected to characters in the play when Mendelssohn re-used them in the subsequent incidental music (composed 17 years later, in 1843). Most notable of these themes is the dance associated with Bottom's transformation, with a lively imitation of an ass's bray – a touch approved of by Marx, who persuaded Mendelssohn to retain it. A rapid descending passage for cellos represents the fly in the garden. The development is now based on the first theme, with a short coda. The overture ends with the four chords that began it.

It is difficult to ascertain how much of the music was intended to be associated with specific characters in the play when Mendelssohn composed the overture. But when he wrote the full incidental music, he made skilful use of elements from the overture in various guises.

CALM SEA AND PROSPEROUS VOYAGE, op. 27

This, the most purely literary of all Mendelssohn's inspirations for an overture, came from two short poems by Goethe: *Meeresstille* and *Glückliche Fahrt*. The first portrays a profound stillness, the ocean lying motionless, windless, a fearful silence, a monstrous waste, over which the anxious sailor gazes. To portray this Mendelssohn chooses an Adagio (a slow movement) in D.

The introduction is based on a theme that appears later; the entire piece is a tone painting of the calmness suggested by the poem. There is little to explain except for the strange flute calls that end it; and these are beyond explanation unless we identify them with the inevitable 'sea-bird'.

The second poem heralds the lifting of a sea-mist and the appearance of a clear sky. A welcome breeze blows, the sails fill and the sailor bestirs himself. The waves divide, and the long-looked-for land grows welcomingly near. In complete contrast, Molto allegro vivace (very lively and vivacious), but still in D, Mendelssohn portrays the ship in action and its arrival in port. Lively passage work pictures the growing breeze, with the opening theme from the first part now providing a basis for development. All is action, with the ship's movement represented in horn and trumpet calls. After a brief recapitulation there is a short coda in which those ashore salute the ship's safe arrival and in the last three bars the vessel slides up to the quay.

EDGAR ALLAN POE
1809-1849

Morbid, passionate and hypersensitive, Edgar Allan Poe was
brought low by desperate poverty, by the tragic early deaths of those
he loved, and by the solace he often found in drink and opium. Yet a
wild and vivid imagination transformed the horrors and obsessions
of his life into potent literary material and he became a master of the
'Grotesque' and 'Arabesque'. His chilling horror stories and
ingenious tales have inspired countless imitators, and he is now seen
as one of the great American writers.

Charleston
(right) When the runaway Poe enlisted in the army under the name Edgar Perry, he was posted to Sullivan's Island at the mouth of Charleston Harbor. This quiet island provided the inspiration for his tale The Gold-Bug.

Virginia Clemm Poe
(below) Poe married his beloved 'Sissy' when she was a bright, vivacious young girl of just 13. But over the next ten years, she fell victim to consumption and died in 1847 aged 24. This portrait was drawn moments after she died, when it was realized that no picture of her existed. The original showed her with her eyes closed, but it was later retouched to show the eyes open.

Poe was soon writing to John Allan, begging for assistance to enter West Point, the officer training academy. Allan did not reply to his letters.

By now Mrs Allan was on her deathbed, and Poe returned to Richmond on 2 March 1829 to find his beloved 'Ma' already buried. In the emotion of the moment John Allan offered to help Poe obtain his discharge from the army by paying for a substitute, and to assist his application to West Point. In the event, Allan gave Poe only 12 dollars for the substitute instead of the 75 he actually cost, and Poe was left owing the balance.

In the meantime Poe found a temporary haven in the home of his aunt, Maria Clemm, who was living in Baltimore with her two children Henry and Virgina. Also sharing the house were Edgar's crippled grand-mother and his alcoholic, consumptive brother. At this time Poe achieved his first literary success – a volume of his verse, *Al Aaraaf, Tamerlane and Minor Poems*, received a good review.

'MUDDY' AND 'SIS'

Poe was enrolled as a cadet officer at West Point in May 1830, and he also published his third book of poems in the same year. But again he proved to lack staying-power. He wearied of West Point, and wrote to John Allan begging for permission to resign. By now Allan was married again, to a woman who convinced him that Poe had not 'one good quality', and once more he did not reply. So Poe deliberately neglected his duties, and in January 1831 was summarily dismissed.

After a cold, miserable month in New York he returned to Baltimore and a warm welcome from Mrs Clemm and Virginia, now aged nine. Edgar's brother Henry died in August, his grandmother was failing fast and Henry Clemm had become a violent drinker; nevertheless Poe found here the family affection he craved. And soon Mrs Clemm and Virginia, his 'Muddy' and his 'Sis', had become the dearest people in the world to him.

The little household in Milk Street was desperately poor, and the sight of Muddy out begging with her basket for scraps stimulated Poe to look for ways of earning some money. Seeing a short story competition in a local newspaper, he took himself up to the chilly garret of the Clemm house and began to write the first of the stories for which he is now best remembered, keeping himself going through cold and illness with the aid of opium.

In July 1832 Poe submitted a number of tales, including *Descent into the Maelström* and *Ms Found in a Bottle*, to a competition in the *Baltimore Saturday Visitor*. The judges were overwhelmed by 'the singular force and beauty' of the tales, and had no hesitation in awarding him the prize. It was the first public recognition of his great literary gift.

Nevertheless, the Clemms' circumstances remained appalling, and Poe attempted one last personal appeal to John Allan, now on his death bed. But as soon as Poe entered the room where Allan lay dying, the embittered old man sat up in bed, waving his cane at Poe and shouting and cursing with terrifying vehemence. Allan died a month later leaving no mention of Poe in his will.

THE YOUNG WIFE

The following year Poe obtained an editorial post on the *Southern Literary Messenger*. But taking the job meant leaving his 'family' and moving to Richmond. Poe was soon lonely and insecure. When he heard that his cousin, Neilsen Poe, had offered to take Virginia into his home, Edgar wrote in incoherent anguish to Muddy, begging her not to agree. At the end of the letter he added a postcript for 13-year-old Virginia which amounted to moral blackmail: 'My love, my own sweetest sissy, my darling little wifey, think well before

Emaciated Beauties

Most of the women Edgar Allan Poe loved died young from tuberculosis – his mother, his foster-mother, his wife – and he remained morbidly obsessed with pale, consumptive beauties. Women doomed to die young appear again and again in his tales – their bloodless skin, blue-veined foreheads and the 'waxen hue' of their pale fingers recalling the fatal symptoms that Poe knew so well.

Maria Clemm
(left) In the home of his 'Muddy' (Aunt Maria), Poe found the family he craved. Poe's young wife Virginia was Muddy's daughter. The three of them lived happily together for a decade, despite their poverty.

you break the heart of your cousin Eddy.'

Poe got his way, and the outcome seemed to justify him. Muddy, Sis and a delighted Eddy moved to Richmond together and led an obviously happy family life. And matters were settled once and for all in May 1836, when Poe and Virginia were married. Virginia's age was evidently an embarrassment, for the affidavit declared she was 'of the full age of 21 years', although she was in fact not quite 14.

The crisis over Virginia had driven Poe to the bottle;

his editor had suspended him from the *Messenger*, warning, 'No man is safe who drinks before breakfast.' But once he was happily settled with the Clemms in Richmond, Poe was reinstated and soon took over editorial control. His stories in the magazine showed that his powers were maturing, and he proved to be a brilliant journalist and an incisive critic. In his hands, the *Messenger's* circulation soared and Poe's name started to become known beyond the South. But 'the drudgery was excessive and the salary contemptible', and he started to drink again. When he was dismissed from his post, Poe and his little family set off to try their luck in the North.

SUCCESS AND DESPAIR

They arrived in New York during a financial crisis and, after a year of hardship, moved on to Philadelphia in the summer of 1838. The years in Philadelphia proved happy ones, and Poe enjoyed a brief period of relative success, although money remained short. During his six years in the city he wrote some of his best tales, including *The Fall of the House of Usher* and the first detective story, *The Murders in The Rue Morgue*. He also consolidated his reputation as a journalist, first as editor of the *Gentleman's Magazine*, and then of *Graham's Magazine*. His critical reviews were generally considered and well argued, although they often included savage attacks on fellow writers that made him many enemies.

In 1842 a devastating blow struck the Poes. One evening in January, Virginia, as pale and large-eyed as Poe's mother, was playing the harp and singing in her sweet, high voice. Suddenly she caught her breath, coughed, and blood ran down her pure white dress. As Poe rushed forward to catch her, he realized with

anguish that Virginia too was suffering from consumption, the terrible disease that had carried off his father, his brother and the women he had loved. Driven 'insane' by despair, Poe took to drinking once more, and as Virginia's condition grew worse, he drank more and more heavily.

Poe's alcoholic excesses wrecked his chances of ever creating a first-class, international literary magazine. They also ruined his chance of becoming widely known by giving a lecture at the White House – he had to be

Long Island Farm
(above) Briefly, in the summer of 1844, the Poes found 'a perfect heaven' in the Brennan Farm near New York. Here, in a study with a vast, carved fireplace, Poe completed his most famous poem. The Raven.

Sarah Elmira Shelton *(above) In 1849 Poe persuaded his childhood sweetheart, now a widow, to marry him. But he died ten days before the date set for the wedding.*

Literary Magazines

In the 1830s and '40s, when Poe earned a meagre living working for magazines such as *Graham's*, across the Atlantic in Britain literary magazines were in their heyday. Journals such as *Blackwood's* and *The New Monthly* had wide readerships among the rising middle class, and featured work by the greatest writers of the age – Dickens, Bulwer Lytton, Thackeray. Their blend of quality and popular appeal impressed Poe, and in his literary stance, learned tone and taste for the burlesque and horrific, he consciously adopted *Blackwood's* style. America, Poe felt, was sadly lacking in comparable magazines – largely because the 'paltry prices' paid by the American editors meant writers could never create 'elaborate compositions'. He was determined that his journal, to be called *The Stylus*, would never exploit writers as he had been exploited.

The English style
When Poe edited Burton's Gentleman's Magazine (left), he emulated English editors such as Bulwer Lytton (right).

Out in the cold
(above, right) The success of The Raven *did nothing to relieve the Poes' poverty, and while the critics of New York sang his praises Poe and his family were freezing in a damp, cold tenement off Broadway.*

despatched from the city in a drunken stupor the very day the lecture was to be given. Even the ever-understanding Muddy and Sis found it hard to forgive him this time. Yet forgive him they did, and soon the Poes were back in New York.

For two years, life there was as hard as ever. Then, in the spring of 1845, Poe's poem *The Raven* was published. Its success was sudden and complete, making Poe a celebrity overnight. Soon fashionable New York literary ladies began to seek him out, and there were rumours of affairs with the established poets Mrs Frances Osgood and Mrs Helen Whitman. Ironically, lack of copyright protection meant that Poe made hardly a cent from his poem, and the Poes continued to live in extreme poverty in a New York tenement.

FRESH SORROWS

Virginia's health continued to decline, and Poe moved out of the city to a cottage at nearby Fordham. It was plain and simply furnished, but Virginia and Mrs Clemm turned it into a neat home, filled with flowers. Although Poe's acid sketches had alienated many of the New York literati, the literary ladies still visited him regularly. Mrs Gove Nichols and Mrs Marie Shew showed particular concern for the Poes' poverty, and Mrs Nichols was distressed to see that on her death bed Virginia had little but straw to keep her warm: 'The coat [Poe's greatcoat from West Point] and the cat were the sufferer's only means of warmth, except as her husband held her hands, and her mother her feet.'

Virginia died on 30 January 1847. Poe was utterly distraught, and his friend Charles Burr claimed that 'Many times after the death of his beloved wife was he found at the dead hour of a winter-night, sitting beside her tomb almost frozen in the snow, where he had wandered from his bed weeping and wailing.' Mrs Clemm would often sit up all night, holding her hand upon his forehead while he lay wracked with grief, or watching over him as he sat at his desk frenziedly writing *Eureka!*.

By 1848, however, Poe was urgently – and simultaneously – wooing Mrs Helen Whitman and Mrs Annie Richmond; Annie seems to have attracted him in a more directly physical way, but unlike Helen she had a spouse who was still very much alive. Poe therefore concentrated on the widowed Helen, who was touched by his sorrows but alarmed by stories about his drinking. However, by December, Helen had agreed to marry him – only to call off the wedding at the last minute. Stung to the quick, Poe vowed to quit forever 'the pestilential society of literary women'.

For the first few months of 1849 he worked furiously, writing poems and tales. But his fortunes were still shaky, and in July he left Fordham for good, leaving Muddy weeping on the dock at New York. His destination was his old home town, Richmond, where he was lionized as a celebrity.

THE FINAL MYSTERY

Poe began to call on his old childhood sweetheart, Elmira Shelton, now a widow, and courted her so ardently that by September they were engaged to be married – on condition that Poe abstained from drink; he agreed and kept his word. Then on 27 September he stopped in Baltimore on his way to give a lecture. What happened there remains a mystery, for he simply disappeared for five days.

On 3 October an old acquaintance of the writer's, Dr Snodgrass, received a note telling him that there was a gentleman named Poe, 'in great distress' and 'rather the worse for wear, at Ryan's 4th ward polls' where a wild pre-election party was going on.

Dr Snodgrass arrived to find Poe in a terrible state, dressed in someone else's clothes yet still clutching a fine malacca cane borrowed in Richmond. He was rushed to Washington College Hospital, where he fluctuated between violent delirium and rambling consciousness for four days. On 7 October 1849 he became quiet, whispered 'Lord help my poor soul', and died, aged just 40.

Mystery And Imagination

In Poe's tales and poems, images of death, violence and mystery combine. Together they express the bizarre but compelling nightmare vision of his morbid imagination.

Although Poe lived in virtual penury for most of his life, his fame and influence as a short-story writer have been widespread, long-lasting and profound. The great French poet Charles Baudelaire, who translated some of his tales, wrote that if Poe had not existed, he would have had to invent him; and his contemporary, Mallarmé, said that he learned English simply to read Poe.

GOTHIC HORROR

Poe wrote in the Gothic tradition – that is, his subject matter deals with the macabre and supernatural, and his style is characteristically heightened and melodramatic. The themes and settings of his poems often coincide with those of his stories, but it was poetry that was his first and abiding love – 'With me, poetry has not been a purpose but a passion.'

In his poetry, Poe aimed to inspire emotion by the musical effect of words. He would have been pleased by one critic's remark about *Ulalume* – that there was no need to understand English to appreciate the poem, provided it was intoned correctly.

Poe was writing poetry in earnest at the age of 14, and already displayed a certain morbidity and a sense of the attraction of death. An early example is the verse he wrote on the

death of Jane Stanard, the mother of one of his schoolmates, with whom he had been infatuated:

> *I could not love except where Death*
> *Was mingling his with Beauty's breath –*
> *Or Hymen, Time and Destiny*
> *Were stalking between her and me.*

This theme was to recur again and again in Poe's stories as well as his poetry. For him, 'The death of a beautiful woman is unquestionably the most poetic topic in the world.'

A gentleman writer
(above) Poe strove to appear a genteel man of letters. One editor, struck by his quiet confidence, said, 'Gentleman was written all over him.'

Fordham retreat
(left) This idyllic cottage was the scene of Virginia Poe's last illness; and here a grief-stricken Poe spent nights composing his prose-poem Eureka.

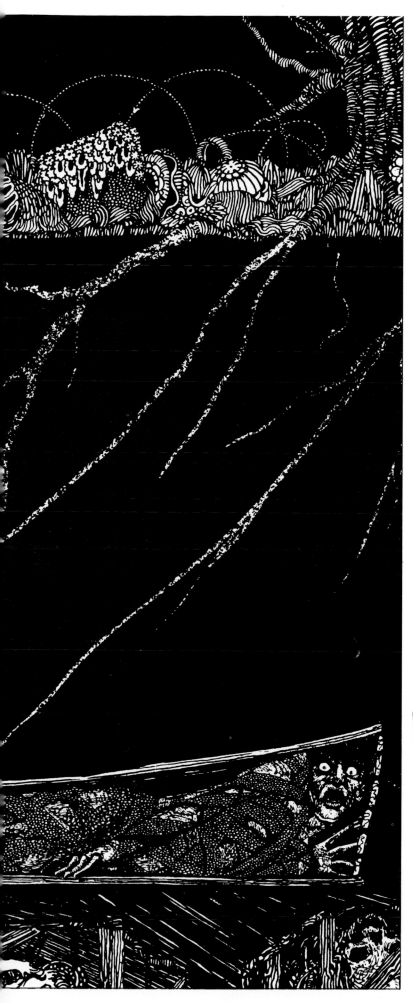

Premature burial
(*left*) *One of Poe's obsessions was the idea of being buried alive. This fear of being confined, while remaining fully and painfully conscious, occurs in several of his stories, one of which is actually called* The Premature Burial. *This illustration for the story conveys the starkness and vividness of Poe's terror.*

Byronism
Most of Poe's literary mentors were British. His poetic manner and sense of isolation largely derived from Byron (left), while Coleridge confirmed his belief in an invisible world.

The intensity of Poe's vision derived largely from his sense of peculiarity and of separateness from others. This is the subject of another poem, *Alone:*

> *From childhood's hour I have not been*
> *As others were – I have not seen*
> *As others saw – I could not bring*
> *My passions from a common spring . . .*

This intensity and singularity reach their most haunting – and certainly their most famous – expression in his poem *The Raven.* Despite being much parodied, *The Raven* has at its centre a sense of pain and despair none the less real for being expressed in a theatrical manner:

> *And his eyes have all the seeming*
> *of a demon's that is dreaming,*
> *And the lamp-light o'er him streaming*
> *throws his shadow on the floor;*
> *And my soul from out that shadow*
> *that lies floating on the floor*
> *Shall be lifted – nevermore!*

The Raven was immediately popular on both sides of the Atlantic. From England, the poet Elizabeth Barrett wrote: 'Your "Raven" has produced a sensation, a "fit o' horror", here in England.' And in his native America, Poe was often called upon to recite it at social gather-

Early successes
(*left*) *Poe's stories were initially published in magazines and newspapers. He won a prize of $100 from* The Dollar Newspaper *for* The Gold-Bug, *but received his first real literary acclaim for his poem* The Raven, *which appeared in the* New York Mirror. *For a few weeks he was taken up by the New York literary world, and gave talks and readings to spellbound audiences.*

211

Deathly beauty
(right) Poe's heroines reflect the nature and preoccupations of his stories. All, from Madeline Usher to Eleonora, are characterized by an unearthly loveliness, a 'gorgeous, yet fantastic beauty'. But their fascination, for Poe and for us, is that their beauty is linked with the remorseless and sinister approach of death.

ings. On occasions when he did so, 'he forgot time, spectators, his personal identity, as the wild hopes and repressed longings of his heart found vent in the impassioned words of the poem . . . the auditors would be afraid to draw breath lest the enchanted spell be broken'.

Poe's preoccupation with mental states took a variety of forms; his liking for puzzles and codes appears in *The Gold-Bug* and led him to write the first true detective story, *The Murders in the Rue Morgue*. The impetus and obsessive concerns of Poe's stories arose in part from his precarious mental state and the facts of his own life. His heroes are, like him, of a nervous, excitable and imaginative disposition. They frequently show traces of madness, which Poe believed to be a sign of higher intelligence. The narrator in *Eleonora* voices Poe's argument:
Men have called me mad; but the question is not yet settled, whether madness is or is not the loftiest intelligence – whether much that is glorious – whether all that is profound – does not spring from disease of thought – from moods of mind exalted at the expense of the general intellect.

Poe's own extraordinary 'moods of mind' led him to focus persistently on the abnormal and terrible in human experience. His control and his author's voice – the voice of reason – draw the reader easily and inexorably into a fascinating but fearful world from which there is no escape.

THE NEARNESS OF DEATH
Because of his wife's illness, Poe had first-hand knowledge of the slow decay of a loved one, and this confirmed his own innate morbidity. For him, death was arbitrary and inexorable. His story *The Masque of the Red Death* is, as it were, suffused in blood:
The 'Red Death' had long devastated the country. No pestilence had ever been so fatal, or so hideous. Blood was its Avatar and its seal – the redness and horror of blood.

To escape it, Prince Prospero segregates himself and his courtiers in an abbey and

entertains them with a masked ball. But despite the revelry, the hourly chimes of the clock cause the revellers to pause:
. . . and, while the chimes of the clock yet rang, it was observed that the giddiest grew pale, and the more aged and sedate passed their hands over their brows as if in confused reverie or meditation.

The sense of impending doom is treated with a poetic restraint which makes it all the more awesome and is continued right up to the fateful climax.

Poe's heroines such as Madeline Usher and Eleonora are all mortally sick, like his wife. Eleonora, for example,
. . . had seen that the finger of Death was upon her bosom – that, like the ephemeron, she had been made perfect in loveliness only to die . . .

His heroines' beauty and their ability to command love are closely bound up with the fact that they are on the brink of death.

Maria Clemm, Poe's main support and comfort during the painful time when he was writing immediately after his wife's death, recorded his feverish method of working: 'he never liked to be alone, and I used to sit up with him, often until four o'clock in the morning, he at his desk, writing, and I dozing in my chair. When he was composing *Eureka* we used to walk up and down the garden . . . until I was so tired I could not walk. He would stop every few minutes and explain his ideas to me, and ask if I understood him.'

HAUNTING THEMES
Even when dealing with tales of adventure, or those based on real or supposed fact, Poe's preoccupations remain central to the story. His fear of confinement haunts his seafaring tales, in which the expanse of sky and water seems to intensify the smallness and frailty of human life. *A Descent into the Maelström* describes how a boat and one of its crew of two are swallowed up by a gigantic whirlpool. In *The Narrative of Arthur Gordon Pym*, the hero is a stowaway, and is hidden first of all in 'an ironbound box

. . . nearly four feet high, and full six feet long, but very narrow, inside the hold.' Like Madeline Usher, he finds himself entombed while still alive.

Human perversity is yet another habitual preoccupation with Poe and is frequently linked with the idea of murder. In *The Black Cat*, Poe describes how a normal, humane man inexplicably turns on those he loves. He begins by torturing and then killing his beloved cat, an act which marks the beginning of a fatal obsession.
And then came, as if to my final and irrevocable overthrow, the spirit of PERVERSENESS. Of this spirit philosophy takes no account. Yet I am not more sure that my soul lives, than I am that perverseness is one of the primitive impulses of the human heart . . . Who has not, a hundred times, found himself committing a vile or a silly action, for no other reason than because he knows he should not?

This theory underlies the whole of Poe's work and has a powerful psychological conviction. It occurs again in *The Tell-Tale Heart*, where a man is murdered for no motive of passion, revenge or greed, but simply because 'He had the eye of a vulture – a pale blue eye, with a film over it'. This 'unfathomable longing of the soul to vex itself – to offer violence to its own nature' was by no means absent from Poe's own life, some of whose disasters were undoubtedly self-inflicted.

Like his hero, the English Romantic poet Samuel Taylor Coleridge, Poe believed in another, invisible world beyond the world of everyday appearances. His own 'other world' is a haunted, demon-ridden one, but he takes care to present it in a detailed and matter-of-fact way. It is Poe's great achievement that he was able to give shape and logic to his tormented vision. D.H. Lawrence was to say of Poe, in his *Studies in Classic American Literature*, that he 'sounded the horror and the warning of his own doom'. In so doing he captured a dark but undeniably real aspect of human experience.

FRYDERYK CHOPIN

1810-1849

Behind the dazzling virtuoso and inspired composer lay other Chopins – the patriotic Pole, the tormented lover, the performer who was terrified by large audiences, and the doomed artist racked by a terrible illness.

More than that of any other composer, the name of Chopin has become associated with a single instrument – the pianoforte. At a time when Europe was well provided with keyboard virtuosi – Thalberg, Kalkbrenner, Moscheles and Liszt among them – Chopin was widely considered to be the greatest of them all, despite the fact that he had no love for the concert platform and gave scarcely 30 public performances in his entire lifetime.

In his music Chopin forged a spiritual link with his country and its people that distance and years of exile could never destroy. The national identity asserts itself not only in the pieces based on Polish dance forms (the polonaises and mazurkas), but in the use of elements from Polish folk music and perhaps, too,

in the pervasive strain of melancholy that seems to linger beneath the surface in even the most serene passages of his works.

Chopin's letters to his Polish friends reveal a lively intelligence and ever-present sense of humour. His accounts of musical and social occasions are incisive and witty; but although he was quick to scorn social and musical pretentiousness in private correspondence, his public behaviour was always kind, courteous and infinitely considerate. No one, having met Chopin, could fail to like him, and it is interesting to note how many of his pupils became staunch companions and helpers in later life when his own physical powers were fading. His foibles, such as his indecisiveness in matters great and small (whether to

Vosges, in 1771. As a young man, Nicolas had left France to seek his fortune, served in the Polish National Guard, became a tutor of French in Polish aristocratic circles and, in 1810, was appointed as a teacher of French at the Warsaw Lyceum; soon afterwards he took a part-time post teaching French at the Military School as well. He had married Justyna Krzyzanowska (born 1782) in June 1806. Their daughter Ludwika had been born in 1807, and Isabella (1811) and Emilia (1813) were soon to follow.

Fryderyk's childhood was a secure and happy one, despite political upheavals that brought most of Poland under Russian rule. The family moved from Zelazowa Wola to Warsaw in October 1810 so that Nicolas could take up his Lyceum post, and were allotted a large apartment in the former Saxon Palace which also housed the school. Justyna was able to supplement Nicolas's small income by taking in boarders, some of whom became Fryderyk's most devoted friends.

From his earliest years Chopin showed a precocious gift for music – he was playing duets with his elder sister Ludwika before he had had any formal training – and also for drawing caricatures, writing verses and, with his sisters, devising comedies which the children performed to celebrate family anniversaries. When he was six, Fryderyk began taking lessons from a local piano teacher, Wojciech Zywny, an eccentric 60-year-old Czech. A violinist by training, a composer and occasional conductor, Zywny channelled Fryderyk's outstanding natural ability, both physical and interpretative, into the German classical repertoire – Bach, Haydn, Mozart and Beethoven – as well as guiding him through pieces by popular contemporary composers such as

Franco-Polish parents
Chopin's parents, Justyna and Nicolas (above), were married in 1806. They settled down in a house on the Zelazowa Wola Estate (below) near Warsaw, and it was here that Chopin was born four years later.

leave Poland, which jacket to wear for a concert), seemed trivial in the light of his other traits, for he was a constant friend, an affectionate son and brother, a sympathetic colleague, and a generous, patient teacher.

EARLY EVIDENCE OF GENIUS

Fryderyk Franciszek Chopin was born at Zelazowa Wola, near Warsaw, on either 1 March 1810 (as Chopin himself believed) or, as his certificate of baptism states, probably erroneously, 22 February 1810. The 1 March date is now generally accepted. His father was Nicolas Chopin, born in Marainville,

had never heard a first-rate company he realized that performances by the Polish National Opera left much to be desired. In 1828, after seeing *Der Freischütz*, he observed: 'The choir kept missing their cues and coming in a quarter beat behind each other.' It would not be long before he felt the need to go abroad in search of wider, more enriching musical experience. Meanwhile, under Elsner's sympathetic eye, he continued to compose for the piano. His efforts to conform to classical structures were less successful, and so were his attempts at orchestration, which Elsner always encouraged. But works such as the flamboyant *Là ci darem* variations, op.2, which exploited his own gifts as a pianist, revealed how fast Chopin was moving towards his mature style. His distinctively fluent and flexible treatment of melody, and his elegant use of keyboard configurations, were already much in evidence.

An opportunity to visit Berlin arose, giving Chopin a chance to widen his musical horizons. Yet although he found himself present at the same function as Zelter, Spontini and Mendelssohn (only a year older than Chopin, but already a prolific and widely acclaimed composer), he lacked the courage to speak to them. A year later, in 1829, he managed to get to Vienna to supervise the publication of some of his early works, and on 11 August he made his true professional début at the Kärntnertortheater, where his performance of his *Krakowiak*, op.14, and op.2 Variations, both with orchestra, had a tumultuous reception. Even better received, however, was his improvisation on a Polish drinking-song! A second concert followed a week later, and then, fired with his success, he returned to Warsaw determined to find a way of establishing his reputation outside Poland.

Hummel (an early influence on Chopin's own compositions) and the great virtuoso Kalkbrenner.

Chopin constantly improvised pieces of his own, which at first Żywny would note down for him. A Polonaise in G minor was published in 1817, and the Warsaw press commented with pride on the child's achievements, both pianistic and creative: 'Geniuses are born in our country also, but lack of publicity stops them from becoming known.' Nevertheless Fryderyk's fame spread rapidly, and local ladies showered him with invitations to play at their homes. Hailed as a second Mozart, he gave his first public performance in 1818, aged eight, playing a piano concerto by Gyrowetz at the Radziwill Palace. In 1821 Fryderyk composed a farewell Polonaise for Żywny, who admitted that there was nothing more he could teach the boy. Soon Chopin began taking composition lessons from Józef Elsner, director of the new Warsaw Conservatoire.

In the summer holidays Chopin, always physically frail, was sent to the village of Szafarnia for country air, food and exercise. Here he heard traditional Polish folk-music – a lifelong influence – and sketched some of his first mazurkas. After three years at the Lyceum (1823-26), he enrolled at the Conservatoire. His Opus 1, a Rondo in C minor, was published in June 1825, and his public performances during his student years included demonstrations on the aelopantaleon and aelomelodicon (hybrid organ/piano instruments). Tsar Alexander I gave him a diamond ring after hearing him perform on the latter.

As a student, and ever afterwards, Chopin attended as many musical evenings, concerts and operas as he could. He admired Rossini's *Barber of Seville* and Weber's *Der Freischütz*, but even though he

Poland's capital
A view of Warsaw (above) around the time of Chopin's boyhood. At the age of eight he gave his first concert here at a charity fête in the Radziwill Palace.

Chopin at the piano
Chopin at the age of 19 – and by now recognized as a rising composer – playing before distinguished guests in the salon of Prince Radziwill in Berlin. Radziwill, himself a cellist and tenor, took a keen interest in Chopin's career. A year later the young composer left Poland for ever, going to Vienna and then on to Paris, supposedly en route for London; in reality the French capital became his permanent home.

Young cartoonist
As an adolescent, Chopin (right), when he was not composing, tried his hand at caricatures. Above is a jolly Polish peasant as seen through the young composer's eyes.

What turned out to be Chopin's last year in his native land was marked by a series of largely abortive plans to tour abroad, and by his love for a young mezzo-soprano, Konstancia Gladkowska, a student at the Conservatoire. During this period he composed his two piano concertos, the first of which (no.2 in F minor) had a slow movement inspired by his passion for Konstancia.

CHOPIN LEAVES POLAND
On 11 November 1830, Chopin left Poland – initially for Vienna, but stopping en route at Dresden, where he improvised for the court. This time, Vienna was less interested in the young Polish genius; during eight frustrating months there he gave only two performances (4 April, 11 June), neither of which had anything like the impact of his earlier concerts. He spent his time hearing as much music as possible, including opera, and in completing an impressive body of work: mazurkas, waltzes (including the Grande Valse Brillante, op.18 in E flat), his B minor Scherzo and his last orchestrated work, the Grande Polonaise in E flat. He also sketched out his first ballade (G minor).

When Chopin left Vienna, it was for 'London, via Paris', according to his passport: years afterwards he would jokingly remind his Paris friends that he was just passing through. En route in Stuttgart he heard

Vieux Paris
When Chopin arrived in Paris in mid-September 1831, he discovered a city of quaint gentility (right). But a few months later, in February 1832, he was whisked into the glitter of Parisian high life when he gave his first, much-acclaimed concert in the capital.

that a Polish revolt had been bloodily suppressed by the Russians, and that Warsaw was in Russian hands. His grief for his homeland overwhelmed him, and it has often been suggested that the news inspired his turbulent ('Revolutionary') Etude op. 10 no 12.

A week later in Paris (September 1831), Chopin took lodgings at 27 Boulevard Poissonière. The city had become the refuge for half the political exiles of Europe, as well as a mecca for artists of all types and nationalities. Through his compatriots – the only people with whom he could feel completely at ease – Chopin came to meet leading figures of the Romantic movement, while Liszt, Mendelssohn, Osborne and Hiller (all pianists) and the cellist Franchomme became his closest musical associates.

Despite being part of such an influential circle, it was five months before Chopin made his Paris début, at the Salle Pleyel on 26 February 1832. There he played, without orchestra, the F minor Concerto and *Là ci darem* variations, as well as taking part in a six-piano extravaganza by Kalkbrenner. For Chopin the concert was an artistic triumph. The critic Fétis wrote: 'an abundance of original ideas . . . His inspiration paves the way for a fundamental change of form [in piano compositions].' The performance was not a financial success, however. Money was a problem, despite the fact that he had acquired a few

pupils from the Polish community, and Chopin described himself at this time as suffering from 'consumption of the purse'. Soon, however, with his appearance at a Rothschild soirée, matters improved dramatically; and now that his reputation as a brilliant musician was acknowledged in fashionable society, he became the most sought-after piano teacher in Paris. Mme de Rothschild herself was one of his pupils.

By 1832 Chopin was said to be the lover of the rich and musically talented Countess Delfina Potocka, who was separated from her husband. The composer dedicated to her the F minor Concerto that Konstancia Gladkowska (now married) had partly inspired two years earlier. (Much later he would also dedicate to Delfina his Waltz op. 64 no. 1, the so-called 'Minute Waltz'.) He found it easier to work, however, when Delfina was not in Paris to consume his time and his emotions. During this period the Etudes op. 25 were Chopin's main concern, but he was also composing nocturnes and mazurkas, completing work on his G minor Ballade, and sketching out some preludes. Liszt had been playing some of his études, with Chopin's wholehearted approval: 'I wish I could steal from him his manner of playing my études', he remarked to Ferdinand Hiller in a letter dated 20 June 1833.

The concerts in which Chopin participated that year (he was not the principal performer) did nothing to further his career. His 1834 performances were likewise few and insignificant, and 1835 saw two performances in April (4 and 26) which confirmed Chopin's aversion to playing in public concerts: the first, which included the Paris première of his E minor Concerto, was damned with faint praise, and although the second, featuring his Andante spianato and Grand Polonaise in E flat (op. 22), was far better received, the hurt of the earlier experience was not forgotten.

Chopin had neither the temperament nor the physical constitution for the life of a concert pianist. He suffered agonies before public performances:

Chopin's home
The drawing-room of Chopin's apartment in the Place d'Orléans (above) to which he moved in 1842. George Sand, who lived next door but one, wrote that 'we are for ever running in and out of each other's houses at night'.

Ignaz Moscheles
(below) A great piano virtuoso, Moscheles brought a crisp and incisive touch to his playing. Yet he considered Chopin's op. 10 Etudes to be nothing more than 'unplayable finger-breaking exercises'.

Dresden affair
When Chopin stopped in Dresden (right) in 1825, he intended to renew a boyhood friendship with the son of the Wodzińska family. Instead, he began a courtship with the 16-year-old Maria (above) which soon became a passionate – though brief – love affair.

I wasn't meant to play in public . . . Crowds intimidate me, their breath stifles me, their stares petrify me, their strange faces throw me into confusion.

That summer Chopin travelled – first to Carlsbad to meet his parents, for the last time, then to Dresden, where he fell in love with the 16-year-old Maria Wodzińska. He wanted to marry her, but the match was not encouraged by her parents and the romance was eventually to peter out. From Dresden he went to Leipzig to meet Mendelssohn, who introduced him to the young Clara Wieck, at 15 already established as a concert pianist. It was at her home that Chopin first met Robert Schumann, the man who had honoured him in 1830 with the famous exclamation: 'Hats off, gentlemen, a genius!' The two were never close. Chopin was embarrassed by the fulsome praise Schumann lavished on him in reviews: 'He exaggerates so much that he makes me look ridiculous.' As he did not much admire Schumann's music, he could not return the compliments either, although he did dedicate his second ballade to him (op. 38). Clara's interpretation of his own work was another matter: Chopin was most favourably impressed.

AFFAIR WITH GEORGE SAND
In October 1836, at the home of Liszt and his mistress, Countess Marie d'Agoult, Chopin was introduced to the prolific novelist George Sand (Aurore Dudevant). He was not instantly attracted to her ('I did not like her face . . . There is something off-putting about her'). George Sand was fascinated by genius of all kinds, however, and musical enough to want to share

Valldemosa monastery
In search of health, Chopin came to Majorca with George Sand and settled in the lovely but isolated monastery at Valldemosa, described by Sand in A Winter in Majorca.

in Chopin's creative life in some way. She invited him often to meet her circle of friends – Alfred de Musset, Heine, the Polish poet Mickiewicz and the artist Delacroix among many others. While he resisted the convention-flouting siren – who not only smoked cigars and wore men's clothes in public but was none too discreet about her many lovers – she began to experience a deep passion for Chopin.

The following summer he refused her invitation to join her and several of his compatriots at her country house in Nohant. Indeed, most unexpectedly, but perhaps because of his depression after the breaking of his engagement to Maria Wodzińska, he left with his friend Camille Pleyel for a two-week visit to London. Here he maintained the lowest profile possible: he played only once, at the house of the piano manufacturer James Broadwood, where he was introduced as M. Fritz. But a mere bar or two of his playing was enough to reveal his true identity.

In the summer of 1838 Chopin at last yielded to George Sand's love – a selfless devotion fired not only by passion but by her desire for a family life (she had two children, Maurice and Solange, by her husband Casimir Dudevant). Conducting their liaison with discretion, they decided to spend their first winter together in Majorca, where, they assumed, the climate would have a beneficial effect on Chopin's health. At first, when they arrived on 8 November, the Mediterranean landscape, the day-long sunshine and the relaxed atmosphere combined to give Chopin a feeling of well-being, and he embarked upon several new compositions. But with the arrival of the damp and windy weather his tubercular symptoms reappeared. He had been very ill in 1835, and the *Warsaw Courier* had issued a denial of his death in 1836; now, once again, he was coughing violently and spitting blood. He had a low opinion of the Majorcan doctors: 'The first said I was going to die,' he recalled, 'the second that I had breathed my last, the third that I was already dead.'

In mid-December, evicted from their first lodgings, they moved to an isolated monastery at Valldemosa, to which a Pleyel piano was at length delivered from Paris. There, while Sand coped with the domestic chores, Chopin worked on his C sharp minor Scherzo, C minor Polonaise and F sharp Impromptu, as well as completing his 24 Preludes. In February 1839 they left for Marseilles, then spent the summer at Nohant.

A PRODUCTIVE PERIOD

Life fell into a pattern: they usually spent their summers at Nohant, but they spent the rest of the year at the Paris apartments which each maintained separately. Chopin had given no public concerts since March 1838, when he had played his E minor Concerto at Rouen to honour a compatriot, the conductor Orlowski; in the same month he had played before King Louis Philippe at the Tuileries. He was to give another command performance for the royal family in October the following year, this time at St Cloud with the Prague-born pianist Moscheles. Moscheles had at first thought Chopin's music 'rather cloying' and 'unmanly', but had since become an ardent admirer. Shortly afterwards Chopin played him his first mature sonata, in B flat minor.

When he was not giving lessons or composing, Chopin spent much of his time with George Sand and her children, frequently entertaining at either his apartment or hers. Besides Polish émigrés, the guests included the novelist Balzac, the composers Meyer-

Ailing artist
Chopin (left) painted in 1848, a year before his death. It was in this year that he performed his last concert in Paris at the Salle Pleyel and saw George Sand for the last time, quite by accident. By this time he was seriously ill.

beer and Berlioz, and the great Romantic painter Delacroix. Though at the height of his creative powers as a composer, in the salons of the nobility Chopin tended to be more admired for his gifts as a pianist, improviser and impersonator – of, for example, familiar figures such as Liszt and Kalkbrenner – than for his composing.

He and Sand were very close at this time: he was a great comfort to her when her first dramatic venture, *Cosima*, failed, and when she accompanied their friend, the mezzo-soprano Pauline Viardot, on a concert trip, Chopin and her children stayed behind to look after each other and mourn Sand's absence.

Sand and son
Maurice Sand (below right) as drawn by his mother George Sand (below left) before he had grown into an irresponsible and conceited young man with a fierce jealousy of Chopin. He was largely instrumental in bringing the lovers' relationship to its bitter and premature end.

A Scottish concert
In 1848, after an exhausting round of concerts and lessons in London, Chopin stayed in Edinburgh (above). Increasingly sick and frequently coughing blood, he gave a concert which created so little enthusiasm that Jane Stirling (above right), his devoted admirer, bought a batch of tickets and gave them away to ensure that there would be an adequate audience.

RIFT WITH GEORGE SAND

Chopin's health was ever precarious; though 5 feet 8 inches tall, he weighed only 6 stone 13 pounds at this time – little more than 12-year-old Solange. None the less, he suddenly decided to yield to his friends' urgings and give a public performance. Then began 'the Chopinesque nightmare' of doubts, fears and indecision. He tried to cancel the concert when he learned that the beloved Pauline Viardot could not appear with him, and he forbade the printing of posters and programmes. As Marie d'Agoult had once remarked, 'Chopin keeps changing his mind. The only constant thing about him is his cough.'

With George Sand's support, the concert, held on 26 April 1841, was less of an ordeal than Chopin had feared. It was a dazzling occasion, producing excellent reviews ('Chopin has done for the piano what Schubert has done for the voice') and raising the fantastic sum of 6000 francs in income. The following February another performance was given at the Salle Pleyel, with Pauline Viardot and Auguste Franchomme. Again the occasion was a triumph, with audience and reviewers united in their rapture ('sheer poetry superbly translated into sound'). It was the last but one performance by Chopin for the next six years.

Chopin's relationship with George Sand now began to break down, partly because, as her children became young adults, the composer became caught in the cross-fire of parent-offspring quarrels, and partly because of an extraordinary novel by George Sand which plainly mirrored their own relationship as she saw it. In her story the actress Lucrezia Floriani – a virtuous lady, devoted to her children – is destroyed by the jealousy of Prince Karol, the lover whom she has nursed through near-fatal sickness. The implication of this tactless literary venture was obvious to all: George Sand had had enough of her Polish lover. Yet, if anything, it was Maurice, George Sand's son, who could most fairly have been accused of jealousy: now an adolescent, he violently resented Chopin's relationship with his mother, and had tried to break it up.

Eventually, after a bitter row in which Chopin tried to arbitrate between Solange, her new husband Clésinger, and George Sand, the nine-year relationship ended. Having sent Chopin a letter of farewell on 28 July 1847, George Sand was never to seek a reconciliation.

FAILING HEALTH

From this time, Chopin's health and spirits began to move on a downward spiral. To give him something other than his pain and misery to think about, his friends again persuaded him to give a public concert. He agreed, and on 16 February 1848 at the Salle Pleyel he managed to walk unaided to the piano and play not only many of his own compositions but also, to start the concert, Mozart's Trio K496 in E.

A former pupil, Jane Stirling, acted as Chopin's mainstay and administrator during the agonizing pre-concert period. Recognizing his need for someone to depend upon, a role assumed for so many years by George Sand, she willingly offered herself in the hope that he would eventually make her his wife. Like George Sand, she was six years older than Chopin; but there the similarity ended. He was grateful to her for her devoted exertions on his behalf, but she appears never to have stirred his emotions.

Chopin had long been planning another trip to England, and on 20 April 1848, with no thought of the possible risk to his health, he crossed the Channel. Soon, in London, he embarked upon a punishing schedule of social engagements and even went to the opera. He played before Queen Victoria and Prince Albert at a glittering evening at Stafford House, home of the Duke and Duchess of Sutherland.

Desperately ill, Chopin lacked the strength to resist when Jane Stirling suggested a trip to Edinburgh. They left London on 5 August 1848. Neither the 12-hour train journey nor the raw Scottish air did him any good: 'I can hardly breathe', he wrote to an old friend. 'I am just about ready to give up the ghost.' Yet he survived to give a concert in Manchester (28 August) and to play in Glasgow (27 September) and Edinburgh (4 October). His other performances were confined to the genteel drawing-rooms of Scottish ladies – all of whom, Chopin reported, commented that his music sounded 'like water'. Jane Stirling both bored and irritated him, and at last, with the utmost diplomacy, Chopin was able to convey to her, via a relative, that there could be no marriage. Soon afterwards providence gave him an excuse to return to London: a charity concert in aid of Polish exiles, held at the Guildhall on 16 November. Although appearing that night nearly killed him, he was little appreciated by the audience and virtually ignored by the press. Using the English climate as a pretext for leaving 'beastly London' as soon as possible, he arrived home in Paris, after a seven-month absence, on 24 November.

A brief remission gave Chopin a few more months' relative happiness surrounded by his friends. Some of the inspiration which had deserted him on his break with George Sand briefly returned, and he produced two mazurkas, which were published posthumously (op. 67 no. 2, op. 68 no. 4). Then came the inevitable relapse. His friends moved him for the summer to Chaillot, from where he wrote asking his sister Ludwika to visit him.

She was with him when, at 12 Place Vendôme, Paris, he died on the morning of 17 October 1849.

An elaborate funeral took place at the Madeleine on 30 October, with a full performance of Mozart's Requiem, as Chopin had requested.

When he had been buried at Paris's Père Lachaise cemetery, Ludwika took his heart back to Poland with her, in accordance with his final wish, and, carefully wrapped, all the letters he had received from George Sand.

Mortally sick
A daguerreotype of Chopin in 1849. Barely 39, he wrote two mazurkas but had not the strength to make legible copies of them.

Informal moments
Chopin, so anxious and shy when put on public display, was most comfortable when playing for friends in the informal atmosphere of a drawing-room. In this charming scene he has evidently broken off in order to chat amiably with a lady who has continued to occupy herself with her lacework while the maestro performs.

Compositions for the piano

Chopin's solo piano compositions have always been admired for their lyricism, passion and beauty. Formally they are works of intelligence and balance, while emotionally they are full of feeling and song.

We should be grateful to Chopin's teacher in Warsaw, Józef Elsner. It was Elsner who advised his former pupil, on his arrival in Paris as an ambitious 21-year-old, to concentrate on composing music rather than embarking on a three-year course of study with his idol, the pianist and teacher Friedrich Kalkbrenner:

The ability to play an instrument perfectly – as Paganini does the violin or Kalkbrenner the piano – with all that this ability implies . . . is still only a means to arrive at the expression of thought. The celebrity which Mozart and Beethoven enjoyed as pianists has long since evaporated.

Chopin took his point. From then on he pursued a career above all as a composer, and before his death at the age of 39 he produced a body of work comparable with that of many longer-lived masters. In fact the development of his style was so rapid that his two piano concertos and his 12 Etudes op. 10, written by the age of 22, are already acknowledged, mature masterpieces.

Though his output was almost exclusively for the piano, Chopin need not be thought of as a limited artist – any more than, say, Wagner or Verdi, who both concentrated on opera. For within the range of his solo piano music, this Polish master (who was also, and significantly, French on his father's side) produced pieces of varying weight and complexity. For example there are the somewhat lighter compositions, which have been called 'salon pieces', after the elegant drawing-rooms in which they were played: the G flat major Etude, the Fantasy-Impromptu and Chopin's waltzes and nocturnes belong in this category. On the other hand, compositions such as the G minor Ballade, the B minor Scherzo and the 'Heroic' A flat major Polonaise are big concert works of great emotional breadth and subtlety.

CHOPIN AS PERFORMER AND COMPOSER

When he played his own piano music, Chopin allowed himself a good deal of freedom, never (it is said) playing the same piece twice in the same way – for example, varying the speed, volume and tone, and even occasionally the notes themselves. His music thus sometimes

The young composer
A portrait of Chopin (right) from the original painted by Ary Scheffer in 1847. This was when the op. 64 Waltzes were composed. Chopin was ill with tuberculosis at the time.

Pleasurable practice
Ferdinand Keller's painting, entitled Chopin *(below), reminds us that Chopin's Etudes, besides being works of art, are also piano 'exercises', designed to make the hands more flexible. Each study addresses itself to different problems of technique: the 'Revolutionary' Etude, for example, is mainly a test of left-hand stamina and agility.*

seems to echo his once-famous keyboard improvisations, in which he actually created music as he went along; in fact he even composed some pieces called 'impromptus'.

Another element in the Chopin style is the display of virtuosity through brilliant passages requiring special technical skill from the pianist – rapid fingerwork, leaps from one point of the keyboard to another, and so on. These give us the same kind of thrill as a gymnastic routine, but can, in the case of lesser composers, amount to little more than that. With Chopin, though, a virtuoso passage is always musically justified, appropriate to the form and content of the piece itself.

PLAYING TECHNIQUES IN CHOPIN'S TIME

The 19th century witnessed great advances in pianistic technique. Chopin, like his contemporary Franz Liszt, was a pioneer in this art. In fact an older pianist, Ignaz Moscheles, pronounced the op. 10 Etudes ('studies') to be 'unplayable finger-breaking exercises'. Today, however, they are within the reach (though never the easy reach) of skilful professional pianists. Chopin dedicated these op. 10 Etudes to another virtuoso pianist, Liszt – a sure indication that the Etudes are musical compositions of the first order, not mere keyboard exercises.

INFLUENCES

The two main influences on the Chopin Etudes were the violinist Paganini and the pianist Liszt. Paganini's music for unaccompanied violin created new technical standards for the instrument which the young Liszt, in particular, tried to emulate in pianistic terms. Chopin was less dazzled by virtuosity than his Hungarian colleague – their temperaments were very different – but he too was excited by Paganini, and above all by Liszt's rapid progress towards becoming a 'Paganini of the piano'. He could at least be sure that Liszt would not find his Etudes 'unplayable': in fact one of his letters speaks of the marvellous way in which Liszt played these very innovative pieces. By contrast, one critic advised pianists to have a surgeon standing by before attempting them.

Another important element in Chopin's style is found in the dreamier pieces such as his nocturnes. These exploit something which in pianistic terms is comparable to the *bel canto* ('beautiful singing') style used by operatic singers. Chopin greatly enjoyed good singing, and the kind of full-bodied yet flexible melody that the right hand plays in a nocturne owes much to what he heard at the Paris Opera. There were piano nocturnes before Chopin (notably by the Irish composer John Field), but Chopin went far beyond his model in depth of feeling and spontaneity. Interestingly, his song-like piano melodies have sometimes attracted words: the op. 10 no. 3 Etude and the Fantasy-Impromptu both lent tunes to 'Tin Pan Alley' a generation ago.

Finally, there is the Polish legacy. In Chopin this was not simply a vague romantic nostalgia for the homeland which he left as a young man. Throughout his life he composed mazurkas – using a Polish dance form in triple time – and polonaises. In both of these forms he quickly learned to convey a wide range of emotions. But although he does very occasionally use a folk melody, for example in the B minor Scherzo, he never became a 'nationalist' composer (unlike some of his contemporaries, who felt it their duty to express their country's musical soul). Even at his most Polish Chopin retains his very individual style.

Influential virtuosi
Chopin's Etudes were influenced by two of the most flamboyant contemporary musicians, Paganini (left) and Franz Liszt (below). Paganini's 'devilish' mastery of the violin had revealed new technical possibilities which Liszt had realized in his formidable piano-playing. Appropriately, Chopin dedicated his innovative op. 10 Etudes to Liszt.

LISZT.

The bel canto style
Chopin's works, especially his Nocturnes and Etudes, were also greatly influenced by his love of opera, particularly the bel canto *style of Bellini and Rossini (above), composer of* The Barber of Seville *(below). Bel canto is literally 'beautiful singing', and Chopin's exquisite melodies can be seen as a pianistic equivalent to this operatic style.*

Programme notes

BALLADE No. 1 in G MINOR, op. 23

Chopin's First Ballade was sketched out in 1831 but not completed until 1835; his fellow-composer Robert Schumann described it as being one of Chopin's 'wildest and most original compositions'. Like the three other ballades which were to follow, it may have been inspired by the ballad poems of his compatriot Adam Mickiewicz, although there is no definite literary 'programme' attached to the music. Nevertheless a musical drama clearly unfolds, and one might call this music a 'tone poem' for piano: indeed, such music as this may well have inspired Liszt to compose his 'symphonic poems' for orchestra in later years. Liszt, Grieg and some others were also to write piano ballades, but Chopin was the first to use this term (borrowed from a type of poetic narrative) for a piece of music.

The introduction to the Ballade no. 1 is slow and ends with the music hanging like a question mark. Then the highly expressive first theme 'creeps in', like a slow waltz, and builds steadily up to a fast, wild passage. This dies away, and there is a sort of 'horn call', alternating two left-hand chords, ushering in the warm (major key) second tune:

Example 1

The rest of the ballade is built up from these two musical ideas. Essentially they are used in alternation and also through various keys. Much of the sheer dramatic tension arises from this harmonic 'straying' from the home key of G minor, and this tension is hardly released by the especially fast and furious coda (closing section) played *Presto con fuoco* (at a faster, fiery tempo) and culminating in rushing scales. On the way, however, the two themes undergo what amount to a series of 'costume changes', appearing sometimes in ballroom splendour (the second theme on its appearance just before the central section), sometimes in dark, mysterious garb (the final statement of the first theme, with a left-hand 'drum-beat' brooding below the right-hand melody). These 'costume changes' contribute greatly to the colour and depth of this passionately expressive music.

'How is gravity to clothe herself', asked the composer Schumann when discussing this work, 'if jest goes about in such dark veils?'; and the English edition of the music actually subtitled it *The Infernal Banquet.*

Chopin indicates that the music is to be played *con fuoco* ('with fire'), and the mood is wild indeed, the pianist's fingers flying over the keys. But a middle section brings a respite and a totally different mood. Here Chopin seems almost to exorcize the fury that has gone before with an utterly simple, gentle tune in the major key: in fact it is a Polish Christmas carol, *Lulajże Jezuniu* ('Lullaby Jesu'):

Example 2

But the wild opening music returns, unsatisfied as it seems, and the final page is demonic in its energy.

GRANDE VALSE BRILLANTE No. 1 in E FLAT MAJOR, op. 18

This, like the Scherzo no. 1 in B minor, was one of Chopin's early works, composed in Vienna in 1831. Vienna, of course, is the home of the waltz, and at this time was in the grip of a passion for light, frivolous music – music that could be played while people ate in restaurants or drank wine in the open air. In a letter home, the young Chopin expressed some slight disapproval of this musical taste, calling the waltz composer Strauss a mere 'dance band leader'; but he was too spontaneous a musician to resist the dance for long.

In this E flat major waltz, more perhaps than in any that he wrote later, Chopin seems to reflect the fashionable Viennese mood: it is sparkling, jewel-like and (said Schumann) suitable for countesses to dance to. Like the Strauss waltzes, it has a main theme, heard right at the start, which gives way to others hardly less tuneful, only to recur brilliantly later on. These themes alternate with each other like dancing partners until the coda is reached. The dazzling final section begins with a crescendo and closes with music that seems to suggest the dancers waltzing off into the distance.

VALSE No. 7 in C SHARP MINOR, op. 64 No. 2; VALSE No. 6 in D FLAT MAJOR, op. 64 No. 1

These two waltzes were written around 1846-47, quite near the end of Chopin's life and when he was already very ill with tuberculosis. Both are more graceful, and less boisterous, than the previous example. The Valse no. 7, in particular, suggests a ballet rather than the ballroom.

Both pieces are in the kind of alternating-section form that Chopin

ETUDE in E MAJOR, op. 10 no. 3

This étude, despite its number in the op. 10 set, was the last but one to be composed, and bears the date 25 August 1832. This was considered by Chopin himself to be one of his finest melodies, and he apparently asked that it should be played at his funeral. Technically it may be thought of as an exercise in *cantabile* (singing style) playing – the pianistic equivalent to the vocal *bel canto* – and the tune must be carefully shaped and sustained above the gently moving accompaniment. Emotionally it is a love song, full of yearning, built on two themes. The impassioned central section is highly contrasted and involves awkward stretches for the hands. However, when this much faster music calms down, a most beautiful passage ensues, leading into a restatement of the melody first heard at the opening.

ETUDE in G FLAT MAJOR, op. 25 no. 9

This light-hearted piece, writen in 1832-34, is often called the 'Butterfly' Study. The key, G flat major, means that much of the playing is on the black notes of the keyboard. That in itself does not add to the difficulty, though: the challenge of this piece is to maintain an effortless lightness (Chopin marks it *leggiero*, 'light') while negotiating large, tricky leaps with the left hand as well as playing the dancing tune with the right. (The right hand is throughout stretched to its utmost, too.) The music builds at one point to a very loud

climax, which is marked 'passionately', but this is very brief and the ending is shimmering, almost feather light.

NOCTURNE in E FLAT MAJOR, op. 9 No. 2

This gentle piece is one of the most loved of Chopin's 20 or so nocturnes. He was still only about 20 years old when he composed it, and was certainly inspired to do so by the nocturnes of John Field – mood pieces evoking candlelit evenings in elegant drawing rooms. The characteristic style is of a flowing and ornate right-hand melody accompanied by a rippling or chordal left hand. Chopin's delicately romantic tune is at first quite simply presented, but becomes steadily more ornamented and passionate. Then, at the point at which his audience would have expected the piece to draw quietly to its conclusion, there is a surprisingly powerful climax. Chopin eventually provides the expected ending, but only after a brilliant flourish, high in the right hand, has transfixed the listener, held him tense, almost in a state of suspended animation, for several seconds: only then does he bring the piece to its wonderfully calm conclusion.

SCHERZO No. 1 in B MINOR, op. 20

This is another early work (1831), the first of the four scherzos Chopin was to write. The style is a far cry from the original meaning of the word scherzo, which implied a playful and humorous quality.

A patriot's music
Chopin's lifelong love of Polish dance forms and his identification with Polish folk music (left) appeared in his polonaises, works of sometimes heroic dimensions.

Night Moods
Whistler's Nocturne in Blue and Gold (far left) is an attempt to express visually what Chopin's Nocturnes express in music. Whistler believed the musical term 'to so poetically say all I want to say and no more than I wish'.

favoured for his waltzes, the C sharp minor being the more elaborate of the two: its shape may be summarized as A,B,C,B,A,B, with A being the main theme, B the rippling sequence of rapid notes in the right hand, and C the slower, sensuous, song-like section in the major key. The D flat major or 'Minute' Waltz has a simpler A,B,A shape: the lyrical tune of the middle section was once made into a popular song called 'Weep No More'. Incidentally, it was never Chopin's intention that it should be played within a minute, at which speed it becomes too much of a rush.

ETUDE in C MINOR, op. 10 No. 2
This is the famous 'Revolutionary' Study. It may have been inspired by the news of the Warsaw uprising and its suppression by the Russians, which occurred in September 1831. We know that Chopin heard of these events in Stuttgart, and was terribly upset and anxious for his family and friends; what is less susceptible to proof is the legend that he instantly sat down and wrote this passionate music; in fact it has been claimed that the piece was composed a year earlier.

Whatever its inspiration, though, the mood certainly fits the story. A flurry of notes in the left hand cascades under right-hand chords and, later, under a searing melody. The whole piece gives a tremendous feeling of ebb and flow, occasionally relaxing only to storm and

protest yet more vehemently. But for the pianist who plays this music there is little respite technically, and much left-hand stamina is required.

FANTASY-IMPROMPTU in C SHARP MINOR, op. 66
This piece was composed in 1835, but Chopin left it unpublished, possibly because he felt it was too much like a work (Impromptu in E flat major) by another composer, Moscheles. Today it is one of his most popular pieces. Over a rippling bass the right hand plays a tune (if it can be called a tune) consisting of rapid notes in a steady pattern; later, certain notes stand out and a more distinct melody emerges. A middle section that seems totally different in mood and theme proves on close listening to be a variant, at a much slower pace, of the initial rapid-note tune, a poigant love song now in the major instead of the minor key: the mood here is like that of Chopin's nocturnes, dreamily romantic. The rushing music returns once more, but just before the end we hear the romantic middle-section melody in the left hand, singing out like a farewell.

NOCTURNE No. 5 in F SHARP MAJOR, op. 15 No. 2
This is another early piece, perhaps written in 1831. Its form is very straightforward (A,B,A). The tune we hear at the beginning is wonderfully relaxed, even languorous; as in the E flat major Nocturne, it tends to become more and more ornamented as a melodic line as the piece progresses. Indeed, in this piece the pianist has a chance to shine with pearly finger technique in some marvellously delicate filigree writing for the right hand. In the middle section the music becomes fast and urgent, building through a long crescendo to an agitated climax. The loudness then subsides, the first tune

returns, and there is an elegent descent, in steps, towards a rustling final chord.

POLONAISE No. 6 in A FLAT MAJOR, op. 53
A polonaise, as the name suggests, is Polish. But it was not so much a dance as a stately ceremonial walk, sometimes even equestrian. There is always something of 'pomp and circumstance' about a polonaise, and something strongly patriotic too. Some of Chopin's polonaises, particularly those in a minor key, are sombre as well as heroic. However, this great A flat major Polonaise is relatively untroubled in mood, although it would not be too fanciful to hear a defiant note in its powerful gestures and swinging melodies.

An introduction sets a note of expectation, even urgency; then an irresistible tune is announced over a bounding left-hand accompaniment. There are other subsidiary tunes, but this main melody is what one especially hears and remembers. Now comes a middle section (in E major) in which, over a galloping left hand – for Franz Liszt, 'the thunder of the Polish cavalry' – a right-hand tune is played that suggests distant trumpet calls:

Example 3

This leads into a somewhat more relaxed, rather wistful passage with a smoothly-flowing right hand. Eventually and quite inevitably, though, the swinging main tune returns triumphantly, in full military splendour, and the ending is one of the most affirmative Chopin ever composed.

ROBERT SCHUMANN

1810-1856

Schumann – composer, critic and intellectual – led a troubled life that was fitfully yet brilliantly creative. A complex character, his decline was foreshadowed in his increasingly erratic behaviour.

Arch-romantic
Robert Schumann (above) was the Romantic composer par excellence. But though he railed against the conservatism of preceding generations, he was a generous and supportive critic of young composers.

Schumann was a prime mover in the advancement of 19th-century Romanticism; in his capacity as founder and editor of the famous German musical periodical *Neue Zeitschrift für Musik*, he was decisively influential in promoting the music of other young Romantics, among them Chopin and Brahms.

Strange as it may seem today, Schumann's music was less well known in his own time than his activities as a writer. His music was the product of a nature so sensitive, and it spoke in so personal an idiom, that it was many years before it began to be accepted by the public.

PERSONALITY AND APPEARANCE

Even as a young man Schumann had two contradictory sides to his character. On the one hand he was extroverted, good company, and energetic in his pursuit of new experiences; on the other he displayed an intense passion for literature, and especially Jean Paul Richter and E. T. A. Hoffmann, that encouraged the poetic side of his nature and turned him into a sensitive, retiring thinker. A by-product of this second side was a secretiveness revealed in his penchant for pseudonyms and the 'cyphers' or coded messages he habitually hid in his music.

Schumann also adopted two parallel personae to

Boy wonder
As the precocious son of one of Zwickau's leading citizens, young Robert Schumann (left) shone at musical and literary gatherings in his home town. He was largely self-taught, however, and did not receive formal musical training until he was 18.

describe himself: Florestan, the passionate hero, and Eusebius, the gentle introvert. These two 'characters' appear and talk to each other in his diaries as early as 1831, when Schumann was 21, and they soon entered his music reviews. Later, they were named side by side as the actual composers of his music.

On occasion Schumann displayed the most outrageous bad manners, especially if he had been subjected to what he considered to be inferior music, or indeed any music incompetently performed. On these occasions he spoke his mind without restraint, or else left the company without a word. With hindsight, these aspects of his nature may be seen as early warnings of the mental disturbances to which he was to fall victim in his last years.

Contemporary reports portray Schumann as a solidly built man, upright but with a curious looseness in his gait, almost as if his broad shoulders were boneless. He tended to narrow his blue eyes in an attempt to alleviate his short-sightedness, for which he habitually carried a lorgnette, and mischievous dimples appeared in his cheeks when he smiled. Long dark brown hair framed, and sometimes partly obscured, a face described as handsome in youth but ruddy and unhealthily chubby in his forties. His dress was conservative and with time became more so: in later years he usually wore black.

Unstable heritage
August Schumann (below right) died when Robert was 16, leaving his widow (below left) to steer her gifted son into a safe career in law. But Robert's nervous temperament was alarmingly reminiscent of his father's, and her efforts were in vain.

The joys of the Rhineland
(above). In 1829 Schumann enjoyed a carefree holiday there, although he kept up his piano practice by pretending to be an interested customer in a piano shop.

EARLY YEARS
Robert Alexander Schumann was born in Zwickau, Saxony, on 8 June 1810. He was the youngest of the five children of the bookseller, publisher and author August Schumann. His education, at first in a private school and later at Zwickau Lyceum, was supplemented by exposure to unlimited quantities of good literature in his father's bookshop, and by piano lessons from a local organist.

In 1826 Schumann experienced a series of sorrows with the deaths in quick succession of his only sister Emilie, whose suicide at the age of 19 released her from life as a total invalid; of the composer Weber, with whom Schumann had planned to study composition; and of Schumann's father, who had succumbed at the age of 53 to a 'nervous disorder'. Some authorities believe that Schumann's later illness was inherited from his father.

However, the young Schumann soon became acquainted with real pleasures, as women began to play a part in his life; and he found happiness, too, when drinking champagne, which he consumed in prodigious quantities from the age of 17 onwards.

CAREER

In 1828 Schumann was pushed into law school by his mother and his guardian. But once ensconced as a student at Leipzig University; he made a point of staying away from every lecture. Instead, he spent his time at his desk concocting literary fantasies in the manner of his literary idol Jean Paul Richter, or at the keyboard practising and improvising. Hearing Schubert's songs at about this time encouraged him to write a number of his own. In August 1828, four months after enrolling as a law student, Schumann began piano lessons with Friedrich Wieck in Leipzig.

Schumann's next move was to persuade his mother to let him spend a year at Heidelberg University. This was ostensibly so that he might continue his law studies in more stimulating surroundings and 'with the most famous professors'; but in reality it was so that he could be with an old friend, Gisbert Rosen. A bonus at Heidelberg was the presence of the 'famous professor' Anton Thibaut – who also just happened to be an enthusiastic musician. Schumann arrived at Heidelberg in May 1829, after a Rhineland holiday that left him penniless but content.

Much of Schumann's year at Heidelberg was spent in socializing and living the unfettered life of an

eligible young artist. Law studies were again low on his list of priorities. After his departure from Heidelberg he returned to Leipzig and again became Wieck's pupil, sharing the master's house for a time from October 1830. Wieck had written to Schumann's mother, telling her that if the young man were to study tenaciously for three years he would become a great pianist; but he frankly doubted Schumann's ability to sustain such a discipline. He suggested a six-month trial period and Schumann's mother agreed, thereby at last releasing him from the pretence that he was studying law. Wieck's attention was concentrated less upon Robert Schumann, however, than upon his own daughter Clara; 11 years old, she had become a brilliant pianist under her father's tuition, and he now took her off on an extended concert tour.

Schumann filled the time by composing, writing, and inventing 'new and more suitable' names for his friends and acquaintances. Wieck became 'Meister Raro', the conductor Heinrich Dorn, who took over from Wieck as Schumann's music tutor, became 'The Music Director', and Clara Wieck became 'Zilia' (short for Cecilia, the patron saint of music). By July 1831 Schumann was calling himself 'Florestan and Eusebius'.

THE INDEPENDENT COMPOSER

By the spring of 1832 Schumann had reached a turning-point. Lessons with Dorn and Wieck had ceased, he had become financially independent on his 21st birthday (when he came into possession of a large part of his father's fortune), and he realized at last that his dream of becoming a great concert pianist would never become a reality. In circumstances that have never been satisfactorily explained, he had damaged one, or perhaps two, fingers on his right hand. Since he is known to have invented a sling device to strengthen the weak fourth finger, this has

Literary mentor
J. P. F. Richter (left), better known by his pseudonym, Jean Paul, was Schumann's great literary hero. 'If everybody read Jean Paul', wrote Schumann, 'we should be better but more unhappy.' Here Richter is shown at work in his garden, a suitable study for a great Romantic visionary.

229

Clara Wieck
From a very early age Clara Wieck (right) was one of Europe's most outstanding pianists and her ambitious father's pride and joy. Friedrich Wieck's resistance to his brilliant daughter's betrothal to Schumann is understandable, for Clara became engaged just at the point in her career when her father was beginning to reap the financial rewards of his daughter's talent and his dedicated tuition. But the malice he displayed was inexcusable.

Lively Leipzig
The marketplace at Leipzig (below), a lively university town. Here it was all too easy for an arch-romantic student such as Schumann to ignore lectures and 'drop out' into a congenial world of wine, women, song and endless passionate discourse on the arts.

been blamed for permanently crippling his hand. Another theory, for which there is not much evidence, is that a treatment for syphilis induced mercury poisoning that affected his extremities. Whatever the truth of the matter, Schumann's damaged hand precluded a concert career, and he turned instead to composition, mainly for solo piano. He also attempted, and almost completed, a symphony, the first movement of which was played on 18 November 1832, at Zwickau, and again, in greatly revised form, at Clara Wieck's Leipzig concert on 29 April 1833.

In 1833 Schumann became severely depressed.

That summer he suffered from persistent fever; in October his brother Karl's wife, 25-year-old Rosalie, died; and in November his brother Julius died. In his letters to his mother he appears to take a morbid pleasure in wallowing in his grief. It was a self-centred grief, characteristic of a man who could confide to his diary that he was 'obsessed by the thought that I might go mad'.

SCHUMANN THE JOURNALIST

Fortunately a constructive influence entered his life at this time: the pianist Ludwig Schunke, a hearty and pleasant optimist, came to share Schumann's rooms, and in 1834 he was among the group, headed by Schumann and including Wieck, who launched the twice-weekly musical periodical *Neue Zeitschrift für Musik*. Most of the editorial chores fell to Schumann and he became happily immersed in the work. His group of friends were the living equivalent of the *Davidsbündler*, or 'Band of David', an imaginary brotherhood devised by the composer to fight Philistinism and the mediocre in music. The members were, naturally, Florestan, Eusebius and Meister Raro, together with any exalted musical spirit – Mozart's Berlioz's – who happened by. The *Davidsbündler* fought out its battles in the pages of *Neue Zeitschrift für Musik*.

Much of Schumann's life revolved around the Wieck household, a centre for the 'real' *Davidsbündler* and a meeting place for composers visiting Leipzig, the attraction, of course, being the widely admired young pianist Clara. Schumann had become engaged in 1834 to Ernestine von Fricken, but a development in the Wieck house caused him to disentangle

himself: Clara was growing up, and she and Schumann began to seek each other's company more and more.

THE WIECK FAMILY WAR

Alarmed at the prospect of what he considered an ill-advised, if not positively unhealthy, match between the wayward Schumann and his 16-year-old daughter, Wieck fought back with every weapon at his disposal. His first shot was a letter forbidding Schumann to call at his house, and he informed his daughter that there would be real shots if the composer disobeyed. Clara herself was confined to the house and told that all the money she had earned during her concert tours was held in trust until her 21st birthday, and that not one penny would be hers if she married before then without his consent.

For her part, Clara was profoundly distressed, for she returned Schumann's love. The couple managed to exchange notes and even a surreptitious kiss at their rare, secret meetings. But for Robert, this was not enough. In desperation he wrote to Wieck, imploring him to relent and make two young people happy. At the subsequent meeting the old man so confounded Schumann by parading a host of arguments, accusations, insults and doubtful concessions that the composer retired in a state of almost suicidal depression.

At length the whole sad business was referred to the courts, where the slow legal process was further retarded by Wieck's refusal to attend hearings. Meanwhile, he did his best to ruin Clara's professional reputation by writing malicious letters, often signed with a false name, to everyone he could think

A true romance
Schumann's passion for Clara Wieck was the very stuff of romance, involving two wonderfully gifted young people, an inflexibly disapproving father, painful separations, a court case, and the ultimate union of the lovers. Unluckily for Robert (above) and Clara (above right), their story did not end with 'they lived happily ever after' but turned into a tragedy.

of. It is difficult to believe that any father could harbour such vicious feelings towards his own daughter as Wieck displayed towards Clara.

The court duly heard Wieck's objections and on 4 January 1840 made its decision. All of Wieck's objections were overruled save one: that Schumann drank to excess. Wieck was required to prove this charge, and when he failed to do so within the specified time, the final decision in favour of Schumann and Clara was given in August 1840, four years after Wieck's declaration of war. By a stroke of ironic timing, the wedding took place at Schönefeld, near Leipzig, on 12 September 1840; on the very next day, her 21st birthday, Clara would have been legally free to marry whomsoever she pleased!

CREATIVITY
Schumann's energies as a composer had been severely depleted by the long battle, but in 1840 he turned from writing for solo piano to produce a whole host of songs, among them his famous *Liederkreis*, *Frauenliebe und -leben*, *Dichterliebe* and many more. When this mine of songs was temporarily exhausted, he turned to the orchestra. His 'Spring' Symphony was written in the depths of winter (23 January to 20 February 1841) and performed in March, and in May he completed his *Fantasie* in A minor for piano and orchestra, which was later to become the first movement of his Piano Concerto. Two other substantial orchestral works were to appear before the end of the year, and his restless creativity, stimulated by the sublime happiness of his new life with Clara, drove him onwards into new spheres: 1842 was to see his two greatest chamber works, the Piano Quintet and the Piano Quartet.

ON THE ROAD WITH CLARA
Meanwhile, Clara followed her own career. This inevitably led to conflicting engagements, as in

Dull Dresden
Compared with Leipzig, Dresden (left), to which the Schumanns moved in 1844, was a stuffy and conservative place, although visually beautiful. But initially it had a calming effect on Schumann's already precarious mental condition.

Clara's career was to be punctuated by pregnancies. The first child, a daughter, arrived on 1 September 1841, and seven more children followed.

In 1843 Schumann turned to choral music, but only one work emerged: *Das Paradies und die Peri*, an oratorio, completed in June. This year also witnessed a reconciliation between Clara and her father and an uneasy truce between the old man and Robert. The first half of 1844 was taken up with a successful concert tour of Russia by the couple. However, it was only successful as far as Clara was concerned, since her fame had preceded her. Despite directing his own 'Spring' Symphony in St Petersburg and attending a performance of his Quintet in Moscow, with Clara playing the piano part, Schumann was conscious of taking second place to his wife.

Upon their return to Leipzig Schumann relinquished editorship of the *Neue Zeitschrift* in order to concentrate on a new passion: opera. All that issued from his tired brain were some pieces based on Goethe's *Faust*, and even this effort, meagre in comparison with the years 1840-42, cost him dearly in mental stamina. The strain of the Russian tour, with its attendant professional frustration, and a general feeling of depression, abruptly crystallized into a total nervous breakdown. Even music, he declared, 'cuts into my nerves like knives'. For a week he was unable to sleep and could barely walk; doctors were powerless to help except to recommend a complete change of scene. Consequently, the family moved to Dresden in December 1844, and Schumann's health slowly began to improve.

Friend Brahms
The inscription on this tender portrait of the 20-year-old composer Johannes Brahms states that it was drawn at the special request of Robert Schumann, who was an ardent champion of the young man's music. Brahms returned Schumann's admiration and also fell in love with his wife Clara, to whom he remained devoted after Schumann's tragic descent into madness and death.

March 1842: the couple were parted – Schumann in Leipzig, Clara in Copenhagen – while Wieck gleefully put about a rumour that the marriage had collapsed. Alone, Schumann gazed into beermugs and studied counterpoint, sometimes simultaneously. However,

A fatal place
Before moving to Düsseldorf (right), Schumann had been perturbed to learn that the town boasted a lunatic asylum, for he disliked hearing anything that reminded him of insanity. His misgivings proved sadly justified, for his mental condition deteriorated seriously in Düsseldorf.

Happy couple
The Schumanns after seven years of an idyllic marriage that took place after a nerve-racking courtship. There were strains on the union, however, due to the competing requirements of their careers – she could not practise while he composed, and his pride was wounded by her greater fame as a pianist.

The asylum
After a final breakdown in 1854, Robert Schumann was committed to Dr Richarz's private asylum at Endenich near Bonn (below), where he died in 1856.

During 1845 he completed the Piano Concerto and began work on another symphony, but this took almost a year to complete. It was during this time that new menaces assailed him: vertigo, and a deterioration in his hearing – further signs of the progressive collapse of his nervous system. A two-month holiday at Norderney, a North Sea island, brought temporary respite, and in November 1846 the couple set off on tour for Vienna in a new mood of optimism.

It proved to be misplaced. The Viennese audiences applauded Schumann's music dutifully, but seemed to have forgotten how welcome they had made Clara some years before. She was still a wonder, but no longer a wonder child. However, in Prague, where the couple gave two concerts on their journey home, they were enthusiastically received, and a subsequent trip to Berlin also encouraged them. Further operatic endeavours occupied Schumann during 1847 and 1848 (*Genoveva*, more work on *Faust*, and the overture *Manfred*), and he entered the most productive period of his life.

LATE INSPIRATION
From this time, music poured out of him for some six years. Even the revolutionary unrest of May 1849 failed to stem the flow completely, although it did force to family to flee from Dresden for two months after a last-minute escape through a back door so that Schumann could avoid being conscripted into a hastily set up militia.

Clara continued giving concerts and Robert's music began to win recognition; but his attempts to consolidate his position in Dresden were unsuccessful. So was his application for the post of music director at Leipzig. However, in September 1850 the family moved to Düsseldorf, where Schumann had accepted the post of municipal music director. After a period of adjustment, and despite further mental and physical debility early in 1852, his urge to compose returned. But he had a number of quarrels with the authorities over his running of the city's musical activities. Schumann was temperamentally unsuited to maintain the training and discipline of his musicians, and a serious lowering in artistic standards ensued.

THE END
The trouble in Düsseldorf and a number of working visits to other musical centres during 1853 finally destroyed nerves worn down by prolonged overwork. In February 1854 Schumann suffered from hallucinations and 'very strong, painful aural symptoms', and his nights were filled with heavenly and hellish dreams. Convinced that his fears of insanity were at last about to be realized, he threw himself into the Rhine, but he was rescued and brought home in a fearful state of mental derangement. Doctors forbade Clara to see him, and on 4 March 1854 he was taken to a private asylum at Endenich, near Bonn. Clara did not meet him again until more than two years later, by which time he was unable to speak intelligibly.

During these two final years Schumann experienced periods of relative stability and corresponded with Clara and with several friends. He even received visitors, Brahms among them. Schumann's mind was still spasmodically active: he continued to compose, although nothing important emerged. Towards the end Brahms discovered him obsessively making alphabetical lists of towns and countries.

On 29 July 1856, at 4pm, Robert Schumann died in his cell. He was 46 years old.

Schumann's orchestral works

Schumann's 'Spring' Symphony and his Piano Concerto were inspired by his love for his wife Clara. Composed during the early months of their marriage, both works reflect the composer's happiness at the time.

Symphony no. 1 in B flat major, op. 38 ('Spring')

The 'Spring' Symphony was composed in 1841, and the Piano Concerto no. 1 was begun in the same year. Robert Schumann had married Clara Wieck, the famous concert pianist, the previous year, and it was thanks to her encouragement that he turned from the intimacy of song and piano music, which had occupied most of his composing activity up to that time, to the 'public' utterances of symphony and concerto. Clara had long felt that the breadth of Schumann's imagination required the wider dimensions offered by the orchestra; but it is unlikely that Schumann needed much persuasion, since the composition of both a symphony and a concerto had been on his mind for a number of years.

Although the 'Spring' Symphony is entitled Symphony no. 1, as early as 1832-33 Schumann had completed three movements and sketched in a fourth for a symphony in G minor. He had also in 1840-41 sketched in four movements for a symphony in C minor which he later used in other works. However, the 'Spring' Symphony, his first completed symphony, was tackled with a far greater feeling of urgency. The entire work was sketched out in four days from 23 to 26 January 1841. The orchestration took from 27 January to 20 February.

FIRST PERFORMANCE

The symphony was first performed on 31 March under Mendelssohn's direction at the Leipzig Gewandhaus, at a concert given by Clara Schumann. After this première, which also marked Clara's return to the concert platform after her marriage, the symphony was performed in 1842 at Bremen and Hamburg, again at concerts at which Clara appeared. But poor Schumann's entry into the symphonic arena failed to meet with the appreciation he had expected, and subsequent invitations to musical centres tended to be for Clara alone. But if the 'Spring' Symphony met with a cool response at the time, today it is one of the best-loved of all Romantic symphonies, its supposed 'faults' of pianistic writing and thick scoring easily outweighed by its charm and ardour.

Young man of music
A lithograph of Schumann in 1839, two years before he composed the 'Spring' Symphony.

Programme notes

Schumann's inspiration for composition came from within, from a desire to widen his creative experience and explore different forms. He was aware that he had temporarily exhausted the rich veins of piano music and song, and, encouraged by Clara's faith, was ready to expand his expressive language. We may even share with Schumann his transition from the smaller to the larger form, for in the symphony we find distinct traces of both song and piano textures and signs of Schumann's developing confidence in writing for a full orchestra.

FIRST MOVEMENT: ANDANTE UN POCO MAESTOSO – ALLEGRO MOLTO VIVACE

The opening notes are based upon the rhythm of a line from a spring poem by Adolph Böttger:

Example 1

This phrase is immediately repeated as all the woodwind and strings join the brass in joyful acclamation. The rest of the slow introduction consists of a series of descents and ascents by lower strings, sharp chords on brass, woodwind and drums, an undulating murmur that starts on cellos and works its way upward through violas and violins. Behind it all there are frequent references to the opening brass fanfare. Gradually the music accelerates, screwing the tension tighter, until it is released by an outburst on four horns, and the main part of the movement arrives.

The Allegro molto vivace (fast, with

much exuberance) starts with that very same fanfare, but played almost four times as fast. It takes off like a March hare, horns in hot pursuit with the fanfare rhythm, but the horns are the first to tire. This brings a moment of repose: a tentative tune with clarinets and bassoons emerges, gradually gaining assurance with flutes and oboes. The music then surges forward once more to an emphatic conclusion.

The development section now begins with the ubiquitous fanfare rhythm, passed freely from strings to wind and back again, until a new theme on oboes and clarinets appears, only to be swallow-ed up amid the general excitement. The fanfare returns, accompanied by a new voice: the triangle, an instrument rarely used in symphonies, adds brilliance as a solo flute plays the continuation.

Soon the new theme reappears, this time giving way to a gradual increase in excitement; clearly something important is about to happen. It is the opening fanfare, back to its original stately tempo but now shouted out by full orchestra – the recapitulation has arrived and the movement retraces its steps. A long crescendo leads not to the final chords, as expected, but to a surprise: for a moment the strings recall Schumann's gently

Spring's awakening
Botticelli's famous painting, the Primavera, *like the first movement of Schumann's symphony, celebrates the awakening of Spring.*

romantic piano music, before the solo flute (with a rising phrase surely borrowed from Beethoven's 'Pastoral' Symphony) heralds the final flourish.

SECOND MOVEMENT: LARGHETTO

Virtually a song without words, the Larghetto is a placid picture of a spring evening of romance. Most noteworthy is the graceful theme played by the cellos, which is later extended to the horns and woodwind. As it subsides, Schumann surprises us again: three trombones darken the mood with a solemn statement, and the music awaits development.

THIRD MOVEMENT: SCHERZO – MOLTO VIVACE

With hardly a pause, the Scherzo bursts in, taking up the trombones' statement in determined mood. Soon, however, the 'surprise' moment of romance, from near the end of the first movement, enters playfully on woodwind, with strings swirling and dancing an accompaniment, before earnestness returns.

Most scherzo movements have a central contrasting section (the Trio) which, in Beethoven's works, often returns to make a double sandwich of the movement. In the 'Spring' Symphony, Schumann harks back to the 18th-century divertimento form and interpolates two entirely different trio sections. The first trio features a simple rhythmic figure played alternately by strings and wind; it seems to suggest the first movement's fanfare, although this never quite emerges. Then the second trio swells and subsides several times before giving way to a brief final reminiscence of the Scherzo. The

Tranquil day
This painting of an orchard scene conveys the dreamy, tranquil mood of the more reflective passages in the 'Spring' Symphony.

Evening calm
Schumann originally entitled the slow second movement 'Evening'. This picture of Springtime *by Alfred East has the same calm, peaceful quality.*

transformed and extended into a grand paragraph that in turn gives way to the development.

The development section takes its cue from the opening flourish and seems to prepare for a solemn climax; but Schumann surprises us yet again. After the music slows to a halt, horns awaken the flute into a delicate cadenza that can lead only to the 'patter song', and the ideas of the movement are restated in the same order as before, but with subtle differences. A tightening of the rhythm and a tying of loose ends, and this joyful, ardent symphony rushes to a close.

Piano Concerto in A minor, op. 54

This is Schumann's only completed piano concerto, though not his first attempt at such a work. In 1829 he was working on a Concerto in F minor which remained unfinished. Between 1829 and 1831 he composed a Concerto in F which was also never completed, and in early 1839 he wrote the first movement for a Concerto in D minor.

Schumann's is amongst the best-loved of all Romantic piano concertos. It is a gentle, sensitive work, yet it lacks nothing

movement closes quietly with fragments of the first trio. This movement could be described as the month of March in sound: in like a lion; out like a lamb.

FOURTH MOVEMENT: ALLEGRO ANIMATO E GRAZIOSO

A brilliant, syncopated flourish – then a giggling, frolicking scrap of a tune like a Gilbert and Sullivan patter song that disintegrates comically amid sharp punctuation. A new idea, borrowed from Schumann's own piano piece *Kreisleriana*, trots in on oboes and bassoons, and is immediately brought to order by the rising flourish on strings. This is soon

Zestful moments
'Merry playmates' was the name Schumann gave to the lively third movement, and Peter Bruegel's Dance of the Peasants *gives some idea of the zest and energy of the music.*

in bravura display. It was written by a pianist for a pianist, and displays a unique understanding of the instrument. Schumann, despite his injured hand, always composed at the piano until 1845, and Clara Schumann often performed the work during her many concert tours.

Schumann completed the first movement at Leipzig in May 1841 as Fantasie in A minor for piano and orchestra; he did not return to it and finish the rest of the concerto until 1845 in Dresden. Clara gave the first performance there in December of that year, with Ferdinand Hiller conducting. She also gave its second performance on 1 January 1846, when Mendelssohn, who is said to have disliked the work, conducted it at a Leipzig Gewandhaus concert at which it was warmly received.

Programme notes

While the 'Spring' Symphony has strong literary associations, the Piano Concerto has no programme (verbal description) whatever to help us understand its 'meaning'. Quite simply, it is a Romantic study in absolute music, although one might be forgiven for reading into it an expression of the love Schumann felt for Clara. After all, Affettuoso, in the first movement, means 'affectionately'.

FIRST MOVEMENT: ALLEGRO AFFETTUOSO

With the minimum of preparation – a single orchestral unison – Schumann's ideas, which occur in great profusion, begin to unfold.

The opening unison comprises a striking statement which tumbles down the keyboard. It gives way immediately to a downward-curving oboe melody, richly harmonized, and extended by the soloist:

Example 2

This is followed by a serious motive upon which the piano and orchestra agree. This in turn gives way to an idea in shorter notes on strings, which the piano is reluctant at first to adopt; but it grows in confidence and is taken up by the full orchestra. A bold piano theme then develops into a restatement of the earlier oboe melody, passionately presented by the soloist and extended in a clarinet-led episode; amidst which occurs yet another idea, a playful tune first on the oboe, then on the piano. A further piano phrase, rising and falling, makes way for a climax.

A change to a slower tempo and a new rhythm (Adante espressivo) ushers in the development, much of which is taken up by a meditative discussion between piano and clarinet. Then all the previous ideas

are recapitulated, in the same order but with slight changes and a more urgent treatment of the opening melody. But instead of building up at the end to an orchestral climax, it introduces a long cadenza for the piano solo. Then the movement closes with a march-like passage led by the oboe.

SECOND MOVEMENT: INTERMEZZO – ANDANTINO GRAZIOSO

A more delicate movement could hardly be imagined. It comes as a perfect contrast to the first movement and forms an appropriate introduction to the ebullient finale, to which it is linked. The first part itself divides into three: a light melody announced by the piano, a more earnest woodwind theme, and a return to the light melody. A graceful cello theme with a delicate piano decoration occupies the central position before the three-part first section returns. This unexpectedly leads to a two-fold recollection of the opening oboe theme from the first movement.

Musical partners
Schumann was inspired to write the Piano Concerto by his wife Clara, a brilliant concert pianist. This lithograph shows the composer listening to her playing.

THIRD MOVEMENT: ALLEGRO VIVACE

Abruptly launched in headstrong mood, the main theme of the finale is a radically transformed version of the opening oboe theme. It dominates the movement, but it courteously makes way for a second subject in cross-rhythm (two beats against three), a leaping piano figure related to the piano phrase at the end of the first movement, and a march which attracts the orchestral strings more readily than the piano, which embellishes it with rapid notes.

When all this material has been restated, Schumann builds an exciting coda upon the rippling piano accompaniment to the march. The end of the concerto is vigorous, joyful and confident.

FRANZ LISZT

1811-1886

Hysterically adored piano virtuoso, passionate lover, man of the cloth and composer of genius, Liszt had a sensational career that epitomized the splendours and excesses of the Romantic movement.

Carl Czerny
(right), Beethoven's most
brilliant pupil, became the
young Liszt's principal
teacher in Vienna. Czerny
was also a composer of
repute, although today he is
best remembered for his
piano studies.

Liszt at 16
(below) By this early stage
in his long and eventful
career, Liszt was already an
acclaimed and experienced
piano virtuoso.

Ferencz Liszt – better known by the German
version of his name, Franz Liszt – was born in
the small Hungarian village of Raiding on 22
October 1811. It was the year of the Great Comet, and
the gypsies who camped nearby foretold a dazzling
future for the baby. His father, Adam Liszt, was a
land steward on the estates of Prince Esterházy.
Haydn had served at the Esterházy court for 30 years;
Mozart's pupil Hummel had been Kapellmeister
there; and Cherubini had been a visitor. Adam
himself could play most instruments, and bought his
son a piano as soon as he was big enough to sit on a
piano stool.

Under his father's tuition the boy made extraordinary progress. At the age of nine he made his first
appearance in public, stealing the thunder from a
titled blind pianist who was supposed to be the main
attraction. Shortly afterwards Liszt caused a sensation with a solo performance at the Esterházy
home. The Princess was so impressed that she gave
him Haydn's name book – unfortunately for posterity, the child promptly lost it. His first newspaper
review declared his playing 'beyond admiration'.
And a group of local dignitaries formed a committee
and provided the young genius with a six-year
stipend so that he could study.

Adam was so ambitious for his son that he
resigned his post and, with his wife Anna, left
Hungary for Vienna, the musical capital of Europe.
He tried to engage the services of Hummel as his
son's teacher, but found him too expensive. So he
settled for Salieri, Mozart's sometime rival, and the
composer Czerny, Beethoven's most outstanding
pupil. Czerny was so amazed at the young Liszt's
gifts that he refused to accept any fee: he noticed with
astonishment that 'Nature had produced a pianist'.
Liszt could play anything at sight, and improvised
brilliantly although he knew nothing of harmony. He
was such a sickly child (attributed in part to the fact
that his mother had fallen down a well shaft when
she was pregnant) that his exertions nearly made him
fall off the piano stool; and he had the most alarming

habit of 'flinging his fingers all over the keys'. Czerny
set out to give the boy what he lacked – control and
discipline – but the 'flying fingers' remained a
hallmark of his playing; it was also an innovation,
since pianists before Liszt played in the same way as
organists, with their fingers curled under like claws.

'IT IS MOZART HIMSELF'
At this time Liszt was presented to Beethoven. An
intermediary is said to have persuaded the great man
to attend one of Liszt's concerts, and although there is
some doubt as to whether Beethoven would have
accepted, since he was very deaf, Liszt himself often
told the story of how, when he had finished playing,
Beethoven got up on to the stage and embraced and
kissed him. Ungenerous critics have dismissed this

foreigners were not to be admitted. But there was a compensation: Sébastian Erard, the famous piano manufacturer, had heard of the young Liszt's prodigious success and, with an astute sense of the value of publicity, he gave the youthful prodigy an instrument of the very latest design which permitted rapid repetition of a single note. Thus equipped, Liszt took Paris by storm. 'Since last night I believe in reincarnation . . . It is Mozart himself. His tiny arms can scarcely reach both ends of the keyboard, his feet can hardly touch the pedals . . . yet he is the first pianist in Europe', enthused one newspaper. Liszt played to the French royal family, he was lionized by the noblest ladies in the land, and his picture was on sale in every shop. Such was the tumult around him that his mother, a simple countrywoman, found it too much to bear and decided to return to Austria.

In 1824 Liszt made his London début. The pianist Moscheles, who had every reason to be jealous, generously affirmed that 'in strength and in his conquest of difficulties he surpasses anything hitherto heard'. Exhausting tours of France and Ireland followed, culminating in a royal command performance before George IV at Windsor.

By the time he was 16, Liszt had been in the limelight for seven years and the strain was beginning to tell. He and Adam took a sea cure at Boulogne. Liszt turned for strength to religion, as he was always to do, but his father, also weakened by their travels, fell ill with typhoid and died. His last words to his son were 'Je crains pour toi et les femmes' ('I'm afraid for you and women'). Adam Liszt evidently had a presentiment that women would be his son's undoing, or at any rate a source of immeasurable complications in his life.

symbolic encounter as pure invention. But Liszt needed no such publicity: his Viennese concerts brought a rash of wildly enthusiastic reviews. 'A young virtuoso has dropped from the clouds,' they gushed, 'There is a god among us.'

When Liszt was 12, Czerny declared that there was no more he could teach him, and recommended that he should continue his studies at the Paris Conservatoire. Before travelling to Paris, Liszt gave a farewell concert in Budapest and repaid the sum that had been donated for his upkeep. Then there was a triumphant tour of Germany, and in Munich he received a second portentous kiss, this time from the monarch.

Initially Paris was disappointing. Cherubini, director of the Conservatoire, upheld the rule that

Gypsy strains
A romantic vision of a gypsy family (above). Similar images inspired Liszt's Rhapsodies *and his other 'Hungarian' music. However, although the composer left his homeland when he was a boy, he never forgot it. The picture on the right shows him dressed in Hungarian style.*

Talented friends
George Sand and her coterie (below). Among the men with her are the painter Delacroix, who stands behind Sand, the unmistakable Liszt, and the bearded dramatist Félicien Malefille, who is declaiming on the right. Chopin, George Sand's current lover, is represented by the brightly-coloured bird perched upon her knee.

FIRST LOVES

After the death of his father Liszt became disillusioned by stardom. Believing that his art was 'debased to not much more than a trade . . . labelled as entertainment for fashionable society', he gave up performing and went to live quietly with his mother, who had returned to Paris. His teaching brought in enough money to keep them both.

It was at this time that Liszt first fell in love. Caroline de Saint-Cricq was his pupil, a girl of his own age from an aristocratic family. When the music lessons led on to romantic poetry readings, her father forbade him to see her again; and she was duly married to a diplomat. To Liszt the loss was a severe blow, and he suffered an emotional and religious crisis that was to last for two years. (This Caroline was to be the only former love he remembered in his will.) He refused food and felt a strong conviction that his vocation lay with God rather than in music. He suffered cataleptic fits and once, when he was unconscious for two days, a Paris newspaper announced his death and printed an obituary.

In 1830 revolution broke out in Paris. 'The guns have cured him' announced Liszt's mother as her son emerged from his lethargy. Within the next exciting year he met three men who were to have a lasting influence on his music: Paganini, Berlioz and Chopin. Paganini's supposed alliance with the devil fascinated the young pianist, as did his uncanny virtuosity. In Berlioz he found another tormented Romantic who had extended the range of the orchestra just as Paganini had extended the range of the violin. Liszt determined to do as much for the piano.

Chopin's influence was different: he calmed Liszt's nerves and introduced him to his first great affair. At an impromptu party at Chopin's home,

Liszt played into the small hours to a select company of artists: Heine, Delacroix, Rossini, Meyerbeer and George Sand. A sixth guest, Marie d'Agoult, was deeply affected. 'His flashing eyes, his gestures, his smile, now profound and of an infinite sweetness, now caustic, seemed intended to provoke me to an intimate assent.'

THE REIGN OF MARIE

The Countess Marie was a 28-year-old mother of three children. She was estranged from her husband, a man of limited outlook some 20 years older than herself, and she led an independent life devoted to the serious pursuit of literature and philosophy. Her liaison with Liszt, whose mercurial nature inclined him towards passing affairs and involvement in long-term relationships only with women made of sterner stuff than himself, lasted for ten years.

To begin with the affair was difficult and scandalous, causing both of them a great deal of anguish. But in 1835 they broke for ever with convention and settled in Switzerland, where their life together became more ordered and their first baby, Blandine, was born. Under Marie's influence Liszt studied Goethe and Dante and applied himself to composition. These were the years of the *Anneés de pèlerinage*, lyrical evocations of his travels with Marie. While he gave free lessons to the young ladies at the Geneva Conservatory, paying as much attention to their charms as to their musical talents, Marie taught him the airs and graces of the fashionable world. In due course, he grew restless to be back in it.

In 1837 a second daughter, Cosima, was born in Italy. (She was destined to marry her father's favourite pupil, Hans von Bülow, and then to leave him for the composer Liszt supported and admired so

First liaison

Liszt's first liaison of any duration was with the Countess Marie d'Agoult (right). Although estranged from her husband, she had avoided entanglements until falling under Liszt's spell. The Swiss scenes and sounds they encountered on their 'honeymoon' in 1835 inspired Liszt's Années de Pèlerinage (below left), a sort of musical diary. Marie had three children by the composer, but failed to control his wanderlust. After he left her, she took her revenge by writing a novel in which he appears in an unflattering light.

Supreme virtuoso

(left) Liszt's lifetime coincided with the great age of virtuoso pianists, who enraptured audiences with their performances on an instrument that was still a relative novelty. Yet even in a select company that included such geniuses as Moscheles and Chopin, Liszt was an unequalled virtuoso, capable of inducing a state of passionate self-abandonment in his listeners – especially if they were female. Like the violinist Paganini, one of his chief inspirers, he was variously regarded as a demon or a divine being.

much, Richard Wagner.) Shortly after Cosima's birth Liszt found the excuse he needed to escape from a domestic setting that he was finding increasingly claustrophobic. He heard news that the Danube was flooding and rediscovered the meaning of the word 'homeland'. 'O my wild and distant country! O my unknown friends! Your cry of pain has brought me back to you.'

ON THE ROAD AGAIN

Liszt rushed to Vienna and gave ten concerts in aid of the homeless. He also visited Hungary for the first time since his boyhood, and heard once more the music of the gypsies, which had fascinated him since his youth. After a long absence from the stage, the adulation he received went straight to his head. Not surprisingly, this was the beginning of the final rift between Liszt and Marie. Although he returned to her, the taste of fame was too sweet, and after the birth of their third child, Daniel, he set off on a glittering series of tours that took him all across Europe.

He raised money for a monument to Beethoven, he raised money for charity, and he earned a personal fortune. Everywhere he received the highest accolades: he was welcomed with frenzied enthusiasm; his concerts were a sensation; his presence required speeches and banquets; he was presented with swords, medals, a title; and his departure was attended with solemn ceremony. His coach was often escorted miles out of town by bands of students. If he had to wait five minutes for a train, the station piano would be dragged out on to the platform so that he could perform to the crowd that always surrounded him.

His social success was equally brilliant, for Liszt's prodigious musicianship was matched by his sex appeal. When his face assumed its remarkable agony of expression, mingled with radiant smiles of joy, and his playing reached a passionate intensity, ladies would scream and faint, or rush the stage to be nearer to his soulful gaze 'like poor little larks, at the feet of a terrible enchanter'. At one concert two Hungarian countesses fell upon each other and rolled over and over on the floor to gain possession of Liszt's snuffbox. At another, a lady retrieved the stub of his cigar, which she kept in her bosom for the rest of her life.

As the superstar of the day, Liszt was the darling of courts and salons, and he wrote to Marie describing his conquests. There was Bettina von Arnim, close friend of Goethe and Beethoven, 'an imp of magnetic intelligence'; Charlotte von Hagn, 'the odalisque of two kings'; Princess Belgiojoso; the singer Caroline Unger; the pianist Camille Pleyel; and Mariette Duplessis, la Dame aux Camélias. Sometimes his affairs got out of hand: his liaison with the tempestuous dancer Lola Montez (later the mistress of mad King Ludwig of Bavaria) ended when he locked her in their hotel room and beat a hasty retreat out of town.

The mass hysteria that surrounded him – 'Lisztomania' as it was termed – may have done little for Liszt's character as Marie's faithful partner, but it did, once and for all, change the status of the musician in society. Previously a pianist had been little more than a servant, his playing providing background music that filled awkward gaps in the conversation. Now he – or she – was a celebrity to be courted, whose status was determined by his talent alone.

But by 1847 the long-suffering Marie had had enough. She ended their relationship in a letter.

Flying fingers
Liszt performs the Galop Chromatique, *the virtuoso stunt with which he nearly always ended his concerts. Addicted to the limelight, he returned to the hectic life of a travelling virtuoso in 1839.*

Liszt in Hungary
In 1839 Liszt visited Hungary for the first time since his boyhood. He played at Budapest and Poszany, and proposed the foundation of a Hungarian national conservatory. On this and later visits in the 1840s he was greatly acclaimed. The programme (left) was for a concert given in 1846; in Hungarian, a person's surname is written first.

'What have I to do with a charming good-for-nothing, an upstart Don Juan, half mountebank, half juggler, who makes ideas and sentiments disappear up his sleeve and looks complacently at the bewildered public that applauds him? Ten years of illusion! Is that not the very sublime of extravagance? Adieu, my heart is bursting with bitterness!' Under the pseudonym Daniel Stern she wrote a novel, *Nelida* (an anagram of their son's name), in which she portrayed him in a clear and unflattering light. Liszt denounced the book as an unjust attack by a scorned woman, but Marie's fictional account of her lover's weaknesses is more accurate than his contemporary admirers cared to admit.

THE REIGN OF PRINCESS CAROLYNE

With Marie eclipsed by other loves, there was now room in Liszt's life for another strong woman, and in 1847, at the age of 36, he met her. She was Carolyne Sayn-Wittgenstein, a 28-year-old Polish princess who, like Marie before her, was married but separated from her husband. Though Liszt admired her for her title and her wealth, they shared deep religious feelings (Carolyne was also a pious Catholic), a love of literature and a passion for cigars. For the princess it was love at first sight: 'I kiss your hands and kneel before you, prostrating my forehead at your feet, laying, like the Orientals, my finger on my brow, my lips and my heart . . .' She declared that henceforth her whole being existed only to glorify him, and she was as good as her word.

Carolyne whisked Liszt off to her romantic castle at Woronince in southern Russia. There, while the snow whirled outside, her servants serenaded the lovers to the playing of the balalaika. In this congenial setting Liszt made a major decision. He renounced his life as a travelling virtuoso and, with Carolyne's encouragement, resolved to devote himself to composition. With this end in mind he went in 1848 to Weimar, where he had had a musical appointment since 1843, determined to live there permanently on a modest salary as musical director.

Liszt was joined there by Carolyne, who eventually reached Weimar after a dramatic chase to the Russian border, which she crossed only moments before officials closed it at the command of the Tsar. (It was difficult for Russian subjects, even aristocrats – and especially independent-minded women – to leave Russia without permission.) On her arrival Liszt was obliged to take his leave of the woman who was sharing his hotel room. He joined Carolyne and her daughter, towards whom he was more fatherly and affectionate than he was towards his own children, in the large villa on the edge of the town that

was to be their home for the next 12 years. Some visitors did not take kindly to the 'irregular' ménage, but as usual in such cases, the criticism was mainly directed at Carolyne. 'She has ensnared him through his vanity, she strews incense about him perpetually, without proportion and without scruple', observed one visitor. Liszt's royal employers continued to address all official correspondence to the hotel at which he had initially stayed.

But the cultivated and strong-minded princess was more than a worshipper and financially supportive of her genius. Under Carolyne's influence Liszt composed the majority of his best piano works, including the piano concertos. She understood him very well. 'It is not genius that he lacks, but the capacity to sit still – industry, prolonged application. Unless someone helps him in this respect he is impotent, and when the consciousness of his impotence takes possession of him he has to resort to stimulants.' This was the period of his musical maturity. Moreover Liszt used his status at Weimar as Europe's foremost musical celebrity to promote the works of other composers, and especially of Richard Wagner. Another of his good works was to allow anybody to attend the free classes he gave three times a week; and everybody did, hordes of aspiring musician flocking to Weimar for an 'apprenticeship' under him.

When the divorce proceedings initiated by the princess finally came to a head in 1860, Carolyne went to Rome to get the sanction of the Vatican for her marriage to Liszt, which was to take place there on his 50th birthday. But on the eve of the wedding, when the church was already bedecked with flowers, a hooded messenger arrived while Liszt and Carolyne were at prayer and, in true operatic style, announced that the princess's in-laws had put forward a further obstacle to their union. (Her husband had no objection to the divorce provided his cash settlement was satisfactory.) The ceremony was duly cancelled. This may have been a stroke of luck for Liszt since, as his daughter Cosima suggested, it would have been like 'a burial service' to a man who sensed that he had another vocation.

This episode marked a turning-point in both their lives. The faith that had united them now parted them. They were no longer lovers, although they remained close friends. Carolyne took a separate apartment in Rome and, with a supply of cigars at her side, began writing religious works, including an interminable project expressing her disillusionment with the Church. It was called *The Interior Causes of the External Weaknesses of the Church in 1870* and ran to 24 volumes. This monumental work took her 25 years to complete, during which time she lived the life of a hermit. In 1887, two weeks after writing the last word, she died.

RETREAT TO RELIGION

In 1862, the year after the marriage débâcle, Liszt's daughter Blandine died in childbirth, and this and the loss of Carolyne turned his thoughts again to religion. Liszt had undergone phases of intense religious feeling as a child and throughout his life, so the reinvigoration of his faith at this stage in his hectic life came as no surprise to those who knew him well. In 1865 he turned this into a lifelong commitment by taking four minor orders of the Catholic Church. (A further three vows were required before full ordination as a priest 'licensed' to hear confession and say mass.) Shortly afterwards he moved into an

Liszt superstar
(below) This caricature gives a delightfully irreverent view of Liszt's superstar status and the behaviour of his besotted lady fans. Their manic acts of audience participation – clapping, blowing kisses, fainting, ogling and showering the maestro with flowers – made a dramatic contrast with the patronizing aloofness which audiences had previously displayed towards the musicians they had hired to entertain them.

Lola Montez
(above) One of Liszt's most exotic admirers, she stormed into a banquet he was attending and danced on the table.

apartment in the Villa d'Este, a superb Renaissance villa just outside Rome, where the beauty of the gardens and the famous fountains gave him a perfect environment for composing.

Liszt's new, black-clad and tonsured image as a devout abbé added to his mystique as well as his personal happiness. But he was to be disappointed by the reception given to his sacred music: Catholics found it too innovative, and in Protestant countries it was regarded with suspicion. Of his new life he wrote to a confidante, 'I have not changed, it is only that my life is ordered more simply.' That he was the same man was to be proved by the fact that the Villa d'Este was the setting for his last dramatic affair.

A young Russian, the 'Cossack Countess' Olga Janina, came to Rome to seduce him. At 19 she already had a colourful past. Her childhood had been devoted to bloodsports, and she had lived among thoroughbred horses. She was married at 15. On the morning after her wedding she horsewhipped her husband and left him. At 16 she bore a daughter. Then she studied the piano and became infatuated with Liszt's music and, inevitably, with the man himself.

Knowing Liszt's weakness for luxury she rented a splendid apartment and bought a complete wardrobe from the Parisian couturier Worth. Liszt the former

Princess in love
Carolyne and her daughter (right). Liszt's relationship with her ended in Rome, where he found his religious vocation. But he continued to live and work in the distinctly unaustere setting of the Villa d'Este (above).

womanizer was impressed, but he said, 'Never speak to me of love: I must not love.' Cleverly, she allowed him to retire to the Villa d'Este and gave him enough time to grow lonely in his meditations. Then she appeared at his door dressed as a gardener's boy and bearing a basket of flowers. 'He showed such joy that I could see how terribly solitude weighed upon his soul, which was so passionately in love with the world and its homage.' Their relationship was tempestuous. Liszt repented of his lapse from celibacy and refused to see her; Olga threatened to kill them both, to take poison, to slash her wrists; after a week he was again her lover.

The end came when Olga, a would-be concert pianist, bungled three attempts at a recital. Liszt was so harsh with her that the audience was saddened and embarrassed; the poor girl returned home to take a dose of laudanum (tincture of opium) and remained unconscious for 48 hours. She threatened to shoot them both, but he persuaded her to leave. Olga, like Countess Marie, consoled herself by writing a book about Liszt in which she revealed the conflicts and contradictions in his personality.

A 'THREE-CORNERED EXISTENCE'

Towards the end of his life Liszt began a strenuous regime, a 'three-cornered existence', dividing his year between Rome, Weimar and Budapest and devoting his time to music, religion and love, not necessarily in that order. The arrangement was satisfactory but exhausting. Cosima had married von Bülow in 1857, but then embarked on a protracted liaison with Wagner, in the course of which she had two children by him; she and Wagner were finally able to marry in 1864. When the scandal first broke, Liszt was loyal enough to his first son-in-law to sever relations with Cosima and Wagner for five years. Eventually, however, he was reconciled with them and became a welcome visitor at their Bayreuth home. Wagner's death in 1883 came as a great blow.

It was en route for Bayreuth, in a cold railway carriage, that Liszt's final illness began. He was sitting in a train with a honeymoon couple who were admiring the moon through the open window – not a situation that a great, albeit elderly Romantic would feel justified in complaining about. Once in Bayreuth he came down with pneumonia. He died painlessly on 31 July 1886.

Man of religion
As the grave Abbé Liszt, the composer's image in old age was that of the artist as a benign patriarch. Here he is shown in his study (below), where much of his time during his last few years was devoted to composing sacred music (above), and at Bayreuth (left) with Cosima and Richard Wagner. He died there in 1886.

Liszt's Piano Concertos

Liszt's dazzling mastery of the keyboard and his love of orchestral effects inspired two of his most important works, the heroic First Piano Concerto and the poetic Second Piano Concerto.

As a pianist, Franz Liszt was a phenomenon. Nobody before or since has combined such dazzling technique with such overwhelming charisma and such remarkable musical insight. When Liszt glided to the piano, tossed his hair and brought his hands down like an avalanche on the keyboard, ladies swooned and shrieked, men wept and other musicians were struck with amazement.

But Liszt was more than a mere showman. His mastery of the keyboard was complete. Nothing seemed beyond him. But, paradoxically, this made it hard to believe that a man with such remarkable powers could be a major composer as well, and there has been a tendency to write off Liszt's piano works as mere pyrotechnics. The two Piano Concertos in particular have come in for considerable abuse. Yet they include some remarkable innovations; they are as complex structurally as any Romantic concerto; and they contain many passages of great beauty and power.

THE PIANO CONCERTOS

Perhaps the most surprising thing about the concertos is just how long they took to complete and how many versions they went through. If Liszt had ever intended them as showcases for his talent on the keyboard, he changed his mind and strove to make them much more than this, long before they reached the final version.

Liszt did not complete the concertos until 1849, two years after he had stopped touring as a pianist. Even then, the E flat Concerto was not premièred for another six years, and the A major for another eight. And both concertos were revised extensively at least twice in the late 1850s.

Liszt first considered writing a concerto when he was barely 19; it was a natural thing for a piano virtuoso to do. The idea for the opening theme of the First Piano Concerto can be traced to a sketchbook perhaps dating from as early as 1831. It may not be a coincidence that Liszt had heard, and had been overawed by, the première of Berlioz's *Symphonie Fantastique* only a few months previously. Liszt's theme certainly has an element of the grim devilry that attracted him in Berlioz's music. Ideas for the Second Piano Concerto probably date from the same period.

Immediately afterwards, however, in March 1831, Liszt heard and was over-

The mature master
Despite some adolescent efforts, Liszt did not actually complete his piano concertos until he was at the peak of his powers (above).

whelmed by Paganini's virtuosity on the violin, and these ideas were abandoned. When he finally returned to them in the late 1830s, he wrote a number of prototypes for both concertos – indeed the First Piano Concerto may well have been completed in one form. But these early versions are perhaps what might be expected of the 'Paganini of the keyboard'. They are virtuoso display pieces with an incredibly difficult piano part. And although impressive as examples of keyboard pyrotechnics, they have little else to recommend them.

During the 1840s, however, Liszt began to mature musically, and to realize that virtuosity was not an essential requirement in an effective composition. Moreover, once he took up conducting at Weimar in 1843, he began to develop a keen ear for other instruments in the orchestra, and to appreciate the importance of proper orchestration.

LISZT AND THE ORCHESTRA

What Liszt tried to achieve in his use of the orchestra in the concerto was, in Schumann's words, 'a new and brilliant [way] to bind the orchestra and piano together'.

In the piano concertos of the period, the orchestra had tended to become a mere bystander, leaving the piano to dazzle the audience and simply filling in the gaps. Liszt sought to redress the balance and make his concerto more 'symphonic'; it is significant that he dedicated the First Concerto to Henri Litolff, a composer who gave his own concertos the title *concertos symphoniques*.

In Litolff's concertos the orchestra carried as many of the musical ideas as the piano itself. In Liszt's concerto this approach is taken further. The powerful pianistic displays are matched by equally powerful orchestration that exploits the stridency of brass and all the rhythmic effects at the composer's disposal; and

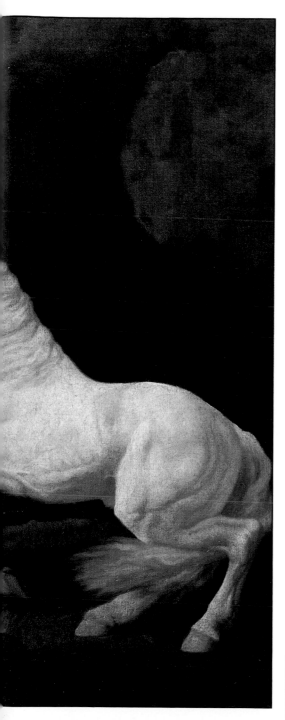

Mighty steed
'As a horse to an Arab': so said Liszt about his piano. The image is a potent one, the horse being a Romantic symbol of energy, used again and again by poets and painters.

First Concerto can be analysed into four main sections, they run into each other without a break; and there are no real divisions in the Second Concerto at all.

In writing a successful single-movement concerto, Liszt provided a solution to the problem that had plagued the Romantics ever since they had rebelled against the rigidity of Classical forms and their strict movements. Without the formal framework it was difficult to maintain a sense of unity over a long piece in which there were many contrasting moods.

Liszt's solution was 'thematic transformation' – that is, one theme would appear again and again during the course of the concerto, transformed each time but sufficiently recognizable to hold the piece together. The idea was not entirely new. Schubert had used it in his *Wanderer Fantasy*. Berlioz's use of a repeated motive (the *idée fixe*), whereby a particular tune on a particular instrument represents a character, hints at it. And other composers had dabbled with similar ideas. But Liszt was the first to use it so thoroughly and successfully.

Programme notes

The grandiloquent First Piano Concerto is a work of heroic proportions that calls for a dynamic performance from the soloist. Liszt himself premièred it at Weimar in 1855, with Berlioz conducting.

Sorcerer at work
Liszt, the 'magician of the keyboard' (below), conjures up a whole world of fantasy.

Piano Concerto no. 1 in E flat major

Liszt leaves no doubt in the score about how he wants the concerto to open. Over the music he has written *marcato* (emphatic), *deciso* (firmly) and *tempo giusto* (in exact time); and the opening bars are indeed decisive. In complete unison the strings launch abruptly into an ominous descending figure, short firm bow strokes etching each note sharply on the ear. A strident fanfare on brass and woodwind punctuates the figure like an exclamation mark, and the strings repeat the figure, descending even further and punctuated by an even more strident fanfare. Clearly Liszt does not intend us to forget these string figures; they are to form the theme (Example 1) that dominates the concerto.

Oddly enough, when Liszt was asked what his theme meant, he went to the piano and played it, singing 'Das versteht Ihr alle nicht.' The phrase means 'This none of you understand'; and of course no one did.

Example 1

Immediately the theme has ended, the piano enters with a resounding thump of a chord, played fortissimo (very loud) with the loud pedal down to give the maximum resonance. And a series of octaves (when the pianist plays the same note in four different places at the same time) roll up the keyboard like a shock-wave. Another hammer-blow of a chord with similar reverberations, and the pianist is away like a conquering hero into a brilliant solo passage.

In few concertos is the piano entry quite so dramatic, and it has a reputation

orchestral instruments are given solo passages to match the delicacy of the piano's more lyrical moments.

Of course, Liszt could never neglect the element of display. Indeed, he believed it was essential to a concerto. When Schumann initially called his Sonata in F minor a 'Concerto without Orchestra' Liszt insisted that a concerto was 'a piece for public performance' and so needed 'brilliant expression and grand style'. True to form, Liszt wrote plenty of piano fireworks into his own concertos.

ONE MOVEMENT
However, the most significant innovation in the concertos is the fact that there are no real movements as such. Although the

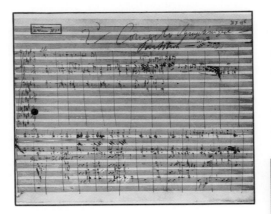

Haunted idyll
In contrast to the dynamic First Concerto, the Second Concerto is much more lyrical and romantic in character. It has the haunting quality of a starry night, although the dreamy mood sometimes borders on the sinister (below).

Disputed work
Joachim Raff (left), Liszt's secretary, claimed that much of the composer's orchestration was in fact his own. Liszt certainly orchestrated the final versions of both the Piano Concertos: above is the score of the Second Concerto, in Liszt's own hand.

among pianists as notoriously difficult to carry off. But in comparison with the almost unplayable early version, it does not make unreasonable demands. Liszt evidently simplified it to ensure that the pianist achieved the effect he desired.

Towards the end of the solo, a high trill runs into a shower of glittering notes, and the mood changes dramatically. A solo clarinet breathes a calming air and ushers in a new melody. The piano passage that follows is one of the most poignantly beautiful that Liszt ever wrote. It seems almost as if, with the tension released, the piano breaks down into impassioned weeping – the pianist is instructed to play *appassionato* while the solo cello which joins in later plays *espressivo*.

But the lyrical mood is soon dispelled. As the strings build up the pace, bassoon and cello hint at the opening theme before it is reintroduced in a massive tutti passage (where the entire orchestra plays, leaving the piano silent). But the piano soon ousts the orchestra with an incredible flight of descending octaves, sparked off by a barely recognizable variation of the opening theme.

Then, after an extended repeat of the opening piano solo, with strings and bassoon again quietly interjecting the main theme, the first 'movement' draws quietly to a close, as if the storm had finally exhausted itself.

QUASI ADAGIO

The slow passage is marked *quasi adagio* ('as if slow') because, although the main melody is slow and lyrical, it is laid over a rapid pulse that adds intensity to the music and gives it an underlying edginess even in the calmest moments.

A moody passage on the strings ushers in an important new theme, which is to reappear many times. Yet its appearance is rather unsettling here because the descending section could lead anywhere.

The uncertainty seems to be resolved, however, when the piano sweeps in and turns the theme into a lovely dreamy melody (Example 2).

Typically Liszt highlights the melody by allowing the pianist's right hand to play only the notes of the melody, while the left hand underscores it with gentle waves of broken chords.

Example 2

But when the strings return with the theme, they corrupt this innocent, dreamy melody into something sinister, simply by changing the last chord and playing it loud and tremolando (vibrating). The chord is in fact a 'diminished seventh' – and ending a phrase with a tremolando diminished seventh was very popular with the Romantics because it was dramatic and created a sense that almost anything might happen. True to form, the piano now launches into a passionate, sensuous sequence. Only when the passion has abated does a solo flute bring a fresh melody to the scene, like a breath of morning air, echoed by gentle breezes on solo clarinet, the oboe and then the cello, while the piano trills like a chorus of birds.

SCHERZANDO

Then, with a little tinkle on the triangle, pizzicato (plucked) strings lead the orchestra away into a merry dance, the triangle running alongside.

In his review of the first performance of the concerto, the critic Eduard Hanslick ridiculed the use of the triangle, calling the work a 'Triangle Concerto'; and the name has stuck. But Liszt stood firm, retained the triangle in all his later versions, and was moved to defend the use of all kinds of unusual percussion effects, thereby anticipating the instrumental eclecticism characteristic of so many modern composers.

The merry atmosphere is chilled as the piano moodily plays the main theme again (Example 1). Rising strings build the pace and drama up to a mighty restatement of the theme on the trombones, followed by the piano's hammer chord from the opening of the concerto. The fresh morning flute theme from the Adagio breaks in but is soon engulfed as the music rises to another climax – this time it is a rapid bugle blast from the trumpets that provides the impetus.

ALLEGRO MARZIALE ANIMATO

The final passage opens with a startling transformation of the Adagio theme (Example 2). Instead of a dreamy nocturne, it appears as a jolly, if rapid, march, sounding almost like a military band (*marziale* means martial) complete with piccolos and clashing cymbals.

But the trombones grimly intervene, finishing off the theme the march had left incomplete, and the piano launches into its most spectacular sequence yet. The pianist takes earlier themes and transforms them until they are barely recognizable, creating a series of glittering passages.

Then, as the march reappears, even faster this time, the music builds to a spectacular climax, accompanied by tremendous octave runs on the piano and a rhythmic repeat of a fragment from the main theme.

Piano Concerto no. 2 in A major

In contrast to the heroic E flat major Concerto, the A major Concerto has a lyrical and poetic atmosphere. It opens not with a dramatic fanfare, but in a dreamy romantic vein, with a quiet, haunting melody on woodwind, the lead moving mercurially from clarinet to oboe, and back to clarinet. A low-key entry, perhaps, but the theme it introduces is to play an important role:

Example 3

Unusually, the piano enters almost unnoticed, stealing on to the scene with a series of gentle arpeggios (a harplike effect in which the pianist runs up through each note of a chord) that spin a dreamy web around the orchestra.

The dreamy mood comes quietly to an end with a deep wistful sigh – an effect created by a piano arpeggio that runs up one note short of the top A, like an intake of breath, and allows the strings to finish off with a sigh to the lower A.

Immediately the piano angrily transforms the theme. But this burst of frustration is soon quelled and the dreamy mood sets in once more. This time, though, the reedy tone of the oboe gives it a slightly sinister edge, and a sense that the mood may be on the point of changing dramatically.

A solo horn enters *träumend* (dreaming), followed by a solo oboe and then a cello, while the piano remains as an accompanist – all this quite typical of Liszt's extensive use of solo instruments – to create an effect like chamber music. But as the emotional intensity threatens to become overwhelming the piano breaks

Brash and triumphant

Ruben's painting A Roman Triumph *(detail) has the same brash, triumphal character as the final section of Liszt's Second Piano Concerto. Some commentators have found this* Marziale *section vulgar but, well interpreted, it can make a magnificent, heady impact on the listener; the closing moments, with their spectacular glissandi, are truly thrilling.*

in with a cascade of chords, running in to its first cadenza.

Now the mood changes dramatically as the piano rumbles right down into its deepest register, an area Liszt seems to have been very fond of. Then with growling, slashing bass chords it introduces a grim new theme with a powerful ostinato (rhythmic) beat:

Example 4

Then, as the piano seems to swell with pride, it bounds off into an accelerating chase, *allegro agitato*. A tumbling piano run leads into a strident tutti (full orchestral passage) dominated by loud trombone blasts. The hunt is really on. But after a fierce exchange between piano and strings, *fortissimo e violente*, the piano takes the strings into a gentle new melody with the three chords from the opening theme (Example 3).

A soothing cello reworking of this theme in a broader, fuller tempo leads back into a slow, contemplative section. A piano cadenza again proves to be the cue for a change of mood, and the ostinato theme (Example 4) reappears in a strutting *allegro deciso* passage. After an exciting, swirling exchange between piano and orchestra, there is a massive climax capped by an avalanche of octaves on the piano.

Immediately the full orchestra bursts in with a stirring martial variation of the ostinato theme (Example 4). Many commentators have found this Marziale section lacking in taste, and indeed, it is less than subtle. But Liszt always believed in making things absolutely clear to his audience in pieces designed for public presentation, and the brash, triumphal sound does provide an effective contrast with the rest of the concerto. It seems to be the finale, but just as it reaches the climax, aided by bell-like trills on the piano, the piano breaks off into its reflective dreamy mood once more.

Earlier themes are transformed and run together by piano and solo instruments before the pace and drama build to a powerful climax. Then with spectacular glissandi (which the pianist executes by running a finger rapidly down the keyboard) the concerto is brought to a triumphant close.

I N D E X

PICTURE CREDITS

AISA: 25(br) Palacio, Real Madrid, 26(t) 31(tl) Prado, Madrid, 27(tl), 28(bl) Hispano-Flemish School, Prado, Madrid, 31(cr) Biblioteca Nacional, Madrid, 65(t), 66(b). **Ann Ronan Picture Library:** 47(br). **Arcaid:** 84(b) Lucinda Lambton. **Archiv fur Kunst und Geschichte:** 16/7(t), 16(l) Erich Lessing, 18(br), 19(tl), 20(c) National Museum of American Art, 21(t), 29(b) National Gallery of Art, Washington, 33(c), 34(t,bl,bc), 35(tl,tr), 36(tr,c), (br) Weimar, Goethe National Museum, 37(t), 38(bl,br), 38/9(t) Schloss Versailles, Musée Historique, 39(br), 40(b), 41(tl,tr,c), 42(t,b), 53(bl), 90(t) Nationalgalerie, Berlin, 91(inset), 96(b) Museum Folkwang, Essen, 117(c), 127(c), 128(tl), 129(l), 130/1(t), 131(r), 132(bl), 132/3(t), 135(b), 138(b), 171(b), 175(tl), 193(t,b), 194(tr), 196(tr), 197(b), 200(t), 215(b), 218(tl), 219(t), 221(b), 222(t), 228(t), 229(b), 232(tl,b), 234(t), 239(c), 240(t), 244/5(b), 247(b). **Arthotek:** 94(t) Joachim Blauel, Staatliche Graphische Sammlungen, Munich, 133(r) Schack-Galerie, Munich, 174(t) Joachim Blauel, Stadelsches Kunstinstitut, Frankfurt, 212(t) Neue Pinakothek, Munich, 222(b) Joachim Blauel, Neue Pinakothek, Munich, 245(b) Joachim Blauel, Schloss Nymphenburg, Munich. **Art Institute of Chicago:** 156(bl) *The Giaour and the Pasha*, Delacroix. **Arxiu Mas:** 24(bl) 27(bl) 29(t) Prado, Madrid, 24/5(b), 27(br) Hispanic Society of America, New York, 30(bl) Collection Villagonzola, Madrid. **Ashmolean Museum, Oxford:** 104(tl) *Tintern Abbey;* Turner; 181(c) self-portrait, 182(b) *Rest of Flight,* 184(b) *Shoreham; Ivy Cottage,* 185(t) *House and Garden at Tintern,* 186(b) View from Villa d'Este, 188(b) *Early Morning,* 188/9(t) *Lake Twilight,* 189(t) *Shepherds Under Full Moon,* 189(b) *Young Man Yoking Ox,* 190(t) *Pastoral with Horsechestnut Tree,* 190(b) *Lonely Tower;* Samuel Palmer. **Barnaby's Picture Library:** 45(br), 46/7(b), 214(b). **Beethoven-Haus, Bonn:** 64(c), 66(tr), 69(t), 70(tc), 70/1(t). **Bildagentur Jurgens/Ost+Europa:** 89(b), 91(b), 230/1(b). **Bildarchiv Preussischer Kulturbesitz:** 89(tr), 93(t), 130(l), 134(t), 191(r), 192(t), 195(b), 196(bl), 217(br) Archiv der Staatsbibliothek, Berlin, 228(bl,br), 228/9(t), 230(b), 231(tr), 242/3(t) Nationalgalerie der Staatlichen Museen Preussischer Kulturbesitz, Berlin. **Bodleian Library, Oxford:** 61(cr), 192(b). **Bridgeman Art Library:** 7(b) British Museum, 9(b) *An Alpine Lake;* Karl Millner; Christie's, London, 14(t) *Place de Molard, Geneva;* Bonnington; Victoria and Albert Museum, 18(t) *Orangery at Versailles;* P. D. Martin, 22(t) *The Taking of the Bastille;* Jean-Pierre Houel; Musée Carnavalet, 23(c) Prado, Madrid, 40/1(c) Faust, *Marguerite and Mephistopholes;* Adolphe Monticelli; Christie's, London, 51(tr) *Satan fighting with Death;* Huntingdon Library, San Marino, 54/5(b) *Tintern Abbey;* F. M. Watts, 59(tl) David Allan, 236/7(t) Roy Miles Fine Paintings, 60/1(t) *River Arno;* Signorini; Gavin Graham Gallery, 66(tl), 86(t) *Battle of Culloden;* British Library, 100/1(b), 105(br) British Museum, 91(t) *Abbey in the Oakwood;* Friedrich; Schloss Charlottenburg, 92/3 *The Stages of Life;* Friedrich; Museen der Bildenden Kunst, Leipzig, 111(b) Tate Gallery, 118(b) *Aeneas telling Dido of the Disaster at Troy;* Guerin,

125(b) 126(r) Louvre, 124(t) Musée des Beaux Arts, Lille, 129(t) *Schubert Evening;* Julius Schmidt; Historisches Museen der Stadt Wien, 142(tl) *St Pancras Churchyard;* Guildhall Library, 148(t) *Destruction of Sodom and Gomorrah;* John Martin; Art Gallery, Scarborough, 159(c) *Victor Hugo;* Leon Bonnat; Chateau de Versailles, 165(t) *Sarah Bernhardt;* Georges Clairin; Musée du Petit Palais, Paris, Giraudon/Bridgeman Art Library, 195(tl) *The Cloakroom,* Clifton Assembly Rooms; Rolinda Sharples; City of Bristol Museum and Art Gallery, 204(br) *Boston Harbour;* R. Salmon, 213 Chopin by Delacroix; Louvre, Paris, 220(tl) *Edinburgh;* Wm. Daniell; Guildhall Library, City of London, 236(l) *Woman and Girl in Orchard;* Sir John Lavery, private collection, 246(l) *The Villa D'Este;* Samuel Palmer; Victoria and Albert Museum. **British Library, London:** 82/3(c). **British Museum, London:** 29(cr), 48(bl), 85(b), 102/3(inset,t), 144/5(t). **Bulloz:** 13(c) Musée de St Quentin, 92(tl), 216/7(b) 243(tr) Musée Carnavalet, 224(tl), 244(tl) Musée de l'Opera. **Castle Museum, Nottingham:** 58(tl). **Charlottenburg Castle, Berlin:** 95(tl) photo – Jorg P. Anders. **Jean-Loup Charmet:** 11(br), 16(bl), 19(tr) 121(r) 161(b) 162(tl) 164/5 Musée Carnavalet, 15(tl,tr), 21(c), 22(b), 151(b), 153(tr), 154(tl,b), 160(t), 161(t), 163(t,b), 164(c), 165(b), 167(t,r), 168(b), 162(tr) 166(br) Maison de Victor Hugo, 164(t) Musée de l'Armee. **Courtesy of Mrs A. H. B. Coleridge:** 54(c), 57(bl,br). **Courtauld Institute of Art:** 185(b) private collection. **I.R. & G. Cruikshank:** 112/3(b). **Delacroix:** 151(tr) private collection. **Dove Cottage Trust:** 53(tl), 55(tl) Margaret Gillies (tr) Wm. Westall. **East Bergholt Society:** 108/9 (c). **Edimedia:** 68(t), 178/9(b) Prado, Madrid, 227. **Edinburgh Bookseller's Society:** 82(b). **Edistudio:** 24/5(t), 27(tr), 30/1(b) Museo del Prado, Madrid, 32(t) Academia de San Fernando, Madrid, 218(b). **Fine Art Photographic Library:** 80/1(b) Alexander Fraser, 84/5(t) S. R. Percy, 140/1(b) A. Nasmyth, 142/3(b) by courtesy of Schillay and Rehs. Inc., 207(r). **Fitzwilliam Museum, Cambridge:** 44(inset), 49(cr), 110(r), 183(b) John Linnell. **Fotomas Index:** 31(tr,br), 98/9(inset), 101(t) Birmingham Museum and Art Gallery, 105(t), British Museum, London. **Friedrich:** 88(tl) private collection. **John Gaisford:** 113(b). **Gesellschaft der Musikfreunde, Vienna:** 73(t). **Giraudon:** 53(tr), 125(t), 152(cl), 225(tl), 158(t) 169(c) Louvre, 70/1(b) 126(l) 155(t,b) 170(tl,tr) Lauros-Giraudon, 150(b) Musée des Beaux Arts, Rouen, 215(t) Malmaison, Lauros-Giraudon, 219(br) 242(l) Musée Carnavalet, Lauros-Giraudon, 219(b) Musée Carnavalet, Telarci-Giraudon. **Glasgow Museums and Art Galleries:** 48/9(b) Stirling Maxwell Collection, Pollok House. **Goethe Museum, Dusseldorf:** 36(tl). **Goethe Museum, Frankfurt:** 11(t) photo – Ursula Edelmann. **Courtesy of Highgate Literary and Scientific Institution:** 56(br) photo – Keith Bowden. **Historisches Museen der Stadt Wien:** 66/7(b), 68(bl), 72(t), 74(tl), 75(b), 128(b), 134(b). **Hulton Picture Company:** 175(br), 210(t) Bettman Archives Inc., 223(r). **ILN Picture Library:** 196(cr). **Imagebank:** 15(cr). **Courtesy of Ipswich Museums and Art Galleries:** 115(t).